Minding the Dream

MINDING THE DREAM
The Process and Practice of the American Community College

GAIL O. MELLOW
and CYNTHIA HEELAN

ROWMAN & LITTLEFIELD PUBLISHERS, INC.
Lanham • Boulder • New York • Toronto • Plymouth, UK

ROWMAN & LITTLEFIELD PUBLISHERS, INC.

Published in the United States of America
by Rowman & Littlefield Publishers, Inc.
A wholly owned subsidary of The Rowman & Littlefield Publishing Group, Inc.
4501 Forbes Boulevard, Suite 200, Lanham, Maryland 20706
www.rowmanlittlefield.com

Estover Road
Plymouth PL6 7PY
United Kingdom

British Library Cataloguing in Publication Information Available

Library of Congress Cataloging-in-Publication Data:

Mellow, Gail O'Connor.
    Minding the dream : the process and practice of the American community
college / Gail O. Mellow and Cynthia Heelan.
      p. cm.
    Includes bibliographical references and index.
    ISBN-13: 978-0-7425-6292-9 (cloth : alk. paper)
    ISBN-10: 0-7425-6292-1 (cloth : alk. paper)
    1. Community colleges—United States. I. Heelan, Cynthia M. II. Title.
LB2328.15.U6M454 2008
378.1'5430973—dc22   2007048201

Printed in the United States of America

♾™ The paper used in this publication meets the minimum requirements of
American National Standard for Information Sciences—Permanence of Paper
for Printed Library Materials, ANSI/NISO Z39.48-1992.

✑ Contents

Acknowledgments

MANY people have been supportive in the writing of this book. I must start with Cynthia Heelan, who first agreed to write this book over breakfast at the Beijing Hotel during the first ever U.S.-China Community College Conference. Her clarity and organization guided our overall approach. We enlisted the librarians at LaGuardia Community College, led by Jane Devine and including Paul Abruzzo and Kenneth Peeples, who made our research possible. Dr. Gail Green-Anderson thoughtfully edited our first draft, and Alumni Honors Fellow Fawad Rahmani edited the bibliography. Our editor Susan Slesinger gave us our first encouragement and was gently at our side throughout the process, correcting and cajoling. Tabitha Kenlon's copyediting showed a precision that would not be lost on a diamond cutter.

My first inspiration for this book came from my teachers at Jamestown Community College, New York, and was deepened by my students and colleagues at Essex Community College, Maryland, and continued when Dr. Bob Miller, founding president of Quinebaug Community College, Connecticut, allowed me to lead a group of wonderful faculty. Above all, I began writing to represent more accurately the stories of LaGuardia Community College in Queens, New York. Our students' heroism shines every day as they navigate complex educational life paths with the precision and grace of dancers. They are partnered with a faculty and staff who are brilliant, innovative, creative, and passionate scholar/practitioners. If this book motivates more people to become dedicated community college professionals, it will have been worth every effort.

Personally, my energy has been nurtured by the Mellow-Bartels family, as Nicole finished her book, Paige completed her degree, and Rafael came into the family in all his glory. There would be no book without my life partner Diana, who knew I was harboring a book years before I did. My heartfelt thanks to them all.

—*Gail Mellow*

I want to acknowledge Gail Mellow, who first conceived of this book. Your dream for writing a book by scholar/practitioners who were loving critics of the field nourished the process. You were a perfect writing partner for me: You pulled me out of my "doctoral research" approach, and I was able to temper your incredible ability to conceptualize and advocate.

Thank you as well to the many people at La Guardia Community College who contributed to the success of this book: editors, technicians, drivers, support staff, librarians… You have all helped make this book come to life.

I wish to acknowledge the faculty and staff of all the community colleges where I have worked. You have been my guides and mentors in understanding and believing in what I do. The faculty and staff at North Hennepin Community College, Arrowhead Community College Region, Minneapolis Community College, and Colorado Mountain College continue to be an inspiration and support for my community college work.

My first president in the community college, John Helling, was my inspiration to want to be a leader, and my professor of community college education, Don Morgan, shaped my passion for community colleges and made me fall in love with them.

I also am grateful to my family and friends who have listened patiently to the book's development and who have shared ideas and provided feedback.

I also want to acknowledge the many people in our field who have done research on the practices and processes of the American community college. You formed the thesis of this book: There are huge successes in our field and some failures; if we replicate the successes you describe on a broad scale, community colleges can be all that we dream.

—*Cynthia Heelan*

❧ Foreword

THE great diversity of higher education in the United States is widely recognized as one of its strengths. From small independent colleges, to the Ivy League, to land-grant colleges and universities, to state colleges and universities, to for-profit institutions, to community colleges, there seems to be a place for almost everyone who seeks an education beyond high school. If there is one of these institutional types that truly exemplifies opportunity, it is community colleges. Now more than one hundred years old, community colleges are a uniquely American contribution to higher education— and one that now enrolls nearly half of all U.S. undergraduates in credit-bearing programs.

Although a recognized component of U.S. higher education, community colleges are distinctive in many ways. Their dedication to open access allows millions of people, who would not otherwise have it, an opportunity to improve their lives and the lives of others. The authors of *Minding the Dream* share many stories of ordinary people who have benefited from this opportunity. But community colleges also count among their alumni Nobel Laureates, successful business leaders, distinguished policy makers, astronauts, professional athletes, and famous actors. Their stories are similar: Community colleges gave them a chance, and these unique institutions give all of us a chance to benefit from the contributions that these alumni make for the betterment of society.

Community colleges are also the higher education institutions most responsive to communities' education needs. State and local policy makers, sometimes with federal assistance, have used community colleges to provide the education and training to transform economies. The contributions that community colleges make to workforce training and economic development have attracted the interest of policy makers and business leaders who are concerned about the future economic vitality of the country. And leaders from other countries are sending delegations to the United States to learn more about these unique institutions.

Unlike their university colleagues, community college educators are focused solely on the scholarship of teaching and learning. Although some community college professors conduct research and publish, significantly higher teaching loads and an institutional culture that concentrates on student learning act as a deterrent to discipline-based research and publication. The "learning paradigm" or the "learning college movement" that has led to increased attention to learning outcomes and their measures throughout higher education has its roots in community colleges, no doubt because of this concentration on students and their learning.

Because of their relative lack of resources, community college educators are exceptionally entrepreneurial, creative, and innovative. Community college leaders often collaborate with other educational institutions, businesses, and government to create programs or to build facilities. This entrepreneurial spirit also extends into classrooms and offices as community college faculty and staff are constantly innovating to help their students be successful. Moreover, community college educators are eager to share successes and to learn from one another at conferences and meetings. Appropriating and adapting good ideas seems to be a part of the community college culture. In the past few years, community college educators have become more open to sharing their problems as well as their successes through initiatives such as the Community College Survey of Student Engagement and Achieving the Dream: Community Colleges Count, the latter a multi-state, foundation-funded initiative intended to improve success rates for students.

In *Minding the Dream*, authors Gail O. Mellow and Cynthia Heelan demonstrate one other uniqueness of community colleges: the passion that has made community colleges a movement. Community college leaders, like Dr. Mellow and Dr. Heelan, often see themselves as missionaries of educational opportunity. But the authors also remind us of the challenges that we face and the problems that we need to solve if community colleges—and the United States—are to realize their true potential. Students who lack financial resources and face other obstacles need more help than is now being provided. Lack of transfer policies discourages many students from moving on to receive baccalaureates, despite evidence of increasing student mobility. Increasing numbers of underprepared students severely tax the ability of community colleges to increase student success rates. And persistent underfunding threatens to undermine this most vulnerable segment of U.S. higher education.

As the authors point out, the dream really does need minding. A new generation of faculty and leaders will soon be taking the reins at these institutions. They must be adequately prepared to be successful, and they must understand—and be able to defend—the unique values of the community college movement and the challenges faced by our students. Adequate resources must be provided both to the institutions and to their students. Community colleges really have accomplished miracles, but they could accomplish so much more if they were not starved of resources.

Although the perspectives of higher education colleagues outside the community college are valuable, those who do not have direct experience with community colleges often leave out part of the story or interpret information differently from those on the inside. The exceptional value of *Minding the Dream* is that it was written by insiders, giving us a relatively rare opportunity to hear from leaders who live the story they have written. They know the successes and they know the challenges firsthand. They are not afraid to address sensitive topics such as undocumented immigration and the failures of the U.S. education system from pre-kindergarten through graduate school, including those of community colleges.

Minding the Dream will be a familiar story to those of us who have served in community colleges—a story that should both make us proud and inspire us to do more. But *Minding the Dream* should also be read by others who can help make a difference: university colleagues who can help strengthen articulation agreements, provide additional opportunities for community college students to have access to baccalaureate education, and prepare the future faculty and leaders for the community colleges; governing board members who influence institutional policy and how resources are spent; local officials, state legislators, and governors who provide most of the resources for public community colleges; federal policy makers who provide much of the need-based financial assistance for students and who shape the tax policies that now provide the most benefit to upper-income students who attend the most expensive institutions; business leaders who can help others understand the vital role that community colleges play in keeping the United States competitive; and foundation officers who can assist community colleges in improving programs and services and increase the success rates of students. I thank and congratulate Gail Mellow and Cynthia Heelan on an important contribution to the higher education literature.

George R. Boggs
President and CEO
American Association of Community Colleges

❧ Introduction

AMERICA as we know it today would not exist without her community colleges. The inclusive, democratic, and meritocratic impulses of the community colleges, and the transparent boundaries between college, work, and social life, have kept alive a promise of advancement and opportunity unlike any other institution in the United States. Without community colleges, America would not have a middle class, and the financial disparities that plague our country would be much more severe than they are now.

Community colleges were created to revolutionize college education in the United States. In community after community, pioneers dreamed it would be possible to break the elitist and narrow frame of colleges designed for the few and the wealthy. They envisioned instead a higher education system in which college is a right instead of a privilege. By their very nature, community colleges dramatically expand the number of people in America with a college degree. A highly educated populace, in turn, advances communities and, collectively, the country. This dream is still alive, but only partially realized. In *Minding the Dream: The Process and Practice of the American Community College*, we extol the dream of community colleges from our perspective as committed practitioners. We expose those parts of the dream yet unfulfilled, because community colleges cannot improve without a realistic assessment of where we fall short. We use the research of our colleagues in the field to provide the most comprehensive and accurate picture of the contemporary state of community colleges. Finally, we use the data to offer a chapter-by-chapter challenge to the field, to overcome obstacles and advance community colleges in the United States.

We chose the title *Minding the Dream* because, like a gardener or parent, tending to community colleges has been our lifelong passion. We have been personally discouraged when students do not succeed in credit or non-credit programs, despite all the heroic efforts of faculty and staff. On the other hand, when someone says, "Do you mind that community colleges are disparaged, or are the orphan children of the American higher education system?" our answer is an emphatic "yes." We take tremendous pride in the work of community colleges, and the against-all-odds thrill of their successes. In part, we write this book because of the see-saw of both of those emotions.

The premise of this book is that community colleges are an essential element of America's democracy and economy. These sturdy institutions manage more miracles than disasters in the face of shamefully low funding levels and dangerous misconceptions about their purpose and goals. Our own experience of the transformative power of a community college education in students' lives runs against the predominant stories of failure so frequently voiced by others.

Just a few stories of students' lives might make our personal experience clearer:

- A group of returning women students shared stories of how spouses tore up their books or papers in a rage about their return to college. Then the women traded tips for how to manage family members' opposition by setting the table before they left for school, and putting an onion in the oven to cook so the house would smell as if dinner was already cooking if they were late returning from school.
- A large, tattooed male student came to the dean's office late one night when she was alone. He had just been released from prison. After sitting down, he leaned forward and glared. "Why don't we have an honor society at this college?" After shattering all her stereotypes, this Vietnam veteran remade his life at the college, and was elected president of the first honor society.
- A 40-year-old mother's life was transformed once she began to study philosophy. She wondered, "How could anyone graduate from college without taking several philosophy classes?"
- Jose, whose English was so poor that he first came to college as a janitor, washing the floor, was inspired to get his GED® credential, passed his basic skills courses, graduated to become a computer programmer, and is now employed at the same college where he once cleaned.
- Moumoud, who moved from basic skills through a business degree, came to my office when his first son was born. "Without this college,

my son would have had a taxi cab driver for a father. Now he has an accountant."

- Virginia, who barely got through high school while living in the local housing project, became inspired by faculty and transferred to an Ivy League college.

Almost half of all college students in the United States now attend community colleges. These 1,202 institutions are the engine of the country's economic development and the builder of its communities. David Breneman of the University of Virginia commented that most higher education research and media focus on the 20 percent of the American student population who go to the colleges that he terms "the snooties." The resulting perspective distorts the picture of the remaining 80 percent of Americans in college today. Yet it is that 80 percent, Breneman maintains, who will make or break America's success in a global, knowledge-based economy (Breneman, 2006). This book is written in celebration of that 80 percent, most of whom go to community colleges. These students are our greatest treasure, and their education our most vexing challenge.

Community colleges are the only distinctly American form of higher education. They have an explicit and implicit commitment to accessibility, community development, and social justice. Not only do community colleges educate almost half of all undergraduates; they also disproportionately educate students from racial or ethnic minorities. On average, community college students are older, poorer, more likely to be part time and working, and more likely to be the first member of their family in college than students at four-year universities. Despite these compelling demographics, few social advocates understand the pivotal role of community colleges in creating a fair and equitable society. Therefore, it is not only the general population who has a dim understanding of the impact of community colleges. Even entities that should be the natural allies of community colleges, including philanthropies, government, anti-poverty advocates, and community-based organizations, often possess an inaccurate or incomplete picture of the power of community colleges.

The purpose of this book is to highlight the impact of community colleges on American life. Community colleges perform minor miracles every day. To get a sense of these miracles, just ask:

- How is it possible that community colleges create academic success for students whom other colleges would not consider "college material"?

- How is a community college able to transform lackluster or even failing high school graduates into academic stars, who then transfer to elite colleges?
- How is it possible that community colleges redress in a single semester or a single year skill deficits in reading, mathematics, or writing that have persisted for students' entire previous academic careers?
- How do community college faculty help students who enter college with low scores on standardized tests to pass high-stakes tests?
- Why do students whose profiles read like a compendium of every demographic "at-risk" factor (part-time status, parenthood, low socioeconomic status, poor high school academic preparation, etc.) actually achieve academic success?
- Why do so many students persist year after year, doggedly attending college classes for as many as 10 years (or more), to graduate?
- Why do so many community college adult students praise faculty for sparking their academic transformation many years after high school?
- Why do community colleges educate almost half of all undergraduates in the United States but receive less than 20 percent of all public money?
- Why is the return on investment of public dollars spent on community colleges so much higher than that spent on four-year colleges—especially when compared to private or for-profit colleges?
- Why do community college students, although the poorest, on average, receive the least amount of public and private financial aid?
- Why are businesses and industries pleased with so much of the noncredit workforce training that community colleges provide?

But these are almost never the questions asked of community colleges or their leaders. It is much more common to be asked:

- Why do so many students fail to pass basic skills courses?
- Why do so many students drop out during the first year?
- Why is it that so few students graduate with an Associate degree?
- Why do so few students transfer?

These questions come from a commonly adopted perspective that makes elite four-year colleges the normative model against which all other colleges are judged. In effect, it asks, "Why don't community college students look, behave, and achieve more like students who enter a four-year college?" This perspective focuses on student deficits and asks how they might be remediated. These are critical questions for community colleges, and real answers must be ascertained, as they will be in this book. Even groups that purport to be about social justice blame the students. They are blind to the structural issues that handicap community colleges because they narrowly consider an outdated, four-year college perspective.

Therefore, the problem is that most of the research and analysis of community colleges focus on what community colleges lack as opposed to what they contribute. *Minding the Dream* is designed to do both. Each chapter is structured to outline the ideal community college, take a look at the rather unseemly underbelly of unfulfilled dreams, and then review the current literature to provide a balanced, whole story picture of the contemporary state of affairs. Thus, each chapter outlines the unique strengths and contributions in the context of areas in which community colleges fail to live up to their promise. The real, balanced story is detailed using research, data, and the authors' collective 60 years of experience. Chapters end with a challenge to the field, inviting practitioners and others to use the best of what we have learned about process and practice to truly mind the dream.

We write this book as critical friends of the community college and as passionate practitioners. We believe in the promise of community colleges. We have celebrated seeing the best of that promise realized in many campuses across the country, and we have grieved when we have seen the worst. We believe the American community college is the single most democratic form of higher education, and that the future of America, especially keeping and educating a middle class, must have great community colleges.

We believe the future of public higher education rests upon a wider understanding of the promise of the American community college. In particular, we hope this is an accessible book for individuals who are a part of the higher learning and especially the community college sphere—board members, faculty, administrators, advocates, students of higher education, policy makers, state officials. The book provides a research- and practitioner-based perspective on the community college in a comprehensive manner that explains its unique functions. For an advocate, such as a trustee member, it might be enough to just read the dream and unfulfilled dream sections of each chapter to get a rounded sense of what is at stake and what is possible when asking state governments or local sponsors for financial support. For faculty or administrators new to the community college movement, the research base will provide a beginning overview of what is best practice, as discovered by practitioners, for students, faculty, staff, and boards.

Because so few current faculty or administrators have themselves attended community colleges or studied within doctoral programs focused on community colleges, we design each chapter to give a flavor of both the potential and the special-ness of our communities and our students. For the serious scholar of higher education, the book is an introduction and not intended to be exhaustive. The challenges to the field that appear at the end of each chapter are intended to focus attention on some of the most critical issues in each subject, areas where directed national, statewide, and local efforts might propel community colleges forward. The closing chapter, "Minding the Dream," collects recommendations for overall policy and practice improvement to maintain the momentum of the community college movement.

We write this book as practitioners because so often community colleges are seen from the "outside." While an outsider's perspective is beneficial, we also want to capture the tangible and powerful changes in students and communities that no other educational institution produces. We want to write as practitioners because we have deep empathy for the ways in which too often the cards seemed stacked against community colleges and the professional faculty and staff who serve in them. The odds can be summarized simply: too much work with too few resources. Yet again and again we have seen achievement against the odds with extraordinary faculty and amazing students.

Like so many community colleges, we hope this book is an amalgam of thoughtful analysis and open advocacy.

Dr. Gail Mellow
Dr. Cynthia Heelan
New York City
2007

PART

I

PROCESS

CHAPTER 1

An Overview of the American Community College

A MERICAN public higher education is one of the emergent success stories in the late twentieth century. As innovation, technology, and speed leap to the forefront of global politics and profit, the investment the United States has made in higher education, beginning with the land-grant colleges and extending through the enactment of the GI Bill and Pell Grant legislation, pays increasing dividends. National issues allow higher education to take an unprecedented place near the center of the American stage. In this overview, we will sketch the evolution of higher education in order to frame the community college movement as an extension of the larger context of college and university development in the United States.

Public perception has simply not caught up with the radical changes that have occurred in the past three or four generations of college students. American higher education has been transformed by the coming-of-age of its community colleges. As such, a much greater focus on community colleges and their contribution to the overall successes and failures of postsecondary education are critical for a balanced view of how higher education today is quite different from the higher education of the 1960s. The changing landscape is not yet encoded in the public's or the press' common framing of the college experience, and few federal, state, or local education policies have caught up to this change.

COMMUNITY COLLEGES AS UNIQUELY AMERICAN

Community colleges express a distinctly American and democratic impulse. They depart radically from the status quo of traditional college systems. Since community colleges are by definition open admissions (anyone with a high school diploma or equivalency is eligible) and therefore non-competitive, they subvert the assumption of college for the select few. Because they promote transfer to other colleges, they foment the modularization of higher education and spur the mobility of student attendance among different colleges or universities for a single degree. In their response to student educational needs, regardless of entry-level academic preparation, community colleges have created an integrated system of educational offerings. This allows students to progress from basic skills, to job readiness, to entry-level employment, to advanced academic degrees. The innovation of open enrollment creates opportunity for an enormously expanded group of the American populace to go to college, a factor that is essential for the advancement of any country in this time, often named the *Knowledge Era*. Community colleges focus on multiple constituencies and increased opportunities for education for larger numbers of both new, traditional-aged students and older incumbent workers. The community college model may form a powerful example for developing countries such as China, Vietnam, and South Africa, which will need to educate an increasing percentage of their populations as well.

ACCESSIBILITY CREATES STRENGTH AND CHALLENGE

The concept of a system of higher education that has open, fluid boundaries between the community and the college is both the community college's strength and its greatest challenge. Great tension exists between the ideals to which community colleges aspire and their achievement of those goals. It is the dichotomy between the dream of community colleges and their current reality that frames this book. The dichotomy between lofty goals and unfulfilled promises demands a rethinking of some of the very values community colleges hold sacred, as well as a rethinking of the fundamental structures and policies that support all of higher education. Here we seek clear perspectives on what community colleges do, how they do it, and why it matters to an American future. In this introduction, we provide a very brief overview of how community colleges fit into the evolution of higher education, and then frame how the chapters that follow attempt to show the dream, the unfulfilled dream, and the current reality of the community college system.

COMMUNITY COLLEGE DEVELOPMENT WITHIN
A BRIEF HISTORY OF AMERICAN HIGHER EDUCATION

Higher education's history is intertwined with the ebb and flow of America's development. Macro trends have propelled the United States from a country that only educated its elite to where we are today, with a nascent push to claim higher education as a necessity for all citizens. College began in the United States with a vocational focus. Harvard University was the first college in the country, emphasizing the creation of clergy able to lead the Anglican Church (the Autonomous Universidad de Santo Domingo in the Dominican Republic claims credit as the first college in the New World, with classes beginning over 400 years ago). From then until now, the range of individuals who need to be educated has grown steadily.

Before the industrial revolution in the 1800s, clergy and barristers (lawyers) were the only professionals who required advanced literacy skills, because at that time even physicians were largely taught through apprenticing with other doctors. As industry developed and gathered workers in factories in the mid-1800s, the great urban centers of America emerged. The move from an agrarian society encouraged the country's educational policy to focus on completing elementary school in order to make sure workers would have rudimentary reading, writing, and mathematical skills to function on the factory floor.

As America became more fully urban and industrialized, higher education entities were partners in the transformation. In the late nineteenth and early twentieth centuries, the land-grant colleges presaged a wave of building the American public higher education system. Land-grant universities were established just as America began this industrial revolution, and they were the source of much of the knowledge and innovation that fueled an international American ascendancy. As industry continued to expand, increases in population, the settlement of the West, the continued mechanization of agriculture, and enormous changes in transportation and communication demanded still more education for Americans to be productive citizens and employees.

As the country moved from local industry to more national corporate structures, and as services became a more common part of the corporate system (finance, real estate, advertising, distribution, sales, etc.), graduation from high school became the universal educational entitlement because it was deemed the basic qualification for most jobs. Although represented as universal, the high school system focused primarily on educating the white males who (with the exception of secretaries) would be the large majority of corporate employees.

American public and private colleges and universities in the early twentieth century began to fuel the applied scientific innovation that was to underpin American economic power. Colleges and universities developed new knowledge that expanded science, social science, and engineering. The two horrific world wars and the attendant industrial advancements, followed by the emergence of American post-war prosperity, propelled social policy, again almost inexorably coupled with expanded access to higher education. The availability of the GI Bill after World War II and the civil rights movement thrust a new wave of students into colleges across the country.

National issues combined with global changes and in 1946 led to the establishment of the President's Commission on Higher Education, headed by George F. Zook. The Commission, later referred to as the Truman Commission, was charged with re-examining the structure of higher education and assessing its ability to deliver the education needed to maintain a post-WW II workforce. It determined that a new system of colleges was needed in order to expand access beyond that afforded by the land-grant colleges. There existed a few private and public "junior colleges" whose mission was to provide the first two years of a transfer program to four-year colleges. There was also a smattering of community colleges with a broader mission that included some occupational degrees, and a range of technical and paraprofessional degrees was provided by postsecondary institutions (such as those focused on secretarial, automotive, aeronautical, engineering, human services, or hospital-based nursing). Comprehensive community colleges, supported by a combination of state and local financial support, were instituted as a result of the Truman Commission. The impetus was to create a national system for this new kind of college, one that would be local, non-residential, and aimed at individuals who in times past would have been able to successfully support a family if they had just finished high school. The new college would be a college of and for its community.

Other national factors in the 1960s and 1970s catalyzed the community college's development from a few fledgling campuses to an explosion of colleges now found across the country. The baby-boom fueled, anti-war movement protesting American involvement in Vietnam in the 1970s taught a generation about political activism and global perspective. The women's movement of the late 1970s through the 1980s opened doors for thousands of women to join Vietnam veterans in storefront community colleges across the country. Thus the civil rights movement, the development of a national job corps, the impact of veterans returning from the Vietnam War, and the women's movement all helped fuel the extraordinary increases in student enrollment in the 1970s and 1980s. At one point in the early 1970s, a community college was opening somewhere in the United States every month. Between 1950 and 2006, more than 900 community colleges were established. Now, nearly every county in the United States has a community college facility that is accessible to the majority of its citizens. The development of community colleges continues, not so much through new campuses, but through structural, diversity programming, accountability efforts, and pedagogical and curricular changes spurred by issues in urban public education, in internationalization, in immigration, and in technology. These forces will set the next agendas for American community colleges.

Where We Are Now

American higher education is spinning from the impact of multiple sets of issues, changes, and problems. Forces such as dramatic changes in public funding, problems with the success of secondary education (especially urban high schools), the pressures of internationalization and immigration, and the transformative dimensions of technology all demand new responses from the country's colleges and universities. It is one of the premises of this book, however, that even considering the challenges listed above, the real story of American higher education at the beginning of the twenty-first century is not known.

The changes within higher education are not uniformly distributed, of course, and not all colleges are different from what they were in the 1960s. Scenes that would conform to a traditional perception of college, the stuff of middle-class American college dreams, persist on a hundred or so campuses. If you walk on the quadrangles of Princeton, Harvard, or Dartmouth, college looks pretty much as it has always looked—populated by young, academically and economically elite students. Some small changes would be noticeable if we compared pictures of a highly selective campus from 1967 with 2007. Many more women would be present, and there would be a slight increase in the number of African-American, Hispanic, Asian, and international students. But little else would be different. Faculty at these institutions are still deeply immersed in research, and are little different in demographic profile from their students. Dorms are comfortable and graced with amenities. All in all, these colleges are a fabulous opportunity for the 2,000 to 7,000 or so undergraduates on each of their campuses.

But this is not the predominant story of college in the United States. Perhaps the American psyche has not caught up with the reality of the college-going student of today because of the media. Popular media represents a reality that is most germane to middle- and upper-class parents and potential students. Since major newspapers and magazines cater to the more affluent, changes to the prevailing paradigm of images of college students are rare. As an example, look at how the "college theme" develops over the year in any magazine or newspaper. The story line begins in November with high school students taking the SAT tests, continues in the early spring with the nail-biting anxiety of waiting for acceptance into the best schools, and culminates in September with images of parents helping students into the dorms. All of this conforms to traditional ideas about college. This is repeated in movies, plays, magazines, and stories told to countless high school students. It just happens to be only a very, very small part of what is actually occurring to the individuals who will be the majority of students in colleges and universities across the country.

A few statistics: Nearly half of all undergraduates, and more than 50 percent of all black and Latino students attend community colleges (American Association of Community Colleges [AACC], 2006). The average American college student (two- or four-year) is over 24 years old and commutes to college (Annual Almanac of Higher Education, 2005). The average student also works, often full time but typically more than 20 hours per week (Adelman, 2006). The average student attends at least two colleges before graduating with a Bachelor's degree, and almost 40 percent of those students do so in two different states (Adelman, 2006).

The average American student no longer corresponds to a traditional stereotype of "college student." It would be as accurate to think of a middle-aged African-American woman who squeezes college into two evenings a week while she maintains a full-time job and cares for her family as it is to imagine a 20-year-old white man drinking beer with his fraternity brothers before the football game. Chapter two describes the fault lines of the dialogue currently occurring in American higher education as the conflict of private benefit versus public good.

The Importance of an Accurate Understanding

It is essential that America begins to understand the college experience of the majority of its students in context. That context must consider the numbers of students, especially minority and urban students, who don't complete high school in their teens, the number of well-schooled and middle-class students who enter but do not complete their studies in four-year colleges, and ultimately the impact of any educational advancement at any level as the United States moves into the future.

If these statistics were routinely examined, they would begin to sketch not only why American higher education has changed, but also why it must change even more. The issue is not who is in college, but who should be in college. The legacy admissions process, whereby children of alumni are given preferential admissions into Ivy League colleges, will ensure that people like the children of the two Bush presidents can continue to go to Yale University. The chances of equally qualified students getting into Columbia University are one in five if the applicant is the child of an alumni, but one in 10 if she is not—a form of "affirmative action" handicapping that rarely riles the public (Marable, 2006). Private boarding schools will still encourage wealthy families to spend huge amounts of money to ensure their children enter a "name-brand" college. Media attention will continue to focus on those high school graduates who get into the most selective 100 colleges in the country, because it is their wealthy parents who are the best target for their advertising. The lucrative industry of test preparation and admissions handicapping will continue.

But Americans must remember that, despite the vast array of support for the small number of students who will become accepted into the elite colleges, the actual life success of those students is probably already assured by the time they enter their first freshman class. There is very little predictive power that accrues to the difference between the ultimate success of the Williams College-educated student versus the Princeton College-educated: Almost all of the students who enter an Ivy League college possess a set of demographic characteristics that are much more predictive of their future success than the difference explained by the college.

The American challenge for higher education is not getting upper-class children into the most highly rated colleges after high school. Nor, despite the many complaints heard in Congress and elsewhere about escalating costs, is paying for college a real barrier to access. The single most important American higher education problem is the powerful way in which the knowledge economy has altered the standards for all of work, as well as participation in local and world polity. The economists Anthony Carnevale and Donna Desrochers say it well:

> "Meeting high educational standards has become a prerequisite for economic growth and inclusion in the 21st century. Knowledge has become the engine of growth among nations, and individuals need a solid academic foundation in order to meet the increasing skill demands on the job. Of course, educational standards are about more than dollars and cents or educating foot soldiers for the American economy. Educators have cultural and political missions to ensure there is an educated citizenry to continue to defend and promote American's democratic ideals.

> *Nevertheless, the inescapable reality is that ours is a society based on individual economic autonomy. Those who are not equipped with the knowledge and skills necessary to get, and keep, good jobs are denied full social inclusion and tend to drop out of the mainstream culture, polity, and economy [I]f [higher education] cannot fulfill its economic mission to help youth and adults become successful workers, it also will fail in its cultural and political missions to create good neighbors and good citizens* (Carnevale and Desrochers, 2005).

And now the obvious question: Who is really doing this type of education? Who is taking the children of the lower economic classes, whose families have no experience with college, and helping them succeed? Who is doing the yeoman's work of maintaining an America that will compete successfully in a world market, as well as continue to keep open a path to the middle class? It's certainly not the Yales and Harvards of the world. The real linchpin of the American education system is its community college network. These issues are further addressed in chapter eleven, "Economic and Workforce Development" and in chapter thirteen, "Programmatic Challenges of Diverse Demographics."

The Key Role of Community Colleges

The community college is the only distinctively American form of higher education. It is uniquely American in its ideals, welcoming anyone with a high school diploma or a high school equivalency certificate (such as the GED® credential). It is committed to trying to create success for all manner of students who enter its doors, with systems of developmental education for students who have a high school diploma in name but who do not have high school–level skills, and with multiple levels of job skills development programs. Because of this, and especially for urban systems of education, it might be argued that community colleges are the single point of effective education for thousands of poorly educated poor kids. In chapter nine, we will describe and evaluate how Developmental Education makes the promise of under-prepared students able to succeed in college a theoretical reality, as well as critique how frequently students in Developmental Education fail to succeed despite community colleges' best efforts.

The openness of community colleges doesn't stop with academic preparation, because it is a system that welcomes students of any age. In their scrappy and under-funded way, community colleges accepted waves of Vietnam veterans after the war, a second wave of women as they entered the workforce in the early 1970s, and currently enrolls the majority of minority and immigrant students in college. Old critiques of the system mentioned that this might just be a capitalist ploy for "chilling out" the poor, making it seem as if a real college education could be obtained but ultimately tossing students out of a revolving door because their academic skills didn't really allow them to take college courses (Zwerling, 1976; Zwerling, 1986).

In many urban areas, more than 80 percent of recent high school graduates, as well as most older entrants to a community college, need some form of remediation. If we measure how many of these students actually complete an Associate degree, the number hovers just around 50 percent. The debate continues as to whether it is better to deny these youth any further education and thereby make high school a one-time, high stakes, singular event of winning or losing in the economic race, or supporting a "second chance" or open-access system where achieving an education is possible for many but not all (McCabe and Day, 1998). Nonetheless, the inevitable conclusion must be that America's community colleges enroll millions of undergraduates, and therefore a clearer understanding of the reasons for their success and failure is fundamental to any accurate conceptualization of higher education at the beginning of the twenty-first century.

The Emergent Trends Affecting Community Colleges

Waves of national and increasingly international forces continue to shape America's community colleges. The changes in U.S. industries, and the relentless trend toward international scope and organizational integration are pushing these "people's colleges" in new ways. Immigration, at an all-time high in terms of the diversity of incoming people, is linked with wholesale economic changes made possible by technology. In every way, community colleges remain both deeply grounded in their community and responsive to the American need to retain a middle class as we compete in a world arena. In chapters ten and eleven, we discuss how students at community colleges access an education that provides essential skills for the new workforce, enhancing both their own and America's ability to stay competitive. As participation in social, civic, and political organizations requires increasing levels of sophistication to engage with multi-faceted issues, the ability of colleges to promote civil and social well-being are also a potential outcome of well-used community colleges. Chapter twelve, which outlines the dramatic increase in English as a Second Language, begins to frame the newer challenges for America's community colleges as they provide a place of integration for immigrant populations. Chapter thirteen looks at what demographic changes portend, examining the impact of immigration increases as well as the needs of a new "majority minority," and the contemporary requirement of advanced education to support global effectiveness.

Chapter three examines the funding of community colleges. It provides a critical overview of what is and what is not provided to community colleges, and examines their ability to achieve their lofty goals in light of the skimpy funding that is so systemic across the country. Chapter four asks the question of how to evaluate a community college's effectiveness, especially if it is to have measures that uniquely assess whether it is meeting its requirements in a distinctive niche of higher education. Chapter five turns to the issues of governance and reviews the role of boards of trustees, state governing entities, and internal governance with a critical perspective that examines how different structures are working for or hindering community colleges.

The power of community colleges for global change is as tantalizing as it is unknown. Perhaps community colleges will inspire the next generation of American citizens to transform and advance their communities. Perhaps a China, Vietnam, Brazil, or South Africa will transform their own societies by implementing a system of higher education that promises access and success to unprecedented proportions of its traditional youth and older students. Chapter eight outlines how a community college model might provide a powerful incentive for the world to change the way in which higher education is conceived internationally.

The world of community college is filled with stories of the students who people its halls. Here is one emblematic of the multiple boundaries that students at community college traverse:

Listening to the deep and soft Bangladeshi-dipped tones of Sayed Iqbal (not his real name), one imagines a Brahmin childhood. His intellectual prowess shines from his eyes, and as he softly tells his story, you are mesmerized by his thoughtful gentleness. Sayed presents the new "Rocky," the prototypical American story about a smart poor kid who succeeds against all odds. By the end of his story, you can almost see him standing at the top of the steps to the Philadelphia Art Museum at the dawn of his new

American life. Sayed grew up in Dhaka, Bangladesh. His family is poor, his father runs a small shop, his mom assists in the shop, and he has seven brothers and sisters. He dropped out of seventh grade for a variety of reasons, including money. His father, troubled by his son's lack of options, encouraged him to go to the United States and get a job with his uncle at a delicatessen in Jamaica Heights, Queens. His uncle helped him enroll in some English as a Second Language classes, and then pre-GED classes offered at LaGuardia Community College in western Queens. He did, and his academic life blossomed. He completed his GED certificate, a sequence of college preparatory ESL classes, and enrolled in a computer science associate degree program. He was elected president of the LaGuardia student body in 1999, and then elected president of the entire 200,000 student body of the City University of New York in 2001. He went on to secure his bachelor's degree in accounting at Baruch College, and has achieved a life-long dream by becoming a New York City police officer.

This is a great story, a very New York City story. And yet the point is something much more complex than an individual immigrant story of triumph. It is a story that may seem exotic to readers living in much of the United States. But it is not exotic, nor (except for some elements) out of the ordinary. What is fascinating about Sayed's story is how increasingly emblematic it is of who is in college today. Other than his immigrant status (although demographers project that about 11 percent of our country will be made up by immigrants by the year 2020), Sayed's path is the path taken to college by almost two out of every 10 college students. If we met up with him in his developmental English class, his situation would be representative of three out of 10 college students. If we began Sayed's story in his first community college class, working part time at the deli and going to an open access college, he would represent between four and five out of 10 undergraduate students in the United States.

Sayed's song will not be recognized by many Americans, although a few of us can at least hum it. Yet it is really the song of our country's American system of higher education. Like Walt Whitman, it is a polemic song of ourselves, the real American story of college.

To frame a college that will respond to the complex and important needs of students like Sayed, two chapters focus on understanding and challenging how we need to change pedagogy (chapter six) and support enhanced leadership (chapter seven) in community colleges.

THE PROMISE AND CHALLENGE

The promise and challenge of community colleges are the primary subject of this book. In the summary chapter, we outline our perspective on leveraging the power of revolution—making the community college dream come true. We seek to make transparent the fluid boundaries and many manifestations of community colleges in this country. Community colleges at their best are the epitome of America, keeping a promise to her citizens that they will be given all the tools to achieve a life of liberty and happiness. Sadly, this dream is not achieved when community colleges fall short of what they could and should be to their students and community. To fulfill the dream of the American community college, we must understand their complex and multiple missions and their expanding and diverse student body. The structure, funding, and implementation of academic policies must be understood in all their local flavors and blended into a sense of the national trends. This book will attempt to give an overview of what is happening, why it is happening, and what should be happening on the more than 1,200 campuses of community colleges throughout the United States.

All of this promise and openness, and the fluctuating boundaries between community and college, are both our strength and our greatest challenge. This opening foreshadows some of the dichotomy between the dream of community colleges and their current reality. Throughout this book the dichotomy stimulates what we need: a rethinking of some of the very values community colleges and the public hold sacred, and a re-commitment to the best of this quintessentially American endeavor.

CHAPTER 2

Community Colleges
Private Benefit or Public Good?

☙ **OVERVIEW**

Who benefits from public higher education? This chapter defines the private benefits received by students, as well as the public community, social, and political gains. We compare educational attainment's impact on crime and imprisonment, culture and the arts, and family and community building in states known for their commitment to higher education versus those with a lower level of support. The changing contract between higher education and the states to produce an educated populace is described briefly. The chapter ends with a Challenge to the Field that encourages more dramatic action for public education around this issue.

INTRODUCTION

"I think only the elite should go to college, don't you?" This comment came from my table companion at a fund-raising dinner party. The handsome, charming young man at my elbow had been identified as a potential contributor to our college. After I explained to him I was the president of a community college and we believed everyone could attend college, we changed the subject. I did not ask him for a sizable contribution to our community college foundation!

This young man, born into a family of the power elite, held firmly to the belief long held by the "Upper 400" that the elite are men of education and of distinction. They possess a certain largeness of view and dignity of character which is inherited from family and nurtured by being educated together in one of a very few Eastern schools. The elite members of the higher circles know one another as personal friends and neighbors; they mingle on the golf course, in the gentleman's clubs, at resorts, on transcontinental airplanes, and on ocean liners. They meet at the estates of mutual friends, face each other in front of the TV camera, and serve on the same philanthropic committees (Mills, 1957). For them, education is a resource and a training ground for future leaders of government, military, and industry. The education of the elite is essential for the public good, since they have been handed the reins of the social world.

We can define "the public good" as a foundational concept for community colleges in at least three different ways. Public good may be defined by strictly economic measures, and perhaps this is the more popular definition since it is appears in the Wikipedia (Wikipedia, 2005). Examples of economic public goods, according to this definition, are related to monetary and labor market concepts, including national defense, property rights, law enforcement, and fire protection. When defined in this way, however, public goods do not include education.

The definition of public good adopted right after WW II provides a more appropriate view of higher education's role in civil society. This definition of public good identifies education as a civic resource, with the understanding that higher education provides benefits that are shared widely across all spheres of society. It is premised on the concept that all people can be members of the elite level of leaders. "Public social benefits of higher education...are benefits that accrue to groups of people, or to society broadly, but are not directly related to economic, fiscal or labor market concepts" (Sosin, 2002).

The public good can also be defined as an ethical code. This definition establishes the public good as a series of tradeoffs and a rationale for making decisions for the greater good. The ethical code guides the weighing of all negative and positive results of an action, and decision making is therefore based upon achieving the greater good for the greatest number. In this regard, education as the public good becomes the moral responsibility of all citizens and requires that every American protect the opportunity of every other American to access higher education. In this book, we will consider "public good" as a combination of the public good as a civic resource and as an ethical code.

When he was president, Bill Clinton clearly articulated the value of education as a public good—the greater good for a greater number—during a 1996 commencement address at Princeton University. He stated, "Today, more than ever before in the history of the United States, education is the fault line, the great Continental Divide between those who will prosper and those who will not in the new economy. Because of costs and other factors, not all Americans have access to higher education. Our goal must be nothing less than to make the 13th and 14th years of education as universal to all Americans as the first 12 are today" (Center on Juvenile and Criminal Justice, 2002).

As community college leaders, we invest our professional lives in this notion of the public good, believing that we serve in "Democracy's College." We create opportunities for individuals who desire a college education, and we prepare them to be contributing members of society at all levels of participation and leadership. Our dream is fulfilled in many small and large ways. Community colleges are a major part of the production of leaders in our country. Successful graduates include mayors of cities across the country, such as Long Beach, California, many Pulitzer Prize winners, military leaders, judges, and stars such as scientist J. Craig Venter, whose company was the first to decode the gnome for an entire living organism, or Rich Karlgaard, a publisher at *Forbes Magazine* (AACC, 2006). No other element of higher education provides more access to more students, embeds its activities and initiatives more deeply in the social and economic fabric of the community where it is located, nor advances the lives of low-income adults more fully than community colleges. We live a dream of nourishing both private benefit and the public good.

Which Definition of Public Good Is Real for Community Colleges?

The community college movement began not necessarily to benefit middle or lower class individuals, but to support the power elite. This support was needed as the elite expanded from those who filled the pulpits, sat on the bench, took part in government, were members of the House or Senate, won success as merchants, manufacturers, lawyers, or men of letters, to men of the military and the corporation. A more broadly educated populace became necessary to support America's productivity and military strength. Separating the masses from the elite became desirable, and so the community college was born to serve, perhaps not so much the greater good, as the economic concept of public good.

This emphasis continues to exist. Increasingly, trustees, for example, look to community colleges to possess the properties included in the definition of the economic public good; that is, to produce a benefit everyone can enjoy without diminishing anyone's enjoyment. Trustees and perhaps government officials attempt to assess the value of the arts, of technology, or of investing in staff development in terms of its direct impact on the bottom line of the budget. This very urge makes the ethical notion of the public good or common good vulnerable to politics.

Public support for higher education relies on a political motivation behind serving the public good. Rod Paige wrote about his role as Secretary of Education: "My job is to be the President's manager of the federal governance relationship [regarding the role of federal education]. I am to reflect the President's vision and to bring that [vision] into reality through this highly decentralized system" (Easley, 2005). This approach to educational policy makes politics completely intertwined with public policy. Most politicians discover quickly that there are political payoffs to keeping alive the notion that colleges are not supporting the public good and they are only focused on expanding the private benefits that accrue to individuals who are educated, or worse, to the private benefits that supposedly accrue to institutions and their leaders.

This confusion between the economic public good and the ethical public good could be a source for the current climate of criticism, decreased funding, and lack of support for higher education in general. If people believe the politicians and media that college students are eating at the public trough of tax dollars without repaying to society, they cannot be supportive of higher education. The confusion between education for the elite and education for the public good continues to be a source of disdain for community colleges (by the educated elite) and for their value as a conduit of American democracy and the common good.

Private Benefits of Higher Education to Students

The private benefits of a college education to graduates are clear, and the strength of the relationship of a college education to economic and professional success continues to increase. The private benefits accrue in almost every aspect of graduates' lives. The U.S. Census Bureau (Day and Newburger, 2002) demonstrates that college-educated people obtain better jobs and therefore greater financial assets, better health and retirement fringe benefits, and have lower unemployment rates. In their jobs, they have better working conditions and greater job mobility. Individuals with a higher education earn more than those with a high school education, and this is true for every group: racial/ethnic groups, women, and men. As a matter of fact, the income gap between high school graduates and college graduates has increased so much over time that a college graduate can pay for full tuition and fees and loss of salary, while going to school, in a very short period of time (Baum and Payea, 2004). The average expected lifetime earnings for a graduate with an Associate degree are $1.6 million—about $.4 million more than a high school graduate earns (AACC, 2006). The case for the private benefits of higher education is clear, and in fact the higher the education, the greater the benefit to the individual.

The Public Good of Higher Education to Society

The more difficult case to make is why higher education, and community college education in particular, is pivotal to the overall health and well-being of a region and therefore our country. In part, this is because "public good" is an abstract concept not nearly as tangible as increases in income. It is multiply defined below, and different aspects are salient to different "consumers." We argue that a community college education is an essential component of the American polity, and indeed the entire rest of the book can be seen as an analysis of the various ways in which community colleges are central to the creation of the public good for America.

ECONOMIC BENEFITS

Critics of higher education who are aware of the economic benefits college graduates experience often overlook the economic contribution of an educated populace to the common good. The public benefits of going to college are extensive, and include increased tax revenue, greater productivity, reduced crime rates, and increased quality of civic life (Institute for Higher Education Policy [IHEP], 1998).

Education results in increased tax revenues because individuals with higher levels of education generally contribute more to the tax base as a result of their higher earnings. Persons with at least some college paid 71 percent of all federal income taxes, despite the fact that they accounted for only 49 percent of all households (IHEP, 1998). Higher levels of education result in lower levels of unemployment and poverty, which results in greater tax revenues and lower demands on public budgets (Day and Newburger,

2002). These trends are magnified when the tax contributions of community college graduates are evaluated in relationship to local community impact, since students and graduates overwhelmingly live in the community where they attend college.

Higher education contributes significantly to greater productivity. American productivity increased only modestly in the last two decades, and nearly all of that growth is attributed to the overall increased education level of the workforce. According to economist Anthony Carnevale, a lack of needed skills in workers and employer demands will produce worker shortages (Gerschwin, 2005). Jobs requiring at least an Associate degree will continue to grow quickly—increasing by more than 40 percent—while the growth of low-skilled jobs will slow (Gershwin, 2005). The current lack of educated workers means that firms cannot meet their growing needs unless community colleges continue to be in the forefront of providing educational opportunities to working people at their worksite, online, and in college classrooms.

In addition, higher education contributes to increased workforce flexibility by educating individuals in generally applicable skills such as critical thinking, writing, and interpersonal communication. These skills are essential to the nation's ability to maintain its competitive edge. While lower skilled work is being sent off-shore or being outsourced, for example, a great deal of national attention is currently focused on the need for highly skilled knowledge workers. In later chapters, we outline the way in which community colleges that are closely responsive to the local employment prospects can be highly successful in maintaining or increasing economic development, to not only create better lives for the college graduates and the companies who hire them, but also enhance the viability of the other dimensions of a community.

Consumer spending increases as individuals earn higher salaries as a result of their increased education. The overall growth in consumption in the last four decades is associated with the increasing education levels of society, even after controlling for income. There is higher consumer spending in a range of categories from housing to food to transportation (Merisotis and Phipps, 2000).

Clearly, the economic benefits resulting from a college education have a direct impact on the greater good of society. It could also be said, reflecting on these benefits, that they impact the economic public good as defined in fiscal, labor market, and economic terms. In addition to these economic benefits contributing to the common good, many social benefits accrue as well.

SOCIAL BENEFITS

Community colleges were often developed from an outpouring of public spirit and community engagement. Public-minded individuals wanted to increase opportunities for potential students and for their community. The benefit of establishing community colleges often goes far beyond the direct educational benefits and their attendant changes in jobs and careers. The social benefits affecting the common good include a decreased dependency on public support, increased charitable giving, increased involvement in civic life, a greater social cohesion and appreciation of diversity, an improved ability to adapt to technology, and a reduced crime rate.

Those who have attended college participate in public assistance programs at substantially lower rates than high school graduates or those who have not graduated from high school (Carnevale and Desrochers, 2003).

College graduates are far more likely to engage in charitable giving and in community service. Sixty-six percent of those with some college and 77 percent of those with at least a Bachelor's degree perform volunteer work. These data are compared to 45 percent of high school graduates and 22 percent of those with less than a high school degree (Carnevale and Desrochers, 2003).

A person with a college degree in more likely to engage in and increase the quality of the civic life of a community. College-educated persons are more than twice as likely to vote than a high school graduate (Baum and Payea, 2004). In addition, higher levels of education are correlated with not only greater civic participation and more volunteer work but also with such simple civic acts as blood donation (Baum and Payea, 2004). Graduates of higher education are concerned about social cohesion, they appreciate issues of diversity, and consequently they have "a massive effect on social connectedness" and appreciation for a diverse society (Baum and Payea, 2004). It seems clear that those with more than a high school education have significantly more trust in civic and community groups and participate in them at much higher rates than others.

Individuals with a college diploma appear to have an improved ability to adapt to and use the technology required for successful contribution to twenty-first century employers. College-educated individuals contribute more to the research and development of products and services that enhance the quality of others' lives, and they promote the diffusion of technology to benefit others.

In later chapters, we will provide extensive examples of the ways in which community colleges benefit the local economy by assessing and responding to local needs. There are multiple models of community college partnerships with the private sector (AACC, 2004). These models improved business and community productivity through increasing worker skills; introducing new technology to improve local business; conducting strategic planning for local economic development that attracted new business to communities; using education to help reduce welfare participation; and increasing successful job participation by former welfare recipients (AACC, 2004).

Higher Education Results in Low Prison Populations

The relationship of education to the general public good is clearly demonstrated in the relationship between incarceration and imprisonment and a college education. Community colleges, by providing access to college to those previously denied, help communities reduce incarceration and lower crime rates. There are 18,929 prisoners with one to three years of high school per 100,000 among the incarcerated, compared to 290 for those who graduated from high school, and 122 for those with at least some college (Lochner and Moretti, 2004). A college education has a noticeable impact on individuals, because they have employable skills and therefore an alternative to a life of crime, but perhaps more importantly because it offers a way of thinking that alters an approach to life. Quality education is one of the most effective forms of crime prevention

The correlation between education levels and crime has been repeatedly demonstrated (Lochner and Moretti, 2004). Sadly, despite these facts, we now spend more money on building prisons than on sending Americans to college. Luckily, community colleges, through their commitment to access, contribute to the public good both in their credit programs and also in the many non-credit and re-entry programs for formerly incarcerated persons and this lowers recidivism. In New York City, for example, six community colleges collaborate to provide structured educational and work experiences for youth who have been recently released from incarceration (Watson, 2007).

Quality education for juvenile offenders—with an emphasis on special education and transition to the community—is a critical component in the reduction of the rate of recidivism among young offenders (National Institute for Literacy, 2001). Community colleges across the country have long been advocates for educational opportunities for incarcerated or released youth and adults, with programs ranging from high school equivalency and

GED preparatory courses offered in correctional facilities to non-credit and credit re-entry skills training.

The potential for community colleges to positively impact the public good is powerful. Community colleges develop national leaders, add power to the workforce, and make visible the positive differences education makes to a community's level of charitable giving and engagement with civic and ethical life. For these reasons, and all those presented throughout this book, we argue that community colleges demand the same public support given to fire and police protection, national defense, and property rights.

Public Support for Prisons versus Community Colleges

Even though evidence would support larger and larger investments in higher education, the current mood among policy makers is to devote more resources to building more prisons, strengthening law enforcement and sentencing policies, and decreasing, stabilizing, or questioning funding for higher education. While the number of arrests has remained relatively stable over the last two decades or so, the U.S. prison population has tripled since 1980 because more arrests have resulted in prison sentences, and the mandatory sentencing has been for a longer term. If this trend continues, the United States will soon have more people incarcerated than in college. Nationally, from 1987 to 1995, general fund expenditures for prison operations increased by 30 percent, while general fund expenditures for universities decreased by 18 percent. The first year in which states collectively spent more to construct prisons than universities was 1995. In fact, there was almost a dollar-for-dollar tradeoff that year, with prison construction funds increasing by $926 million to $2.6 billion) while university construction funding dropped by $954 million to $2.5 billion (National Institute for Literacy, 2001).

This comparison between prison populations and publicly supported higher learning is an important barometer in analyzing policy choices. Unlike other elements of state budgets, higher education and corrections are essentially state mandates. Hence, they are often viewed by budget analysts as dominating a state's "discretionary spending" Center on Juvenile and Criminal Justice, 2002). At the same time, while state spending veers away from higher education, so does federal support.

Federal support for higher education is shrinking. A primary form of federal support for higher education is financial aid. Financial aid is moving away from need-based grants to student loans as a predominant means of support. As an example of this, between 1980 and 1998, the value of the Pell Grant award shrank 24.2 percent (Trombley, 2000). In addition, 1992 Pell regulations reduced the number of community college applicants who were eligible by 3 percent because of a new rule that severely limited independent (self-supporting) students (Hungar and Lieberman, 2001; IHEP, 1995). This new policy eliminated 60,000 students of higher learning, primarily from community colleges where students are more likely to be self supporting.

The example of the relative private or public benefit of community college investment as compared to prisons is but one of many that could be made. The point that must be stressed is that, whether it is healthcare, housing, or a range of other social needs, there often accrues both a private AND a public good. The need to maintain the focus on both units of analysis—the individual student and the well-being and viability of a community as a whole—will be framed in the next sections.

CHALLENGES TO THE FIELD

- Community college leaders are called to advocate policy decisions that include education in the definition of the economic public good.
- Community college leaders and advocates can use information generated by research and collected in this chapter to influence the politics of education as a common good.
- Community college leaders and advocates can use the information generated by research and collected in this chapter to influence public policy to provide greater support to higher learning and less to prison construction and incarceration.
- Publications of institutions of higher learning can include information about their direct contribution to the common good of the country.

CONCLUSION

The parallel between declining state and federal support for higher education and the increase for prisons is most unfortunate. Given the mountain of evidence supporting the positive public impact of a college education, it seems clear that supporting higher education is a significant means of expanding the good of American society. Higher learning in community colleges increases public social, economic, and governmental good. It produces leaders and contributors toward the public good. It decreases drains on public expenditures. It would be sound public policy to expand spending at both the state and federal levels for higher education in general and for community colleges in particular. What could be the reason for the apparent blinders worn by public policy makers?

Perhaps the explanation introduced earlier is at play. Perhaps political office seekers need a negative story based on fear (i.e., we need more prisons) in order to be elected. Perhaps voters are moved more by fear than by evidence. Perhaps the elite, forgetting the importance to their own standard of living of education for the masses, still want only the elite to be educated. Perhaps we, as leaders of democracy's colleges, can do more than we are to help the elite and policy makers remember that their lifestyle depends on an educated populace.

Financing Community College

෨ OVERVIEW

Community colleges began with a radical premise—everyone should be able to afford college. The financing of community colleges is where the dream becomes reality. Community colleges realize many of their aspirations, and they have lower tuition than any other form of higher education.

But affordability is eroding. Trends in student aid, and in particular the recent introduction of for-profit colleges as aid recipients, alter the funding landscape. The true affordability of community colleges is eroding because of the consequences of low levels of public funding, which results in lower percentages of full-time faculty, more students attending part time, and low levels of intensive academic support for at-risk students. The culminating challenge to the field presents ways to work toward improved funding practice.

THE DREAM

Cost is the bright line separating different strata of higher education. The most selective colleges in the United States are, by and large, the most expensive. Eliminating cost as the barrier to college attendance requires community colleges to extend affordability beyond tuition and fees. Developing the dream of true affordability draws on several elements that comprise total student cost. Students must be able to afford books, supplies, uniforms, calculators, and anything else they need for class. Community colleges are predominately commuter campuses, so at first glance the traditional expenses of dormitories or food service don't seem to apply. But this framework applies only for traditional-aged students living with parents. Independent adults, or even traditional-aged students from poor families, may not have sufficient funds to afford both college and living. Financial support must broaden to include money for the necessities of life—paying for health care, child care, the rent, and groceries. If college participation takes time away from work, then affordability must include a way to replace lost wages. There are established mechanisms for employer support, including tuition assistance, paid time off from work, or both.

Ample financial aid that covers both tuition and living expenses produces real affordability. This is especially true if the aid is flexible financially, applying equally to an Associate degree or to non-credit courses designed to help students (especially low-income adults) enter the workforce. Since enrollment patterns of community college students are often part-time and episodic, the best financial aid is not time-limited or available only to full-time students. Large numbers of community college students require developmental education or ESL classes before taking credit courses, so financial aid should cover all the credits needed to complete a degree or certificate. This would require, on average, an additional semester of aid (Heelan, 2005).

Community colleges need additional funding of basic services to be affordable. Tutoring, advisement, and services for students with disabilities increase academic success, and therefore must be fully funded for true student achievement. Since most community college students are at risk of not completing their college degree, and since financial constraints rank high in that risk, these support services should be more plentiful than those offered at traditional four-year campuses with fewer at-risk students.

Affordability is an empty concept if a low-cost education is of low value. The ideal is to provide a high-quality education with plenty of full-time faculty who have the time to attend to the demands of at-risk students as well as create the intellectual atmosphere through research and scholarship that is the foundation of a college experience. The college must have sufficient faculty and other resources to teach students how to develop critical thinking and make a beginning connection to their disciplines. An affordable college education is therefore not sufficient if it cannot provide enough full-time faculty, quality teaching, excellent academic libraries, or up-to-date laboratories. The best community colleges have faculty who engage students in high energy academic activities and help students access plays, musical performances, and art galleries. The dream is to have affordability not compromise quality.

Holding costs low and keeping quality high are primary reasons for the development of community colleges. The dream presumes low cost applies to non-credit and customized training as well as to programs leading to an Associate degree and transfer. Easy physical access is linked to affordability, and community colleges' ubiquitous presence in nearly every county in the country helps to keep costs low. Typical tuition, fees, and living expenses at highly selective Ivy League campuses exceed $40,000 annually (Chaker, 2005). If the promise of community colleges to welcome a huge swath of American students is to be upheld, tuition has to be low, almost ridiculously

❧ M'SHELL WHITE'S STORY

M'Shell White's husband had become so abusive that she and her two children left her apartment in a Midwestern city. With no place to go, they spent more than two weeks sleeping in a city park. Friends had told her of a program at a local community college, but when she entered the building she was so overwhelmed with the chaos of her life and her fear of another failure that she sat in an un-used stairwell and began to sob. The director of COPE, a program to support public assistance recipients as they move from welfare to work, found her. COPE stands for Challenges and Opportunity to Prepare for Education, and was focused on helping public assistance recipients attend college. The program helped M'Shell apply for public assistance, maximize her tuition assistance from the state, and get the maximum financial aid from the federal government. The COPE program also worked closely with the city's public assistance office, making sure that students met all requirements and applied for all available sources of city support, such as food stamps and child care assistance. M'Shell started at college living with her children in a shelter for battered women, but she was soon able to share an apartment with another COPE program participant. The counselors at the program closely followed her academic progress, making sure that she maintained all the necessary credits to obtain her financial aid. M'Shell graduated from the human service program, and went on to receive both a Bachelor's and Master's degree in social work. She now works for the city's department of aging, rents her own apartment, and recently had the joy of being able to hire one of the graduates of the COPE program to work for her.

low when compared to the Ivy's. However, the requirements of running a high-quality college at a bargain price for students, and providing financial aid for a wide range of needs, places significant claims on public dollars. Localities that support community colleges establish them as a part of the public good, as necessary as roads free of tolls. With adequate financial support from an entire community, colleges can make real the dream of affordability for all.

THE UNFULFILLED DREAM

While the reality of funding for community colleges falls far from the ideal, community colleges have made tremendous advances in making college education affordable to a large proportion of the American public. At the same time, just as the United States reaches a point of overwhelming consensus that some college is required for each citizen to be productive (Carnevale, 2005), public funding for higher education has begun to erode. The erosion is most pronounced for colleges whose purpose is to serve the poorest or least prepared students, and it is most visible on the state and local levels.

Like all dreams, affordability is a fluid concept. Enormous amounts of public funding are provided annually for community colleges. Given the amount of money provided by federal, state, and local sponsors, it is the rare student who cannot afford tuition and fees at a community college for a degree program, since if a student is truly poor, federal or state support is usually available. This is not true for the low-income student seeking short-term education leading to certification, however, because non-degree educational entities are rarely eligible for federal financial aid (Pell Grants), state tuition assistance, or scholarships. Nor is it true for most part-time students, who make up a large percentage of community college students.

The picture is more complex for living expenses, where there is an annual gap of almost $8,000 between what students need to fund their education at a community college (including living expenses) and what they receive (*Institutional Profile*, 2004). The single most common reason community college students self-report as the reason for dropping out of college is financial (Braunstein, McGrath, and Pescatrice, 2000-2001).

Most community college students work to afford college. Students at elite campuses tend to arrange their lives so they can enjoy an uninterrupted focus on academic work. Community college students' lives are more likely to be tethered to bus, work, or childcare schedules. Far too many community college students squeeze college into the margins of complex lives. They do not have the money that would buy them the luxury of uninterrupted time to go to class, study in the library, and leisurely debate new ideas with fellow students. Affordability, when looked at from this perspective, remains a half-full glass.

The quality of an education balances on the fulcrum of money, and community colleges run on a shoestring. Budget constraints hobble community colleges' ability to offer needed services. This shows up in many ways. Community colleges pay their faculty less, on average, than four-year institutions and use a much higher percentage of part-time faculty *(Annual Almanac of Higher Education,* 2005). While the quality of classroom teaching is equivalent between full- and part-time faculty (Roueche, Roueche, and Milliron,1995), there is no doubt that an intermittent workforce cannot provide the program development, academic advisement, nor participation in students' lives that lead to high levels of academic and career advancement. This is despite the many efforts to involve adjunct faculty as much as possible in the ongoing activities of the campus. Community college faculty teach more classes each semester than faculty at four-year colleges, and therefore the students who most need individualized attention from faculty because of past academic deficiencies are least able to receive it. Many community colleges across the country struggle to supply the necessary technology, science equipment, library resources, and academic support services for under-prepared students.

The dream of a totally affordable college for everyone is thus real but flawed. The hundreds of thousands of students who participate every day in credit and non-credit courses attest to the reality of community colleges' low costs. Nevertheless, the dreams deferred are a testament to the ongoing economic challenges, and can be counted when we examine the number of students who drop out or stop out because they do not have the financial wherewithal to continue.

THE REAL STORY

Sources of Public Funding

At the macro level, the funding equation for American community colleges consists of some combination of public tax dollars and student tuition. However, the way in which public funding is provided is so variable that, while the following sections provide an overall description, there are few uniform patterns across the country.

◈ ALEXANDRA SANTIAGO'S STORY

As an adolescent, Alexandra came to the United States from Peru. She attended a high school for two years, but she never really learned to speak English well. Bright, she taught herself enough about computers to work in her cousin's computer repair company, but could not be sent on repair calls because of her lack of English skills. She enrolled in a local for-profit ESL school that was heavily advertised in her community. The $7,000 annual tuition was completely covered by state tuition assistance. She learned to speak English quite well, but the program did not focus on reading or writing. When her cousin returned to Peru, she could not get another job in the field without an academic credential. She enrolled in an open-access for-profit business college in her neighborhood, also heavily advertised, and again used financial aid to pay the $8,500 annual tuition. She was enrolled in English, business writing, and two computer courses. She did not see the value of the English classes, and stopped going to them. The business college went bankrupt after her first semester. The community college in the area reached out to the students, and she went to enroll. The admissions process was sobering. Never having taken a placement test, she was surprised to learn she needed at least a semester of developmental education. She had already used one and a half of a two-year eligibility for financial aid. Moreover, since she did not complete two of five classes at the business college, in her first semester at the community college she would be required not only to complete the developmental classes but also to make passing grades on at least three classes for college credit in her degree program. Discouraged, she left college and went to help her sister clean offices at night.

There is no national standard for public funding of higher education, and therefore the state statutes or local provisions that structure funding at individual campuses are as diverse and idiosyncratic as the communities they serve. Public tax dollars are commonly segmented into local support and state support. Differences occur in how colleges receive both operational funding (financial support for the ongoing costs of personnel, programs, and building maintenance) and capital funding (dollars used to build buildings). The rules that govern those contributions, and the relative weight each bears in the final funding level, differ dramatically across the country. While there can be consistency within a state, regional differences can be dramatic. Reviewed from an historical perspective, there is some trending from local sponsorship as the primary source of funding to state dominance (Fischer, 2005). Overall, there is an increasing dependence on student tuition and decreasing levels of public institutional support, as is true of all of higher education (Fischer, 2005).

Public Funding for Community Colleges Compared to Other Educational Institutions

There are strikingly different levels of public funding per capita among all sectors of public education. To gain a clear perspective of the slim financial margin on which community colleges operate, the following compares their expenditures with those for K-12 and four-year public colleges. The median state expenditure per full-time-equivalent student (FTE) for elementary and secondary schools in 2002, averaged across the country, was $7,380 (Cohen, 2004; Park, 2005). Community colleges spent an average of $6,208 per FTE (Harmening and Douglas, 1999). *Thus community colleges receive $1,100 less per capita than the average elementary and secondary school.* While K-12 education still struggles to determine how to raise sufficient money to support students over multiple socioeconomic communities (Olson, 2005), it remains striking that they have more than $1,000 more per pupil to spend than the community colleges, which often do so much to remediate student academic success upon graduation from high school.

In 2004, national expenditures for public two-year colleges were $24,447,430,000, or less than 20 percent of the $124,877,518,000 expended by public four-year colleges and universities (*Annual Almanac of Higher Education*, 2005). The comparison of costs, then, highlights that community colleges, despite enrolling almost half of all undergraduate students, spend more than 80 percent less than their public four-year counterparts. When analyzed on a per-student expenditure basis, the difference is even more striking. *The average per-student expenditure for all four-year institutions is $26,378, while for all two-year institutions it is $8,430, for a whopping 68 percent difference (National Center for Education Statistics [NCES], 2006). When just public institutions are reviewed, the percentage changes only slightly, with per-capita spending for four-year public colleges averaging $27,973 and two-year public community colleges averaging $9,183, meaning that four-year colleges spend three times as much as community colleges per student* (NCES, 2006).

This is probably the most important funding story about community colleges. When compared to any other educational sector in the United States, they receive fewer dollars. When this under funding is juxtaposed against the implications of educating students who are disadvantaged in many ways, from not being successfully prepared in high school to being out of the educational system for many years, the return on investment of these few dollars is enormous. Community colleges, which enroll almost half of all undergraduates in the United States, receive less funding than local high schools and a fraction of the funding provided to four-year colleges. Their success against these financial odds is nothing short of miraculous.

State Funding Models

The combination of state and local appropriations for community colleges ranges from a high of $1,200 per capita for Wyoming to less than $10 per capita in Alaska and Vermont (*Annual Almanac of Higher Education*, 2005). The following examples are provided to give a sense of different models in three varied parts of the country. They illustrate how different funding structures and local sponsors influence individual campuses. A comprehensive review of all community colleges across the country would give other kinds of variations; those selected here simply provide a national flavor:

1. *California community colleges* are funded by the state through an allocation formula based primarily on enrollment, and in a minor way on physical plant requirements. Funding is allocated from three primary revenue sources: a state aggregate of local property tax, the state's general fund, and students' tuition and fees. After Proposition 13 passed in 1978 and severely limited increases in property taxes, state policy was re-written to limit fundable growth in FTE to a specified amount. For many colleges, the allowable allocation limits growth to 1 percent per annum. In one case (the City College of San Francisco), the community college and the local school district won a referendum to receive a portion of the municipal sales tax to create a larger local revenue source. Small amounts of additional dollars come from state lotteries. The state mandates tuition and fees, which are the lowest in the country. Capital costs are competitively allocated across the 109 community colleges in California by the State Chancellor based upon the submission of a campus building proposal. All proposal costs (architectural, engineering, etc.) are self-funded, and if approved, the state provides

50 percent of capital costs. These funds are available if and only if the college is then able to pass a local bonding initiative to pay for the other 50 percent.

2. *Michigan community colleges* have a great amount of local autonomy (Haring, 2005). Each local board of trustees has the authority to set tuition and fees, to create bond initiatives, and to levy local property taxes. State support comes to each community college directly, presumably through a formula that establishes need, although the state has never fully funded the formula. Individual campus need is determined by examining tuition, fees and other revenue, making an adjustment if a campus' tuition is above or below the state average, and deducting the amount of local taxes. The association of community colleges, which consists of one board of trustee member and the president of each college, makes recommendations for the distribution of state funds. There has never been enough money to adequately fund each campus, which has lead to increasing internecine competition for these funds and funding formulas (Haring, 2005). Capital projects are funded with a 50/50 percent state and local match. The state allocation is a political process, which annually approves individual campus projects. Local capital must be raised through bond or tax initiatives (sometimes for a set period of time), and the language of the enacted legislation provides guidance for how the capital funds can be used. The state is reluctant to approve projects unless the local match is already ensured.

3. *New Jersey community colleges'* funding is guided by a state statute that identifies the ideal as an equal tri-partite contribution from local, state, and student tuition for operational costs. Since the statute does not mandate the equal participation, the balance among the three sources fluctuates throughout the state. Each campus sets tuition policy locally. The state reimburses on an FTE basis guided by actual enrollment numbers from the prior year. Each college works with its county legislature in a politically negotiated process to establish annual local sponsor contributions, which are typically allocated in a single lump sum after a county-level review of the college's proposed budget. Capital costs are born 50 percent by the local sponsor and 50 percent by the state. Local capital funding must be formally approved by county legislators before state match can be sought. The state sets an annual capital budget, and a statewide coordinating council establishes capital funding priorities and attempts to distribute statewide on these priorities. The variability of local match requirements makes this a somewhat fluid process.

PATTERNS OF STATE AND LOCAL FUNDING

There is no one standard for the relative contribution of state and local funding to community colleges across the United States, and the presumptive standard deviation among patterns of funding is large. Survey data provide estimates of the median percentages of funding derived from each of the primary categories. These categories are usually termed:

- local sponsor (overwhelmingly a city or county)
- state (with federal making a small contribution)
- tuition and fees
- grants and gifts (Douglas and Harmening, 1999)

In 2004, the national average for the percentage of overall revenue provided by tuition and fees was 20 percent, state appropriations constituted 39 percent, local appropriations 18 percent, grants and contracts 12 percent, and private gifts and endowment income 1 percent. Auxiliary enterprises and independent operations produced close to 7 percent, and a variety of additional sources produced about 10 percent (*Enrollment in postsecondary institutions, fall 2004, graduation rates, 1998 & 2001 cohorts; and financial statistics, fiscal year 2004*, 2006).

But the actual balance among these sources in funding any individual college is quite variable. Tuition and fees can make up less than 15 percent of revenue to over a third. The median that colleges receive is just about 26 percent (Douglas and Harmening, 1999) . On average, state appropriations consistently were found to be a larger share of the revenue pie, with percentages ranging from just under 30 percent to 60 percent or higher (Douglas and Harmening, 1999). The median state contribution is just under 50 percent of colleges' total budget (Douglas and Harmening, 1999). Local appropriations tended to be lower, and in a very few cases there is no financial contribution from a local sponsor. Although it can be as high as just more than a quarter, the median is 12 percent. The revenue derived from gifts, grants, and contracts, despite large overall increases on individual campuses, are still a relatively minor part of the overall complexion of community colleges' budgets, with a median contribution of 7 percent. Thus the general pattern of relative contribution is for state appropriations to be the largest share, tuition and fees to be frequently second and local funding to be the smallest. But the variability is enormous; for example, one college in Colorado is supported 68 percent by local property taxes (Douglas and Harmening, 1999). Urban community colleges tend, on average, to be under-funded relative to their suburban and rural counterparts in public dollars (Dowd, 2004).

TRENDS IN PUBLIC FUNDING

Although trying to find trends in data as variable and as locally determined as the weather is probably suspect, some national patterns in the funding of community colleges emerge. The total amount of public funding of community colleges is decreasing in both real dollars and as a percentage of state and local budgets. This, in turn, means that larger percentages of the total cost of education are being born either by students directly, by grants, contracts or gifts, and/or by a range of entrepreneurial enterprises. While community colleges received less in regular governmental appropriations per student in 1994 than in 1989, total revenues per student increased because institutions were able to generate more revenue from such things as increases in student tuition and fees, one-time specialized government grants and contracts, or private fundraising (Watkins, 1998).

This pattern continues. Rizzo (2004) looked at the long-term decline of state spending for higher education from fiscal years 1976-77 to 2000-01. He determined that the share of state discretionary spending allocated to higher education fell by 6 percent, with higher education being the only major category of state funding to decline continuously since 1989 (Okundade, 2004). There is a concomitant trend to give the money directly to students instead of institutions. Considered in this light, the decrease in real dollars for public community colleges is even more substantial. While a state would count the money given directly to students as a part of its support of higher education, it has resulted in an additional 4 percent reduction in state appropriations to higher education. Rizzo states that together, the declines translate into real institutional appropriation losses of $2,800 per FTE for an average state—significantly more than the $1,700 increase in real average public four-year in-state tuition since 1977. In the last 20 years, states have systematically decreased spending on all of higher education (from 46 percent in 1980 to 34 percent in 2000), and community colleges have felt the overall impact of decreased state funding. Thus community college students, who are the least able to pay for college, are increasingly called upon to fund their own tuition.

The following sections point out how changes in financial aid are indicative of the changing nature of the implied contract in higher education between the state and the individuals who need support to get a college education. As access to higher education becomes more significant to the country's ability to be effective, a lesser percentage of public dollars supports students, who now increasingly rely on their own resources. The clear implication is that education in the eyes of public funders is turning into a private benefit as opposed to a public good. There are many underdeveloped countries in Africa and South America where private education is the only place for most to receive a college education. Unfortunately, it looks as if the United States may be moving in that direction. Theoretical models have demonstrated that states can encourage students to begin their studies at community colleges by managing tuition costs and cost differentials between four-year and community colleges (Hilmer, 1998). Yet few do so.

STUDENT TUITION

There are large differences in rates of student tuition charged by colleges. The variation appears most dramatically when compared across states, but sometimes varies within states as well. In every state, community colleges are less expensive than their public four-year counterparts, often by significant amounts (*Annual Almanac of Higher Education*, 2005). State tuition levels between the two sectors are highly correlated within any one state, with both standing in the same relative position to the national averages for each sector. Overall, community college tuition averages $1,379 for full-time, in-state students, ranging from a low of $316 for California to a high of $4,324 for New Hampshire *(Annual Almanac of Higher Education*, 2005). Four-year publics average $8,552, ranging from Oklahoma's low of $6,000 to Vermont's high of $12,836. Thus, states pay an average of $6,837 more per year to four-year colleges for each student in attendance than if the same student attends a community college. This difference has profound implications for how the states and federal government differentially support higher costs at four-year campuses, as well as significant implications for state expenditures on state financial aid, since aid is structured to be tethered to tuition.

FINANCIAL AID

The barrier high tuition creates for low-income students is eliminated if financial aid is plentiful. From a cost/benefit standpoint, governments are well served if students in community colleges are successful since, credit for credit, governments pay far less if they educate their students for the first two years at community colleges. This is especially true for the federal government, which provides the largest amount of tuition assistance (National Association of State Student Grant and Aid Programs [NASSGAP], 2004). Effective use of tax dollars is compounded by sending students to community colleges when states also provide tuition assistance to private (non-profit and profit) colleges, because their tuition is much higher on average than the publics *(Annual Almanac of Higher Education*, 2005).

Student tuition assistance programs have a large impact on students' out-of-pocket costs regardless of the actual level of tuition and fees charged. Because of this, there are paradoxical aspects to both federal and state policies for student tuition assistance. In some cases, the complexities of the rules cause community college students to pay *more* out of pocket for their lower-priced tuition than students at private or for-profit colleges. This disjuncture has not gone unnoticed by those who wish to find a way to make a personal profit from the billions of dollars that are spent on college each year. The difference in public dollar support for higher as opposed to lower tuition is probably central to the growth of the for-profit sector in the United States (Marchese, 2000).

Pell Grants are the single biggest source of federal financial aid, spending upward of $12 billion annually, dwarfing any other source of funding (Spence and Kiel, 2003). Although overall Pell allocations continue to increase, the difference does little to make college more affordable to the low-income adults who are most likely to attend community colleges. The reasons for this are multiple, including the overriding focus on tuition, the constraints of the Pell formula, which is based upon dependent students without income (resulting in working adults being denied aid), and the inadequate support for part-time aid. This combination of factors explains the differences in utilization, with just 20 percent of community college students compared to 46 percent of four-year college students receiving Pell Grants (Spence and Kiel, 2003).

While community college tuition costs are low compared to public colleges, they are small enough to seem almost ludicrous when compared to selective colleges. The average private college tuition of more than $20,000 a year towers above the community college average of $1,379 (*Pricing and Financial Aid*, 2004). The community college student pays, on average, *$18,621 less each year* than a student attending a private college. The perspective that is argued here will be that, despite the hue and cry about the runaway increases in college costs, the country is increasingly paying more for college educations than is necessary. Because financial aid policies, at both the state and federal level, are indexed to tuition at individual colleges, the highest-cost colleges derive the most benefit from public financial aid. If the focus of financial aid is to assist students who would not otherwise be able to go to college, these policies are flawed. This is especially true for low-income and minority students, for whom attending a community college increases the probability that transfers will go to more elite colleges than they would have had access to based solely on high school level achievement, and this is true for every income level (Hilmer, 1997).

Since students in a community college receive an education equivalent in quality to the first two years of college in comparable four-year institutions (Melvine, 1977), more tax dollars spent for equivalent or less than equivalent education is misspent. Current policies provide more public money to private or higher cost education because of the indexing of tuition to assistance.

There are human factors in the setting of tuition—and in particular in the process of tuition "discounting" that is conducted by private colleges, but not by community colleges. The process of discounting tuition is available to all private colleges and some public four-year colleges. It basically allows admissions staff to determine how much a prospective student is able to pay for college and lower the amount of tuition that the student will need to pay. In almost all cases, the discount is presented as a scholarship.

It is important for any analysis of tuition policy to try to quantify the psychological impact of getting a "scholarship" of a significant amount of money. It is difficult to believe that there is not a differential effect. Imagine first-generation students telling their parents, "I received a $6,000 scholarship." It feels much more exciting than saying, "The community college will cover all of my tuition." The first feels like a huge collegiate prize, and the second has the whiff of the free high school they attended. The difference is that the private college will now receive significantly more public dollars to support this student than the community college.

To examine this process in more detail, the following data are taken from the College Board's report on average tuition and fees (*Pricing and Financial Aid*, 2004). Students attending a four-year public college receive $3,000 on average in public financial aid; at four-year private institutions they receive an average of $10,700 in public aid; and yet community college students receive on average only $2,076 in public financial assistance. Community college students are at a disadvantage because the system, tied to tuition costs, provides the least amount of money to the poorest students, who overwhelmingly attend low tuition community colleges.

Community college students receive, on average, **81 percent less financial aid than they would if they went to a private college and 37 percent
less than if they went to a public four-year college.** Moreover, a family's
financial ability to pay greatly impacts the availability of financial aid, and
if the first child goes to a private four-year, the family's ability to pay for a
second child is lessened and therefore eligibility for financial aid goes up.
This math lesson is well understood by private, for-profit institutions, and
is fundamental to understanding the significant increase in the number of
for-profit colleges in the United States (Blumenstyk, 2005).

Further compounding the movement of tax dollars to support the highest tuition is the way tuitions are set. Private colleges can discount tuition at
the discretion of admissions officers, while public colleges typically have
tuition set by public entities in a politically charged atmosphere. For the
most selective institutions, scholarships are often plentiful as well. Overall,
this combination of factors leads to more state money going to higher priced
colleges. In New York, for example, while for-profit colleges educated only
about 2 percent of the population, they obtained 7 percent of the state's gen-
erous tuition assistance program (Smith, 2005).

Sources of Student Financial Aid

The sources of student financial aid for community colleges are the same as
for all of higher education—namely federal, state, private, and personal
resources. Aid can be categorized as being based upon need or upon merit.
Need-based grants are the largest category in both federal and state tuition
assistance plans. There is little data at national or state levels that separate
tuition assistance for community colleges, so much of the subsequent discussion looks at all of higher education.

Just over 20 percent of community college students receive federal
financial aid (through the Pell program), compared to 46 percent of all four-
year colleges (Olson, 2005). State-based financial aid is more comparable
between the two sectors. Fourteen percent of community college students
and 18 percent of four-year college students receive state tuition assistance
(NASSGAP, 2004). States awarded $6.9 billion in all forms of financial aid,
an annual increase of more than 9 percent in 2003-04 (NASSGAP, 2004).
The majority of state aid is awarded as grants, with more than 3.2 million
students receiving state tuition assistance (NASSGAP, 2004).. State financial
aid policy has been neglected as a way to increase transfers, but incentives

could be developed if states linked policies to characteristics that are positively related to transfer, such as increased aid for good GPAs, for completing an Associate degree, for extending time-to-degree, or for part-time enrollment (Long, 2005).

Need-Based Aid

Declining need-based aid is the national trend, and this again hits hardest at the lowest-income students. In part, this is because there is a strong correlation between family income and test scores (Carnevale, 2005). In 2001-02, there was a 2 percent decrease in needs-based aid (Rizzo, 2004). Student aid is not uniform, and six states (California, Illinois, New Jersey, New York, Pennsylvania, and Texas) account for 63 percent ($2.5 billion) of all state aid. States provided about $1.1 billion in non-grant student aid, including loans, loan assumptions, conditional grants, work-study, and tuition waivers, which accounted for 62 percent of tuition assistance in 2001-02 (NASSGAP, 2004). New York State, for example, provides an average of $1,007 per FTE, making it the national leader in need-based undergraduate aid (NASSGAP, 2004).

The nature of tuition assistance is complex when viewed in relationship to overall cost and student ability to pay. But in an atmosphere of declining resources for higher education, it is important to see the way in which state dollars are inappropriately directed to higher priced colleges. This is compounded by the lack of institutional support for community colleges. While just 4 percent of community college students receive any kind of institutional aid, more than 17 percent of four-year college students do (*Pricing and Financial Aid*, 2004).

POLICIES AFFECTING TUITION AND FINANCIAL AID

Aid for Wealthy Families

The shift in financial aid policies to increasingly target money for merit as opposed to need-based aid results in a distribution of aid to economically well-off families (Rizzo, 2004). This trend is compounded by the increasing numbers of students attending college, making more households eligible for Pell Grants and placing added pressure to slice the federal money for student aid even more finely.

Tuition Related to Financial Aid

There is a straight line decrease in proportionate public funding for higher education in America, and most colleges make up the difference by increasing tuition (Rizzo, 2004). These trends have the effect of sanctioning local tuition increases to capture federal grant aid. Debates at the federal level as the U.S. Department of Education examined the Higher Education Reauthorization bill in 2004 make this issue clear. Representative Howard "Buck" McKeon, a California Republican, says that every increase in Pell awards is an open opportunity for colleges to raise tuition (Burd, 2004).

Aid for Developmental and ESL Learners

Policies for the distribution of aid can also disadvantage community college students who require ESL or developmental courses. While all states allow use of public allocations to fund remediation, 11 percent of states do not allow students to use state financial aid for remediation, and Maryland alone requires all remediation to be completed before a student can be eligible for financial aid for credit courses (Jenkins and Boswell, 2002). State financial aid policies that require students to pass a specific number of college credits each semester can be disadvantageous to students who need to take a semester or more of developmental courses for which no college credit is given. Policies that limit the number of semesters students can receive aid also place developmental students at a disadvantage.

Additionally, policies that will provide aid only for those courses required in a specific major limit students' ability to explore new disciplines and may force a premature selection of a major. When students receive their credential from a state-sponsored GED or high school program, it is difficult for community college administrators to then tell these students not only that they must spend up to a year in remediation,, but also that the remedial courses may be only partially reimbursed under the requirements of Pell.

On the other hand, there has been federal legislation, such as the Hope Scholarship tax credit, that allows students tax credits for an array of educational expenses in their first two years. These and other state-based policies expand opportunities, although they disproportionately benefit middle- and upper-income brackets who attend the most expensive institutions in the country, rather than providing any benefit to low-income students who attend community colleges.

ALTERNATIVE REVENUE SOURCES

As public dollars for higher education decline, community colleges search for financial resources in addition to tax dollars. Colleges use alternative sources of revenue for both operational and capital needs, and try to augment existing activities, as well as seed innovation, or expand services with these more flexible dollars. The variable, episodic nature of alternative revenue sources, however, makes them difficult to rely upon to fund recurring costs.

Alternative sources can take several forms. A common form is grants and contracts for specialized educational services sought from local, state, federal, or private sources. Another is philanthropic activities that seek contributions from individuals, businesses, and foundations. A third source is revenue from entrepreneurial activities. Finally, community colleges provide a tremendous amount of education and training through non-credit structures that bring in revenue.

Grants and Contracts

Grants from local, state, private, corporate, and/or national sources are becoming an indispensable part of community colleges' ability to serve a broad swath of their community. Grants fund anything from a new academic program in bio-tech engineering to customized degrees for telephone company employees. Government grants and contracts, amounting to more than $1.2 billion, rose ten-fold between 1980 and 1996, with every indication that this is a continuing trend (Keener, 2002).

Grants greatly expand a community college's ability to provide human services as well as workforce development needs (Shulman, 2005). Total grants provided to individual community colleges average from $366,504 at small colleges to $3.9 million at large urban ones (Keener, 2002). Sixty-nine percent of the colleges reporting had grants offices (Keener, 2002).

Philanthropy

Philanthropy is a more recent part of the community college funding strategy, beginning to make a small but significant impact on overall revenue. The annual Voluntary Support of Education Report, the major source of information on higher education's private fundraising, has data on just 10 percent of community colleges nationally (*Voluntary Support of Education 1999*, 2000), making data on the true extent of external funding speculative. Historically, community colleges receive only 2 percent of private financial support (Pulley, 2001). But they are decisively entering the world of raising revenue through gifts, with 93 percent of colleges now staffing a foundation office and reporting an average total revenue of $993,296 (Keener, 2002).

The model for philanthropy for community colleges will be quite different from the standard four-year focus on alumni and parents. The most academically successful community college alumni often make new ties when they transfer to a baccalaureate granting institution, which then competes for their philanthropic allegiance. On the other hand, the services a community college provides to a local community, and particularly the way in which its efforts are fundamental to the economic development and social viability of that community, make it an ideal recipient of local business and foundation support (Begin, 2005). Thus, community colleges have unique development opportunities and challenges (Jackson and Glass, 1998). The link to businesses and individual community philanthropists might be the reason for the size of total endowments, which survey respondents reported as more than $680 million, with an average endowment of more than $2.3 million (Keener, 2002).

Entrepreneurship

Entrepreneurial actions are those activities colleges mount that serve their community and provide additional revenues for the campuses. The revenues gathered by entrepreneurial community colleges are even more difficult to quantify, and there is no national measure of the amount these endeavors contribute to a college's overall budget. Increasingly, community colleges are developing a range of activities that create revenue streams. Some examples include:

- Cuyahoga Community College in Cleveland has a wellness consulting service in which the college works with local employers to evaluate employees' health and then provide a wellness program to lower employer health costs.
- San Diego Community College's business services program at its downtown campus, which provides a range of business consulting and an on-site location for business development and incubation.
- Kirkwood Community College's Community Training and Response Center, which houses the National Mass Fatalities Institute, the Hazardous Materials Training and Research Institute, the Midwest OSHA Center, and the Linn County Emergency Management Agency, funded through college, county, private, and local industry.

If the trend in decreasing amounts of public support continues, it is likely that the range and financial contribution of these innovative forms of revenue generation will continue to proliferate.

NON-CREDIT REVENUE SOURCES AND FUNDING

Non-credit courses are educational offerings not appropriate for college credit. They teach content as basic as literacy or as advanced as highly technical medical procedures. Although offered by almost every community college, summary statements about the national state of funding for non-credit courses regarding either their overall revenue impact or the mechanisms by which they are funded are impossible to make. Beyond an individual state's or locality's practices for funding non-credit courses, there is no national data collection for non-credit courses comparable to the U.S. Department of Education's Integrated Postsecondary Education Data System (IPEDS) reports for credit courses. It is with these non-credit courses that the responsive mission of community colleges is perhaps best expressed and most difficult to codify.

Complicating the collection of any financial information is a lack of clarity. No single definition of a non-credit course exists, and therefore no standard unit of measurement analogous to a credit or a full-time-equivalent student (FTE) can be derived. Even a relatively simple thing such as the number of enrolled students is not clear for non-credit courses. While some colleges might report the overall number of registrants annually, the variable nature of the courses might lead to the same person enrolling in multiple non-credit courses. Without the conventions of the FTE student metric, there is no standard way to represent the duplicate number of non-credit students taking multiple courses in a single number. It is common for community colleges, when they report non-credit student participation, to count number of registrations, but this number often contains duplicate headcounts.

Financial aid is rarely available for non-credit courses. Federal tuition assistance is offered only for postsecondary educational experiences leading to an academic degree, and state tuition assistance is most often offered only in specialized cases. Grants and contracts for non-credit work typically provide a small amount of indirect fees that support the overall campus bottom line in addition to payment for the services provided.

Performance-based contracts, an increasingly popular model of grants from state sources, make the ability to quantify the net value of funding more complex (Graves, 2004). In these funding structures, full payment of the cost of providing the educational services is acquired only after the individual has received the training and been placed in a job, often for a specific amount of time at a specified rate of pay. If the student is not successful, the college is not fully paid for the cost of providing the service, leaving open the possibility that the program will run at a deficit.

While the variety of cost and revenue generation patterns for non-credit courses at community colleges make accurate classification difficult, the bulk of offerings and their funding structures might be categorized in three ways:

1. *Professional or paraprofessional development courses* are offered either through open enrollment or specific arrangements with a funding agency. Examples include a series of courses designed to prepare for a real estate certification exam, or a program of technical courses to train chefs, oil refinery operators, or emergency medical technicians (EMTs) to sit for licensure examinations. These courses can be funded on a fee-for-service basis paid by the students themselves, or through a grant that specifies who will be served (displaced workers, for example).
2. *Courses customized solely for a particular business or organization* that pays for and determines who enrolls in the courses. For example, an engineering company might contract for a specialized course in geo-positional systems to enhance field engineers' skills, or a large company might outsource all of its professional development to a community college to deliver programs in multiple cities in three different countries. Colleges often devise the cost structure so that the operational costs and some indirect costs are covered.
3. *Enrichment courses* that are provided to improve the lives of individuals who voluntarily enroll. These kinds of courses run the gamut from basic literacy and GED certificate courses to swing dancing and calligraphy. While some non-credit courses for academic skills improvement are state supported, the pure enrichment courses are usually provided on a fee-for-service basis.

Revenue from Non-credit Courses

The revenue for non-credit courses is highly variable. Colleges often hire permanent administrators, but it is not common for there to be a permanent instructional staff. The changing sources of funding, as well as the evolving nature of the content of the education and training provided, makes adjunct faculty appointments more common, either as an additional assignment for the college's full-time credit faculty or from external sources.

Non-credit programs are a part of the diversified revenue stream for community colleges, where they might prove to be constant, episodic, revenue-neutral, or even (in the case of performance-based contracts) a drain on revenues. The most successful community colleges are aggressive about the development of the non-credit courses because the potential is not just for increased revenue, but also for augmented services to a broad range of businesses and organizations. Large colleges can derive millions of dollars of revenue from continuing education offerings.

While there are not reliable data, it is likely that a number of credit students begin as non-credit. The ability to serve business and organizations through non-credit offerings also solidifies a community college's connection to a broad range of constituents and assists in spurring economic development throughout its catchments area. In these and other ways, the actual benefit that accrues to community colleges from non-credit offerings is both direct and indirect, with unmeasured impact on the total revenue picture.

VARIABLES INFLUENCING LOW COST OF COMMUNITY COLLEGES

Why are community colleges less expensive? While the foregoing should caution the reader from deriving uniform or consistent perspectives of community college funding, the different funding mechanisms do not fully answer the question. With a mission that is more expansive than either the high schools or most public colleges, how is it possible for community colleges to function with less funding per FTE than many high schools and most state colleges? What follows are some beginning answers.

Physical Plant

Most community colleges, for a variety of reasons, are able to function with fewer resources allocated to buildings when compared to other educational entities. The overwhelming majority of community colleges are designed to be within commuting distance of all students, by and large allowing them to forgo dormitories, extensive student development, expensive athletic programs, or opulent student activities facilities. At one extreme is the Community College of Vermont, which has almost no permanent educational facilities and leases space in 13 small town centers. Community colleges do not typically require faculty to conduct original research, lowering the cost of maintaining specialized research laboratories.

On the other hand, many community colleges do make extensive investments in their physical plants. Community colleges in California, Michigan, and Texas can look every bit as spacious and gracious as four-year colleges, with extensive grounds, burgeoning sports programs, ample recreation facilities, and expansive libraries. To diversify revenue streams, some colleges include a conference or business center on campus. Companies co-locate on community college campuses to provide easy access to incumbent worker training. Therefore, while it is common for community colleges to have lower expenditures per FTE on physical plant than comparable four-year colleges, it is not always the case.

Instructional Costs

Community colleges have lower costs of providing instruction. This is interesting because few community colleges have the enormous lecture halls or a graduate student teaching staff, practices which lower costs at universities. However, compared to four-year institutions, community college faculty are not expected to have an earned doctorate degree or focus on research, translating into lower beginning average salaries. For public postsecondary institutions, the average community college salary was $48,240; the average for four-year college was $54,255; and the average for universities was $63,595 (*Annual Almanac of Higher Education*, 2005). Community college faculty have much greater teaching loads, in part because of the decreased expectation for research and publication. Community college faculty teach more classes each semester than any other sector of higher education. The national average course load for community college faculty is 30 credit hours a year, or five three-credit courses each semester (*Fast Facts*, 2005).

Community colleges employ many more adjunct faculty, which also lowers costs. In 2001, 72 percent of the faculty at public four-year colleges were full-time compared to 33 percent of community college faculty (Harbour, 2003). These braided requirements for faculty (more teaching, fewer credentials, less research, higher part-time status) combine to keep labor costs more modest than on four-year campuses, and teaching productivity (i.e., the number of credit hours taught by each full time faculty member) high.

CHALLENGES TO THE FIELD

Community colleges are at the end of a long line of outstretched hands when it comes to public, private, or philanthropic support of education. On every index, community colleges receive less money from every funding system, whether state, federal, or locally sponsored. Without the innovation and entrepreneurship of most community colleges, many of them might not have survived. The pop singer Cyndi Lauper tells us, "Money, money changes everything," and it is interesting to speculate how many of the criticisms lodged against community colleges might be different if sufficient funding were provided for faculty, student support services, and student financial aid.

But recommendations for more money are neither practical nor likely. As public funding for higher education continues to diminish in the United States, community colleges will continue to be in a race for financial support with all other educational sectors. The suggestions that follow focus on providing the data support for a more comprehensive understanding of the value of a community college degree, on developing systems of national benchmarks, and on systems of support for the multiple missions of the community college.

1. Data Collection
   - Create national benchmarks or indices, similar to a Standard & Poors rating scale, that evaluate the relative contribution of local, state, and federal dollars.
   - Create national benchmarks or indices that create a value standard that relates tuition to educational value that can be used by students and elected officials to determine the best use of tax dollars in higher education.
   - Establish a definition and collect national data on non-credit courses and workforce development activities and use this information to fund non-credit courses that could move low-income adults to college and ultimately to greater employment and productivity.

2. Funding Support
   - Close the funding gap between community colleges and the rest of public higher education.
   - Use the national benchmarks scale to structure state and local statutes that regularize the funding for community colleges to create greater consistency of funding. These benchmarks must take into account local cost-of-living indices and could be used as the basis for creating a pool of equity dollars that could be distributed using equalizing factors.
   - Increase availability of state and federal tuition assistance for community college students' living expenses, indexing the entire need and making equitable allocations that ignore tuition differentials.

- Create mechanisms to provide tuition assistance for non-credit courses.
- Ensure that states provide funding, at a minimum, that creates equity on a FTE basis between high schools and community colleges.
- Re-evaluate and recalibrate federal and state tuition assistance programs so that greater number of tax dollars do not automatically flow to the most expensive programs.

CONCLUSION

The financial picture of community colleges is quite complex. On one hand, despite great disparities between community colleges and their four-year counterparts, this sector has created a vibrant and viable system. Tens of thousands of students take advantage of low tuition and supportive services to achieve an Associate degree and beyond. Thousands of businesses are served by customized training, and communities thrive when workforce development grants funneled by community colleges create new sources of economic activity.

On the other hand, community colleges accomplish their goals against the odds. With less than 20 percent of the dollars spent on higher education, it is difficult to provide the levels of support needed to make dramatic differences in the lives of too many of their most disadvantaged students. Increasingly, they are fighting with private and for-profit colleges for their share of state and federal tuition assistance programs. While entrepreneurial activities are important additions to the bottom line, they rarely provide for the ongoing operational support that builds quality educational organizations.

A deeper understanding of the ways in which state and federal policies affect community colleges, and mechanisms to benchmark best state and local funding practices, are some beginning steps on the path to regularizing and rationalizing the crazy quilt of funding structures across the country. Finding ways to close the disparity gap between two- and four-year, and between public and private colleges, will be increasingly important if community colleges are to continue their efforts to serve almost half of all undergraduates. Given what community colleges have been able to accomplish on a shoestring, it is exciting to imagine what might happen to half the learners in America if community colleges were provided equitable and consistent funding.

CHAPTER 4

Measuring Community College Effectiveness

◌ OVERVIEW

We yearn for a true measure of a community college. Is it possible? To be accurately evaluated, community colleges must develop distinctive measures of effectiveness. Many standard yardsticks for four-year colleges (time to graduation, acceptance rates, national statistics which measure "first-time, full-time students" exclusively) do not give a true measure of a community college's effectiveness, yet comprehensive measures which might provide some insight (percentage of developmental students who graduate, percentage of students who pass certifying examinations, percentage of students who complete college mathematics, percentage of non-credit students who move to credit courses) have not been used nationally. This chapter presents an overview of the range of current evaluation strategies that are used to determine, at a macro level, the effectiveness of community colleges.

The chapter also critiques both what is and what is not measured. It provides an overview of the ways in which better calibrated measures might be used to more consistently evaluate areas of success and failure, along with a survey of the emergent national assessments. It concludes with an analysis of where distinctive measures would improve the ability to assess accurately the value of a community college to its students and its community: a challenge to the field.

THE DREAM

A goal statement about ideal measurement of academic success at a community college can be stated with almost elegant simplicity: precisely assess each student's level of skills, match them to a set of pedagogical and curricular experiences, measure the student's level of education upon completion, and follow the student to the next phase, where those skills are to be applied (work or further academic classes), and then measure again. The initial assessment would include demographic indicators so colleges could make sure that different categories of students (i.e., various ages, races, socioeconomic statuses, genders, etc.) did not have differential outcomes. In this chapter, we argue that this dream is as elusive as it is deceptively easy to articulate.

The dream of ideal measurement becomes more complex conceptually when community colleges expand from evaluating only the students who enter into the school to measuring whether the college itself is making a positive impact on its community. Metrics would then include the identification of all the constituencies that comprise a college's community and the goals for serving each one. Measures might be developed, for example, to answer why a college offered one specific program as opposed to others, and if the program had the intended impact on the community. A community college's contribution to economic development might be assessed through an analysis of data on indices such as the number of new business starts, increases in the business tax revenues, number of new jobs created, increases in jobs that pay a living wage or offer health benefits, increases in new companies in emerging industrial sectors, etc. A different college, whose mission focused more on community development, might collect indices of the number of individuals who owned homes, the number of parks created, increases in cultural offerings or community-based organizations, the success of students in elementary school, decreases in incarceration or crime, etc. The only way to get accurate measures is to tie indices directly to the college's activities and programs.

Ideal measures are iterative and cyclic. The best colleges will want to know more and more about the impact of their educational programs. As questions are answered (i.e., which developmental sequence do data suggest is best for those who have not been in a mathematics class for more than twenty years but progressed through algebra versus students who have completed elementary calculus), other questions emerge (does it make a difference if those individuals ever took any on-the-job training related to quantitative reasoning?). Assessment must be iterative so that the cycle of analysis and measurement continues as new students, new programs, and new faculty refine and create new educational offerings.

The dream is for measurement to help establish effective benchmarks about what is possible as well as what is standard for community college education. If high school graduates are reading at a sixth grade level, what can we expect as the average in one semester of developmental reading? Does it differ for writing or mathematics? How effective are the best community colleges at graduating students with an Associate degree if they begin with a GED credential? Having benchmarks that could outline national averages for what can be expected, what the best colleges can accomplish, and how individual colleges can develop realistic standards for their success would propel community colleges into the future of effective academic measurement.

THE UNFULFILLED DREAM

The reality of measuring the effectiveness of community colleges is mixed and troubling. When the few metrics that four-year colleges have established for themselves (or that have been forced upon them by federal or state mandates) are applied equally to community colleges, the outcome seems dismal. The overwhelming majority of students who enroll in degree programs at community colleges don't graduate. It is common for only just over half of all students whose first class is a developmental reading, writing, or mathematics class to progress beyond that first class. These statistics are more true for low-income or minority students than for middle-class or white students. There are virtually no statistics that can even hint at the efficacy (or lack thereof) of non-credit programs.

Community college practitioners, however, point to the successes within these data. They remind us that none of these students would succeed if it were not for the community colleges, and that students who do graduate and transfer to baccalaureate programs progress at the same rate as students who began at the four-year college. It is evident that wholesale application of four-year metrics to community colleges is ludicrous, since four-year colleges weed out everyone who they do not believe will make it, and community colleges accept everyone and create miracles.

The issues of how to measure, what to measure, and when to measure continue to confound community college systems. The number of differing federal, state, and local agencies that want to understand the effectiveness of community colleges make data collection difficult. The time and money spent to collect these data further exacerbate community colleges' difficulties. What might seem simple at a residential four-year campus—for example, collect the home addresses of students—can become a nightmare for poor urban students who move frequently between the homes of different family members. Community colleges rarely have the extensive institutional research capacities to provide adequate data, and it is a rare local sponsor who wants to fund this kind of activity.

The reality is that data collection often comes at the end of a long list of wishes for community colleges. When scarce resources are spread thinly, even campuses that recognize the value of collecting information have a hard time choosing between tutoring students to pass algebra classes and funding an institutional research office. The local control of community colleges also makes a "one size fits all" data collection protocol hard to establish at a national level.

The influence of non-credit courses on overall enrollment and the lack of a single definition of a non-credit student analogous to a full-time-equivalent student (FTE) also make data collection blurry. Much of what might be evaluated in terms of workforce development is mandated by the grants that a college receives, but there is no parity between data that the U.S. Department of Labor, the U.S. Department of Education, or the local Workforce Investment Board wants colleges to collect. The default position is often to just collect what is necessary for one grant program, without the resultant ability to generalize data across different populations or different programs.

THE REAL STORY

Why Measure? The Dynamic Political Landscape of Higher Education Measurement

Issues of measurement and accountability emerged in the 1990s and 2000s as an animating principle for higher education in the same way that the critical analysis in *A Nation at Risk* galvanized the K-12 sector in the 1980s. The argument about measuring higher education effectiveness now traverses a familiar landscape: legislators complain about the costs of higher education, employers complain that college graduates cannot do high-level critical thinking or innovative management, while college leaders explain that education is an internal process not intended to be closely aligned with the bottom line.

When legislators argue that greater accountability would create incentives for colleges to become more like businesses by streamlining costs and improving "product" performance, educators retort that corrupt businesses like WorldCom and Enron, which misuse funds and deceive the public, would be the result of simplified expectations of easy to measure learning

outcomes. In lofty language, colleges assert that the goal of creating an educated citizen is complex and not easily reduced to simple numbers. When
elected officials complain that tuition has outpaced the cost of living, educators respond that there has been a wholesale dis-investment in public
higher education, along with an increasing reporting burden, that has
strapped colleges. Bruce Johnstone, former chancellor of the State University of New York, the coordinating body for all New York State community
colleges, wrote, "Planning and decision making [in higher education] are
often exercised in a veritable cauldron of political theatre, posturing, and
political agendas..." (Nettles and Cole, 2001).

The battle lines of accountability are thus clear, and tensions still flare
up on a regular basis. The conversation at the end of the Bush presidency is
that the U.S. Department of Education is interested in imposing an examination along the lines of No Child Left Behind for colleges and universities
(Arenson, 2006). There is no sign that this tension will decrease, because
there are so many competing state interests. Community colleges are caught
between perceptions of elected officials as spending more and more tax dollars on what might be called discretionary education, and the business perspective that education is becoming too important to the economic health
of the country to be left to the intellectuals (Nettles and Cole, 2001).

State-level assessment of public higher education remains an entangled
process marred by lack of clear goals or even clear roles for the different
state-level players (Nettles and Cole, 2001). There is some evidence that
explicit focus on a narrow set of outcomes might displace more traditional
goals of accessibility and affordability (Nettles and Cole, 2001).

What is rarely discussed in the political roil of accountability is the need
to be accountable to ourselves. If community colleges do not look squarely
in the eye of the most troubling statistics—progress of students in developmental education (or lack thereof), students whose credits will not transfer
to the local state college, or workforce training programs that do not make a
measurable change in graduates' wages—then they are operating at sub-opti-
mal levels. Community colleges have reached a level of sophistication at
which we can no longer rely on anecdotes to form the foundation of our *rai-
son d'etre*. Above all, the accountability movement must propel colleges themselves to evaluate their ability to make real the promise of higher education.

In 1984, the Study Group on the Conditions of Excellence in Higher
Education at the National Institute of Education issued *Involvement in
Learning*, which argued that extraordinary breakthroughs in learning could
be achieved if faculty used the research on teaching that demonstrated that

high expectations, active pedagogies, and frequent feedback produce significantly improved academic results (Ewell, 2005). Two years later, co-authored by a man who would shortly be elected president of the United States, the National Governor's Association published *A Time for Results*. In this report, Governors Bill Clinton, Lamar Alexander, and Tom Kean exhorted colleges to create clear standards for the kind of educational results that both students and the public could expect, and then measure themselves on their ability to achieve these standards (Ewell, 2005). Both reports spurred the development of the ideologies of assessment and accountability.

Peter Ewell, while acknowledging that politics instigated the accountability pressure, argues that higher education is well served by articulating standards by which we should be measured as a matter of public trust (Ewell, 1994). Others have a more sinister view, asserting that accountability is a political ploy and an expression of a conservative move toward making higher education function in a capitalist market in the same way that health care has functioned in the past twenty years (Ohmann, 2000). This darker view believes assessment is a convenient cover for a more explicit intention of challenging progressive movements on campus (Ohmann, 2000). Whether it is an asset, a tool, or a bludgeon, every indication is that accountability measures are increasing and are here to stay (Petrides, McClelland, Nodine, 2004; Sanchez and Lanaan, 1998; Serban, 2004).

The political nature of accountability measures will undoubtedly become more volatile if states or localities use measures to limit funding, close programs, or combine campuses. As the state and local fight for funding becomes increasingly pitched, fueled by the twin combustibles of tax cuts and runaway costs in health care, community colleges will be challenged to develop and deploy outcome measures as never before. The best colleges will craft meaningful metrics, use them consistently, and make sure that they are transparent and completely understood by the politicians and the public.

Community colleges must also push for measures that indicate how states or localities themselves can be held responsible for providing the necessary conditions for success. This kind of measurement is exemplified by the State-by-State Report Cards issued by the National Center for Public Policy and Higher Education (Callan and Finney, 2005). Yet another measure might document the way in which the country itself is falling behind in overall measures of higher education in international comparisons. For example, the United States lags behind other countries in several important educational indicators, trailing in the percentage of the population under 25 who enroll in some form of postsecondary education, according to data from the Organisation for Economic Co-operation and Development in 2003 (Callan and Finney, 2005). Only governmental action can have a meaningful impact on system-level measures such as these.

APPROPRIATE MEASURES FOR COMMUNITY COLLEGES

Community colleges (and public colleges in general) were seen throughout almost the entire twentieth century as a public utility, and no evaluation beyond the perception that the public was well serviced was sought (Sanchez and Lanaan, 1998). The accountability movement for all of higher education has disputed the effectiveness of grades as measures partly because colleges began to be perceived as no longer serving the public effectively and partly because a strategic investment of so many tax dollars should provide an adequate return.

The question of what should be measured depends in part on who is asking and the purpose for which the data will be used. Community college audiences for outcome measures include federal, state, and local governments, boards of trustees, philanthropic funders, program-specific agencies, and regional accreditation agencies. Institutional accountability can be typified by some combination of legal accountability (compliance to standards), negotiated accountability (collaboratively determined data demonstrating responsiveness to constituent needs), anticipatory accountability (metrics for advocacy), and discretionary accountability (measures to assess self-determined elements of mission) (Kearns, 1998). Responding to this multi-leveled group of constituents is amazingly complex and very difficult to fund (Shaw and Rab, 2003).

How community colleges use funds is a common measure of legal accountability (e.g., percentage of federal grant dollars used to purchase equipment, or percentage of students eligible for financial aid), while a negotiated standard might consist of mutually agreed upon measures with a state department of education, such as an appropriate student pass rate for a state licensure exam. Anticipatory metrics are represented by such measures as the number of students who remain in a community college district and pay taxes after graduation (always good for a lobbying day with the legislature), while a "Diversity Scorecard" might be an example of a discretionary metric that seeks to evaluate differential rates of attrition for African-American males versus females (Bensimon and Soto, 1997).

The autonomy enjoyed historically by community colleges in what they measured is a thing of the past, particularly when all of higher education faces a decline in public and political trust (Richardson and Smalling, 2005). In the wake of the No Child Left Behind legislation, most states want easy and comparable measures of learning and some, such as the community colleges in New York City, have mandated both passage of standardized basic skills assessment tests for entrance and rising junior exams before graduation to appease politicians (Ewell, 2005).

The potpourri of measures at community colleges currently reflects a range of federal, state, and local priorities. Only a few states develop measures and funding mechanisms to evaluate teaching and learning effectiveness, such as Georgia's Special Funding Initiatives or the Illinois Performance-based Incentive System (Richardson and Smalling, 2005). Some states, such as Arizona, identify very appropriate priorities for community colleges to measures, such as transfer, but then do not hold the four-year campuses equally responsible (Richardson and Smalling, 2005).

Preliminary analysis of national IPEDS data find that individual student characteristics are much more predictive of successful completion of degree or certificate programs than institutional data, so the unit of analysis is always important in understanding how to measure an effective community college (Bailey, Calcagno, Jenkins, Kienzl, Leinbach, 2005). Nonetheless, the indices by which community colleges across the nation are currently measured can be described by a taxonomy of

- inputs
- processes
- outputs
- outcomes (Burke, 2005)

Despite the rhetoric of measurement, less than 20 percent of the measures used are actually outcomes (Burke, 2005). To achieve a higher percentage of actual outcome measurements, colleges would include such things as evaluating student learning through a standard such as passing national examinations, submitting portfolios for review by external evaluators, succeeding at transfer institutions, achieving job placement, or receiving an increase in wages upon graduation. Almost half of the kinds of things community colleges measure are process indicators, such as class size or the percentage of instruction provided by full-time faculty (Burke, 2005). There is a presumption that smaller classes or more full-time faculty lead to improved student performance, but this is not measured. Rather, community colleges (and all of higher education) tend to measure what is easy to measure: enrollment, numbers of students receiving financial aid, and numbers of students enrolled in developmental education. The few true learning outcome measures that are almost universally evaluated by community colleges across the United States are graduation rates and passage of professional licensure exams. Other common measures include:

- transfers from community colleges
- use of technology
- faculty teaching loads
- credits at graduation or time to degree
- faculty/staff diversity
- job placement rates
- preparation of entering students
- non-instructional costs as a percentage of overall costs
- program duplication
- satisfaction surveys (alumni or employers)
- sponsored research dollars obtained
- student test scores
- workforce training indicators (Burke, 2005)

Accountability measures at community colleges are increasingly influenced not just by political agencies, but also by regional accrediting agencies. Regional accrediting agencies are critical to the funding of community colleges because federal financial aid is predicated on their approval. While in the mid-1990s most regional accrediting agencies included assessment measures as evaluation standards, these measures tended to evaluate the overall institutional effectiveness as organizations rather than focusing on students' ability to function as employees and citizens, the latter being a more traditional state perspective (Ewell, 2005). Critics of accrediting agencies argue that the agencies are more interested in whether colleges establish metrics for measurement than if the colleges actually use the measures for improvement (Ewell, 2005). The local focus of community colleges results in measures that are not comparable nationally, and often not even comparable across different counties in the same state.

DATA NEEDED FOR EFFECTIVE MEASUREMENT

If community colleges are to be measured effectively, the measures must be tied to the reality of students' lives and the colleges' multiple missions. Over the past decade, many suggestions have been made. Measures of community college student learning outcomes tend to cluster around four areas: progressing toward academic goals, achieving general education, overcoming educational deficits, and preparing for transfer (Alfred, Ewell, Hudigns, and McClenney, 1999). In addition to student learning outcomes, community colleges should also be held accountable for workforce development, economic development, and related measures of responsiveness to community needs (Alfred et al., 1999). Currently, none of these goals are measured consistently across the country, and few have commonly agreed upon data elements. An overview of this research can be categorized in the following ways: academic goals, general education, student engagement, intellectual qualities, basic skills, transfer rates, economic development and community responsiveness, and workforce development.

Academic Goals

When students enroll at Dartmouth as freshmen, their goals are clear: graduate with a baccalaureate degree in four years. This is not true for the typical community college student. Students may come to community colleges with goals unrelated to getting a certificate or degree. They might wish, for example, to take three courses on marketing and finance to improve their ability to manage a business they own, or to take enough classes in developmental writing to pass the U.S. Air Force test. Community college advocates argue that the multiplicity of goals for students must be considered when evaluating success. Critics maintain that community college officials cite these less-than-degree goals to make low levels of degree attainment palatable.

A clear measure of student goals, assessed every semester, could provide an accurate benchmark of goal attainment while at the same time determining whether colleges were successful in increasing student aspirations. Progress toward goals could then be calibrated in a time-sensitive manner. Measures might include academic standing (grade point average), number of courses attempted versus those successfully completed, and consistency of registration, in addition to the most common degree completion rates (Alfred et al., 1999). The Beginning Postsecondary Students Longitudinal Study of 1996-2001 does attempt to identify student goals and gives evidence that, while some students attend community college for skills upgrades, many aspire to an Associate degree and higher (Bailey, Calcagno, Jenkins, Kienzl, and Leinbach, 2005; U.S. Department of Education, 2003). There is some evidence that, when community colleges conduct the necessary data gathering to link student goals to educational outcomes, colleges can effect modest levels of improvement in student performance (Harris, 1998).

Currently, graduation data are calibrated in years to degree, and the standard is full time plus 50 percent (typically three years for a two-year degree). This standard is promulgated by the federal government in its IPEDS data requirements. Degree and certificate completion rates, however, should at minimum be linked to student attendance patterns. Thus, proportionate part-time status should be translated into expected completion rates and measured against this timeframe. The critique of the federally required Student Right to Know report of enrollment and graduation data is that it not only studies the cohort of "first-time, full-time students" who comprise less than half of all students nationally, but also that no calibration of data is allowed when students shift to part-time, as frequently happens among community college students (Bailey, Calcagno, Jenkins, Kienzl, Leinbach, 2005, 2005). An Associate degree student who takes one class a semester would be expected to graduate in 30 semesters (or almost 15 years). Community colleges that were successful in helping students gain successful completion of more courses a semester to achieve, for example, a graduation in 10 years instead of 15 should be commended.

General Education

Although measuring general education has been on the national agenda for years, little substantive progress has been made. How can community colleges measure their effectiveness in both remediating the general education that high school graduates have not received and providing a solid basis for the first two years of college? The answer remains elusive. Despite the heightened public need to assess a student's capacity to function within the liberal arts and sciences (skills in computation, analysis, and communication as well as general knowledge), there is less agreement on a national basis than ever before on what constitutes the appropriate frame of general education (Rust and Reed, 2004). The need for clarity and sharpness of definition for learning goals for colleges is of paramount importance, and a few testing companies are attempting to develop standardized measures (Burke, 2005).

The so-called soft skills that employers expect to be the result of a college education—such as leadership, teamwork, ability to tolerate ambiguity, ability to function in different cultures, creativity, initiative, capacity for continuous learning, along with the much-beloved skill of multi-tasking—are even more elusive (Rust and Reed, 2004). On the other hand, measurements of licensure and certification pass rates provide a standard assessment of specific skills associated with particular degrees, often providing a clear national standard. The National Council of State Boards of Nursing's NCLEX examination, required across the country for Registered Nurses (RNs) to practice, is one such example. Measures of critical literacy and numeracy skills, augmented by citizenship skills, have been suggested but not generally embraced as ways to evaluate general education (Alfred et al., 1999).

Student Engagement

A different and promising approach has been promulgated by the Community College Survey of Student Engagement (Community College Survey of Student Engagement [CCSSE], 2006). While it does not attempt to measure learning outcomes per se, the rigorously developed and nationally normed test attempts to assess quality in community college education by surveying students in randomly selected classes about a campus's educational practices that are correlated with high levels of student learning and retention (CCSSE, 2006). The survey is intended to identify areas for improvement, and is grounded in research about what works in strengthening student learning and persistence; it includes national benchmarks (CCSSE, 2006).

Intellectual Qualities

Rust and Reed (2004) identify what they term "next generation state accountability reporting and federal research." The Pew Charitable Trust is working with states to generate state-based data about the intellectual qualities of their graduates through a standardized test designed to be incorporated into the "Measure Up Report Card" from the National Center for Public Policy and Higher Education. The National Governor's Association is identifying best practices in state-level metric systems, and the National Assessment of Adult Literacy test administers to a nationally representative sample a test that examines proficiency in English language prose and document and quantitative literacy skills (Rust and Reed, 2004). These tests and initiatives may be the beginning of an emerging consensus about what to measure and how to measure it, although again the focus is usually framed by a four-year college perspective.

Basic Skills

Nationally, community colleges are much more likely to have measures of how many students attend and successfully pass through developmental education. This is because assessment of high school level skills takes place, whether through the commercially available assessment tests such as ASSET or COMPASS from ACT (ACT , 2006) and ACCUPLACER from the College Board (Accuplacer, 2006), or through home-grown tests. Thus is it common for community colleges to be able to indicate the number or percentage of incoming students who must take developmental education courses, and often the number of students who subsequently pass successfully into college-level courses. However, there is still no national standard for passing—even for the nationally normed tests—and it is not uncommon for different standards to be held by different community colleges in the same state or region. These data are therefore rarely collapsed for a national benchmark or measure of the average pass rate out of developmental education.

A more robust measure would be one that includes measures such as the number of developmental students who pass the content course subsequent to passing out of remediation, or the relationship between the percentage of entering students who need developmental education and the percentage of graduating students who began their studies in remediation. The issue of definitions is also at play here, since some colleges identify English as a Second Language courses as development and others do not. As outlined in chapter twelve, students in ESL classes range from those holding Master's degrees from home countries to those who are almost illiterate in their native language. How to depict accurately their participation in developmental education is problematic.

Transfer Rates

Transfer preparation would be a much more straightforward measure if all campuses (two- and four-year) identified, in a national database, the schools to which students transferred. This has yet to be achieved, and there are critics who fear the "big brother" aspects of having a single national database that lists all students and where they attended college. Without this, however, data on student transfer will be more or less complete. Since it is very common for community college students to stay local, transfer data are more available than other metrics, and the most common "sending to" institutions are usually known to any one community college. Again, what is often lacking is the next level of data that would indicate actual success in transfer—the performance of community college students in the institution to which they transfer. These data require cooperation from the campuses to which students transfer, sometimes easy to obtain and sometimes not. It is also important for four-year colleges to be held to the same standard, as many students transfer from a four-year to a community college, but the four-year college is never asked to account for student success.

Other measures important for a national understanding of transfer success or lack thereof would be for four-year colleges and universities to report what percentage of their graduating class began their studies at community colleges. For many public institutions of higher education, the numbers of transfer students are larger than native students. At least one college in the country reports these data, where the data demonstrate that the very best juniors are the students who transferred from community colleges. They are doing better than the native juniors (Heelan, 2006).

Transfer can also be expanded as a national measure for four-year institution to establish benchmarks about transfers into their institutions. For the community college student who wishes to transfer to a competitive college, this is a critical issue.

A more important measure could be to track who in the community *should* be going to the community college. This might be conceptualized as having two dimensions. The first would be to look at local GED certification and high school graduation rates to determine the number of students who are admitted to the community college immediately or closely following degree achievement, and monitoring this percentage over time. The second dimension would be those adults in the community who have no or at minimum less than two years of college. Because the changes in workforce needs correlate this measure so closely with poverty, the community college that is responsive to its community should be developing strategies to successfully help these adults enter and complete certificates and degrees. Again, the creation of a national benchmark would spur this evaluation.

Economic Development and Community Responsiveness

One of the ways in which community colleges are most distinctive is their mission to serve the cultural, workforce development, and economic development needs of their locality. Yet there is no clear answer to the question of how to measure economic impact. However, as community colleges do more and more in this realm, several proxy measures are beginning to emerge.

One important measure is employer assessment of students. These surveys are increasingly used, both while students are enrolled through assessment of internships, and then after course completion through alumni surveys and surveys that assess employers' evaluations of the success of customized training and related initiatives (Alfred et al., 1999). Most students attend the community college with an express interest in furthering their economic status. Thus, a measure of the economic benefit of community college education is a critical individual factor, and one that can be averaged across individuals. State and national level analyses, however, currently do not provide sufficient measures to evaluate the impact of community college on income levels. United States census measures of educational attainment do not include two-year colleges as a separate category, and state efforts to collect such data have been uneven (Peterman, 1999). One powerful tool, linking community college administrative records with unemployment insurance, has allowed states such as Washington, Florida, and North Carolina to track earnings in three-month intervals, although other states' policies prohibit linking data in this way (Peterman, 1999). Even this measure undercounts the self-employed, federal employees, or military personnel (Peterman, 1999).

Economic development can be viewed as the larger category into which workforce development activities can be situated. However, for this section, economic development refers to the range of services that are provided to companies that result in the creation of wealth for businesses and organizations. Community college activities that enhance economic development are various. Some include activities that help businesses, cultural institutions (museums, theaters, artists' collectives), or community-based organizations (CBOs) to:

- increase the numbers of employees and/or increase employee wages,
- expand into new markets,
- maintain market share in increasingly competitive markets,
- improve profitability,
- improve a business's ability to offer health insurance or other employee benefits,
- increase taxes paid to the local community,
- access more governmental services or funding (small business development loans, tax abatements, program initiatives, etc.).

While these activities and their results can be measured, there is no national standard or set of indices that would allow for comparisons across colleges, and there has been no attempt to develop standards that would allow colleges to make self-assessments or strategies for improvement. Individual community colleges often give some sense of these activities in annual reports, press releases about individual projects, or internal campus planning documents. The opportunity for local municipalities to develop these standards and work with community colleges to expand their impact exists, as does the potential leadership of state departments of commerce or labor. The ability to define a national metric will probably need to wait until more local, regional, or state measures can be identified. This work is so central to the community college mission and has so much potential positive impact on a community that the lag time until standards emerge is regrettable.

Workforce Development

Workforce development in this section refers to those activities undertaken by the community college that provide skills and resources to individuals in the community, with the express purpose of making these people more employable. The range of activities commonly undertaken by colleges includes programs using vouchers for skills development funded by the federal Workforce Investment Act (WIA) or related government programs, customized training for incumbent workers, and credit programs for beginning accountants, veterinary technologists, allied health professionals, and other paraprofessionals. It must also refer to transfer students whose first two years at a community college allow them to complete a baccalaureate (and beyond) on their way to becoming business owners, doctors, and professors. Some of the ways to measure economic benefit to individual students are known but difficult to effect (such as unemployment insurance rates tied to student identifiers, measured indices of economic viability among sectors of businesses with which colleges had collaborated in comparison to overall financial data for a region, etc.). Yet without standards, and especially without encouragement to seek and collaborate with local economic development agencies to gather actual data, the metrics available are infrequently used and rarely developed into standards against which a college could measure itself in relationship to other colleges.

Toward a Definition of True Community College Effectiveness

Ties to Local Community

A college that is effectively tied to its community should be able, over time, to demonstrate its impact. Educational levels should rise, and increasing numbers of individuals should go to college and/or upgrade skills. The best measures would hold an institution accountable for being an active player in the improvement of its community. Because standard measures of higher education are focused on four-year colleges (time-to-degree, applied to admitted ratios, external research grants obtained), the real value a community college adds to its locality is missed. The problem with this is two-fold. First, since those who establish the indices do not ask us to measure what we value, the true value of the community college is never included in the appropriate indices. In fact, local politicians have sometimes deliberately misused community college data to make the colleges appear much less effective than they are (Arenson, 1999).

Second, it is difficult to measure what would happen if a community college was not in a specific community. While it is true that many students graduate from high school without high school level skills, rather than measure the deleterious impact these low-skilled individuals would have on a community, we now measure the percentage of these low-skilled students who enter but do not complete a degree at a community college. It is also difficult to evaluate the impact of going to college on someone's life-outlook or readiness to work. If there was no place for disabled workers who needed specific support to achieve economic self-sufficiency, what would happen in a specific community? Right now, the best we can do is assess things such as wages after training, but the deeper personal and social implications are not evaluated. The social attributes identified in chapter two as being associated with college attendance, although difficult to measure, are the very ones at which community colleges should excel. Thus a college should be able to show that lower dependence on public assistance, lower rates of incarceration, and higher participation rates in positive community activities such as philanthropy and political and civic life are attributable to community college attendance. Sadly, these important effectiveness measures will probably never be employed.

Ties to Regional and National Economic Health

A more pernicious problem is that these measures matter more now than ever before. While a male college graduate's first job typically paid 33 percent more than that of a male high school graduate in 1973, the difference has more than doubled to 81 percent (Rust and Reed, 2004). It is estimated that in the next twenty years, businesses will need between 12 million and 14 million more employees with high level skills than the United States currently produces (Rust and Reed, 2004). If community colleges were more widely seen as central to the effort of sending more students to college successfully, and were financially supported to achieve these goals, it is possible that the United States could add $230 billion in national wealth and $80 billion in taxes annually. With no measures that hold community colleges to high national standards, the ability to diminish the almost 20 percentage-point difference in educational attainment between white and Asian baccalaureate attainments and Latinos or African-Americans is probably dismal (Rust and Reed, 2004).

Cohen (2001) notes that measures of community college effectiveness were presumed to be managed at the state level, and therefore few colleges established the sort of robust institutional assessment centers that might begin to frame appropriate answers to the questions posed above. Without measures of student learning and institutional effectiveness that not only connect to public understanding of what colleges do but also actually re-educate the public about the real impact of community colleges, it is probable that states and the federal government will not change their four-year bias. Unless community colleges are able to talk about what they do, how it impacts students and the community, and how they are redressing many of the concerns that have been voiced about K-12 education, community colleges will continue to be the forgotten partner in higher education.

CURRENT ACCOUNTABILITY MEASURES - FEDERAL, STATE, PROGRAM

Federal Measures

What is measured and how to measure are usually based upon who is asking. There are at least three very different constituencies who should comprise the "who": students, the business community employing the students, and the government funding the programs (Shaw and Rab, 2003). In 1994, the American Association of Community Colleges established a list of thirteen core indicators of community college effectiveness. In general, community colleges were exhorted to develop measures that demonstrated their successful transactions with external agencies, be able to compare results achieved to the measured needs and expectations of their constituents, and provide information about performance in ways that build understanding of the community college mission (Lanaan, 2001a). The thirteen core indicators included measures for student achievement, transfer, persistence, citizenship and placement rates in the workforce (Lanaan, 2001a). Other than this almost 10-year-old document, there is little on the national level that attempts to specify what an institutional measure of success should be.

While there are federally mandated measures that relate to specific activities on campus (for example, the Student Right to Know Act regarding crime, Americans with Disabilities Act regarding accessibility, and Titles IV, V, and VII regarding financial aid and other specific funding formulas), no attempt has been made to articulate what the nation expects of its community colleges. Is a 50 percent pass rate in developmental education great or problematic? Is it acceptable that almost 70 percent of students do not graduate with a degree or a miracle if a community college can get its graduation rate up to 30 percent in four years? Is 90 percent passage on the national nursing certification exam terrific, or wasting a community's precious resources on the 10 percent who failed? No agency of the federal government, nor any national educational association, has even begun to outline what would be quality standards for a community college. Conversely, many fear the establishment of standards if they are based upon a four-year model.

Use of National Data

Community colleges must respond to federal requests for information on students. There are two primarily federal measures: the Integrated Postsecondary Data Systems (IPEDS) submissions, which provide data on student enrollment and demographic characteristics, and the Student Right to Know, which provides information on crimes on campus.

IPEDS, the single most common data collection process in higher education, is based on assumptions that are out of date for all of higher education. The outmoded data categories are particularly problematic for community colleges. The principal focus of IPEDS student data is on the measure of "first-time, full-time" students. This measure works adequately for the most selective institutions, where nearly all students entering college are first time (there are very few transfer students) and full time. It does not function effectively for community colleges for several reasons.

Part-time Student Status

On average, 62 percent of students are part time (*Fast Facts*, 2006). Thus, by definition, IPEDS ignore the majority of community college credit students. Patterns of typical community college course-taking make the IPEDS' focus on first-time/full-time less helpful because it is the rare student who, even when beginning full time, is able to stay full time (*Institutional Profile*, 2005). While the reasons for changing attendance status are many, primary among them is student need to work in order to pay for college and life (*Making sense of the retention puzzle*, 2005). Because community colleges now enroll 45 percent of all first-time freshman (*Fast Facts*, 2006), the U.S. government dramatically under-measures the characteristics of its college students when it focuses solely on first-time/full-time students.

Retention

This problem is then compounded with the other IPEDS measures that describe the student experience. Retention, arguably one of the most important measures of the success of a community college, is evaluated only on the return of first-time/full-time students from fall to fall. Graduation rates are calculated only on first-time/full-time, and are calculated for four years only, despite the evidence that many students successfully graduate in five or more years (*Institutional Profile*, 2005).

Financial Aid Awards

How a college distributes scholarships, and how financial aid is provided, is measured for first-time/full-time only. One of the most intractable problems for the low-income students who attempt college is access to part-time aid so that they can remain employed and respond to family responsibilities, but the federal government currently does not track information that would allow for the creation of national guidelines or standards for community colleges.

Credit versus Non-credit Enrollment

A final reason that IPEDS is problematic is its focus on credit students only. In 2005, there were 6.6 million credit students and 5 million non-credit students in community colleges. Defining college students as only those intending to achieve a college degree is clearly appropriate for the federal government and IPEDS duly does so. The complexity emerges for community colleges when all campus expenses and revenues are applied to credit FTE only. This overestimates the amount of money community colleges have available to support credit students, since many campuses have significant revenues associated with their non-credit activities.

Additional Federal Measures

Other federal measures of community colleges are embedded in longitudinal studies of college students undertaken by the U.S. Department of Education. These on-going research projects contain much more descriptive data about community college students, and the information detailed in reports based upon these data sets is much more effective in providing a national perspective on community college students. They include the National Educational Longitudinal Student Survey and the Beginning Postsecondary Students Survey. Clifford Adelman (Adelman, 1999, 2000, 2003; Adelman, Daniel, and Berkovits, 2003) has determined several important national dimensions that clarify the complexity of accurately measuring aspects of community college student life. Some of the dimensions include the need to carefully understand graduation rates, the need to measure transfer rates only after grouping students by intentions to attempt college (typically, by completing 12 or more credits), and the need to identify the multiple ways in which students access higher education across city, state, and sometimes even national boundaries.

However, the kind of thoughtful studies that are undertaken with the data sets do not provide the information that IPEDS could—information that links dollars, scholarships, and student success. Nor are they available to be used annually for colleges to understand where they are in relationship to national averages, or for the government to track trends as they occur.

The data that Adelman has highlighted points to another potential role of the federal government in tracking students across institutions and across states. Increasingly, the National Student Clearinghouse in Virginia provides this data for groups of students. More than 90 percent of the colleges and universities in the United States participate (National Student Clearinghouse, 2006). If the federal government mandated that all students enrolled in any college, public or private, were entered into this database, community colleges would be acknowledged for the educational foundation they provide to many students who subsequently complete degrees on other campuses.

STATE MEASURES

Linked to Funding

State level measurements are typically linked to funding, as mentioned above. There is a difference between measures that are mandated and consistent across all sectors of higher education and those that are specific to community colleges. For example, accountability measures in New Jersey which were used as the basis for small amounts of performance funding were not specified, leading to some interesting disjunctures. Under Governor Christine Todd Whitman in the late 1990s, time-to-degree was of paramount importance (Scott, 2005). Time-to-degree is typically an upper middle class preoccupation since an additional semester at a high-tuition college is difficult for parents, but often wonderful for their fully supported children. On the other hand, community colleges that help students persist to degree while working full time over many years are to be commended, not penalized. The disjuncture thus occurs in this measure between paying for college (a common community college student activity) and graduating fast (a common desire for younger students whose parents are paying for every semester).

Transitory and Political

State-based measures can be perceived as transitory because of they are often established based on the particular interests of politicians at a specific time. Since many community colleges have very stable faculty and staff over many years, this can encourage foot-dragging. "College faculty and staff have seen specific external requirements come and eventually go. In an environment in which the state fiscal picture and the attention of state legislators can change rapidly, internal delaying tactics, such as resisting efforts for a specific program assessment because it is assumed that the requirement will be dropped eventually, are quite effective." (Petrides et al., 2004)

Accountability measures that are linked to funding are usually established at the state level. The measurement is developed to either reward good performance (incentive funding) or provide additional resources for improvement. Performance-based funding in higher education was first introduced in Tennessee in 1978, with large increases in the late 1990s (Petrides et al., 2004). While the total amount of state dollars allocated through an accountability-linked measure is small, about half of the states currently allocate some performance-based funding (Petrides et al., 2004), and three-quarters ask for performance-based reports (Lanaan, 2001a) For example, in 1989 California asked its community colleges to develop accountability metrics tailored to their mission. The colleges assessed categories such as transfer rates, student satisfaction, occupational preparation, and the financial conditions of colleges, but attention to these measures lessened as funding for measurement as well as incentive funding dried up in 1990s budget shortfalls (Lanaan, 2001a). There are few substantive evaluations of the impact of performance-based funding on actual outcomes. The analyses that currently exist suggest that the impact has been moderate (Petrides et al., 2004). North Carolina has experienced an iterative process, with a small amount of state funding distributed via performance measures, but the potential for increased state control of local allocation decisions is possible (Harbour, 2002).

Mandated Measures

States mandate that colleges collect certain measures with the goal of creating positive change in those statistics. Actually achieving the desired change can be elusive. To improve all community college performance in a state is predicated on a number of things. Because college is a people-intensive activity, the success of a large-scale program can depend on the perceptions of the individuals charged with responding to the assessment data. Surveys of faculty and staff perceive mandated accountability measures as anything from an opportunity to demonstrate success to a situation that calls for dedicated resistance to bureaucratic meddling (Harbour, 2005). Sometimes mandated accountability measures lead to self-defensive actions, and often they are hobbled by the lack of realistic assessment data (Petrides et al., 2004). "You're asked often by the chancellor or the president to improve rates of under-prepared students, and you have a really difficult time even identifying who is under-prepared...You can't be accountable if you don't have the data, and that's what we're finding" (Petrides et al., 2004).

One qualitative study found that community college leaders responded with a variety of different actions to performance funding, with outcomes ranging from program changes grounded in the data derived from performance measures, to complete apathy and no appreciable change, despite the state funding that was linked to successful outcomes (Harbour, 2005). It is unclear, therefore, whether performance-based funding produces the large-scale improvements often touted as the reason for their imposition. The variability of outcomes indicates that some colleges respond as if performance-based funding is an effective goad or incentive, and others seem absolutely unmoved.

PROGRAM LEVEL ASSESSMENTS

It is at the program level where accountability measures are most highly developed in community colleges. Occupational or vocational programs typically have the clearest standards and assessment protocols. There are a variety of programs assessed according to national standards. Programs assessed in this way include health care (such as the National League for Nursing, the Commission on Dietetic Registration, the American Occupational Therapy Association, Inc.), and applied technology (such as ABET, Inc., for programs in applied science, computing, engineering, and technology). For many of these programs, student outcomes are also tracked by national examinations. The accountability measures are specific, didactic, and linked closely to program improvement. As such, they function as de facto national standards for colleges. Critics would argue that their rules are often over-determined, and that the ability for program innovation and institutional flexibility is hobbled by their standards. On the other hand, many would agree that the rigor of self-assessment, data collection, and continuous program review of improvement keep many of the occupational programs at community college at high performance levels.

The program level assessment weakens considerably when there is no external standard. It is hard for a program coordinator to make state or national comparisons when almost no data on program level assessment exists. Indeed, at the community college level there is no real definition of "program," since the word is loosely used to refer to a course of study, a group of courses within an academic department, developmental education across disciplines, or a degree program (Bers, 2004). Yet it might be at the program level that assessment is strongest at the community college within specific disciplines. When the National League for Nursing specifies the criteria for faculty-student ratios, clinical hours, or curricular mandates, colleges adhere or risk losing the program-level accreditation. The inclusion of national examinations, such as the National Council Licensure Examination (NCLEX) and typically state-mandated pass rate levels also creates a level of accountability that is much more difficult to achieve in the liberal arts.

Program-level assessment has significant room for improvement, especially when the alignment between community colleges programs and practices are reviewed in light of their sending high schools (Orr, 2001). Unfortunately, it is rare to find a program that coordinates program-level evaluation of student success with what is taught to high school students in order to facilitate movement into college. Even the assessment tests so frequently used as entrance level measures for incoming freshman are not aligned with high school mathematics, reading or writing, and the scores (which might have diagnostic utility at the high school level) are rarely communicated between the two systems (Orr, 2001).

CHALLENGES TO THE FIELD

It is tempting to state that many of community colleges' problems would be solved if only it were possible to actually quantify the effectiveness of outcomes that relate to the real services offered. While hyperbolic (and unnecessarily self-serving), community colleges will never be accurately depicted if they are unable to set the terms of measurement, and then have actual data to assess individual and statewide levels of success.

The following recommendations are an expansion of those proposed by Rust (2004):

- Create coordinated strategies across states and regions and establish national indices and benchmarks as a beginning accountability measure;
- Collect and focus on improvement of teaching and learning, but ensure that information on learning success is then publicly presented in clear language;
- Be articulate about community college's distinct mission, and then link all accountability metrics to those roles;
- Have the federal government and the states distinguish between institutional-level and state-level accountability, with special attention paid to how students flow across institutions, including from high school to college and between colleges as well as patterns of returning adult student enrollment and graduation between public, private and for-profit college;
- Establish campus-level standards for learning, especially for general education, and how these learning outcomes can be measured. Then consistently report on these outcomes to the general public;
- Help the federal government revamp IPEDS data to include measures that respond to community colleges. While the federal government must also maintain focus on educational equity, federal data collection must improve its ability to track students across institutions across the country. Also, the federal government must improve national research—the equivalent of clinical trials research—on student learning;
- Develop a national metric for non-credit education that takes into account both duration and head count; and
- Articulate a national benchmark for economic impact on community that measures both credit and non-credit impact on wages, business start-ups, provision of benefits, and related measures of social or organizational development that can be tied to a community college.

CONCLUSION

When it comes to measurement, all community colleges should try to come from the state of Missouri's perspective: show me! Community colleges have languished for too long being battered by data more appropriate for four-year campuses, while at the same time hiding behind the excuse that our students have goals other than graduation. We must have measurement that takes into account students' lives at an appropriate level of granularity, so that meaningful changes in pedagogy and curriculum in credit and non-credit education can be made, and the impact of these changes measured. There are too many students whose success is not heralded because we do not know how to measure it effectively, and too many students who do not succeed at community colleges. It is time for a clear community college role in national benchmarking to allow a transparent measure of success.

CHAPTER 5

Governance

Governance defines power in a system. Good governance empowers student learning. In this chapter we examine the process and product of internal and external governance systems of community colleges. The chapter begins with a critical analysis of the process of local control as expressed by a board of trustees and the difference between the hypothetical or ideal role and the actual role of local boards. Several models of board organization are reviewed, as well as the ways board actions limit or support community college initiatives. We review various state-level organizational bodies that shape community colleges across the country and their success or lack thereof, and review internal college governance structures. Challenges to the field call community college advocates to action.

THE DREAM

Community colleges ideally frame governance as a process that can open up significant decisions to multiple voices in the community and stay close to the college's higher purpose as conceived by dedicated and knowledgeable faculty and staff. The best governance induces a college to grapple with significant educational issues and provides a gentle correction to limit initiatives which move the college away from its primary mission. Governance is ideally a process of structuring the conversations among different internal and external constituencies to instigate a collaborative process of problem identification and critical issue clarification. It should provide a thoughtful analysis of alternative directions, and ultimately guide decisions based upon clear facts and transparent goals and objectives.

All community colleges have boards of trustees, although their structure can range from a single board for one campus to a single board for all community colleges in a state. In addition to boards of trustees, most community colleges are responsible to a variety of quasi-governing entities, whether it is the local county government or the state department of higher education.

Internally, governance at community colleges has a variety of mechanisms that structure how decisions are made. Colleges' internal governance structures embody academic traditions of broad consultation and strong faculty participation in the decision-making process. Senates are a common form of internal campus governance, with well established traditions and practices to structure conversations about major campus-based decisions. Governance is most likely to be faculty-dominated on issues related to credit degree programs and curriculum, and least likely to be so on issues of budget and fund raising.

The composition of governing bodies—from boards of trustees to subcommittees of faculty senates—will ideally be a selection or election of the best and the brightest people. Participants in governing bodies should come to their tasks with a single purpose: to maintain and advance the community college. Thus, the ideal governance has processes which seek out and select individuals on the basis of intellect, wisdom, expertise and the purity of their intentions. When individuals are selected for their connections to other individuals of influence or wealth, they will agree to serve only to the extent that they can use their wealth or prominence in a community to accrue to the betterment of the college. In the best governance, no aspect of an individual's service is aimed at personal gain.

Ideal governance systems assume that service on governing bodies requires orientation and education, and therefore they create activities that provide for the ongoing professional development of their members. These principles hold not only for the college's board of trustees, but for state-level organizations, local advisory committees, and the college's own internal senate, council, or related structures. It is still rare for a governing body to have a significant number of individuals who themselves have experience with community colleges. Therefore it is crucial for a governing body to have frequent interaction with students, to learn about the principle of an open-access institution, and to develop familiarity with workforce development and community activities in order to advance the college's mission. Terms of office are set to take advantage of growing levels of knowledge and effectiveness as a governing representative. Ongoing evaluation of members ensures that those who are not sufficiently active or knowledgeable no longer serve.

A great board becomes a group of knowledgeable advocates. The members, in their various civic and professional roles, represent the positive qualities of the college in such a way as to enhance the reputation and awareness of the college. They build bridges to other constituencies that the college uses to expand and deepen its service to its students.

In sum, the ideal governance at a community college is a future-oriented structure that moves the college toward a better tomorrow. Internally, campus governance makes wise decisions about development of programs and use of resources to advance its ability to serve students. Staffing of the governance bodies is undertaken seriously to attract the most qualified individuals. Processes used to make decision are open, and the dialogue it instigates provide the basis for sound decisions, where every action adds to the value of the college and its goal of advancing higher education for its community.

THE UNFULFILLED DREAM

Each element of the governance structure is by definition in flux, since almost all of the members of governing bodies are appointed or elected cyclically. As such, in every state and every college, one can find examples of governance bodies that are very close to ideal as well as some of the worst.

The reality is that governing bodies run the spectrum from selfless to selfish. Local boards of trustees may consist of dedicated individuals who volunteer their efforts in the sole interest of making a good college better. The countless hours of selfless contribution by hundreds of board members across the country must stand in balance to what is listed below.

Because the ideal was outlined in the dream section, this reality section will be skewed toward the negative. On every campus, one can probably find an individual who has lived through some of the best and some of the worst. At the risk of making the reality more bleak than it is, what follows are some of the possible pitfalls of poor governance on the community college campus.

Boards of trustees are variously selected through a public election or appointment by a political body. Some board members seek these positions because they are knowledgeable and supportive of a local community college. However, many board members seek a position in order to represent a local legislator's controlling hand, to position themselves for a future political career, or to open up sources of patronage jobs or contracts to friends and colleagues. For elected board positions, the process of running a campaign can also put a particular political perspective (militia, anti-abortion, pro-gun control) before a local community, despite its near irrelevance to the governing of a college.

Poorly motivated board members are pernicious actors in the governance process, with agendas contrary to the best interests of the college. The ways in which poorly intentioned board members exert their influence are many, from demands for patronage jobs to advancing positions antithetical to higher education. Actions such as seeking to limit funding to the college, curtailing a broadly conceived curriculum, or awarding a building contract to the most politically connected construction company are easily found among board actions. The interlocking system of board appointment by politicians and board control of fiscal and hiring decision can be a formidable threat to good governance and the integrity of any college.

Unfortunately, boards of trustees of community colleges have received almost no attention in academic research or analysis. Anecdotal evidence from endless conversations about inappropriate board actions is common among community college presidents. The following examples have been personally related to the authors, but in the interest of protecting both the presidents and the colleges, citations will not be given.

- A president receives a call from a board member who says that, unless a politically connected accountant is hired by the college, the president's contract will not be renewed for the upcoming year.
- Hopeful board members see the college as an increasingly successful and visible entity and seek to use it as a springboard to higher office. This includes generating fear and negativity about the college in order to win elections.
- A president is told by a group of board members that, regardless of the open-bid process, the architect for a multi-million project must be the firm that has donated the most money to the local Democratic Party (the party currently in control of the local county's legislature).
- A president is told by a group of board members who owe their election to the campus' faculty union that they must promote a specific union-connected internal candidate to academic vice president.
- A female African-American president is taken for a boat ride with several male board members and told to remember that the Klu Klux Klan is still active in the state and therefore her attempts to remove two maintenance workers after a negative performance evaluation must stop.

- A president is required by a board member to form an alliance with a for-profit business college in which the board member has a controlling business interest.
- A president is required by a board member to choose an insurance company which the board member owns.
- A college staff person who, after due process, was fired from the college, gets the ear of a board member who generates a campaign to fire the president.
- At the instigation of faculty, a newspaper abundantly covers the perspectives of college staff who do not want to implement new strategic initiatives, and are then able to convince board members to terminate the president.

Governance, as with all politics, is local. The old joke is that politics and making sausage have a lot in common—no matter how delicious a sausage is, watching it being made up close is distasteful. So the small "p" politics of community college governance can be as appalling as any other form of political intercourse. The governance of community colleges lies in the interstices between local control and the increasing centralization/federalization of education in the United States. Community colleges that were started either by local boards of education or local engaged citizens maintained the concept of a lay board of trustees to provide distance and protection for the college from the vicissitudes of local politics while at the same time being very close to local conditions and needs. Unfortunately, local control can often turn to parochial strangleholds.

There is increasing pressure for those who are appointed to community college boards of trustees to align closely to the political ideology of those who appointed them. This leads to significant concerns in community colleges that board members are more concerned with cost cutting than with serving a community, or with creating distance between faculty involvement, academic freedom, and decision making (Zumeta, 2001).

In an odd way, the increasing political activism of boards of trustees is a positive sign, indicating the growing awareness that the ability of community colleges to deliver on their promise of opportunity to learn for a large segment of the community is the foundation of a community's ability to grow and prosper. On the other hand, attempts to limit the sweep of education to a pre-determined set of politically motivated agendas will gut the power of American higher education to deliver on promises of prosperity, creativity, and democracy.

Similarly, internal college governance systems can be examples of very different standards and orientations. Some college senates are a beacon of proactive, rational dialogue which maintain the direction and effectiveness of a campus. Yet some colleges have internal governance bodies that are merely puppets of the faculty union or the college administration. Some colleges have internal governance where one faculty member has chaired for decades, or where it is impossible to get the best, most engaged faculty and staff to run for office because so little is fought over for so long. Internal governance systems can reify the status quo, provide lax tenure and promotion standards, or maintain out-of-date degrees for the ease of particular groups of faculty or staff. As in all politics, personal animosity can play a disruptive role. The only way in which some of the college governance processes are potentially more troublesome than in other organizations is that the consultative nature of academia provides a greater opportunity for blocking progress, and for a small personal disagreement to turn into a major campus-level squabble.

Governance at any community college at any time is likely to be a rich mix of the best of the ideal and the worst of the reality. Many board members are motivated by civic and philanthropic concern for their community, and can be credited with establishing, building and enhancing community colleges across the country. Yet community college faculty and staff know of individual board members, even those active in national organizations, who exhibit the worst traits of governance and are selfish, petty, and destructive. In like manner, for every engaged faculty council that puts students first and worries about how to best support innovative pedagogy, there is a faculty council dedicated to their own personal advancement and comfort.

The reality for governance of community colleges in the United States is that they are good and bad, with traditions of either rapid turn-over or stasis, as likely to be extraordinarily effective in governing as they are to be only effective at creating chaos and conflict. The reality of community college governance is that it can be subverted for personal or political reasons that limit the college's ability to effectively serve the higher education needs of the community. Perhaps it is simply enough to say that, in this way, it is potentially no different from any other human system.

THE REAL STORY

Why Boards of Trustees? Governance and Local Control

To quote the legendary Speaker of the House of Representatives Tip O'Neill, all politics is local. This is as true of governance of community colleges as it is of any other form of political interaction. The principle of local control was established by the early groups of citizens or school boards that began community colleges (Cohen, 2001), but is increasingly curtailed by the growing federalization of education in the United States (Zumeta, 2001). Lay boards of trustees, comprised of a group of concerned citizens, are presumed to shelter community college enterprises by keeping them at an arm's length from the volatile rough-n-tumble of local politics (Zumeta, 2001). This very American invention stands in marked contrast to boards of higher education in Europe or Asia, which are formed by faculty guilds or national governmental agencies with proscriptive oversight of colleges in a region or a country.

The lay board of trustees is predicated upon the idea that membership will consist of citizens selected upon the basis of their ability to assist the college. In particular, lay boards are expected to bring expertise in fundraising, fiscal administration, and organizational management. It is in the area of management issues in particular where local boards of trustees are presumed to exercise their greatest influence. College presidents, historically selected for academic prowess, were presumed to lack the corporate knowledge of fiscal and administrative management, and thus would form a mutually beneficial bond with their boards. The tension that begins around lay boards is that colleges are stubbornly independent yet require large amounts of state and federal money to operate (Lingenfelter, 2004).

The local nature of community college trustees also poses a unique set of complications, since trustees are as likely to interact with families, special interests, co-workers, and neighbors who have a stake in the college as with formal structures (Polonio, 2005). This makes them both more interested than might be ideal, and minimally requires community college trustees to have a higher level of confidentiality and tact than other college trustees.

Who Serves on Boards of Trustees?

Approximately 6,500 individuals serve in publicly elected or appointed positions as trustees in more than 600 community college governing boards across the United States (*Fast Facts*, 2006). Elections occur for trustees in about 20 states, although low voter turn-out can result in individuals being elected who represent small or extreme special interest groups (Davis, 2000). Some critics question the quality of governance provided by elected or appointed boards, in particular when a board does not do a good job of discharging its duty to protect and advance the interests of the college (Davis, 2000). A variety of problems at individual campuses have been noted, including not paying sufficient attention to the evaluation of the colleges' outcomes, policies, personnel, or finances; ethical or conflict of interest debacles; or board members using the position to advance actions for the wrong people or for the wrong reasons (Davis, 2000). These problems can stem from a trustee's motivation to serve on the board for reasons that do not relate to the advancement of the institutions. Some inappropriate motivations include personal motivation (i.e., my daughter didn't get into the nursing program), labor union sponsorship, desire to get preferential treatment, or to create a new pathway for a political career (Polonio, 2005).

Some reviewers highly extol community college board members. George E. Potter writes, "It would be rare indeed to find a more important or more difficult role, carried out by more dedicated, selfless public servants, than that of a governing board member of a community college" (Association of Community College Trustees, 2006). Potter's perspective is based largely on anecdotal evidence, on his consulting experience with college trustees, and on his involvement with a national community college trustee organization. Very little research or analysis exists on community college boards of trustees. Although there are standards promulgated by national organizations as well as state and local authorities, there is little evaluation of the extent to which these standards guide the appointment or election of community college board of trustee members. The role of the president in the selection varies from making the single nomination (that is, virtually selecting the board member) to having no say in who is nominated, whether the position is appointed or elected (Richardson and Smalling, 2005).

The Association of Community College Trustees (ACCT) was established to promulgate national standards of best practices and to coordinate state and national advocacy efforts (*About ACCT*, 2006). Its goal is to provide professional development activities for individual community college board members to promote higher levels of ethical leadership through a strong regional presence and a fledgling international constituency. Yet without data, it is difficult to say with any certainty who serves, or to name the specific qualifications or competencies in service.

LOCAL BOARDS' POLICY AND FISCAL ROLES

Board of trustee mission statements and orientations often emphasize the manner in which the boards should exercise influence over policy issues and fiscal administration. "Tough strategic decisions...[s]trong leadership and effective governance...are crucial ingredients for success" for boards of trustees (*About ACCT*, 2006). These are tall orders. Often there is confusion as a board member sorts out the "ownership-representative" nature of the appointment, because it can be unclear who legitimately owns the college and whose interests should be represented (ACCT, 2006). The ACCT provides a national forum and advocates activities to enhance board members' ability to serve a college well and to govern effectively in a difficult world. The organization encourages board members to be keenly aware of ethical behavior, the need to embrace diversity, and how to effectively provide policy leadership for community economic development. The ACCT helped to instigate the development of theories of community college "trusteeship."

A beginning primer on effective theories of governance was outlined in the early 1980s by George Potter (ACCT, 2006), and later expanded upon by John Carver and Miriam Mayhew (Carver and Mayhew, 1991). The ACCT endorsed the board policy process of Carver and Mayhew, termed Policy Governance®, as an ideal process for boards to use as a guide for actions and interactions with the campus' people and practices (ACCT, 2006). Briefly, Policy Governance maintains that lay board members should be active leaders on behalf of the community, while simultaneously giving the president of the college as much autonomy and authority as possible. The ACCT's endorsement, however, is based more on theoretical than empirical reasons—little research on the positive impact of Policy Governance or its ability to create more effective community colleges has been conducted. And despite the national endorsement, little has changed across the country in terms of effective board processes (ACCT, 2006).

Policy Governance presumes that board effectiveness is improved when boards create a set of specific policies that clearly guide the level and purpose of their interaction with the campus. The policies are intended to allow boards to clarify and establish expectations regarding ownership (to whom is the board responsible), outline the board's actions and responsibilities to each other as a group, and determine the permissible actions of the board chair, the board's committees and the CEO of the organization (Carver, 1990; Carver and Mayhew, 1997). Policy Governance is distinctive in that it also attempts to limit board actions to those that allow boards to focus on what are termed *ends determination* (where the board defines results for specific groups at specific costs) and *means determinations* (where the board specifies processes to be used to achieve the ends within articulated bounds of action by the CEO) (Carver, 1990)..

The Policy Governance theory encourages boards to develop policies and practices for

- creating a consent and work agenda
- performing board self evaluations
- governing board-foundation relationship
- orienting new trustees
- connecting with the community and evaluating impact
- evaluating the president's performance
- conducting effective political advocacy
- developing a budget and financials
- maintaining trustee ethical practices
- bargaining as a collective

Anecdotally, presidents and board members who embrace the process are pleased with the conceptual framework, particularly as it clarifies the relationship between the college president and the board (Day, 2004). Unfortunately, other than the endorsement of the ACCT and individual testimonials, the actual data supporting the effectiveness of adopting Policy Governance is slim. And there are other anecdotes of situations where community college boards, after extensive orientation and participation in developing the Policy Governance framework, quickly lapse into administrative decision making. A frequent problem is they sometimes see themselves as acting on behalf of employees and special interests rather than owners—usually the community.

Advocates for community colleges have created national initiatives to promote better board governance, such as the ACCT Select Committee on Exemplary Governance (ACCT, 2006). In general, advocates stress that boards work best when they are not another layer of administration, but rather a standards-setting system that uses clear standards and practices to represent community interests and hold colleges accountable for effective educational results (Smith, 2000). Some systems, such as North Carolina's, have established a robust orientation and guidelines program that assists boards in creating good practices, including ethics and conflict of interest policies (Dowdy, 1996). Illinois allows community college boards of trustees to conduct annual assessment of board members in closed executive sessions to promote a more honest evaluation of board performance (Polonio, 2005).

THE BOARD'S RELATIONSHIP TO THE COLLEGE PRESIDENT

The most difficult terrain traversed by a community college's board is the recruitment, selection, and oversight of the college's chief executive officer, the president. The healthy balance of both supporting and challenging a president or system chancellor is the ideal to which boards strive, but in reality the relationship can be characterized by everything from micro-management to absolute laissez-faire (*About ACCT*, 2006).

Recruitment of new presidents has become increasingly professionalized, with many colleges using specialized search firms to identify candidates and help manage the search process. Searches can take from six months to years, and make significant demands on the volunteer board members' time (*About ACCT*, 2006). Unlike corporations that spend significant amounts of time and money on institutional succession planning, community colleges rarely try to grow their own presidents from inside the institutions. Recruitment often means a national search, and a set of on-campus and off-campus meetings to review candidates' credentials and "fit" for the institution. Once the offer has been made, there are a variety of ways of handling terms of office, contracts, payment, and other aspects that the board or its designees must negotiate with the incoming president.

Oversight and evaluation of presidents is one of the board's most important roles. If board members have extensive corporate experience, evaluations tend toward managing to a set of expected outcomes that are mutually established between the college president and the board. Yet many presidents never get honest feedback, get information only about how they are doing in a political sense, or have their first real evaluation when board members inform them that they will not have their contract renewed.

The local control aspect of the board also makes the relationship with the president fraught with pitfalls. When special interest pressure on the board members is strong, it will happen not only at board meetings but in grocery stores and bank lines. Community college presidents in small communities are sometimes among the most prominent or highly paid individuals in the area. When salaries are set, or when the president makes considerably more than board members, the public outcry can be disconcerting at best. Managing these elements of oversight so that a college president is appropriately compensated and protected from undue intrusion is important.

Board members often encounter a complex interaction in determining how to relate to the college president in contrast with their interaction with other members of the college community. Most best practices advise that the board should relate directly only to the president. But this wonderful advice can be naïve for board members appointed by local political entities. A community college's board members are by definition members of a local community, and the information that they have about personnel and fiscal matters can be difficult to keep confidential from friends and family. It can also make it difficult for them to refrain from meddling administratively at board meetings. In a small community, the college can be the most significant employer, and a lay board member's "insider" knowledge is all too often an open secret.

ACTIVIST BOARDS

The phenomenon of 'activist' college boards involving themselves in administrative agendas emerged in the early 2000s and challenges the presumptive "arms-length" orientation of previous boards. The State University of New York (SUNY) Board of Trustees, which oversees most of the state's two- and four-year colleges, decided without public review to mandate the course content necessary to fulfill general education requirements (Higginbottom and Romano, 2001). Faculty groups across the state, usually unchallenged in governance control over degree requirements, publicly expressed dismay and opposition to the decree (Higginbottom and Romano, 2001). Other examples across the country continue to signal that boards may be actively pursuing agendas dictated by political orientation rather than strict adherence to local community needs. The intensifying circles of political ambition and public higher education oversight, fueled by the political fractionalization of the United States, foretell the potential of even greater changes in the future for local boards of trustees (Zumeta, 2001).

QUASI-GOVERNING PUBLIC ENTITIES

Community colleges are also accountable to a variety of state and local entities that have varying impact on their ability to govern themselves. Whether loosely structured as advocacy groups or strictly bound by state statute to mandates ranging from curriculum development to fiscal policies, colleges throughout the country must negotiate relationships with state and local entities in order to remain effective practitioners in their communities.

State Boards

The interface agency of many states between individual boards of trustees and campuses is the state board of higher education. There is no single, national organizational structure of either state boards or their regulatory relationship to community college boards that is common to all community colleges (Richardson and Smalling, 2005). State boards are another uniquely American institution that have experienced an erosion of the traditional role they played in protecting community colleges from political intrusion (Zumeta, 2001). When state boards are effective, their presence can help spur a coordinated effort to align state budgets and policy initiatives and focus attention on the interests of the state (Lovell and Trouth, 2002). By hiring expert education professionals as their staff, state boards can elevate the academic focus of higher education by providing sophisticated support and guidance to the appointed public members (Zumeta, 2001). State boards are likely to provide academic program review and oversight for statewide planning, identification, and implementation of policies. They are also likely to be involved in state-level resource approval or allocation, as well as institutional assessment and/or accountability. (Zumeta, 2001). Each of these oversight activities varies considerably from state to state (Lovell and Trouth, 2002). Community colleges often have to deal with a plethora of quasi-governing entities, with a California study finding more than 22 offices and agencies that shared governance responsibilities with colleges' boards (Lovell and Trouth, 2002).

The variability in the actual structure of state governing boards has led to several proposed taxonomic models. These models try to differentiate the various state structures as they are influenced by the amount of control they have over community colleges (Tollefson, 1996), by their main purpose of planning, governing, or serving (*State Postsecondary Structures Sourcebook*, 1997), or by the way they govern in a federated, unified, or segmented manner (Richardson and de los Santos, 2001; Richardson and Smalling, 2005). While so much diversity limits the ability to talk about a general model, there is an emergent tendency to place community colleges under a statewide governing body within higher education as opposed to K-12, or by itself (Lovell and Trouth, 2002).

The intrusion of local political ideologies and perspectives appear to be ascendant nationally. As politics becomes more predominant in the governance of community colleges, the likelihood increases that policies will begin to swing widely in response to changes in elected bodies over a very short time period, even as brief as from session to session (Zumeta, 2001). These changes are too infrequently based upon a thoughtful analysis of what community colleges need (often more funding) and are more likely to substitute the "flavor of the day" educational fix or political hot-button issue.

State and local boards of trustees for community colleges are at a critical juncture. A free and sometimes free-wheeling academic purpose has ultimately shown itself to be the saving grace of intellectual, political, and business endeavors, and remains commonly perceived as the reason for the

United States' ascendancy on the world stage (Kirp, 2003). Balancing the public's need to understand deeply the purposes to which their tax dollars are put to use with the need to insure, by their daily interaction with specific policies and colleges, governance boards, impacts the future to a great extent. The academic freedom to pursue new intellectual pursuits has clearly produced real progress in the United States (Zumeta, 2001). While community colleges are less likely than universities to be making the break-through discoveries that lead to new knowledge and innovation, nonetheless they are a critical participant in educating the citizens who will fuel and partake in progress in the social, cultural, political, and economic realms. The ability of community colleges to respond rapidly to changes in the workplace also demonstrate how highly centralized management is less responsive to the rapidity of the external environment, particularly within a knowledge economy (Zumeta, 2001).

Potential for Positive Action

Politically, the mid-2000s have seen increases in political calls for affordability. Yet community colleges really make higher education affordable (at least as far as tuition) for most families. And affordability has emerged as a political issue just at the time that public investment in public higher education has dropped precipitously. As David Breneman notes, "The economic—as opposed to political—fact is that true *affordability* remains a problem primarily for students from low-income families, which simply means that the promise of access has not yet been met. Ironically, achieving *affordability* in this current political definition means competing for resources that might otherwise increase access—a situation that cries out for correction" (Heller, 2001, viii). These are the issues in which community college boards could take the lead, with powerful public dialogue, pointing out the ways in which decreases in public funding have made community colleges less able to serve their communities and that the majority of federal and state financial aid is provided to higher cost education rather than to the community colleges (see chapter two). But the political nature of most state boards has muted or silenced this potential. Moreover, as state boards and national higher education organizations attempt to balance the needs of elite and private colleges with the needs of public and open access institutions, they end up saying little that might push state boards to be active in promoting the very standards and initiatives that would raise the status of community colleges and produce truly affordable higher education. The complexity can also lead to misunderstandings about who has the proper authority over decisions, the state board or the local campus's board of trustees (Wyoming Community College Commission, 1999). Conversely, some state boards, such as those in Iowa and Florida, have bravely tackled what had seemed to be intractable problems, such as transfer among a state's community and four-year colleges, and have produced positive changes (Lovell and Trouth, 2002).

Community College Coordinating Entities

Several states have entities that coordinate statewide activities for community colleges, with little governing power outside of the ability to foster collaboration. New Jersey and Michigan have statewide coordinating committees, which meet regularly to come to consensus on policy and fiscal issues. Massachusetts has an even looser organizational structure, with dialogue primarily on coordinating political strategy. These entities are commonly funded by proportionate assessments paid by each campus. These organizations appear most effective when they are able to determine clear goals and strategies for requesting state funding or policy changes.

The coordinating bodies often meet to determine internal allocations for capital funds. This is true in Michigan and New Jersey, for example, with the rules for distribution collegially set, and more or less adhered to. However, state funding can also be changed by the ascending or descending power of an individual state legislator. In such cases, a capital project can be awarded or stopped for an individual campus in the legislator's district. This is also linked to the consensual nature of the process—no actual legislative authority backs up the prioritizing that the coordinating body has established. The lack of legislative authority is not always problematic. For example, in Georgia, where the state coordinating body has state constitutional status, community colleges are disadvantaged in the internal competition for resources, because the coordinating body must serve several systems of higher education (Richardson and de los Santos, 2001).

In most states, the community college's closest link is to their local sponsor (a county or city) with the state coordinating organization focused on working directly with state legislatures and the governor's office (Richardson and de los Santos, 2001). The trend appears to be moving away from coordination, with a push to develop statewide organizations that have oversight and are able to deliver to politicians data emerging from mandated accountability standards (Richardson and de los Santos, 2001).

INTERNAL GOVERNANCE

Community colleges, like all institutions of higher education, have traditions of consultation and dialogue on decision making. "Faculty governance is broadly defined as the procedures, processes and structures that allow individuals with instructional responsibilities access to the decision-making process of the institution" (Pope and Miller, 2000). Community college's internal governance structures are designed to encourage consultation, sometimes with faculty only, and sometimes with a broader range of institutional constituencies, in order to gain input and support for strategic direction, policies, and funding (Pope and Miller, 2000). For example, one campus created a tri-cameral system consisting of a council for professional and support staff, another for administrators, and a third for faculty, all coordinated by a joint council chaired by the college president (Asonevich, 2005). At non-union campuses, college senates might make recommendations about wages and work conditions, but at all campuses they are a collective voice that can have a powerful impact on the course and direction of the institution.

Interestingly, there is very little empirical work on college governance structures, and even less on community colleges'. While governance structures at community colleges are as diverse as any other structural entity, it has been asserted that community colleges' governance functions are quite similar to their four-year counterparts (Pope and Miller, 2000). In general, the consultative or recommending role means that these bodies are constituted to offer advice or direction but they function with neither the authority to control the final outcome of a decision nor the responsibility for seeing a decision enacted. Approximately 75 percent of community colleges have some form of staff involvement in college governance (Gilmour, 1991). The membership in college governance is highly individualized by campus. In some places, the structure reifies long ago fights (Lee, 1991). For example, a campus governance was so shaped by faculty distrust of a long-gone president that the senate leadership focused almost exclusively on process to the exclusion of outcomes twenty years later (Lee, 1991). More recent theoretical and empirical literature seems to favor leadership, trust, and positive relationships as crucial elements of an effective college governance rather than any particular type of membership structure, although again most studies look only at four-year colleges (Kezar, 2004; Pope, 2004). It does not appear to matter at what point faculty, in particular, have input into decision making (department, division, campus, or union) when the actual outcome of a campus decision is measured (Kaplan, 2004a).

Faculty senates have distinctive issues and challenges. For example, they must represent their peers' views as well as coordinate activities with the college's administration (Pope and Miller, 2000). For this reason, research has confirmed that the best members of the faculty senate are great communicators, since they are in effect in the middle of the decision-making process. However, it is rare for faculty or administrators to believe that the best individuals are attracted to serve on the governance bodies (Gilmour, 1991). It has also been recommended that faculty or college senate leaders receive leadership training, since this role is distinctive from the teaching or administrative professional roles for which individuals were hired (Pope and Miller, 2000). One empirical study found that more than two-thirds of faculty governance leaders were male, and one-third were involved in liberal arts (Pope and Miller, 2000), although it is unclear how reliably these data may be generalized.

Birnbaum and others hypothesize that it is the ability to communicate effectively, whether in formal or informal ways, that makes a governance structure work (Birnbaum, 2004). As such, it is important that college governance groups remember to maintain effective communication with all affected constituents and ensure that Web sites and other sources of information are accurate and current in order to engender trust and credibility in the governance institutions (Birnbaum, 2004; Tierney and Minor, 2004).

Nationally, survey results have a large percentage of faculty consistently expressing lack of approval of relationships with administrators and with campus governance beyond their own department level, although these data are not broken out for community colleges (Lee, 1991). Despite the complexities of the relationships among faculty, staff, and administrators, there is in actuality a large body of agreement between presidents and senate members with regard to authority, roles, and perspectives on campus issues (Gilmour, 1991). Over the past twenty years, college governance bodies have increased their participation in policy making with formal recommendations to administration (Gilmour, 1991). Indeed, a court case in New York City found that the administration was so likely to wholly take the recommendations of its college senates that the senates were required to adhere to the city's open meeting laws (Schaffer, 2005). Faculty and staff who are able to make the college's adherence to its core values apparent in its decisions, whether directly through governance or indirectly through relationships and informal leadership, maintain the integrity and consistency of a college (Birnbaum, 2004). "Like democracy itself, shared governance is ungainly but effective in holding on to the larger moral purpose" (Birnbaum, 2004).

Shared Governance

Internal governance structures are typically involved in the dialogic process of shared governance. While discussed frequently on campus, there is little consistent interpretation of what shared governance really means. Definitions range from a system of collective self-government to a system where anyone can participate in any decision. Other definitions outline a more limiting process of defining the roles each constituency (faculty, staff, administration, board member) must play within a set of mutually understood areas of responsibility, accountability, and cooperative action (Alfred, 1998). Alfred defines shared governance as "collegial decision making or the process for distributing authority, power and influence for academic decisions among campus constituencies...including but not limited to faculty, staff, students, administrators, the faculty senate and unions" (Alfred, 1998).

The most intensively discussed area of shared governance in community colleges is in California, where in 1988 Assembly Bill 1725 was passed, which mandated participatory governance. Lack of definitional clarity led to many conflicts over how to exactly enact the sentiment embodied in the law. Alfred maintains that one of the outcomes, almost by definition, is a slowing of decision making because more individuals must be consulted and because faculty schedules do require their presence on campus for three to five months of the year (Alfred, 1998). Others say it is exactly this slowing of decision making that allows an institution to keep its value system intact and not be needlessly tossed by the whims of the market or local politics (Birnbaum, 2004). Shared governance can be hampered if sufficient weight is not given to decisions that assess factors such as responsiveness to students or the community (Alfred, 1998).

Faculty or college governance structures, when well conceived and led, have the potential to greatly enhance engagement of the faculty and staff and actively participate in the actions called for (Alfred, 1998; Kezar, 2004).. The whole campus benefits from a college governance body that produces wide-ranging dialogue that promotes the development of consensus. This process can engender a deeper understanding of issues across campus constituencies and inculcate a simultaneous sense of empowerment and collective responsibility (Alfred, 1998). The best governance structures are characterized by a dialogue that encourages divergent points of view, rational analysis, and a growing sense of compromise and prioritization of the issues most critical to a campus (Birnbaum, 1991).

Unfortunately, it appears that college governance frequently does not display these characteristics (Birnbaum, 1991). Very little data is available that singles out governance on community college campuses, but some of the disadvantages that are attendant to college governance systems are the ways in which effective or efficient management is curtailed and the quality of decisions are degraded by seeking opinions from those not qualified to speak about issues (Alfred, 1998). College governance has been characterized as bureaucratic oligarchies, and as likely to create conflict as to create consensus (Birnbaum, 1991). Some believe the functioning of most campus governance structures is so compromised as to be only symbolic rather than functional (Birnbaum, 1991). One of the most troubling critiques is that college governance does not focus on the primary responsibilities of the campus: teaching and learning (Alfred, 1998).

The major recommendation that emerges from several studies of academic governance is the importance of college administrators' support for the existing college structure of internal governance (Gilmour, 1991; Kezar, 2004; Lee, 1991; Williams, Gore, Broches, and Lostoski, 1987). Without leadership support, college governance systems can slow institutional development; become overly focused on the process as opposed to the outcome of decision making, or disguise self-serving agendas or political maneuvering of faculty and staff—all leading to polarization and adversarial relations among faculty, staff, and administrators (Alfred, 1998). And without an engaged administration, including formal and informal relationships with the president or provost, where issues are mutually framed and the authority of the college governance body is acknowledged, effectiveness is diminished (Lee, 1991).

Role clarity is usually clearest in governance control of decisions regarding curriculum and degree requirements (Alfred, 1998). It does not appear to include assessments of teaching effectiveness, however. "Faculty frequently proved distinctly anti-intellectual when it came to examining evidence about performance that might question their professional authority to determine what was best to teach and how to teach it" (Ewell, 2005). A case where faculty senates proactively examine assessment "as a natural part of academic discourse and governance" (Ewell, 2005) has yet to be documented. Faculty senates appear reluctant to undertake a process such as assessment that "... inherently questioned the premise that individual faculty members should decide on their own what to teach and how to do so" (Ewell, 2005).

There appear to be some differences among community college faculty who do and do not actively participate in college governance. Interestingly, both involved and less involved faculty agree on the characteristics of ideal governance and faculty roles in that governance structure, while they differ on their perceptions of shared governance's effectiveness (Miller, Vacik, and Benton, 1998). Sometimes younger faculty are encouraged to avoid governance service in order to focus more on teaching and learning, or because of the perceived insufficient rewards for service (Williams, Gore, Broches, and Lostoski, 1987). Since membership is fluid and fluctuates as interest in particular decisions changes among faculty and staff, governance is sometimes more chaotic than is ideal (Williams et al., 1987). The former general secretary of the American Association of University Professors, I. J. Spitzberg, perhaps summarized college governance challenges best when he said "Our current challenge is to make collegiality real in a world where many constraints are set off-campus and where past collegial expectations are made less operative by collective bargaining, the growth of administrative bureaucracies, and trustee control" (Williams et al., 1987).

Unionization of faculty and staff at community colleges sometimes makes the role of shared governance more difficult to separate. Unions represent about 51 percent of full-time and 27 percent of part-time faculty at community colleges (Lovell and Trouth, 2002). The contract itself can have a considerable influence over governance systems, and in some states the activities controlled by governance are decided in contract negotiations (Lovell and Trouth, 2002). The college's governance structure is specifically referenced in about 60 percent of union contracts (Gilmour, 1991). While some parties would argue that unions can create governance problems by tying decision making to protocols that favor employees over students, others maintain that unions play a protective role in governance, especially because the leadership of the two entities often overlap (Alfred, 1998; Lee, 1991).

Alternative Ways to Enhance Internal Governance

New modes of action and interaction have been used throughout the country by community colleges to enhance internal governance. These methods seek to solicit the perspectives of multiple campus players and ensure that those most knowledgeable about an issue are granted particular freedom to articulate the dimensions of problems and solutions. Community colleges of the future must possess organizational resilience to achieve long-term organizational success. Their internal governance structures must have strategies for sustaining innovation and allocating human and fiscal resources to support an organizational ethos of renewal (Hamel and Valikangas, 2003).

Providing new kinds of processes that engage the campus spur a non-traditional form of consultation that can augment internal governance. A process used by several community colleges called "whole system" is characterized by goal setting and decision making procedures. Theoretically indebted to social psychologist Kurt Lewin, strategies have been formulated for large-scale participation by Marvin Weisbord, Kathleen Dannemiller (Dannemiller, James, and Tolchinsky, 2000; Lewin, 1951; Weisbord and Janoff, 1995), and others. These processes expand the notion of governance by making sure that as much of the campus as possible (students, faculty, the administration, the board of trustees, and every level of staff from security to program directors), and external participants (elected officials, community-based organizations, local businesses and industries, feeder high schools, and the colleges to which students transfer) are invited to take a more comprehensive view of which decisions must be made for what purposes.

Albert Einstein said, "The significant problems we face today cannot be solved at the same level of thinking we were at when we created them." New methods of governance and decision making require that campuses create new structures that honor the academic tradition of dialogue, consultation, and shared governance. Many colleges use cross-functional task forces whose members are carefully drawn from across the campus and given an explicit charge and specific timeline to avoid the "just another committee" syndrome. Campuses report that these new governance-like structures allow campuses to tackle various difficult issues (Mellow, 2005).

The late Japanese economist Jiro Tokuyama said, "The hardest thing is to unlearn the secrets of your past success." Another change in governance and collaborative decision making at community colleges is an increased focus on data that promote a detailed and often fresh look at existing issues (Mellow, 2005). Appreciative Inquiry has been used as a process that changes the questions asked of an institution from "What's wrong?" or "Where have we fallen short of achieving our goals?" to "What is working well that we want to build on for the future?" and "Where are the resources and energies for change?" (Cooperrider, Whitney, and Starvos, 2004; Talmadge, 2006).

These new structures allow for greater levels of participation by faculty and staff, thus creating the next generation of leaders (Mellow, 2005). They also increase the number of direct paths for multiple communications across multiple modalities, which encourages continued interest and the development of a shared community vision (Mellow, 2005). Perhaps most critically, these newer forms of governance and decision making seem to be more able to sustain the deep and lasting changes that allow a community college to support innovation and nurture new initiatives.

CHALLENGES TO THE FIELD

Governance of community colleges in the United States stretches all the way from the state level to the students participating in campus decisions. It is the point at which a campus is mandated to interface with external players, as well as the place where a college often claims its distinctive decisions about curriculum or academic practices. It can be parochial or international, rational or irrational, innovative or historically determined. The challenge is to find ways to selectively take the best of the community college's history, regional flavor, political support, and dedicated employee engagement while jettisoning intractable practices, cronyism, self-serving agendas, unnecessary complexities, and untimely decisions. Accomplishing all the positive that governance can offer while eliminating all the negatives that can accrue is highly unlikely. Therefore, these recommendations are offered in hopes that the dialectic process of change and balance remains a vibrant part of the continued evolution of community colleges across the country.

1. Recommendations regarding strengthening supportive actions of boards of trustees:
   • Create clear guidelines for selection of board members based upon skills and competencies.
   • Create oversight mechanisms that help diminish self-serving agendas of board members or their sponsors in board service.
   • Establish national guidelines for state sanctions of boards that do not adhere to minimum standards of professionalism. Likewise, provide rewards for boards that exceed these standards.
   • Expect boards to support institutions and to gain perspective on the major issues of the day through effective environmental scanning, assessment of inherent risks, and potential benefits in future endeavors, and focus board meetings on discussions of strategic issues.
   • Ensure regular board orientation and evaluation.

2. Recommendations regarding strengthening state boards and related entities:
   • Ensure state boards focus on the most pressing state (and national) issues, with adherence to the core academic ideals of community colleges.

- Create educational mechanisms so that state board members are regularly informed about best policies and practices that ensure the state's interests are being effectively responded to by its community colleges.
- Create clear guidelines for state board members that establish selection based upon skills and competencies.

3. Recommendations regarding internal governance structures:
   - Develop leadership development programs that encourage all levels of faculty and staff to become active in college governance and do so at the highest level of rational engagement.
   - Actively promote multiple forms of communication to capture both the formal and informal ways campus participation can inform decision making.
   - Explore the use of multiple forms of decision making that have emerged to enhance the ability of constituencies to become informed and involved in governance issues.
   - Clearly identify areas of responsibility before decisions are made, and make explicit areas of responsibility and authority for all involved, to enhance the effectiveness of internal governance.

CONCLUSION

It is possible community college governance is the one area where there is the least amount of distinctiveness between four-year and two-year colleges. The traditions of the lay board, internal faculty, or college senates, and a state oversight mechanism are common to all forms of public higher education. While there may be a slightly greater tendency for community colleges to define "local" more narrowly, the intents and purposes of the governance entities from the state board to the campus remain remarkably consistent.

Therefore, the real challenge of the community college is to ensure that "local" is defined as integrated and responsive, as opposed to embedded and parochial. The most difficult challenge at every level of governance—from the state to the local board of trustees to the internal governing body—is to prevent narrow perspectives from controlling decision making. The local community's needs must be addressed, and at the same time colleges must avoid self-serving decisions made in favor of small-time local politicians or friends of faculty or board members. Governance that holds as sacred the deeper purpose of higher learning in a community is central.

CHAPTER 6

A Changed Pedagogy

꙳ꙴ **OVERVIEW**

We can no longer teach as we have been taught (New Jersey Virtual Community College Consortium, 2006). The external world and the nature of our students require a more engaging form of pedagogy because it is imperative for America to provide a college education to a greater percentage of its population than ever before. Changing our pedagogical approach to achieve the dream of community colleges is vital. Current research suggests student learning can be advanced by implementing approaches which support teaching as a fundamental discipline, and by providing leadership and new structures for enhancing the scholarship of teaching. This chapter gives examples of new pedagogical methods for the community college learner and organizational approaches that support learning. New methods are summarized at the end of the chapter in the form of challenges to the field.

THE DREAM

Higher education is about transformation, about deep change, about moving the hearts and minds of learners. We have a responsibility to help our students be critical thinkers who become informed and active citizens. While better teaching and learning at the college level are important for all sectors, improved pedagogy is essential if community college students are to overcome the barriers to success we have outlined elsewhere in this book. Community colleges are unique institutions, not simply lesser versions of four-year colleges. Their faculties will ideally take the lead in developing distinctive pedagogies for the new populations of learners who attend America's colleges.

Any good pedagogy focuses clearly on four aspects: teaching, learning, knowing, and doing (Woolis, 2006). Community colleges dream of perfecting the practice of great teaching so that every student succeeds. Ideally, community colleges transform students who are not "college material" because of inadequate prior academic preparation, significant language barriers, or past failures in traditional school settings offering traditional pedagogy, into engaged thinkers and scholars who can use their considerable experience to actualize a lifetime of opportunity as intellectually sophisticated citizens.

The old pedagogy, i.e., broadcasting methodologies such as lecturing to students who are presumed to be "empty vessels," has had moderate success, mostly with teaching the few students of elite stature who previously made up the bulk of college students. The elite were of traditional age when they entered college, immediately after high school. Their family's finances allowed them to go to college full time. These elite students were a mostly homogenous group whose prior educational experience had all the hallmarks of college success: rigorous academic preparation in secondary schools, rich cultural environments and contacts, years of academic success upon which to base high educational aspirations, and parents (indeed, often generations of family and friends) who graduated from college. They entered college with positive experiences, with traditional approaches to learning, and not surprisingly they found college teaching methods adequate.

Very few community college students have even one of these privileges, much less a combination of such factors. The profound difference in student background and demographics calls for a very different pedagogy. In this unique learning environment, faculty might be as likely to be working with students who have shattered egos and feel hopeless because of past academic or social struggles as they are working with academically talented students. The dream of a perfectly effective pedagogy is one that engages hearts and minds as well as provides the intellectual tools to overcome past educational missteps.

Community college faculty are ideally suited to become experts in the scholarship of teaching, modeling for all of higher education the best educational practices for the critical first two years. The perfect pedagogy is a seamless integration of practice and experience. The best practices lead to a conscious and continuous analysis of what learners learn, and how they learn it, because the skills of learning emerge as essential as any specific kind of knowledge in today's complex and networked world.

If community colleges are correct in thinking of themselves as "democracy's colleges," our pedagogy must reflect those democratic values. The word democracy comes from the original Greek *demokratia*—combining *demos* "the people" and *kratia* "power or rule." Democracy values each individual and his or her freedom equally under the rule of law. Democracy has three major characteristics: diversity, interactivity, and multiple ways for citizens to engage in the exercise of civic power. Community colleges must develop the student's ability to claim a rightful voice in the discourse of civil society. The best pedagogy provides a basis for the learner to develop a perspective not only on what one should learn, but also how they learn it, because self-awareness of the intellectual process of continuous learning is ever more imperative in a complex and networked world. Community colleges support democracy's diversity by preparing a great range of learners to be active citizens, voters, volunteers, parents, leaders, and workers. Learners need to be able to cope with and live in the real and internationally connected world, and at the same time, understand their role in transforming it.

There is general (but rarely specific) agreement about the areas in which students should develop proficiency. Students need to gain experience in a variety of specific knowledge areas and skills, including communication, information gathering and application, critical thinking, logical and quantitative reasoning, and the ability to learn independently as well as in teams.

Ideally, the entire college campus has a role in sustaining and improving student learning. Incredible learning can result when faculty work together with student support staff to create a total focus on learning, knowing, and doing within the institution. Learning is guided by specific goals that articulate levels of competency, goal achievement, and assessment.

ꙮ MIDWESTERN COMMUNITY COLLEGE I

Midwestern Community College I changed their mission statement to reflect a focus on learning. This focus began to drive learning activity in the college. Several consultants worked with the college faculty and staff to help them understand fully the implication of being a learning college.

Faculty members developed a set of learning goals that reflected what students should know and be able to do once they had earned an Associate degree. Each learning goal had a set of competencies for minimal and then for optimal achievement. Faculty members created assessment guidelines to ensure the curriculum and teaching methods were achieving their purposes. The primary assessment tool was individual student portfolios. When program-wide assessments found students were not learning at the desired level, departments made changes in their curriculum and in their teaching so students would "get it." Faculty members created the Center for Teaching and Learning, and faculty development became an integral part of the teaching and learning process. Great teaching and great teachers resulted.

Faculty and student support staff worked together to create a Freshman Experience (cornerstone) course. This course prepared first-year students for the rigors of higher learning and introduced them to the learning goals, thus taking the first steps toward building a learning community. Faculty also created a capstone course. During this course, faculty worked as cross-disciplinary teams to assess student learning across the curriculum and met with students to review their portfolios.

Eventually, the college changed its organizational structure to incorporate several concepts. First, a dean of student learning replaced the instructional services dean. Positions were created for a dean of student success and a chief information officer (CIO). The person holding the latter position would provide faculty development to support the use of technology applications in the teaching/learning process. Strategic initiatives were selected to focus on student learning and on college excellence, and they were data driven.

The CIO specifically supported learning processes for the college and became responsible for helping the college purchase and implement new instructional software. This task included all the groundwork needed to ensure instructional, student, and business support services. A strong focus for the technology effort became, "How can we support student learning?"

THE UNFULFILLED DREAM

While there are institutions and even entire states that have implemented new pedagogy and structures, there are many community colleges that still demonstrate only the most traditional of pedagogical approaches. The reasons for stasis on the part of colleges in the face of greater student need can be grouped into two general categories of factors: those that emerge from the students or institution itself (internal constraints) or those that impinge from outside the campus (external constraints).

Internal Constraints

Students themselves can resist new teaching strategies. New pedagogies can strike students as threatening. Community college students can resist an additional course or new classroom structures that appear to encumber an already complex set of graduation requirements. Education has often been a stressful and unsuccessful endeavor in their past, so students hesitate to embrace anything that places even more pressure on them to perform. Since students feel relatively powerless in academic surroundings, they can find comfort in the old traditional structures, even ineffective ones. Students are accustomed to being able to be passive in class, not required to reveal how much they really understand until they (privately) fail an examination. They can be very resistant to strategies that demand engagement of any sort, such as active participation in the development of a lesson or a task. Students may be hesitant to engage in group work because other students' lack of engagement might lower their grade. Traditional students in classrooms where faculty use engaged pedagogy can initially feel cheated, realizing that the instructor isn't the only source of knowledge. We have heard students say with disgust, "She didn't teach me anything. I had to learn it all myself."

Faculty may have other reasons for not using new pedagogies. They may ignore the focus on student learning, presuming that it is a new fad that will soon fade. Faculty might look forward to the day when they can get back to the much more comfortable position of pronouncing their own thinking rather than trying to determine if their techniques work for their students. They prefer to teach the way they were taught, as though they were teaching people like themselves. Community colleges rarely reward faculty for undertaking pedagogical innovation, and there are even fewer penalties for using out-of-date methods. Union leaders are adamant about not linking student performance to faculty evaluation, further limiting incentives available to initiate new strategies to reach higher levels of success.

When faculty do embrace a learning focus, they may do so only partially. For example, faculty may prefer not to work together to create learning goals for the college curriculum as a whole, since it is much more common for faculty to develop learning goals only for their individual classes. Faculty may have come to their profession hoping for opportunities to discuss issues of substance; they soon discover that having enough enrollment to conduct class may be as critical as their in-depth analysis of a topic. They can be discouraged by the need to learn how to work with a new breed of students who are not interested in learning so much as in getting a job, or in just getting by. There are students who need special attention in other ways that remove faculty from their dream of engaged students who embrace the material on their own and come to class eager to discuss it.

External Constraints

Administrators of community colleges, focused on declining budgets, staff retirements, and enrollment growth, are beside themselves attempting to keep the college boat afloat and on an even keel. Providing support to "trendy" topics when they are already awash in conflict among their various stakeholders can be out of the question. Administrative performance is almost never measured by the college's engagement in a new pedagogy. Presidents and vice presidents barely have time to take note of the radical changes occurring around them: new students captivated by new technology, increasingly diverse students whose cultures and experiences are not validated in the curriculum, and new faculty members who are energized with new ideas but floundering for lack of experience both in the classroom and in the charged environment of faculty politics. This reality is reflected in Midwestern Community College II.

⟨⟨ Midwestern Community College II

At Midwestern Community College II faculty members and counselors do not communicate with one another. Faculty members, for the most part, do not value the work of counselors very much and consider their work to be, at times, distracting for students. For example, counselors developed a Freshman Experience course in order to orient new students to college life and to foster a sense of community among faculty and students. Counselors could not recruit enough faculty members to actually create this learning community and intense interaction with students, so the effort eventually failed.

When students complained about this new class, faculty members told students they agreed the course was a waste of time. The course

(Continued)

---

became an institutional squall, and even data demonstrating student success could not convince faculty members that the new course could produce dramatic results in student learning.

College deans believed that spending money on technology was a money pit and a waste. They decided to continue to be the best possible college at offering the Associate degree, in the classroom, in a traditional manner, and they vowed to recruit students who preferred a traditional pedagogical approach to learning.

Faculty decided that teaching was more important than learning, and they rejected the learning college concept and any attempt to introduce new curricular or organizational shifts.

One new faculty member attempted to conduct a new multicultural literature course. He believed it was crucial for learners to understand the thinking of diverse groups: those who had a disability, were of diverse ethnic and racial groups or diverse sexual orientation, and were living in diverse regions and nations of the world. His colleagues disagreed with his definition of diversity. In addition, they had worked hard for several years to introduce a new course on Eastern Literature to supplement the traditional Western Lit course, and believed they had done their part to broaden student awareness.

Another new faculty member learned there were significant numbers of students who found it very difficult to attend class for 10 weeks from 10 AM to 11 AM, the time his required psychology class was offered. He volunteered to teach a four-week course, three hours a week on Saturdays morning for this group. He was quietly visited by the union president, who told him that if he followed through on this idea, he would jeopardize the long-term agreement in place between the union and the administration regarding the hours of instruction that were acceptable to the union.

The college president spent every possible moment meeting with legislators to broaden state understanding of the college's funding crisis or conducting fundraising to supplement the college's budget. He listened to all sides of every argument and nodded his head to each of them. Overall, seasoned faculty and staff felt safe in the knowledge that they had, once again, survived the gales of the pedagogical sea-change.

THE REAL STORY

Principles of the Learning Focus

While there is no national agreement on what college students should learn, and even less on the methods by which they should be taught, there is a long history in higher education of attempting to delineate pedagogical perspectives. Although pedagogy is the most common term to describe all manner of teaching practices, some practitioners argue that andragogy is a better term for collegiate education because it indicates that adults, not children, are being taught. Current practices are influenced by Bloom (1956), who introduced a taxonomy for learning; Knowles (2005), who first introduced a definitive approach to adult learning in the early 1970s; and Barr and Tagg (1995), of Palomar Community College in California, who, after a call for a new vision by president George Boggs, argued for a paradigm shift in college education from teaching to learning. Barr and Tagg (1995) frame learning holistically, recognizing that the chief agent in the process is the learner, not the teacher. They maintain that teaching has not really occurred if learning isn't the result, shifting the perspective from inputs to outcomes (Barr and Tagg, 1995). Over the same time period, pedagogical trends went from behaviorist approaches, to cognitive emphasis, to a current focus on constructivist and engagement strategies (Summers, Beretvas, Svinicki, and Gorin, 2005).

These approaches may exist in individual classrooms or in institutions as a whole. Several principles mark an institution where learning is the primary focus: changing individual learners substantively; engaging learners as full partners in the learning process; creating options for learning, including collaborative learning; teaching from the perspective of a learning facilitator, directed by the needs of the learners; and documenting the learning (O'Banion, 1997). Each of these learning principles is exemplified in the pedagogical values described below.

Substantive Change in Individual Learners

One of the most important reasons for higher learning opportunities is the transformation that occurs as students learn to question and explore the assumptions they have acquired throughout their lives. Most community colleges organize their general education curriculum to provide this liberal learning. It is in understanding assumptions and their sources that allows individuals to make changes in themselves and in their cultural environment. Contemporary society abounds with assumptions needing exploration, including the areas of ethnic and racial understanding, sexual orientation, geographic differences, gender, age, and class differences, and religious diversity. When campuses change from a teaching to a learning paradigm, they re-frame their definitions of what is taught. The learning focus demands that faculty understand that the transmission of current knowledge, while essential, is no longer sufficient for a college-educated individuals. For community college students who have attended high schools that emphasize rote memorization and silence in class over any empowered engagement in an analytic perspective, the need for elements of an education beyond simple transmission are even more important.

TYPES OF EMERGENT PEDAGOGIES

Community college faculty must identify those elements of each intellectual discipline or philosophical theme that make the most sense for the collection of learners on their campus. There is not yet a singular standard for the content of a college education that extends beyond the broad outlines above. The same is not true with pedagogy, however, because certain approaches are particularly suited to a community college student profile. Many of these approaches are considered best practice but do not have the breadth or depth of supporting data that would conclusively establish their effectiveness. They can overlap in focus or intention, and the typology given here serves only to provide a general overview. Much more research is needed to determine if these practices are as promising as some faculty and staff believe, and if there are other approaches that are especially suited to a particular discipline or for students with a specific profile. The emergent types of engaged pedagogies include:

1. *Reflection* – strategies that change the purpose of learning from simple memorization to one of deeper analysis by combining questions, individualized goals and values, and multiple perspectives on the knowledge gained.
2. *Integrated Learning* – strategies that link across intellectual disciplines and help students fabricate a coherence in their individual learning which has occurred over time in multiple settings, such as classes in different disciplines, in internships, and in life experiences. Integrated learning strategies encourage students to create an intellectual frame-

work, which is likely to reveal the lack of grounding in certain areas of students' prior academic preparation as well as demonstrate students' ability to see relationships among different disciplinary learning over their time in college.

3. *Collaborative Learning and Learning Communities* – strategies that create communities of learners, virtually or in person, premised on the belief that learning is socially constructed, so that students experience the process of creating social knowledge as well as working together. Learning communities or collaborative learning experiences typically adopt active or constructivist learning techniques, which incorporate students' prior knowledge and advance this knowledge based upon active interaction with what is currently known.

4. *Narrative* – strategies that use the creation of story as a foundational pedagogy in order to include the multiple aspects of students' lives and cultures. Creation and use of narrative is a mechanism to study the specific within a general understanding, allowing for personalization of information and analysis by example.

5. *Applied Learning* – strategies that use real-world situations that students experience through cooperative education, internships, or service learning, where theoretical knowledge is applied to actual behavior or implementation. Included in this approach are strategies to award credit for college-level learning that occurs outside of traditional classes.

6. *Technology* – no longer a separate strategy, but an increasingly integrating focus of multiple pedagogic strategies. There are emerging analyses about effective practices in virtual or online modes, as well as thousands of ways in which faculty integrate technology into teaching. Discussion of technological innovations will be integrated into the other above categories as well.

1. Reflection

The ultimate goal of all college teaching is to advance the quality of students' thinking. While the thinking is usually directed at understanding information and gaining knowledge within a specific discipline, college is intended to enhance the overall quality of students' ability to think. Pedagogies that emphasize this aspect of a college education are as concerned with the systematic application of the thinking as they are with the ability to do so. There is a high level of general agreement that deep analysis and reflection are positive attributes to inculcate in students, but it can be difficult to actually define what a deeper level of thinking is and how to measure it (Rodgers, 2002).

Critiques of college-educated students from employers are often directed at this skill when they complain that students come with good grades but seem unable to apply the theoretical information from classes to actual situations or to generalize from a present situation to undertake better action in the future. Reflective pedagogies help students develop the skills to look at themselves and what they are learning in class, integrate information from many sources, and develop a higher-level personal understanding that can then result in informed action (Bringle and Hatcher, 1997).

Students develop habits of mind that allow them to reflect upon and possibly change or challenge underlying assumptions, create a new intellectual framework, and then use this more complex understanding of the world. Educators can also use active techniques (experiments, real-world examples, problem solving activities, dialogues) to introduce students to information and issues and then encourage students to reflect on and talk about what they did and how their understanding is changing. The duality of exchange these techniques evoke can be very important for community college students, whose life experiences can often enrich a classroom with learning that occurred outside of traditional classes. Moreover, since community college students are the most diverse of any college sector, an engaged process will bring into the classroom distinctive perspectives, cultures, and histories. This pedagogy often utilizes collaboration and peer criticism as a way of facilitating students' abilities to reach a new level of understanding (Arcario, Eynon, and Clark, 2005).

Critical thinking is a crucial portion of the learning agenda within a reflective practice. It involves recognizing and researching the assumptions that guide thoughts and actions. At its core, critical thinking is hunting down and checking these assumptions (Brookfield, 2005; Chaffee, 2006a).

Community college faculty who use reflective pedagogies do so in a variety of ways. Critical thinking might be articulated in a college's core learning objectives and outlined and measured in multiple ways. LaGuardia Community College, for example, uses a faculty-created critical thinking rubric that measures student progress in critical thinking over time and within specific courses (Katopes, 2007). Other campuses have critical thinking courses or require that critical thinking perspectives be inserted into every syllabus. The critical incident approach, where students uncover and research their assumptions by exploring a particular moment, situation, or incident in their lives, is one more example of a pedagogy whose intent is the development of critical thinking skills (Brookfield, 2005).

Many pedagogical innovations nurture critical thinking. As community colleges re-conceptualize their core curriculum, being locally responsive to the students creates a new opportunity to integrate history, circumstance, and community. For example, a global/transnational, multicultural literature course might introduce the value of an alternative aesthetic, and simultaneously focus on the self-understanding in the context of the diversity of human experiences and the multiple layers of connection among them (Clem, 2005). The composition of community college classes make them uniquely able to establish a class that is rich in the potential for personal transformation. When coupled with explicit faculty development and careful assessment, improvements in student learning, retention, and enthusiasm result (Arcario, Eynon, and Clark, 2005). Other strategies include the development of cross-disciplinary capstone courses, cross-disciplinary internships, travel programs, and interactive online courses with students from other countries (Arcario et al., 2005). All these efforts can deepen learning through an explicit focus on global perspectives while simultaneously developing critical thinking abilities.

Reflective pedagogies require faculty to rethink their own assumptions about teaching. Faculty who are used to lecturing often move beyond the idea of the infallible lecturer and demonstrate the notion that they have explored their own assumption about how to best learn (Brookfield, 2005). This change is especially productive for community college students whose previous education is likely to have been lackluster, and/or with faculty who are not self-reflective practitioners (Brookfield, 2005).

2. Integrated Learning

Integrated learning strategies emerge from faculty perceptions that, although students take a variety of courses across several disciplines to help them function in a multidisciplinary world, the curricular structure often creates fragmentary knowledge (Huber, Hutchings, and Gale, 2005). Integrated learning advocates believe there must be clear goals about how to incorporate multiple perspectives and experiences if students are to develop a holistic understanding of the knowledge presented over many classes and experiences. "Contextuality, conflict, and change are the defining parameters" of integrated learning as students learn that all knowledge is contingent (Klein, 2005). Creating structures for integration are particularly important for community college students, because the approach can link life experiences in and out of the classroom with the theoretical or disciplinary perspectives in any one course (Arcario et al., 2005). Community college students' greater repertoire of life experiences contribute significantly to this strategy.

Thus, integrated learning is not so much a coherent pedagogy as it is a structural approach to college learning. "Integrative learning comes in many varieties: connecting skills and knowledge from multiple sources and experiences; applying theory to practice in various settings; utilizing diverse and even contradictory points of view; and, understanding issues and positions contextually"(Huber et al., 2005). Interactive pedagogies in community colleges focus on helping students not only to learn to ask better questions about complex knowledge, but also to be able to understand that different perspectives use distinctive kinds of information to answer the questions posed (Klein, 2005). Ultimately, an integrative approach helps students develop increasingly sophisticated frameworks in which to situate their own understanding of the world as they use, compare, and contrast different patterns of knowledge associated with different perspectives (Klein, 2005). Evidence of integrated learning might be an insight that a student achieves when she is able to combine information from multiple resources. For example, she might use classes in different disciplines (art history and economics) in combination with an internship in a local economic development agency (Huber et al., 2005). Some campuses coordinate integrated learning efforts by creating a matrix that uses skills and knowledge as one axis and classes that should require students to use and develop those attributes on another axis; i.e., to specify a system of repeated exposure at increasing levels of achievement (Bierman, Ciner, Lauer-Glebov, Rutz, and Savina, 2005).

Community colleges assert that each student should enter the institution and be able to take steps toward educational advancement. Teaching for powerful learning uses a range of methods so each student can work up to his or her potential. Individuals turn information into knowledge through a process of translation, but their styles of doing so can differ widely. For some people, visually oriented learning strategies work best, for others it is aurally or conceptually, and for still others it is first-hand experience. Both reading and hands-on work—doing research or art, performing music or drama, serving local community groups—can deepen knowledge.

E-Portfolios are increasingly used to provide an intellectual scaffold and process that encourages integration of student learning over multiple classes within an electronic framework *(Researching Electronic Portfolios and*

Learned Engagement, 2005). The best e-Portfolio programs offer students a way to collect and showcase accomplishments, and then require students to make personal intellectual connections through a reflective process. Early research indicates that as students electronically represent—literally "re-present" themselves—the engaged process leads to deeper and more holistic learning (Arcario, Eynon, and Clark, 2005). For community college students who are generally from groups who are not represented in media or the public consciousness, this self-narrative is a powerful means of learning and of creating educational aspirations (Arcario, 2005). It also has the unintended positive consequence of allowing first generation and immigrant students to open up the academic process to family and friends, creating digital resumes to send to employers and transfer institutions, and connecting educational goals with personal experiences (Eynon, 2006a). Students populate their e-Portfolios with integrated essays, poetry, original paintings, drawings, oral interviews, family photographs, annotated resumes, and a range of projects that represent who they are as students and emerging scholars (Eynon, 2006a).

The best e-Portfolio processes are faculty-led learning projects, with changes in student learning and subsequent student success and graduation as the ultimate goals (Eynon, 2006a). The integration simultaneously provides an intellectual framework, created by faculty, that helps students to see connections among their work from different classes or different educational experiences, and a prompt for students to take more responsibility for their learning. Evaluation can be embedded in e-Portfolios, whether for holistic student or programmatic assessment (Eynon, 2006a). The e-Portfolios themselves can be evaluated by reviewing the quality of writing, especially the reflective writing, the clarity of intellectual annotation, and the completion of different sections. The student's digital literacy can be assessed through the quality of the design, ease of navigation, or the quality of the multimedia presentation.

Pedagogical innovations can require different kinds of support systems. The e-Portfolio project at LaGuardia Community College, where more than 5,000 students maintain e-Portfolios, developed specialized computer labs, a peer mentor program in which technologically savvy students mentor faculty who are implementing e-Portfolios in their classes, and instructional design assistants who help faculty and students with more advanced e-Portfolio applications.

Grounding learning in specific learner experiences allows the learner to draw comparisons and to go from the known to the unknown (Arcario et al., 2005). Community college students from minority communities or lower socioeconomic groups rarely see their perspectives represented in traditional texts. Integrating learning across outside work or in the community creates perspectives in the classroom that allow for a richer and more complete academic experience for all students.

3. Collaborative Learning and Learning Communities

When students are actively engaged with college faculty and staff, with other students, and with the subject matter they study, they are more likely to learn and persist toward achieving academic goals (McKlenney, 2006). Therefore, student involvement is a valuable yardstick for assessing whether an institution is using educational practices likely to provide this result (McKlenney, 2003-2006). Adult learning paradigms point to the key elements of interaction and application as especially helpful to adults (Knowles, Holton, and Swanson, 2005). Collaborative learning pedagogies and learning communities seek to engage students with each other in the social creation of knowledge and understanding.

Collaborative learning is based on the assumption that it is the interactive group activity that produces the learning (Baker, Hanson, Joiner, and Traum, 1999). While there are many specific definitions and ideas about the kinds of activities and measurements that are necessary for collaborative learning, it is generally understood to be a coordinated process in which the intellectual interaction between the students and faculty helps to construct knowledge, define a problem, and create a solution (Dillenbourg, 1999).

Collaborative pedagogies require much more than having students together while in class. Since these experiences lend themselves to allowing the most verbal students to manage a discussion, the collaborative interactions need to be organized so that each person gets an opportunity to speak, think and learn (Brookfield, 2005). Collaborative classes may appear somewhat chaotic to the casual spectator, but the best consist of a tightly orchestrated set of activities that balance individual and group learning and assessment. Collaborative learning assumes that learners must be active discoverers and constructors of their own knowledge into frameworks or wholes (Barr and Tagg, 1995). Knowledge is not seen as cumulative and linear, like a wall of bricks, but as nesting and interacting frameworks (Barr and Tagg, 1995).

"Learning communities" is a term used to describe a range of pedagogical structures or practices (Smith, McGregor, Matthews, and Gabelnick,

2004). All learning communities intend to use interaction between and among students and faculty to create a more social process of learning. Loosely coupled learning communities are groups of individuals whom faculty encourage to work together or study together, sometimes linked by common elements such as similar major or class standing. More tightly developed learning communities integrate two or more classes and have a cohort of students attend all classes, with some level of coordination between the faculty in the different classes. The most structured learning communities have cross-disciplinary faculty work together to integrate syllabi, class activities, projects, and often classroom teaching into a coherent theme. Such themes are fascinating just to list: "Beauty or the Beast?" (philosophy (bioethics), biology, science-fiction literature); "Harlem on My Mind" (literature of the Harlem renaissance, introduction to jazz, introduction to sociology); and "Graphic Stories" (introduction to design, geometry, the graphic novel). Whether the learning community is focused on developmental studies or if it is an honors community, research consistently finds the communities induce positive student engagement and success, especially for community college students (Smith et al., 2004).

The techniques associated with these approaches use a mix of individual and collective classroom activities that teach students about independence, interdependence, and engagement. The group projects nurture negotiation skills, conflict resolution, teamwork, collaboration, and a practical understanding of people from diverse backgrounds, in addition to a social construction of knowledge. Since no one discipline monopolizes particular learning outcomes, a powerful education repeatedly exposes students to multiple teaching methods across the curriculum. Technology-based instruction that engages the learner can supplement and complement more traditional methods, just as learning by doing can enrich learning from lectures. Effective teachers use scholarly work on motivating a class as a resource to improve performance (Association of American Colleges and Universities [AAC&U], 2002). Several studies at community colleges have demonstrated the effectiveness of learning communities or related cohort models of education, with particular success with developmental students (Bloom and Sommo, 2005; Pascarella and Terrenzini, 1991).

Organized peer groups for learners are an example of a loosely coupled learning community where opportunities for learning are enhanced through dialogue and through interaction with other learners. Even these more loosely structured learning communities are important learning resources for students, and may be particularly helpful to community college students who need additional critical debate and dialogue, and whose complex lives make this difficult to obtain.

Metropolitan Community College uses learning communities in its Developmental Studies program, where integration across developmental disciplines and the use of a retention counselor help students improve basic skills, develop sound learning strategies, and set realistic goals. The college retention counselor meets with the faculty who guide the learning community to provide case management services for students (Raftery, 2005). Cy-Fair Community College in Houston, one of the few new colleges built from the ground up, used the principle of collaboration not only as an organizing principle for learning, but also as an inspiration for its architecture. It created a variety of learning spaces sized to accommodate individuals, teams, small groups, large groups in formal classrooms and labs, and informal indoor and outdoor spaces (Design Share, 2007).

4. Narrative

Using narrative by incorporating written, oral, or digital stories into teaching honors the centrality of narrative structures in human experience. Narrative and storytelling pedagogies are seen as particularly useful for adult learners because they acknowledge the students' wealth of life experience and adeptly provides a space for diverse cultures (Rossiter, 2002). The inherently interactive dimension of stories told by multiple students can create multiple perspectives from which to frame understanding and decipher assumptions (Eynon, 2006b). Narrative structures are constructivist because students develop and use a story to connect and elucidate knowledge, and to connect new knowledge into the schema of a lived experience (Rossiter, 2002).

Community college students rarely see their lives depicted in the curricular materials that are common in undergraduate education. Narrative structures can therefore be transformative when the diversity of the lives of community college students changes the application and understanding of

---

FACULTY PERSPECTIVES ON DIGITAL STORIES

Juan (sociology faculty): The key to learning and remembering is associating new information with what you are already familiar. Nothing is more familiar than our lives and our stories.

Admani (non-credit faculty): I think students will get to know a lot about other cultures and understand that while there are differences, there are also similarities. But most of all, understanding why people behave in a certain way and why they migrated to the United States is important. Often students are either too shy or afraid to speak up in class and share their stories; creating digital stories is a way to have them get actively involved in their learning while sharing with others.

Nanci (English faculty): … Students [can] create digital stories which parallel a personal statement for college or graduate school … the goal for the large majority of my students

Frank (business faculty): I use the storytelling especially in the topics I consider difficult to understand to the students, e.g. how to record an initial investment of a company. Students will fully understand the principles of a procedure or activity because story telling is a concatenation of visual ideas that stay a long time in our memories.

Mark (English faculty): It helps students with formulating [an] overall structure that relates not only to the digital story but to writing in general. The formulating of ideas into communication depends on structure and logical organization and this process furthers that creation.

Meg (ESL faculty): Creating a story about themselves is an important step, but creating a story that communicates the message, the experience or particular opinion that they want to express is another skill. I want them to think in an organized, consecutive manner that they can use to express who they are confidently on English.

Rodney (communication faculty): It's the wonderful view from the top of the mountain. It's the combination of process and product. It's a journey of self-discovery for the students and for the instructor and appreciation of what students bring to class and who they are as individuals.

Names changed; adapted from Eynon, 2006b

knowledge frameworks. As faculty use narrative to structure learning, they get a more complete picture of their students. Moreover, the tacit learning of a diverse student population expressed in narrative enriches the entire classroom experiences as it helps to alter the implicit one-way orientation of faculty as "all knowing" by acknowledging the wisdom of adults who have lived rich lives. Including narrative structures in a community college class-room also allows faculty to deepen their own understanding of the cultures and intellectual traditions from which their students emerge.

Digital storytelling—that is, having students construct the story using multi-media and commonly transmitting the story electronically—provides additional learning for community college students. By telling an integrated story of their own life, which includes how they learn and contextualizes the role of education within it, the story itself becomes an intellectually ground-ing scaffold that they can carry with them through the rest of their educational life. Faculty have found that the process of digital storytelling helps students move from description to analysis and interpretation as they place their stories within fuller cultural and social meanings (Eynon, 2006b).

Community college faculty have a responsibility to help students under-stand that education has a utility leading to a job or an enhanced career, and narrative techniques not only help students chart this journey but also encourages the development of the mind that allows critical consciousness to fully blossom. Panel formats and bringing in former students to talk about the connection between their study and their work are both ways to suggest the importance of current education and future work and to stress the sig-nificance of a topic and the diverse approaches to thinking about it. Since community college students overwhelmingly will live in the community upon graduation, the expansion of an understanding of how to critically reflect on one's life and place in a community has the potential to transform that community as well as an individual.

This focus on the learner's previous experience also lends itself to tai-loring learning strategies to individual learning styles. For example, profes-sors intentionally expect students to move from the specific to the general only after demonstrating they are able to go from the general to the specific. Approaches tailored to different learning styles include learning by doing or learning by visualizing, in addition to reading and listening activities as ways to understand content (Sperling, 2003). While all of higher education can benefit from these approaches, the potential increase in student success for community college students is multiplied by the likelihood that community college students have not succeeded with traditional pedagogical methods in the past. Using the perspective that the average community college student has not responded particularly well to prior educational experiences is key to finding ways to fundamentally change community college educational approaches and achieve dramatically improved academic success. This is also incredibly difficult, because it is unrealistic to expect that community college faculty, which face such a range of abilities, can customize approaches to so many needs.

These alternative approaches to learning focus on learners and on how to help them integrate personal experience with new encounters. Each of these approaches also lends itself to enhancement through integrating new technology. But more importantly, community college students require a new kind of pedagogy if colleges are to be successful in moving them past the damage of past poor or unsuccessful schooling, over the hurdles of time that distance them from high school, or beyond the barriers of race, class, and/or immigration status. It is in the engaged pedagogies that the future of community college students' academic success lies.

5. Applied Learning

Simulations, case studies, internships, and service learning activities all engage students in experiential learning. Experiential learning, or finding ways to give credit for prior college-level learning, provides a way for the experience-rich background of the older community college student to be recognized in a parallel to the way being good at taking standardized tests privileges students just coming out of some high schools. Experiential learning opportunities include role-playing, individual projects, group projects, computer-based activities, simulations, case studies, thought questions, analogies, cultural exchanges, mini-lectures, and lectures (Ennis-Cole and Lawhon, 2004). There are also extensive internship and service-learning activities, for credit or not, which enrich a community college student's life and expand the ability to apply theoretical knowledge in a specific context (Kolomechuk, 2006).

Service learning is a program that began in the mid 1980s to redress the perceived lack of students' acceptance of civic responsibility in their personal lives, and encourage elite college involvement in the issues of the communities beyond their campus walls. Begun at Brown, Georgetown, and Stanford, service learning soon spread to community colleges (*About Campus Compact*, 2007). Service learning programs are essentially volunteer opportunities in the community, often stand-alone, but they are sometimes linked to a specific course or curriculum that provides students with experiences with people or groups in their community who need their help (Zlotkowski, 1998). The purpose is to develop the habit of involvement in community activities as well as to expand students' intellectual and personal repertoires. One of the early leaders is Brevard Community College in Florida. Here, service-learning is touted as "an opportunity to enrich and apply classroom knowledge; explore careers or majors; develop civic and cultural literacy; improve citizenship, helping, learning and occupational skills; enhance personal growth and self image; develop job links; and most of all foster in students a concern for social problems, sense of social responsibility and commitment to human service." (Brevard Community College, 2007). Brevard College faculty facilitate service learning through assisting in the placement and review of students, providing one-credit hour experiences either as a stand-alone, or as connected to a specific social science class that has faculty oversight and student provision of class work that reflects on the experience (Brevard Community College, 2007).

Assessment of prior learning is a particularly suitable process for community colleges, whose students may have gained knowledge through decades of work and independent study. The Community College of Vermont adopted a system in the mid-1970s that requires students to take a three-credit portfolio development class where they learn epistemology, assessment, and presentation skills, and gather information that documents their prior learning, which is then evaluated by appropriate disciplinary faculty (Community College of Vermont, 2007). The process has been enormously successful, with retention to degree of these students averaging over 70 percent, far exceeding the average adult student (Warren, 2007).

6. Technology

Technology can enhance student learning by allowing learning to be experiential and interactive. It is important to apply the measuring stick of engagement to technology-assisted learning. Technology can transform learning both in the classroom and in the silent kitchens or dorm rooms where students are online at 2:30 in the morning, but technology itself is not the answer unless it incorporates active engagement. The least effective use is when students simply employ technology to take in information and then reproduce it on a test, or when faculty use technology as little more than an electronic flash card (Dirks, 2005). "When it comes to technology and teaching and reaching students, we have to be sure not to use technology for the novelty, but for the utility" (Milliron, 2003).

The intense arguments between the high-tech and the high-touch advocates have for the most part dissipated, with strong agreement that technology can be very effective in the community college classroom as long as the focus is on how the technology expands or enhances the teaching-learning process. Faculty incorporate technology in classrooms so that as students write papers, they can engage in on-the spot research, solve assigned problems, and receive expert guidance for linear or sequential problem-solving, or simulate use of clinical or technical skills as in, say, a CAD program. Anatomy and physiology students review for a test with an interactive Web site of the body's system with flash animation. Students writing their first essay use writing sites to look up questions of grammar, to understand a faculty member's diacritics on their paper, to guide them through a staging of their writing process, or to use an error analyzer program to suggest where their first draft might be improved.

Technology in career programs is used to gain deeper understandings of reality and find multiple answers to complex problems. Interactive nursing technology presents multiple points of information within clinical cases so that nursing students understand the relationship and critical evaluations necessary to be a good nurse (as well as pass the national NCLEX exam). At its best, the internet permits access to information that would be difficult or impossible to physically obtain; allows users to select relevant information representing dissonant viewpoints; presents current, real-time data; and enables file sharing. Students can visit the Louvre in Paris, use the Library of Congress, view current satellite data, or contact experts (Ennis-Cole and Lawhon, 2004). For community college students whose ability to travel (either to libraries or within study abroad programs) is usually limited, the best faculty significantly enhance students' exposure to the world through technology.

Specific technology-mediated activities can increase both student learning and student satisfaction. Students who engaged in chat room conversations and exchanged as few as two email messages a week with their faculty member learned more and were more satisfied because they were more engaged (Oleks, 2005). Using common online platforms such as blackboard allows community college students to make more connections than is sometimes possible in person because of students' complicated schedules. A faculty member who mandates that students participate in online interactions about homework problems or group projects can facilitate not only intellectual development and deeper dialogue, but also create a place for students to come to know and enjoy each other as colleagues and co-learners.

Technology in instruction can include computerized tools, hardware, and application-oriented software, e.g., GIS software, audio-visual products, multimedia presentations, visual materials, and end-user products. Internet access, distance learning capabilities, and applications software are all tools that can make the learning experience more rewarding, enriched, and relevant (Ennis-Cole and Lawhon, 2004, 586). Integrated into a curriculum, technology and good teaching practice increase positive gains in student motivation, retention, attitude, and learning (Coughlin, 1999). Since motivation, time constraints, and academic connection to college can be difficult to achieve for a community college student population, the use of technology as an integrated and integral part of a community college pedagogy is exciting and potentially very fruitful.

Mobile applications advance the potential to immerse students in learning. The current formats include mobile phones, laptops, and increasingly wireless technology—everything from personal digital assistants to podcasts of lectures to handheld gaming applications. At a peer level, students could use mobile computing for collaborative learning as they now use it for their own social purposes, by coauthoring content or share big files electronically while talking quietly (Alexander, 2004).

Use of an electronic portfolio (e-Portfolio), whereby students are required to collect, select, and connect ideas from across different disciplines, creates multiple forms of engagement. Students do the critical thinking necessary to make intellectual connections across disciplines and assignments, to publish authentic student work for review by peers and employers, and to conduct the critical reflection that changes information into knowledge (Arcario, 2003). Students who use e-Portfolio were more engaged, had higher retention scores, and reported greater motivation for learning than a comparison group (Arcario, Eynon, and Clark 2005). Engaging students as mentors to assist faculty in the use of technology, as well as helping peers, has led to powerful learning environments (Arcario et al., 2005).

These approaches to technology-enhanced pedagogy allow for some of the best of what we know about student learning: student engagement, peer support, and grounding learning in the learner's experience. Work products generated by students occur in a digital environment so everything is stored and available for review and class participation (Woolis, 2006).

Distance learning uses a variety of modalities, such interactive television, satellite courses, video-based conferencing, Internet-based discussion groups, chat rooms, and courses, to make new content available to learners. Estimates vary, but it is likely that more than 30 percent of adult students in community colleges will use an online course at least once in their educational career (Parker, 1999). Coastline Community College in Southern California was established in 1976 as a campus without walls, and has continued to lead in the use of technology to deliver not only course content, but also a virtual library, student support systems, and other mechanisms to buttress academic success (Coastline Community College, 2007).

The use of distance learning, increasing in community colleges as in all of higher education, can still be contested terrain. Interestingly, faculty are often much more negative about online courses than students (Inman, Kerwin, and Mayes, 1999). While some educators maintain that this delivery system is an ideal solution for many community college students, others worry that the motivation, self-discipline, and broad academic skills necessary to be successful in the individualized world of the online learner are less likely to be present among community college students. Studies of online learning suggest that a self-selection process occurs so that students who are highly motivated to control their time and the pacing of course content are more likely to choose an online course (Roblyer, 1999) Some systems ask that students take a self-reporting assessment test, to at least provide students with information about their likelihood of success when using this modality (New Jersey Virtual Community College Consortium, 2006). This is critical, since attrition rates for community college students enrolled in online courses tends to be higher than students in traditional face-to-face courses (Parker, 1999).

The pedagogy used within an online course can range from traditional (lectures online, multiple choice tests, etc.) to highly innovative. Research suggests that the best asynchronous online courses for community college students build communities through consistent rules that guide interaction (student to student as well as student to faculty) so that there is a high level of communication and contact at regular intervals (Swan, Fredericksen, Pickett, and Pelz, 2000).

Technology is also an important factor in linking faculty who are interested in pedagogical innovation. The League for Innovation maintains a website for "Transformation Learning Connections," where multiple sets of resources for curricular enhancement and development are vetted and grouped for easy faculty access (League for Innovation, 2007).

DOCUMENTING STUDENT LEARNING

It is exciting to implement new ideas for student learning, new pedagogies, and to enhance the experience with technology. For so long, we in community colleges have, for the most part, implemented new ideas without assessing the impact of our strategies and experiments. The emphasis on quality and on a data-oriented environment encourage a new focus on assessing how new ideas work. Are students really learning more because they use their personal digital assistants or work in learning communities? Are these technologies increasing learning, knowing, and doing? Do they integrate the hallmarks of democracy: diversity, inclusivity, and interactivity? This assessment requires more than looking at student grades in individual classrooms. Does teaching really occur if the students don't get it? True assessment of student learning needs to illustrate whether or not students "got it"! Colleges truly concerned about increased student success in learning are building a culture of inquiry that goes far beyond grades, to document actual student progress along the road of transformation.

Colleges are beginning to buzz around this topic, although critics maintain that they seem to not be doing very much about it (Milliron and de los Santos, 2004). Accrediting agencies in the nation are an important impetus for more rigorous assessment. With their renewed focus on learning and on quality outcomes, accountability standards and practices are changing. .

One of the first requirements for assessing student learning is for a college to agree on what a student should learn—not just in individual classes, but as a result of earning an Associate degree. In other words, what should a student know and be able to do as a result of participating in the general education curriculum required for all Associate degree curricula? The American Association of Universities and Colleges describes some of the appropriate learning goals for the student educated by a liberal arts curriculum:

- communicating in diverse settings and groups, using written and oral communication, and in more than one language;
- understanding and employing both quantitative and qualitative analysis to describe and solve problems;
- interpreting, evaluating, and using information discerningly from a variety of sources;
- integrating knowledge of various types and understanding complex systems;
- resolving difficult issues creatively by employing multiple systems and tools;
- deriving meaning from experience, as well as gathering information from observation demonstrating intellectual agility and managing change;

- transforming information into knowledge and knowledge into judgment and action; and
- demonstrating intellectual agility and managing change by working well in teams, including those of diverse composition, and building consensus (American Association of Colleges and Universities [AAC&U], 2004).

Learning goals like these need to evolve within a college through dialogue among faculty members. Faculty members at Arrowhead Community College Region in northeastern Minnesota forged such a set of learning goals for students in 1988. A college-wide group of faculty members, along with union representatives, explored, shared across disciplines, and finally presented their work to the faculty at large. These learning goals have evolved over time along with levels of competence required for minimal and optimal performance. A statewide dialogue among university and college faculty occurred. Minnesota eventually developed a statewide set of learning goals that allowed for easier student transfer, because Associate and baccalaureate graduates all had engaged in the same set of knowledge and skills.

Approaches to assessing student learning require a great deal of research in order to find effective and economic methods of documentation. For example, student portfolios and capstone courses have been found to be very effective means of interdisciplinary assessment and integration for learners. They are also the most challenging to implement. Very few faculty evaluation systems are linked to the amount and quality of student learning.

Assessing student success can also occur through performance benchmarking, whereby colleges evaluate the resources or inputs applied to the learning process and the outcomes achieved (Dowd, 2005). The National Community College Benchmarking Project is a model for this type of effort (Dowd, 2005; Hurley, 2002). Diagnostic benchmarking uses research-based survey questions to determine college/student interaction and explicitly take into account student responsibility for their own contribution to outcomes. The Community College Survey of Student Engagement has begun to achieve broad appeal because it benchmarks those activities associated with deep student learning (CCSSE, 2007). Process benchmarking is very complex; it compares institutions and their student learning outcomes (Dowd, 2005). Benchmarks have also been developed for distance education, where colleges seek to identify effectiveness in overall institutional support, course development, methods of teaching and evidence of learning, and student support (Phipps and Merisotis, 2000).

Faculty who are engaging in the scholarship of teaching and learning are developing the spirit of inquiry specifically tailored to a community college setting. They are asking questions of one another like, "What do we know about motivation?" "Why do some people want to learn while others don't?" "What practices promote high motivation over time?" "Must we teach under-prepared adults differently than more traditionally aged students?" "Can community colleges significantly enhance retention and graduation through new pedagogical techniques?" They are digging into the theoretical literature, and then conducting proactive research around those ideas (Sperling, 2003). These faculty members are role models and can change the face of pedagogy for all community college faculty members, or perhaps all of higher education.

The heart of assessment is that it is characterized by a primary concern for student progress in the learning endeavor and asks important questions about what it is a student has learned. New pedagogical approaches require equally innovative methods to assess effectiveness, and will ultimately demand new roles for the faculty member in a community college.

TEACHING TO FACILITATE LEARNING

Teachers in today's learning environment play different roles than in the past, and the requirements are far more demanding than earlier teacher preparation assumed. Instructional roles include: lecturer, expert, mentor, reflection facilitator, group discussion guide, intensive workshop leader, consultant, leader of intensive problem-based experiential learning, software developer or adapter of off-the-shelf software, and partner with co-curricular educators. Carol Twigg found the best approach to knowledge development was in a large room with a "guide on the side" supporting student learning by doing (Dowd, 2005; Oleks, 2005).

Teachers who use new pedagogies must be learning-centered and organized as they assume the new role of mentors, coaches, and motivators in the learning process. Effective teachers sequence content; they begin with prerequisite skills and progress to applications of theory and demonstrations of students' mental models of the subject matter. Successful instructors balance organization with flexibility; they are aware of students' concerns and incomplete knowledge, and they redirect questions, reword discussion points, and restructure content to match the needs of individual learners. Incidental learning, humor, hands-on experiences, and connections between current information and newly forming knowledge are often found in the classrooms of good instructors (Ennis-Cole and Lawhon, 2004).

Effective teaching that truly transforms student learning involves setting and reaching goals, bridging the gap between theory and practice; using listening and other effective communication skills for student engagement; and utilizing students' prior experiences and reiteration (Sanford, 1999). Faculty members need to attend to active student participation, fair evaluation procedures, respect for student rights and needs, and activities for different learning styles that are logical/deductive, verbal/visual, or visual/kinesthetic (Ennis-Cole and Lawhon, 2004).

Clearly the role of community college faculty is evolving with our understanding of how learning occurs, and the evolution is both challenging and exhausting. As we hire new faculty members, we need to select faculty who approach learning in these ways, and continue to provide faculty development and ongoing rewards for this important work. Community college faculty will require significant changes in orientation and support to develop and implement new pedagogies. This will be particularly true in community colleges that have not heavily invested in faculty-inspired and faculty-led professional development programs.

LEADERSHIP FOR A NEW PEDAGOGY

Community college leaders first need to be aware of learning and teaching research and the mandate and requirements for implementing a new pedagogy. They need to understand the pressure placed on faculty members, both experienced and newly hired, to integrate new approaches and need to continue their own learning to enable effective implementation if we are to achieve better educational outcomes. A changed pedagogy also requires strong leadership to support faculty innovation as they implement new pedagogy. .

Leaders need to provide opportunities to have conversations about learning and they need to provide in-classroom and institution-wide support for true learning to occur. Leaders need to create an environment in which dialogue is desirable and where each college member can speak from his or her heart and be heard. An important leadership characteristic for this role is the ability to motivate. Greenleaf called this persuasion, the most important characteristic of the servant leader (Greenleaf, 1982).

Leaders need to develop an environment and culture of inquiry and exploration and dialogue. This culture is important so that all members of the college realize that no one has all the answers. Everyone wants to grow and learn on an individual path, whether it is as administrator, faculty member, or staff. At the same time, there may, at times, be a need for aggressive action on the part of leaders.

ORGANIZATION FOR A NEW PEDAGOGY

When learning is taken seriously, it implies far-reaching change because college becomes a place where people learn, rather than where they teach. Focus on learners involves discovering the kind of organization students crave and the structural pieces that support new pedagogies.

Moderate Organizational Change

Discovering student desires and needs for the learning environment involves talking with them. Midwestern College I, described earlier, created focus groups of learners both at the beginning of their college experience and at the end. There, students are encouraged to describe their optimum experiences and then to assess their overall learning experience based on the stated learning goals and their personal exposure to the pedagogy and practice implementing them.

The structure to support new pedagogies and their technological enhancement can involve some tweaking of current organizational structure, or it can be a massive overhaul. Learning communities are increasingly a structural change found at community colleges. LaGuardia Community College has a variety of learning communities for first-year students, including liberal arts clusters, ESL pairs, the New Student House, and First Year Academies. The LaGuardia liberal arts clusters date from the 1970s; ESL Pairs and New Student House were conceived in the early 1990s, and First Year Academies were first piloted in 2006. LaGuardia's learning communities are faculty designed, and while they are not team taught, they are highly integrated: faculty teaching in learning communities plan a coordinated program of themes and related activities and assignments. The joint faculty planning and resultant connections strengthen both the curricular learning and academic support (Smith, McGregor, Matthews, and Gabelnick, 2004).

The term "learning communities" can also be used as a way to designate more loosely defined groups. At Metropolitan Community College in Nebraska, faculty members are given an extra stipend to support and facilitate learning communities among developmental students. This kind of organizational support can be essential because learning communities can involve intense faculty/student interaction outside the classroom (Lieberman, 2000).

Faculty can organize themselves as mentors for new instructors, to help them adapt to the environment, promote professional and personal growth and success, increase productivity, and create a faculty network. Mentoring can help new faculty achieve professional goals and develop new teaching strategies (Ennis-Cole and Lowhan, 2004) . Supporting incoming faculty will be increasingly important for community colleges as new faculty are hired to replace retiring baby-boomers.

To help faculty members adapt to the changes in pedagogy, faculty development is increasingly crucial. Faculty can work with instructional designers, librarians, and other institutional members involved in the educational process to ensure technology and course delivery are focused on student learning (Lieberman, 2000)

Colleges can organize the physical/technical environment of the college to support teaching. New equipment, distance learning capabilities, access to the internet and computer laboratories can be made available. Creating the right technical support staff is essential for keeping technology functional, updating hardware and software, and for faculty development (Ennis-Cole and Lowhan, 2004). These changes require resources and still are an adaptation of what already exists.

Large-Scale Organizational Change

A more sweeping physical change to accommodate technology comes when a college asks the questions: "How does a campus look when students are accustomed to reaching the Internet from wherever they stand, stroll, or lounge?" We already see the decline of the lab and the rise of the multi-configurable classroom. For example: a growing interest in mobile chairs, desks, and displays, and an increase in blended or hybrid learning (such as Internet access and collaborative learning) are enhanced by technology. Another change is creating new learning spaces such as information commons, where wireless, mobile connectivity admits the full range of the Internet into any space used for learning. Older spaces can take on new pedagogical meaning. For example, wireless cafes allow class work to occur over coffee and a bagel. Students Google® a new term, upload a comment to a class blackboard, and check for updates to an assignment—all while wandering around the college campus or waiting for friends at a meeting place (Alexander, 2004).

Traditionally, collegiate practice has separated general education, study in the major, and electives from each other. In the new academy, curricula will integrate general education and study in the major, including pre-professional programs, so that they form a consistent whole. But this does not mean that all students will take the same set of courses or that such a common core will provide all the necessary integration. The goals of liberal education are so challenging that all the years of college and the entire curriculum are needed to accomplish them. Responsibility for a coherent curriculum rests on the shoulders of all faculty members working cooperatively (AAC&U, 2002).

Course times and formats can change. Six-week formats, shorter terms, and more intensive workshop formats can also facilitate learning (Lieberman, 2000).Just as time is seen differently in an education focused on learning, so, too, is place. Learning happens during formal classroom study, but also in other ways. So while two semesters may not produce competence in a second language, many other pathways might do so: a longer series of courses, living abroad, growing up in a bilingual family, or studying in an immersion environment. Likewise, leadership skills can grow by theoretical study, leading a group in class, holding office in the student government, or being captain of a sports team. With a stress on learning, a student's capacity or proficiency matters more than the subject matter taught, courses completed, or credits earned (AAC&U, 2002).

The value of the credit unit comes into question. Do credits earned, which equate to time spent in class, really certify learning? Does sitting through and passing two three-credit courses mean a student can communicate well enough in a second language? If the triple goals of intellectual and practical skill mastery, knowledge gain, and personal responsibility growth are what count, shouldn't how long it takes to acquire them become secondary? With learning truly as the center of education, the current practice of fixing a constant time for learning could logically give way to a more flexible model in which students are allowed variable time to achieve the outcomes desired (National Panel Report, 2000).

The cost of massive curricular and physical plant changes can be prohibitive both in terms of financial and human resources. Lieberman and Guskin (2003) suggest additional models useful for accommodating pedagogical changes in higher education. They suggest seeking partners among various external sources: other institutions, community and work environments, non faculty members, co-curricular educators, and libraries.

CHALLENGES TO THE FIELD

Colleges deeply focused on the learner and learning can create policies that motivate and support new pedagogies.

1. Require pedagogical innovative, inquiry-based liberal education.
   - Ensure multiple educational experiences across courses and semesters to help students move toward achieving general learning goals.
   - Integrate courses required in specific areas of knowledge with skills so that students simultaneously develop competencies (like writing), use modes of inquiry (like deductive reasoning), and engage with selected themes (like science and society).
   - Encourage creative combinations of classes such as applying quantitative skills in a humanities course.

2. Utilize the emergent pedagogies of engagement
   - Assess faculty use of engaged pedagogies, providing incentives for their use.
   - Document the effectiveness of specific pedagogies for particular populations, making sure to identify which kinds of students learn best with what combination of engaged pedagogies.
   - Provide space and encouragement for faculty experimentation with new pedagogies over several semesters to allow for initial student resistance and faculty tentativeness to dissipate.
   - Provide incentives for faculty to continue to evolve the emergent pedagogies with stipends, professional development, and release time to research and codify pedagogical improvements.

3. Eliminate administrative barriers to innovation.
   - Reconsider class size policies to allow for creative new class options.
   - Evaluate whether course cancellation policies force innovative projects to be scuttled before they have a chance to become known by the word-of-mouth so common in community colleges.
   - Provide sufficient space and administrative support to integrate technology into innovative curricula, engage the learner and to take maximum advantage of immersion in multiple technologies. This could involve outsourcing or co-sourcing technology efforts.
   - Seek new funding sources to address the pressures on education for a learning emphasis and for the resources required to keep small class

sizes, offer low-enrollment courses, implement innovative technology, and make large-scale organization changes to support a new pedagogy.

4. Support faculty development for pedagogical development and innovation.
   - Establish faculty development experts as guides at community colleges to support new faculty roles and to help faculty to learn the skills of the assessment of student learning.
   - Create an environment in which faculty and staff come together and speak from their hearts about issues of substance: student learning, new roles, and new learning strategies. These conversations of consequence can be part of a general culture of inquiry and quality engendered by the leader.

CONCLUSION

Higher learning, the transformation of individuals in their learning, knowing, and doing, continues to be a challenge for community colleges. Sixteen years after we first explored the role of learning as opposed to that of teaching, we continue to focus more on the needs of our teachers (hours taught, courses taught and time spent directly with students) than on the needs and outcomes of students. We have learned much in sixteen years about ways to increase student progress along the road of transformation. We have discovered and implemented new pedagogies that are truly democratic in their diversity, entry points, and interactivity. New technologies enhance the learning process, and faculty roles have evolved. Leadership roles continue to be important; and organizational changes that support technology are still needed. While the knowledge exists for a more responsive pedagogy, our practice and the funding for implementation lag far behind.

CHAPTER 7

Leadership to Guide the Dream

OVERVIEW

Leaders are both the bane of and a boon for guiding the dream of community colleges. Leading a community college has traditionally been very different from leading a four-year school. This chapter suggests the characteristics of those who have been the leaders of the movement, who the leaders are now and who might they be in the future. It describes the preparation of community college leaders and various paths to the presidency. Diverse modes of leadership are discussed, including current trends in leading complex organizations. The chapter ends with a challenge to the field and a call for action to leaders, faculty and staff, graduate program administrators, and trustees.

THE DREAM

The leaders who guide the dream of community college must understand the student population demographics—the higher proportion of racial/ethnic minority groups, first generation college students, and high-risk learners—and be able to develop close ties to representatives of each group. The ideal leader is a clear-eyed financier who can increase financial resources, a gifted communicator who is as at home in academic discourse as in business and workforce circles. In general, the senior leader must have a certain amount of expertise in all the issues addressed in this book, including developmental studies, emergent pedagogy, governance, global challenges, and accountability. To be effective, leaders use these skills as a set of tools that focus colleges on the important issues and move systems forward.

The ideal leader has vision, makes expert use of data from the field, and builds a team that can implement the necessary foundation to achieve the dream, solidly based on the evidence of what works. Effective leaders build on the first generation of community college presidents' efforts by expanding the movement's vision and making educational success a reality for the many people who otherwise would never have the opportunity to attend college and for the many who still experience a community college as a revolving door. These leaders inspire the hearts and minds of faculty and staff to be responsive to the community college audience, and they move the hearts of the larger external community to support and commit to the community college mission.

In sum, the ideal leader understands with exquisite sensitivity the distinctive nature of the community college and binds it to the complex process of running a college in the modern world. Presidents who lead in this way experience the joy of truly serving all the constituents of the community college. They celebrate with graduates of every age and cultural group and they enjoy the collegiality of true partnership in their communities.

Competencies required for a transformational leadership team include skill in organizational strategy resource management, communication, collaboration, community college advocacy, and professionalism (AACC, 2004). The competencies identified for the next generation of leaders have certainly marked many leaders in past generations as well. The field has multiple examples of first, second, and third generation leaders of community colleges who are models of the kind of leadership needed to initiate the dream and then to nurture it.

THE UNFULFILLED DREAM

Community college leaders, faculty, and administrators are retiring in droves. The generations of leaders who created and sustained the community college dream are leaving and taking with them their vision and their passion for the movement. A doctoral student in a community college seminar reported that young professionals did not want to hear about a movement. It did not rouse them. We are concerned about keeping alive passion for the community college mission.

Many faculty and staff at community colleges have not themselves been educated about, nor do they understand, the community college mission. At worst, they see their role as biding their time until they can get a better job in a four-year college or university. There are administrators and faculty who know that success statistics would be higher and classes easier to teach if we abandoned open admissions. There are faculty who feel that teaching

President Boon led his college for 23 years. During that time of great stability, he built the college from one campus to 15 campuses and served a population of more than 500,000 students. He created non-traditional campuses and programs and led one of the first colleges to reach students electronically via radio and television.

Although President Boon was fairly role-conscious in the beginning of his presidency, as times changed he was able to empower his faculty and staff, and those creative and committed people brought to him new and innovative ideas. He "turned them loose" to implement those ideas. When they worked, he was able to share those successes with the rest of the country to serve as models that could be replicated at other community colleges. Innovative programming included customized workforce training, art and cultural events, a strong transfer program, aggressive technology investment, creative resource development, and leadership development programs for both an internal audience of faculty and staff and an external audience in the community.

President Boon further enriched his background in and passion for community colleges through the award of a Kellogg Fellowship and his involvement in a community college degree program funded by the Kellogg Foundation, a significant funder of the bourgeoning community college movement in the 1970s. He met and worked with a cadre of leaders that had fallen in love with the community college movement, and he worked tirelessly to invent, innovate, and implement the programs that could support successful community college students. President Boon may be viewed in contrast to the sometimes darker unfulfilled dream of community college leadership.

Developmental Studies is beneath them. There are administrators who do not want to reach out to communities and offer services in workforce education. There are deans who believe that if their college could just be the best at offering liberal arts courses for the Associate of Arts degree in their classrooms and would not have to bother with vocational education, the educational work would be simpler.

Other leadership challenges facing community college leaders include the changing nature of the compact between government and its colleges, the increased politicization of curricular development processes, the evolving the world of work and accompanying pressures of globalization, the dramatic rise in corporate and business partnerships, the growing competition of the for-profit sector for public support, and the emergent need for private philanthropy. These issues construct a demanding environment in which leaders must bring together many divergent opinions around difficult endeavors in order to respond to change. The public pressures on leaders at every level include public castigation, personal threats, e-mail bombardments, and unending lawsuits. For many, the risks of exposure are too high Within one year, twelve presidents were fired by their boards, with some of these unfortunate leaders indicating that their board's agenda for change produced dynamics that became too hard to manage (Fain, 2006). Internal constituents often reject change and ignore efforts to make our colleges more responsive to the community. We have heard comments such as, "The community knows where we are; if they want something, they can call us" or "if we do workforce development, we are compromising our integrity as an institution." Leaders who need to move an institution forward on all aspects of its mission wrestle with individuals on campus who want to reproduce outdated or narrow ideas of what a college should be.

The original community college leaders were grounded in the vision of great thinkers like B. Lamar Johnson, a professor of higher education at UCLA who reached out to provide models of teaching, learning, and leading to the emerging community colleges in the 1960s. They were supported and sustained financially by the Kellogg Foundation, which created fellowships and doctoral programs that shaped the thinking of two generations of leaders. The retirement of almost all of these Fellows, who were steeped in the understanding of the community college as a movement for social justice and democracy. leaves a void in commitment to this movement. At the same time, then, there are both difficult challenges facing community college leaders and a declining number of those leaders.

THE REAL STORY

The Leadership Crisis

The leadership challenge is staggering. In 2004, it was projected that nearly half of those who were presidents at that time would retire by 2006; 600 of that generation's presidents had already retired (AACC, 2004). In addition, presidents projected that one-fourth or more of their administrators and their faculty would retire (AACC, 2006). Community colleges are in the midst of a leadership crisis of large proportions. We can estimate the need to fill 600 presidencies and about 1,800 vice presidencies and dean positions (if each of the 600 colleges has, say, three or four vice presidents and/or several deans), not to mention 15,000 faculty positions (assuming that each of the 600 colleges has an average of 40 to 60 faculty members and one-fourth of them retire).

There is a decline in the number of candidates presenting themselves for middle- and senior-level administrative assignments, and candidates are relatively poorly prepared (Piland and Wolf, 2003). Meaningful interventions are required to augment the size and quality of leadership pools (Piland and Wolf, 2003). At the same time, new presidents admit they are unprepared for the overwhelming nature of the job, the level of politics involved, and the amount of relationship-building they are expected to accomplish (Shults, 2001). Current doctoral programs, with perhaps one or two graduates per year, barely make a dent in the need to hire thousands of new leaders for community colleges. Therefore, while a leadership vacuum is evolving, there are fewer opportunities to support and sustain new leaders.

The reality is that while many presidents are well prepared, like President Boon, many are not. Presidents are hired without a background in the community college mission and movement, and are judged by boards of trustees to be saviors if they have business acumen, close ties to politicians, or access to corporate or philanthropic dollars. New presidents can be entrepreneurial and eager to take community colleges in directions that have traditionally been avoided because they did not fulfill the mission. These new directions might bring colleges into the future, or push them into chaos. Some entrepreneurial presidents want to offer the baccalaureate degree or become exclusively workforce colleges. Some want to screen out the most at-risk learners, avoid English as a Second Language programs, or skimp on Developmental Studies programs. Emerging leaders risk having their energy for supporting their college and contributing to the field in general siphoned off by heavy commitments to fund raising, the petty politics of elected officials, the unending grind of scarce resources, and the antics of board members who do not understand the role of holding an institution in trust.

The example of President Bane illustrates the underside of the community college's leadership reality.

President Bane was eventually removed from his last college by a state coordinating committee. This was not before he had written many articles

President Bane has led several community colleges—each for about two years. He is a skilled and articulate speaker, and is heralded as a tough and savvy fresh wind by the boards who hire him. Sadly, in the wake of his multiple presidencies, the campuses are left roiled in controversy and internally divided. President Bane successfully convinces hiring committees that his entrepreneurial dreams of greatly expanded enrollment, streamlined organizational structures, and new ventures will lead the college into a rosy future. These unfortunately never materialize.

President Bane was a history professor and mid-level administrator at a community college. Over time, he began to cultivate a group of nationally known professionals, whom he met though conferences, to tout his skills and build his resume. The word-of-mouth from these well-placed references helped him to quickly advance through the administrative ranks as he moved through several colleges. A voracious reader, at each new college he would announce a creative idea to frame his first year. Sadly, he possessed neither the implementation nor the people skills necessary to inspire faculty and staff to work with him. His were the only ideas that were ever seriously considered. President Bane would hire one or two "sidekicks" who would command obedience to the new processes President Bane developed through intimidation and budget manipulation.

Although never successful internally, President Bane was continually on the conference circuit with his sidekicks, talking about the wonderful new programs he had instituted. A quick political study, he filled each campus he led with political "puts"—poorly qualified individuals hired as patronage favors.

on his putative success and had promoted sycophants to high-level administrative positions in the colleges he left behind. Externally, President Bane's legacy looks visionary in the articles he writes—technology applications, creative marketing strategies, and organizational innovation. Internally, faculty and staff still shudder when his name is mentioned, and too many of the poorly qualified administrators still hold power in several colleges. He worked tirelessly to aggrandize his reputation, and he found the community college process of selecting presidents one that he could manipulate for many years.

THE CURRENT LEADERSHIP

Demographics of Leaders

The majority of community college leaders are Caucasian. The total number of ethnic minority leaders rose by 4.1 percent from 2002 to 2004, increasing from 14.3 percent in 2002 to 19.9 percent in 2004 (Vaughan and Weisman, 1998). This is substantially more than the representation of minority leaders in four-year colleges, yet still dramatically less than a proportion that would parallel the ethnic representation in the student body. Hispanics and Asians are the most under-represented groups among presidents. The Hispanic student population was 14.5 percent in 2004 and the percentage of Hispanic presidents was 6.8 (Vaughan and Weisman, 1998). The low success rate among ethnic minority students may be just one of the outcomes of this lack of role models in high-level positions (see chapter twelve).

The Route to a Presidency

The route to a community college presidential position is predictable. More than 90 percent of community college presidents have the earned doctorate, with more than 60 percent of those degrees in higher education (King, 2007a). Almost one-third of community college presidents are internal candidates, as compared to only one-quarter of four-year college presidents (King, 2007a). Popular opinion among those presidents is that there are several unwritten rules for achieving the position. This folk wisdom includes: do not alienate a sitting president; show progressive movement through the administrative ranks, but stick to the academic side as opposed to student affairs, administrative services, or advancement; apply for a presidency upon reaching the vice-presidential level; and interview well with trustees and faculty members (Vaughan, 2004).

LEADERSHIP COMPETENCIES

To become outstanding community college leaders, aspirants need the ability to help their colleges identify and meet community needs. In this book, we acknowledge that there are administrators who are not concerned about fundamental community college issues such as provision of non-credit literacy and workforce development, basic skills, or open access. We know that diverse learners do not succeed as well as traditional-aged, economically affluent students. In other words, the challenge is not just to create leaders but to forge a generation of leadership that can address the challenges of guiding the community college dream into the forefront of American higher education. The next generation of leaders must be even more innovative and creative, and much more successful at implementing new structures and pedagogies than their predecessors. Current wisdom suggests that leaders are not going to be able to stand on their desks or within their roles and give orders—if they do, they will meet with, at best, malicious compliance. Although community colleges employ many people who understand and respond to calls for change like the ones established in this book, there will also be people who will find ways to sabotage anything that looks like a mandate.

A survey by the American Association of Community Colleges (AACC) of current presidents summarized required presidential skills (AACC, 2004). The ability to manage resources in service to the college mission requires, by equal measure, balance between actions that sustain the human, procedural, and information resources of the college, while making sure that the buildings, equipment, and finances are adequate. Effective leaders have communication styles that are as focused on listening as on speaking and writing, and they can deploy these skills in order to promote open dialogue through the college. The best leaders seek multiple ways to engage the community in a dialogue that promotes the academic success of the widest array of students possible. Increasingly, leaders must be able to select and develop partners with appropriate internal and external entities in order to derive mutually beneficial collaboration. These partnerships are complex, and a recent scandal regarding colleges' relationships to loan companies remind leaders that partnerships must hold to the highest ethical standards and aim to nurture diverse aspects of community and student success. Expert and aggressive advocacy among stakeholders and the public has long been a necessary leadership skill. The sitting presidents noted that personal professional efficacy is an internal standard, and that leadership requires the insight and self-reflection to identify high standards and commit to continuous improvement. Feedback is a valuable part of self-improvement, and leaders must honestly evaluate every sector of the community college, including the president, staff, and governance structures, all for the creation of a clear accountability to and for the institution. These leadership capabilities function in the interest of the long-term viability of the college and community.

This is a daunting list of competencies. No wonder new presidents who were surveyed felt they might not be up to the task! If we are correct in asserting that leadership in a community college is as much a calling as a job, it is important to understand the approaches or styles one might use to live out these competencies.

LEADERSHIP STYLE

Leaders are individuals who significantly influence the thoughts, behaviors, and/or feelings of others, and therefore are found throughout all levels of a community college (Gardner and Laskin, 1995). There is no distinctive community college leadership style. Although most colleges trace their roots to times of change and organizational innovation, no research suggests that community college leaders, as a group, are any more experimental, participatory, non-hierarchical, or collegial than any other group of leaders. Nonetheless we argue in this book that great community college leaders must understand and celebrate the visionary foundation of the community college. Holding true to a dream of open access and egalitarian community development implies that leaders must develop a distinctive style that exemplifies the best values of the community college mission. Among the thousands of daily personnel and budget tasks, leadership style is an important skill for the next generation of community college leaders who wish to be both effective and transformational. Leadership in turbulent times of change requires strong relationships of trust among all levels of an organization. "Those organizations that will succeed are those that evoke our greatest human capacities—our need to be in good relationships, and our desire to contribute to something beyond ourselves. These qualities cannot be evoked through procedures and policies" (Wheatley, 2004). The best leaders appear to use a style that develops strong decision-making processes, involving the stakeholders who are affected by decisions, and thereby strengthening trusting relationships (Wheatley, 2004).

Leadership can also be defined as a subtle process of mutual influence that connects emotion and action by fusing intellect, emotion, and action to produce cooperative effort that serves the goals of both the leader and the led (Bolman and Deal, 1997). These seemingly divergent definitions perhaps best describe the visible differences between the generations of leaders who have led community colleges for the past 40 to 50 years: concern for people versus concern for completing a task.

Current presidents and other leaders express a certain amount of angst when they try to implement their values of inclusion, but the campus responds with foot-dragging or cynicism. It can be discouraging for individuals to express a heart-felt opinion they believe should guide the college's future only to hear five or six counter opinions. As Cleveland discussed in his 2002 publication, developing a consensus and finding order among the chaos is important for leaders. Effective consensus builders find areas of common interest, identify next steps, and help others live with a decision once dialogue has occurred. Consensus emerges when, rather than suggesting that all constituents, (with their diverse opinions) totally agree, the reality is closer to "acquiescence of those who care, supported by the apathy of those who don't" (Cleveland, 2002). Too often, when there are strongly divided opinions, leaders simply listen and nod, but resist making a decision that will be unpopular with some groups, often resulting in no action (Cleveland, 2002). While the college remains at peace, communities go unheeded. At this juncture in our history, community colleges need action and change to meet the challenges of social justice and community need; building effective consensus is a skill of the first order for college leaders.

Numerous researchers have explored the divergence in leadership style between task- and people-oriented leaders. Community college leaders are counseled to integrate both task and process into a coherent intellectual framework for leadership (Argyris, 1999; Goff, 2003; Sullivan, 2001). Different groups of people are brought to collaborative action through different strategies (Sullivan, 2001). Because community college leaders connect with a range of constituencies, a multiplicity of approaches is important.

Sullivan, in his 2001 publication, explains that leaders must understand and create appropriate administrative structures (formal roles and rules), while at the same time centering leadership activity around human resources that value people and their skills. Leaders must cultivate political acumen to build coalitions, be excellent strategists, and develop the easy give-and-take of effective negotiations. (Sullivan, 2001). Finally, Sullivan continues, community college leaders must understand how to deploy symbolic approaches using ritual and stories to motivate people and build a thriving community (Sullivan, 2001). While these skill sets are common to all leadership to some extent, the nature of the community college—fractured because of larger numbers of part-time faculty and students; flexible boundaries between work, college, and community; and ongoing public derogation of the community college's place in higher education—demands greater attention to these issues. The best community college leaders must understand these skills within different contexts, crossing many more borders than a president of a four-year college.

The competencies needed to be a good president are clearly complex and sophisticated. One aspect too little commented upon in leadership training programs is the need for leaders to build trust among faculty and staff. Having a vision for the future is an element of moving a campus forward, but without a committed faculty the task of educating half the country cannot be achieved. Leaders must create an environment where people feel safe to speak from their hearts. At the same time, skill in accomplishing both of these tasks requires diverse abilities in a spectrum covering hierarchical, political, social, and symbolic activities.

LEADER PREPARATION

Several institutions and organizations have begun to respond to the need for a large influx of leaders who are better prepared for leadership positions in community colleges. Successful candidates for the presidency use mentors, formal degree programs in community college or higher education leadership, short-term leadership programs, and seminars offered by universities, national higher education associations, or state and local programs (Shults, 2001).

National community college organizations have created task forces to address leadership issues, suggesting ways to recruit, prepare, and support new leaders and recommending a set of competencies leaders need to be successful. New leadership programs such as Leading Forward and the President's Academy (for new presidents) and the Future Leaders Institute (for community college staff showing leadership potential) were implemented by the American Association of Community Colleges. The Executive Leadership Institute was established by the League for Innovation in collaboration with a university (League for Innovation, 2007; AACC, 2006).

Doctoral Degree Preparation Programs

There are 140 university-based degree programs that have at least some coursework in the area of community colleges, although there was a 78 percent decline in the in the number of advanced degrees in community college administration from 1982-83 to 1996-97 (Boggs, 2003; Shults, 2001). Some research suggests that doctoral training within a discipline provides candidates with a greater ability to move into leadership roles than narrowly conceived leadership training or doctorates in higher education administration (King, 2007b).

There are no national standards for doctoral programs for mid-career professionals, but organizational task forces have suggested criteria such as:

1. Portability – including distance learning and competency-based programs and internships;
2. Mentoring – for effective role models and for networking;
3. Just-In Time Education – for working professionals who need immediate advice and guidance (modeled after effective MBA programs);
4. Reflection – an analysis of personal qualification and goals; and
5. Accessibility – low cost and high quality (Heelan, 2001).

Several new degree programs have been created, or a community college emphasis has been added, integrating these criteria, with some recent examples such as Fielding Graduate University and Walden University.

Non-Degreed Preparation Programs

There are various non-degree programs intended to prepare leaders for the work of implementing the community college dream. Universities offer professional development for leaders, and the Community College Leadership Program (CCLDI), initiated by Claremont College and taken over by the University of San Diego, is just one example. In 2000, Claremont College created a leadership program based on the principles that leaders should be:

- grounded in an understanding of the community college, their history and strengths, their multiple missions and values;
- cognizant of the agility needed to collaborate with K-12 systems, senior higher education institutions, community-based organizations, and industry; and
- focused on improving the organizational capacity to conduct the collective work of community colleges rather than focused solely on improving the ability of individual leaders.

The most effective programs use multiple modalities of instruction. A program might include an on-site leadership academy with somewhat traditional classroom-based instruction, policy seminars over a specified time-frame or offered electronically, executive coaching or other modes of individual support, and research dissemination that evaluates and quantifies what works (Romero, 2004). There are currently more than thirty of these short-term, non-degreed leadership development programs, many offered by councils of national organizations or universities (Boggs, 2003). These programs, along with the National Institute for Leadership Development (NILD), have been influential and productive in preparing people for higher-level leadership positions (Boggs, 2003). Attendance at training sessions raises awareness of an individual's interest in leadership, and institutional selection and support of individuals for attendance signals the college's intention of a potential promotion.

In addition to these regional or national programs, some colleges have small, usually sporadic programs to develop their own leaders through in-house internships or staff development activities. These programs tend to be poorly funded, loosely organized, and they add more responsibilities for someone in the organization. Colleges with such programs rarely see themselves as preparing the next generation of community college leaders, but rather as developing leaders for their college (Piland and Wolf, 2003).

FACULTY LEADERS

Recruiting community college faculty members for leadership positions is a logical place to look for committed and knowledgeable leaders. Faculty interaction with students provides the best understanding of the power and pitfalls of community colleges. The ongoing interaction with the diverse student body expands their perspective, and most community college faculty have supported (or struggled with) under-prepared students, or brilliant students, or students whose home lives are marred by poverty and violence. In short, community college faculty quickly come to understand the community at a deep and nuanced level through their interaction with individual students. However, advancing faculty into administrative leadership roles presents its own special issues.

Faculty members often feel the pull of leadership from the moment they enter community colleges, a pull that increases as they become more senior in their departments and divisions. They often move from roles on committees and senates into positions such as department or division chairs, deans, or provosts as their careers progress. Given the graying of the senior faculty, who are preparing to retire in record numbers in the next few years, the mantle of leadership will increasingly fall on junior faculty, underscoring an even greater need for appropriate leadership development among this sector of the campus community (Cooper and Pagotto, 2003). Unfortunately, for the purpose of increasing community college leaders by promoting faculty members, too many community college faculty members do not view leadership as a particularly attractive opportunity. Faculty members refer at times to administration as the "enemy," as in "our colleague has gone over to the dark

side" (Cooper and Pagotto, 2003). This view of administration as an opposi-
tional force to faculty concerns emerges from multiple and long-standing traditions on some campuses, and is inflamed by old-fashioned unions on one
side, and faculty-bashing administrators on the other. But college environments that persist in the view that administration is antithetical to faculty
instead of collaborators in the creation of a learning environment limit the
likelihood of recruiting faculty for leadership positions.

A variety of personal and situational factors can motivate faculty members to become leaders. The acceptance of a leadership position can occur
because of organizational deficits, such as being the default person as a result
of a leadership void, or because of personal deficits, such as not being able
to say no (Cooper and Pagotto, 2003). However, other faculty seek leadership positions as an opportunity to learn more about their institution, as a
prelude to a greater decision-making role, and because they have a desire for
more influential leadership positions (Cooper and Pagotto, 2003). Leader-
ship-seeking faculty acknowledge the inherent challenge of leadership, but
their commitment to their institution is coupled with an ability to envision
a better institution that inspires them to make a difference. They understand
that leading implies being able to view their college from a larger perspective, and are anxious to push their institutions forward (Cooper and Pagotto,
2003). One study found that more than one-half of community college faculty members in leadership positions were there because they had been
invited to do so, suggesting that a personal invitation can be crucial (Cooper
and Pagotto, 2003).

LACK OF NATIONAL COORDINATION

Leader preparation for community colleges would be substantially improved
by better regional and national coordination. Professional development programs and individual college programs could be coordinated on a state-by-
state basis so that one could begin where the other ends. This level of
integration is unlikely to occur because collaboration is rare in graduate education. Among community colleges themselves, independence and local
responsiveness are signature concepts that lead to resistance against uniform
or national standards. Minimally, clear statements about need, model programs, and effectiveness of specific types of education could provide some
national-level guidance. An occasional graduate program could connect with
other leadership development experiences. For example, Fielding Graduate
University in California, using very specific criteria, grants graduate credit

for some classes taken at another institution, such as Cornell University's Institute for Community College Development. All those who care about the future of community colleges, however, must continue to find ways to encourage faculty members to consider leadership positions by appealing to the greater good, enlightened self-interest, creation of incentives, and support of a range of leadership experiences.

CHALLENGES TO THE FIELD

The following challenges for community college leaders represent recommendations of the authors as well as those contained in the research used for this chapter.

- Distributed education or distance learning programs for mid-career professionals are essential for preparing persons already employed in community colleges.
- Current leaders need to support the field by assisting in the research to determine which are the best leader behaviors to implement the crucial competencies and needed for community colleges. Successful leaders need to share their stories with their colleagues, telling their successes and their joys, and to analyze together what works.
- College leaders need to employ a diverse set of behaviors and styles in order to relate to the many constituents and opinions operating in their milieu.
- Colleges need to find ways to persuade faculty members to consider leadership positions by appealing to their sense of the greater good as well as to their enlightened self-interest.
- Colleges need to formalize a leadership development policy and program to prepare future leaders among faculty, support staff, and administrators, representing every ethnic group. The program needs to be assigned to a responsible individual, perhaps the staff development officer. Elements of policy that would be worthy of attention include: sabbaticals, extended leave for administrators, and financial support for persons pursuing longer-term leadership programs including advanced degrees. It would be valuable for the common good if colleges would consider these programs a service to the entire field as well as to individual institutions.
- Graduate universities need to explore creative and collaborative ways to offer graduate credit for national, regional, and statewide leadership programs.

- New leaders need trained mentors and coaches as guides as they travel across a changing and tumultuous collegiate landscape.

CONCLUSION

The leadership crisis in the American community college is truly one of blockbuster proportions. The number of people prepared to be presidents and other leaders, the ethnicity of presidents and other leaders, the commitment of community college leaders to the community college mission, the competencies required, and the leader behaviors needed are all crucial issues. Although a great deal has been done to address the crisis, more is needed in terms of preparation programs and knowledge regarding the kind of leader needed for this century.

CHAPTER 8

Global Adaptations
International Implications of the American Community College Model

ꙭ OVERVIEW

Global awareness at a time when China has the most English speakers in the world is beyond a mandate—it's a basic skill. In this chapter, we study the inter-section of the multiple aspects of community colleges and the trend toward glob-alization in contemporary society. We begin by examining postsecondary institutions throughout the world that are comparable to the American com-munity college, their effect on expanding higher education opportunities, and their similarity to or difference from the American model. Many U.S. commu-nity colleges now offer educational and training services in other countries, serv-ing both American and "in-country" students. This is part of the response of community colleges to the implications of globalization, and this chapter focuses on the impact on work and citizenship. The chapter closes with an analysis of the potential contribution that an open-access higher education system can offer to enhance democracy and opportunity for individuals around the globe. Chal-lenges to the field suggest future directions for global engagement.

THE DREAM

Around the globe, countries must squarely face H. G. Wells' dictum: *History is a race between education and catastrophe.* The educational mandate applies to all countries, from non-industrialized countries in Africa, to troubled areas in the Middle East, to emerging world powers like India and China, as well as to highly industrialized countries like Italy or Germany. Each country expresses its own history in the forms and structures of its higher education institutions and systems. Yet globalization washes over the world like a tidal wave, soaking everything and everyone in different ways. The American community college's philosophical commitment to universal education holds great potential as a contributor to world-wide economic growth and promotion of democracy. At the same time, a system of community colleges could safeguard and encourage elements of existing identity and culture, such as that promulgated by 13 Southern African nations (Sehoole, 2004). Local autonomy in education can maintain local customs, crafts, and traditions in a way that imported higher education systems cannot.

The dream is that countries that have not tried to bring large segments of their citizenry to college will begin to do so. It is beginning to happen in places like Hong Kong. The Hong Kong system is developing new Associate degree programs that are directly linked to social and economic capacity-building. It is using these new degree programs as its central strategy for its newly re-cast relationship with mainland China and concomitant need for an educated workforce (Lee and Young, 2003).

As the Knowledge Age advances in the twenty-first century, technology increasingly defines the kinds of work that will be available. The tradition of reserving a college education only for the elite is falling everywhere, even in highly developed industrialized countries like Germany or Hungary (Mellander and Mellander, 1994). However, the concept of an open access college that caters to an adult and/or part-time student is still very new in many parts of the world. Even more radical is the American notion of transfer from a community college to a four-year school, especially to a country's elite campuses. China, the Middle East, Africa, India, and the Southeast Asian sub-continent have demographic growth patterns with large numbers of traditional-aged college students and little infrastructure to support them. The dream is that the community college model, adapted and integrated with local traditions, can reshape access to higher education across the globe.

Perhaps the American community colleges should pay special attention to supporting nascent systems around the world that educate adult, poor, and low-skilled individuals. Since these are the individuals now providing much of the United States' goods and services, we have a moral debt to help the emergent community college-like institutions succeed in other countries. We need to support these institutions to continue the development of management skills and internal career ladders that can improve international standards of living. However, community colleges must undertake a role in international educational development with careful sensitivity to America's place on the world stage. We have an unfortunate history of forcing international structures into an American mold that thwarts indigenous and sustainable development. There is much we need to learn from other countries, both developing and industrialized. We cannot go in as saviors, but rather as learners and supporters in ways that countries request.

The social justice orientation of community colleges is perhaps best expressed when education creates a path out of poverty. Of particular importance is the hope that educating women will allow countries to fully realize their social, political, and economic potential. Even as the first women leaders emerge in places like Chile (Bachelet, 2006) and Liberia (Polgreen, 2006), economists agree that poverty in developing countries will continue unless women are more fully educated (Lindsay and Daalder, 2005). Community colleges hold promise on the international stage as the foundation for transforming the role of women in developing countries.

There is opportunity for community colleges in the United States to work with colleagues globally. If the world's educational level rises, the benefits to all countries is synergistic and multiplicative. We can create relationships to make conscious connections to the development of community colleges across the globe, which in turn can spur pedagogical and economic progress in the United States. In an ideal future, community colleges can learn how to incorporate the perspectives on teaching and learning from other countries into our common approaches.

Globalization is changing the face of America as relentlessly as it is China or Indonesia. Most manufacturing of goods for the American market occurs in other countries, and increasingly, a variety of administrative services are "off-shored." The American community college must respond to these changes by advancing the American worker skill level to undertake the higher-skilled jobs that remain, and to do so with an emphasis on creativity and innovation (National Center on Education and the Economy, 2007). The best community colleges embrace the ideals inherent in the saying "think global, act local." Since community colleges have been calibrated to be responsive to the needs of a local community, it can seem counterintuitive for a college to embrace an internationalist theme in curriculum and outlook. Yet it is this perspective that is critical for any community to establish itself as a player in a relentlessly connected world.

Community colleges have a responsibility to know and understand the challenges and successes of our higher education colleagues around the world. We must teach our students to be aware of global issues, and prepare entrepreneurs to actively participate in a global marketplace. Just as importantly, students and faculty must become critically aware of the unintended negative consequences of out-sourcing and off-shoring. Community colleges can be places where students begin to understand their role in sharing wealth and creating sustainable structures both here and in other counties.

THE UNFULFILLED DREAM

There is no one overall "reality" that sets in motion actions for the development of two-year, postsecondary, or open-access institutions. The pressure for developing further educational institutions and systems comes from many directions, with each country confronting its own specific set of issues and problems. The current capacity of nations is being stretched due to budget limitations and changing roles of government. Developing, non-industrialized countries need robust systems of higher education to advance socially and economically, although some critics maintain that remnants of colonialization combined with policies of international institutions such as the International Monetary Fund or the World Bank do not provide sufficient resources for these countries. The current conflicts based upon religious affiliation push back not only secularism but also modernism.

Industrialized countries have their own sets of problems. For example, South Africa has a solid infrastructure of colleges and universities which might assist the development of community colleges, but their history of apartheid and the Africanization of higher education has created an internal "white flight" to private institutions (Sehoole, 2004). Japan's junior college system was cast as a finishing school by U.S. occupation forces (Starobin, 2002) and struggles to shake off its legacy. China's higher education system is tightly controlled by the central government and still contains strong remnants of an interlocking set of communist party perks as students are assigned to majors and post-graduate employment (Mellow, 2005).

The dangers of aggressively establishing community college systems in many countries must be recognized. An educated workforce, particularly if liberal arts and sciences are a part of the education, is more likely to be critical of entrenched power. Some scholars maintain that dictators like Antonio de Oliveira Salazar of Portugal or Augusto Pinochet of Chile deliberately limited access to higher education to curtail challenges to their regimes (*Dictators of the World*, 2006). An open-access college is a direct threat to concepts of elite or privileged access to all sources of power and wealth, as well as the current higher education status quo. The participation of women in higher education ranges from 35 percent among 25- to 29-year-olds in the United States, to less than .2 percent in Sub-Saharan Africa (National Council for Research on Women, 2006). Changing who is in power, changing the traditional relationships between men and women, or providing the intellectual skills to challenge an entrenched oligarchy or monarchy are among the most dangerous activities that can be undertaken. A community college system could foment some or all of these trends.

American communities can be surprisingly xenophobic. We know of community college presidents in the United States who were fired because they supported international travel for students and faculty. Immigration is changing hundreds of communities across the United States, and there is increasing resistance to opening up sources of education for individuals whose tax dollars did not pay for the development of these systems. The American Association of Community Colleges (AACC) after much dialogue and disagreement, first accepted global interaction as a strategic action area in 2001.

Groups such as the Association of Scholars and think tanks such as the Heritage Foundation actively promote the idea that teaching international perspectives is a threat to the American way of life, and to democracy itself. Organizations and institutions such as these perceive an international perspective as inherently challenging Judeo-Christian religious values and a Western Civilization perspective on human values. These are formidable forces of resistance that can make attempts to incorporate global perspectives in education and training at community colleges a politically volatile subject.

THE REAL STORY

Community College-Like Structures Around the Globe

In every country, the development of community college-like structures is in a dynamic process of change. Some countries' educational structures are created by the private and/or the for-profit sector, while others are centrally planned by the government. The following examples, while not intended to be exhaustive, provide a flavor of the kinds of structures that are emerging internationally. Like all developing systems, as each new community college-like system grows in strength, resistance is mobilized to maintain the status quo. The tensions of history, colonialism, war, and power are played out in the development of any new postsecondary educational system. But the seemingly inexorable movement toward higher-skilled work and the liberation of women and other oppressed peoples throughout the globe is an impetus toward continued development.

Japan

Japan provides an interesting study of how history and current conditions can impede the development of a community college. Junior colleges were developed in Japan during and immediately after the occupation of Japan by U.S. forces, and were established primarily as finishing schools for women seeking marriage and as a way to enact General MacArthur's desire to eliminate any remnants of imperial universities (Starobin, 2002). In the 1960s, the establishment of technical college and "special education" systems was geared to help the male population prepare for work in business and industry. Unlike many industrial nations through the 1970s and '80s, female participation in the labor market in Japan remained low. Junior colleges, although slightly expanded in terms of curriculum, remained more than 90 percent female through the 1990s (Starobin, 2002). Now they face extinction due to drops in enrollment related to the rising status of women and the concomitant change in traditional colleges' acceptance of female applicants' admission, along with precipitous drops in the number of traditional college-aged students.

Thus, Japanese junior colleges never served the community college purpose of either first, two-year preparation for a baccalaureate degree, or second, job-focused vocational training. In this context, they are extremely unlikely to be perceived as a partner in the higher education system. The junior college system in Japan retains few commonalities with the U.S. system.

Jordan

Jordan, on the other hand, explicitly modeled itself on the American system, as have Saudi Arabia and Oman (Al-Tal and Ashour, 1993). Begun in the late 1980s, community colleges developed as an explicit response to the need to educate more than the elite few who had access to a university education in the past (Al-Tal and Ashour, 1993). By 1993, there were 22 private and 30 public two-year institutions in Jordan. There is significant national government oversight, with most colleges controlled directly by the Jordanian Ministry of Higher Education or other governmental agencies such as defense, social services, or the central bank. Several of the community colleges are single-sex institutions.

The Ministry of Higher Education promulgates rules that all public and private institutions must adhere to, and a Council of Higher Education (CHE) acts like a national board of trustees, concerned with all matters institutional (programmatic, fiscal, and operational). The CHE sets enrollment levels and assigns students to each college. It also mandates that 75 percent of the faculty at community colleges have the minimum of a Master's degree, 25 percent must have Doctorates, and 80 percent must be full-time.

While Jordanian community colleges have a range of academic specializations that parallel what would be found in the United States (e.g., business, computer science, allied health, engineering, agriculture, hotel and restaurant management, etc.), the curricula are prepared at Jordanian universities by faculty who are appointed by the Minister of Education (Al-Tal and Ashour, 1993). The CHE allocates few admission slots in baccalaureate-granting institutions to community college graduates, regardless of graduates' grades or passing exit exam, so while articulation agreements exist they are rarely effective (Al-Tal and Ashour, 1993). The comprehensive exit exam is also problematic for most students (Al-Tal and Ashour, 1993). Remediation is not offered at any of the community colleges (Al-Tal and Ashour, 1993).

Hong Kong

A very different example is provided by Hong Kong. As it moved from a British protectorate toward re-connection with China, an ambitious target was set to increase the percentage of secondary school graduates who went to higher education from 30 percent to 60 percent over 10 years (Lee and Young, 2003). The government called for the development of a "diversified, multi-channel, multi-layer higher education system" (Lee and Young, 2003). The only university in the territory, University of Hong Kong (HKU), established the first Associate-degree granting institution in March 2000 (Lee and Young, 2003).

The Hong Kong Associate degree was explicitly designed to articulate the British educational system, admitting students who complete Form Six or Seven (roughly equivalent to U.S. high school graduates) and providing potential transfer to the second year of the British-style three-year university curriculum (Lee and Young, 2003). Innovations of the system also included a broad-based curriculum which links basic skills, liberal arts, and vocational education (Lee and Young, 2003). The government has centrally determined aspects of the curriculum. For example, the Associate degree must contain at least 20 percent general education, consisting of courses in English, Chinese, Putonghua, quantitative skills, basic information technology, communication/interpersonal skills, and analytic and problem solving skills (Lee and Young, 2003). This is less than the standard liberal arts focus in university, but more than in postsecondary technical institutes. Greater pedagogical innovation is more likely in these institutions because they are not so tightly bound by the strictures of the A-level examinations (Lee and Young, 2003). Students tend to be older, and part-time or taking only evening classes (Lee and Young, 2003).

Like American community colleges in the early 1960s, few Associate-degree-granting institutions in Hong Kong have campuses, usually meeting in community facilities such as town centers. The government recently developed a system to provide interest-free loans to build facilities such as libraries, so their structure is changing. Similarities also exist between the problems in Hong Kong's Associate degree institutions and those of the United States. Critics contend that curriculum is too narrowly technical, and colleges bemoan the lack of transfer/articulation agreements and spaces (Lee and Young, 2003). Yet Hong Kong's employers, especially the civil service branch of the government, have given Associate degree graduates broad acceptance (Lee and Young, 2003).

INSTITUTIONAL MISSIONS

As the above examples illustrate, the emergent international two-year degree-granting institutions develop with the intention of serving a broader group of potential students than the traditional-aged or the traditionally prepared. As the need for broader and deeper education continues, there appears to be a growing consensus about mission and purpose, even though these institutions are variably named and situated within a country's higher education system. Internationally, community-college-like institutions are grouped under a variety of terms, including

- junior colleges
- technical, teknologi, or technological institutions
- district or regional colleges
- further education institutions
- advanced education institutions
- fachhochschulen or folk high schools
- higher schools
- workers' colleges
- short-cycle institutions (Brawer, 1996)

These variously named institutions are situated within different parts of a country's educational system. In Indonesia and Denmark, for example, the secondary school system coordinates the postsecondary, non-traditional offerings. New Zealand ties its Associate-degree-like institutions to polytechnic or technical institutes, while Canada has a separate, nationally coordinated system of community colleges (Brawer, 1996).

The actual form of the Associate-degree-like institutions and curriculum also ranges widely. For example, in Austria, "upper second schools" are integrated with workplaces in internship-like arrangements, while Ireland's are linked together in a regional technical college system (Brawer, 1996). China might call an institution a community college, but what is taught ranges from classes that would be found in a YMCA or community-based organization in the United States to a relatively advanced two-year technical college (Mellow, 2005). Australia, Britain, Denmark, Germany, and Norway emphasize lifelong learning and cultural education in addition to the occupational focus so common throughout the world (Brawer, 1996).

The dynamism of community-college-like institutions across the globe can be seen in their continued growth and change. The proposed or newly developing systems are often targeted to support very specific economic goals. For example, in Ukraine, "junior specialist courses" are part of the country's reform efforts to advance the educational level of its populace, while in Belarus and Bulgaria postsecondary institutions focus on business and entrepreneurial skills (Brawer, 1996). Yet these dynamic institutions also face resistance from traditional sources. In a criticism that is all too familiar for those of us working in U.S. community colleges, Israel has questioned whether a "second-chance" institution has any place in a higher education system, and if the Israeli community college system can deliver on its promise of increased access and social equity (Brawer, 1996).

International systems have varying degrees of cooperation with or focus on the United States community college model. For example, community colleges in New York and California have partnered with South Africa, which is trying to integrate existing colleges and tecnikons, which are higher educational institutions that offer degrees in engineering, computers and other technical areas, but do not offer a liberal arts curriculum, with a community college system to eliminate the legacy of apartheid in the educational system (Williams, 2005). Community colleges have been contracted by several counties, such as Hungary and the Dominican Republic, to either establish community colleges or to make suggestions about potential structures to launch a system (Burcham, 2004; Mellander and Mellander, 1994).

KINDS OF INTERNATIONAL EDUCATIONAL SERVICE PROVISION

The multiple ways that a college education is delivered in developing countries include:

- Delivery of education from outside the country, through distance learning or other virtual learning structures;
- Delivery of students to another country to study;
- Establishment by external institutions of a presence in another country, through satellites and branches, partnerships, and/or franchising arrangements; and
- Guest educators, where faculty travel to another country on a temporary basis to provide service (Sehoole, 2004).

These modes can create local pressures for U.S. community colleges when a local sponsor is wary of international provision of services. For example, one rural community college president had a public conflict with the college's board of trustees when it became clear that there was a vibrant international student exchange program. The board publicly maintained that there was no need to use local tax-payer dollars to support international students or international travel (Viniar, 2001).

Some U.S. community colleges have established branches or partnerships in other countries, where they have conducted successful programs over many years as faculty and students partake in studying abroad. Pasadena City College in California and Brookdale Community College in New Jersey have facilities in Italy and Ecuador, respectively. These programs tend to remain small, and funding for students who do not have their own personal financial resources can be difficult. However, powerful connections are made in exchanges with foreign countries, and faculty development is an important benefit of these programs. The programs also establish connections that translate into ongoing economic development activities. City College of San Francisco has expanded its work with the San Francisco International airport for terminal activation and aircraft maintainer training into a contract with China to train China's air mechanics, who come for several weeks to train in the United States (Day, 2006).

INTERNATIONAL TRADE AND DEVELOPMENT

As technology spawns the delivery of higher education throughout the globe, trade policies become increasing important in shaping how countries can create a strong postsecondary system of education and training. The international policy setting agenda created through the General Agreement on Trade Services (GATS) might provide the impetus to liberalize education in non-Western and Western countries alike. As countries such as South Africa identify increased educational attainment as critical to the country's advancement, it is time to use systems of international relations to advance the economic and social imperative inherent in these goals. Like any other public utility, it is unlikely that impoverished countries will be able to build viable state-supported higher education institutions unless they tap into strong market incentives. It is here that U.S. community colleges, as well as U.S. businesses and consumers, can play a supportive role.

Any unregulated international market has the dangerous potential of "cherry picking" students so that the elite are educated and the rest of a country's citizens are left behind. Although countries are beginning to state publicly their belief that lack of an educated citizenry hinders both economic and political development, many are placing all of their trust in the use of private providers to respond to the pressures in order to rapidly increase access. In China, where this occurs, the quality of private college "vendors" ranges dramatically, and there does not yet exist an accrediting process to establish standards of educational quality (Mellow, 2005). While countries that have advanced systems of quality assurance might help countries who are building community-college-like institutions develop oversight mechanisms, too often the only assistance that developed countries are providing to less developed countries comes from private corporations, all too happy to provide services to a newly enfranchised middle- and upper-class students for a nice profit.

To manage the tensions inherent in allowing private education providers to increase the availability of college, but at the same time to frame the relationships to provide tangible benefit to the country as a whole, some regions have begun to outline protocols that regulate the new college offerings. For example, 13 Southern African leaders have joined together regionally to harness cooperation in social, economic, and political spheres, 12 of whom signed the Protocol on Education and Training in 1997 (Sehoole, 2004). This protocol is designed to pool resources in order to increase access to all levels of education, and relax some policies (like immigration) to promote freer movement of students and faculty. While it does not specifically promote the development of a community-college-like system, it does advocate the creation of a system of interchange or transfer which would provide evaluation of equivalence of education and training systems (Sehoole, 2004).

The global trade in higher education makes for multiple complications as countries seek to both expand access and hold on to control of their countries' educational systems. In 2003, the United States, Norway, Kenya, New Zealand, and Australia made bids at the GATS negotiations for South Africa to open up to foreign higher education and to change the burdensome requirements to foreign universities seeking to operate in South Africa (Sehoole, 2004). South Africans resisted, worried that their educational system would not maintain an African focus. This is an area where local community colleges might be part of the answer—to avoid the hegemony of Western capitalistic educational entities flooding a local market.

ROLE OF COMMUNITY COLLEGES IN THE AMERICAN RESPONSE TO GLOBALIZATION

Community colleges, like all American institutions in contemporary society, are both a buffer for changing requirements in the workplace resulting from globalization, and are themselves buffeted by the dramatic changes that have occurred over the past 20 to 30 years. And the responses from the colleges are as confused as any other part of the economy. So many changes hit the working people of a community, who are often the students and businesses with which community colleges work most closely. While manufacturing has led the way, the current off-shoring of a range of services (from relatively routine data entry to sophisticated engineering and computer programming) impacts the workforce of a community in multiple ways. When manufacturers began to take production to lower-wage markets in India, China, and elsewhere, community colleges were often involved in trying to re-train displaced workers or help local manufacturers advance technologically to stay ahead of the skills/wage curve. While the U.S. Department of Labor for several years touted "High Skills/High Wage" as the best mantra to keep Americans working, this strategy does little when the work that is off-shored begins to be highly sophisticated (National Center on Education and the Economy, 2007).

The community college's role as a player in the international scene must be one of outreach so that other communities can understand how education and training may enhance the lives of people who are working in newly created factories. On the other hand, this may seem like colleges are seeking to take work out of American hands. Yet the reality is that much of the "knowledge work" of innovation and creation that can remain in the United States requires a level of education and sophistication that makes an Associate degree an essential ingredient for a community's workplace. With Toyota now building more cars on American soil than Ford, it is also important for community college curricula to incorporate international perspectives so that graduates are suited for the kinds of cultural competencies and sensitivities that may be required as they work for a global company. Colleges that wish to produce the next international leaders do well to think about the new kinds of competencies, such as collaboration, synthesizing, localizing, or adapting, which will be required of anyone entering the workplace anywhere (Friedman, 2006).

If graduates of community colleges are not aware of global issues, and if we cannot help them to become the citizens and entrepreneurs who understand the intended and unintended consequence of out-sourcing and off-shoring, no college education will be sufficient.

Can Community Colleges Promote International Economic and Social Advancement?

If community-college-like structures are able to achieve some of the goals outlined in the dream section above, there is real hope for those structural changes to have a dramatic impact on the lives and livelihoods of millions of individuals across the globe. Community colleges have a role to play in changing global inequities. Two billion people currently live on less than $2 a day (Hughes, 2007) In order for American community colleges to make a difference in a global movement to increase educational attainment, it is critical that we begin to know and understand our higher education colleagues from around the world. International travel, international conferences, web conferences, symposia, or any gathering that begins to pull together a commonality of community college supporters is critical to sustaining this potentially positive impact.

Without commitment, support, and struggle, there is little impetus for our students and ourselves to work globally to create wealth and encourage a higher standard of living. The potential is great, but the fight is long and difficult.

CHALLENGES TO THE FIELD

The challenges of international development are as large as the world itself, or as small as helping a local business understand the power of importing raw material from a new source in a developing country. American community colleges might become essential messengers to the rest of the world about the power of equal education opportunity to improve the human condition. However, the emerging social and economic powers of countries like China and India should caution restraint in believing that American community colleges have this form of education all worked out. There is much to learn from other educational entities across the globe. The following ideas are therefore only suggestions, in the hopes of furthering the dialogue.

- American community colleges should continue to expand dialogue with partners around the globe to deepen an understanding of the opportunities and restrictions of open access college in other countries.
- American community colleges should promote internationalization in every aspect of their campuses—credit courses, exchange programs, and non-credit services.
- American community colleges should use the freedom of speech and media to continue to promote the necessity of creating educational opportunities around the globe for individuals who have been denied access—especially the poor, women, and individuals of minority status in differing parts of the globe.
- American community colleges should increase activities that create linkages among individual programs, faculty, and campuses to develop a network of trust and knowledge that can ground future international collaborative initiatives.

CONCLUSION

The American community college movement is one that symbolizes American values and aspirations. It will be interesting to see what values—community or spiritual or social order—will form the foundation for open-access college educational systems in other countries. While there is no doubt that the Knowledge Age will require increasing levels of education from people across the world, how this can be delivered, and the mechanisms needed to fund and develop these systems are unknown. As the American workforce responds more directly to international markets and outsourcing, the kinds of curricular and workforce programs offered at community colleges will change. The intersection of technology and education will be a frontier across which many of our students traverse. It is up to community colleges to fully engage our students and our communities in the global challenge of understanding world cultures.

PRACTICE

CHAPTER 9

Developmental Studies

⤳ **OVERVIEW**

Developmental Studies (preparing the unprepared for college-level work) forms the centerpiece of the dream of opening higher education to all Americans, regardless of prior educational opportunity or success.

The "remedial" function serves as the "clean-up batter" for many public high schools, and the "pinch hitter" for American industry. Data from a variety of research reports verify student success in GED® preparation, transfer student competitiveness, workforce success and developmental course completion. The success of these students keeps alive the promise of democracy in our country; their success makes higher education inclusive, diverse, and accessible from many directions.

The reality of Developmental Studies in an open door setting is that too many students never "graduate" from basic skills. It is the program attempting to embrace high school drop-outs, adults returning to school after a long absence, students with learning disabilities, and many other under-prepared learners. It is the program that many community college staff do not believe in, and that politicians and pundits revile as a waste of taxpayers' money.

This chapter reviews approaches to developmental pedagogy and to educating adults, and illustrates the added value created by Developmental Studies in community college education. Diagnostic tools, student background, who needs remedial help, how long a program takes, the various forms of developmental programs, and who are the teachers are all described in this chapter. Also reviewed are data regarding the impact of developmental education, including developmental students who proceed to a degree, who are involved in their community, who transfer successfully to a four-year college, and those who do not. The chapter ends with an extensive list of Challenges to the Field.

THE DREAM

Other institutions of higher learning achieve excellence by keeping people out. Most four-year colleges skim the "cream" of learners for their student bodies. Community colleges, on the other hand, achieve their excellence by allowing adults who desire an education to enter higher education at whatever skill level they have achieved. When these students leave the community college, they are "cream"—prepared to enter any baccalaureate program they desire, whether it is U.C. Berkeley, Yale, Colorado State University, or Vassar. Developmental Studies is *the* program that assists students who are unprepared for college to become "cream." By stating that the *remedial function serves as the "clean-up batter" for many public high schools,* we are demonstrating that community colleges achieve the high-school-level preparedness that students did not achieve previously. And by claiming Developmental Studies as the entity that is *the "pinch hitter" for American industry,* we are reminding the reader of the power of providing basic skills instructions to adults who cannot work effectively without possessing (minimally) reading, writing, computing, and critical thinking skills commensurate with the needs of industry. It is the singular invention and ongoing refinement of Developmental Studies that has allowed community colleges to provide this essential underpinning to the American learner landscape.

Developmental Studies gives learners the basic reading, writing, and mathematics skills either not achieved in or not retained from high school. This program allows community colleges to welcome students whose backgrounds (poor high school grades, a long lapse between high school and college, poor English skills, poverty, uneducated parents, employment status, age) would have prevented their entry into traditionally structured colleges. The Developmental Studies program is the backbone of the community college founders' dream of access to the middle class for all. In many ways it demonstrates the profound impact extra time to learn and focused learning support can have on an individual's life, and ultimately on the public good.

Developmental Studies, in many colleges, is a comprehensive process that looks at learners holistically. It focuses on the intellectual, social, and emotional growth of the learner, and grounds its practice in current learning theories. Developmental Studies assumes all learners have talents that educators can identify and nurture so that students prepare for success in the next (collegiate) phase of the curriculum and in other parts of their lives (Casazza, 1999).

Developmental Studies is the program that actuates the community college dream. It equalizes the opportunity for under-prepared students to be successful and to achieve the American Dream. Under-prepared students have many different faces. Some students are bright and talented but have trouble in math. Some students are math whizzes, yet have difficulty with reading or writing. The returning displaced homemaker may not be able to study at first, and the person from a first-generation college family may not understand academic jargon and the challenges of earning an academic degree. Many students are in their 30s and 40s, and suddenly realize they "wasted" their high school years. Development students all share the ability to take the new chance offered by Developmental Studies to help them achieve their goal of improving their lives and reaching for the American Dream. The ideal community college makes a commitment, without apology, to help under-prepared students overcome academic deficiencies and acquire the skills they need to become effective, independent learners (Commission on the Future of Community Colleges, 1988).

Just as high school dropouts tend to have children who drop out, Developmental Studies faculty often see that parents who start studying have children who start studying. Parents who are college graduates have children who complete college. Given these benefits, abandoning remedial efforts in higher education would reduce the number of people gaining the skills and knowledge associated with postsecondary education, and it would be unwise public policy.

With this wisdom in mind, the ideal Developmental Studies program would be supported by all faculty and administrators within the community college world, and public policy makers would find ways to buttress it so it could maintain affordability for both institutions and students. All students who entered a Developmental Studies program would gain from it, the pass rate would be nearly 100 percent, and a student who enrolled in Developmental Studies would be as likely to graduate with an Associate degree as a student who arrived at the community college with college-level skills. Funding structures would be developed so that students would not place financial aid for college at risk while they gained needed skills, and colleges would be able to provide the additional kinds of support services (tutoring, greater access to faculty, academic advising, mentoring) that are correlated with academic success for at-risk learners (McCants, 2004). Without these supports in place, it is amazing that almost half of all developmental studies students actually pass and move on to college-level courses.

The following story provides an example of the dramatic, long-term changes Developmental Studies can have on an individual and on an entire family.

❧ EDNA'S DEVELOPMENTAL STUDIES SUCCESS STORY

Edna, a woman in her late 40s, appeared at a community college in the West, distraught and overextended. Her son, imprisoned with a fairly light sentence for a drug offense, was killed in prison. He left a wife and three children, and his wife, Edna's daughter-in-law, was addicted to drugs and was unable to be a mother to her three children, including a toddler. Edna, with anxiety and a sense of dread, took in the three children, thinking it would be a short-term solution until the children's mother became healthy again. Health never occurred for this mother, and Grandmother Edna became a full-time mother at the age of 40.

Teachers began to call Edna to let her know of the school-aged children's poor school performance and behavior problems. Edna admitted her frustration and anxiety to the teachers and counselors, and they recommended a non-credit parenting course taught at the local community college. She enrolled in the course and learned of the importance of education for children; the instructors emphasized the value of education for parents as role models for children.

Inspired by this course, Edna enrolled in the college's GED® program. She began to go to the Learning Lab (part of the Developmental Studies program) to increase her reading, writing, and math skills as a support to passing the GED Tests. Edna was so successful in her GED work that she became the speaker for the GED graduation that year. She had become so inspired by her Developmental Studies work and so imbued with the value of higher education, that her speech contained a passionate appeal to her fellow GED credential recipients to continue their education and to earn a college degree. She talked about her story and her new children, and about the positive impact her college work was having on the school-aged children in her care. When she studied, they studied; when she read, they read, and their enjoyment of school soared and so did their grades. Edna earned her Associate degree with high grades and went on to earn her Bachelor's degree. Her grandchildren continue to earn good grades in school, and they too are talking about how college can support their career goals when they graduate from high school.

THE UNFULFILLED DREAM

There are many aspects of the reality of Developmental Studies in community colleges. For many students, Developmental Studies are both their entrance into and their exit from college. Students who come with very poor skills, often coupled with non-existent study habits, weak educational aspirations, few or no role models, and complicated personal lives often fail to make academic progress. Some of these students leave developmental classes mid-way through their first semester, and some try for a year, but their rate of academic progress is limited. For some students, the height of the hurdle of mastering academic writing, critical reading of serious texts, or algebra is simply too high. Because of its open access policy, community college is sometimes recommended by advisors of a small fraction of students with intellectual developmental disabilities who have "aged out" of high school but for whom there is no real alternative. In communities where from 30 percent to 80 percent of the students who graduate from high school with a diploma lack high school–level skills necessary to succeed in college, it is the rare Developmental Studies program where more than 60 percent of the students remediate their basic skills deficits.

Other realities concern how incoming students' developmental needs are assessed. Although entry-level skills testing is overwhelmingly conducted in contemporary community colleges (using nationally available or home-grown tests), few of these tests provide the kinds of diagnostics that would allow a college to customize a curricular sequence. While some community colleges, such as Miami-Dade Community College in Florida, mandate that all basic skills be remediated before beginning credit work, many community colleges separate linguistic from mathematic basic skills. This can result, for example, in students succeeding in one area, but then spending several semesters trying to pass an algebra course as their final six credits for a degree. At the other end, there are systems, such as the City University of New York's community colleges, which use nationally normed assessment tests as exit examinations and prevent even the students who pass a developmental course from taking the credit classes unless a set score on the examination is achieved. Interestingly, the national testing companies do not set "passing" scores for their basic skills assessment tests, nor do they publish results—not even a national average, suggesting that the political and economic realms might not be in harmony.

Structural considerations for developmental programs within community colleges are quite variable. No consensus has been reached for how to configure Developmental Studies—about half create separate departments, and half embed developmental classes within departments that offer college-level English or mathematics. While some data have determined aspects of developmental pedagogy that are helpful, there is no generally accepted protocol for curriculum development, and only slightly more agreement about support services.

Another reality is the internal and external politics that affect Developmental Studies and the faculty and staff who teach basic skills. While there are many faculty members who are passionate about educational access and who devote their professional lives ensuring student success by providing Developmental Studies and services with thoughtful care and design, there are also faculty members who harbor hope in their hearts that Harvard will eventually call. This latter faculty thinks teaching developmental courses and developmental students are a black mark on their resume, and look down on faculty who do so. An example is the biologist who said, "I only want to teach people like myself." Developmental Studies faculty and staff read the literature and thoughtfully plan their program; however, they often cite lack of support from their college administration. One such leader bemoaned the variation of support at his college. He described the lack of support by one president, the extensive support of the next president, and then a new president and again limited support. Program strength waxed and waned depending on moral and financial support, and strong programs existed only at the campuses where the deans supported it (or at least saw that it brought in funding) or where a strong faculty member pushed constantly for the program.

Externally, influential conservative leaders believe that not all people should go to college, and education should be reserved for a very few. An economic force in one community college town said, "Only the elite should go to college." This opinion infiltrates the halls of state legislatures and Congress as well as the halls of higher education.

There also is a physical/social reality that limits the success of Developmental Studies. There are students who have extraordinary limitations to their ability to benefit from education, for example, students who have severe mental and learning disabilities, students whose English skills are not adequate, and young people whose focus is elsewhere.

Drug and alcohol use has had a profound influence on a student's ability to learn. Eighteen-year-old freshmen used to arrive at colleges and experiment with alcohol and drugs; they now come as full-fledged addicts. All of these students might enroll in Developmental Studies, and they are a part of the program's failure because they need more time, lower-level courses, or some other service requiring more than a college can provide.

The sad reality is that, of all those learners who enroll in Developmental Studies, only half of them complete their courses, move on to college-level work, and graduate with an Associate degree, get a job, or transfer to a four-year college or university.

The internal and external politics and issues of ability to benefit are not researched or discussed very often. They are facts of life in the Developmental Studies reality, and will be developed more fully, along with recommendations for community colleges, later in this chapter.

The following story describes the impact college faculty and staff commitment can have on the Developmental Studies area.

~ THE PRECARIOUS NATURE OF DEVELOPMENTAL STUDIES PROGRAMS

One campus in a multi-campus district had a flourishing Developmental Studies program. A highly committed faculty member participated regularly in college-wide training for Developmental Studies faculty, and he was a strong advocate for the program, along with other faculty, the campus, and the college-wide administration. Because of the nature of the campus, and the students it recruited, Developmental Studies courses were usually full, the Learning Lab was a thriving entity, and faculty were pleased with the skill level of students who came to college-level classes from the Developmental Studies program.

The faculty member retired, and the campus administration had other priorities and did not pay attention to the Developmental Studies program. A person without adequate skills was hired to replace the retiree, and inadequate funding, little moral support, and too many responsibilities for the new person in charge of the program all took their toll on the program's quality. Not many courses were offered, the GED® program became half-time, and faculty discontinued their participation in staff development activities. Faculty members now complain about the decline in student competence when students leave the Developmental Studies program and enter college-level courses.

THE REAL STORY

What Is Developmental Studies?

At its most basic level, Developmental Studies provides a remedial function by working with students not prepared for college-level reading, writing, or arithmetic. Developmental Studies has evolved as a collection of courses or a program of studies and also embodies a collection of services. Developmental Studies is a comprehensive and holistic process. It focuses on the intellectual, social, and emotional growth of the learner and uses learning theory to inform the process (Casazza, 1999).

Developmental *courses* include freshmen seminars, critical thinking, study strategies, orientation courses, some freshmen composition classes, and pre-college reading, writing, and low-level math courses (Boylan, Bonham, and Rodriguez, 2000 in Kozeracki 2002). Developmental *services* include assessment, placement, orientation, tutoring, advising, counseling, peer support or supplemental instruction, early alert programs, study skills training, and support groups and learning assistance centers (McCabe and Day, 1998). One of the many controversies surrounding Developmental Studies concerns the structure of these courses, programs, and services. The question is, should basic skills be offered separately and be contained in separate organizational units or embedded within existing course syllabi and be housed in regular departments (Boylan 1999; McCabe 2000; Oudenhoven 2002; Perin, 2002; Roueche and Roueche 1999; Shults 2000)?

ORGANIZATION OF DEVELOPMENTAL STUDIES PROGRAMS

On one hand, these researchers argue that *stand-alone remedial courses* in a department by themselves negatively affect students' attitudes and expectations and force students to take longer to finish degrees. The experience of being only with other remedial students lowers student self-concepts and makes it more difficult for students to shed the image of being at-risk learners. At the same time, this method appears to be superior with regard to teacher motivation and experience. On the other hand, some experts argue that *mixing prepared and under-prepared students or mainstreaming students* in the same classroom does a disservice to both groups and can lead to low morale for both students and teachers. However, the method of mainstreaming does seem to have more positive student reactions, and overall demonstrates higher quality. Fifty-four percent of higher education institutions mainstream reading, 59 percent of colleges mainstream writing, and

62 percent mainstream math (National Center for Education Statistics [NCES], 1996).

The disagreement around the best approach to structuring Developmental Studies is an important issue. As more and more students are enrolled in such programs, more states (21) are mandating attendance in developmental courses if students do not meet the minimum college-level performance criteria (Jenkins and Boswell, 2002). It is important to understand which approach is truly more effective, and at this time research supporting either approach is not conclusive.

WHO NEEDS DEVELOPMENTAL STUDIES?

This chapter addresses important issues and questions about who needs Developmental Studies, how long the program takes, who finishes, what kinds of Developmental Studies exist, whether they have an impact, who teaches these courses, and how they are taught.

Developmental Studies (often termed remedial) is not a new phenomenon. Such courses have been offered in higher education institutions since the mid-eighteenth century (Breneman and Haarlow, 1998). Harvard College provided tutors in Greek and Latin for under-prepared students entering the ministry. In the mid-eighteenth century, land-grant colleges instituted preparatory programs or departments for students with below-average skills in reading, writing, and arithmetic (Payne and Lyman), and in 1849 the University of Wisconsin offered its first remedial courses in reading, writing, and arithmetic (Breneman and Haarlow, 1998). By the end of the nineteenth century, when only 238,000 students were enrolled in all of higher education, more than 40 percent of first-year students were enrolled in pre-collegiate programs (Ignash, 1997). After WWII and the advent of the GI Bill, and during the 1960s through the '80s, competition for students (enabling open admission) and government funding allowed thousands of under-prepared students to enroll in colleges and universities. During this time, more than half of the students enrolled in Harvard, Princeton, Yale, and Columbia did not meet entrance requirements and were placed in remedial courses (Payne and Lyman, 1996).

As a result of the growth in under-prepared students enrolling in college, state agencies are increasingly concerned about Developmental Studies and are trying to engineer public policy to eliminate some of the cost. The number of institutions offering developmental programs is declining. During the early 1980s, 82 percent of institutions offered remedial education in the areas of reading, writing, and math. By 1995, 78 percent of institutions offered all three areas. At the same time, enrollment in higher education increased by approximately a half-million students, while the percentage of students enrolled in Developmental Studies stayed basically the same (Hoachlander, Sikora, Horn, and Carroll, 2003).

Developmental Studies is a significant part of helping many groups of students achieve educational success and access to the American Dream. These programs also fail many students who should achieve the same. The community college dream is based on the belief that adults can learn, and that given the right support system and enough time, older adults can return to the education system that may have failed them in the past, and succeed. These adults are now 40 percent of the developmental population. Community colleges dare to believe they can support adults' dreams of postsecondary education to achieve new career goals, to retool for their employers, or because they finally have time and resources. They may be rusty, or they may never have learned the information the first time around (Cronholm in Oudhoven, 1994; Ignash, 1997). Employment-related forces cause older students to return to college because the growth rate in jobs between 1994 and 2005 was the greatest for those categories that require at least an Associate degree (Boswell, 2002). Service to business and industry forms a sizeable proportion of developmental work at 21 percent of all education institutions. More colleges offered mathematics (93 percent) than reading (81 percent) to industry employees (Parsad and Greene, 2003). These courses are offered to already employed adult learners, and they are evidence of the role of the community college as pinch hitter for industry. Recent high school graduates are another large group of community college learners needing remedial reading, writing, and arithmetic help.

High school faculty members have many demands on them. They are required to be therapist, parole or police officer, parent, and teacher to their students. The act of teaching is often the last role they are able to implement. One of the outcomes of the shortage of support for high schools is the shortage of college-level skills in high school graduates.

Nationally, 51 percent of African Americans, 79 percent of Asians, 52 percent of Latinos, 54 percent of Native Americans, and 72 percent of Caucasians graduate from high school (Education Watch, 2004). Many others are earning a GED® credential and then seeking a college degree in a community college. In 1982, *A Nation at Risk* reported that only 14 percent of high school graduates took the college preparatory curriculum. Today, *one-half* of them do so and nearly *two-thirds* of all high school graduates attempt college at some point (NCES, 1996). In the early days of higher education, only about 20 percent of high school graduates ever attempted college (the cream?). Then, over time, the next 20 percent of high school graduates attempted college, then the next 20 percent, and then the next 20 percent. Community colleges dare to dream that all these levels of high school graduates and dropouts are able to learn and succeed in college, too. This radical idea drives community college educators, inspires the passion of Developmental Studies educators, and shapes the "rule book" for the "big league game" of Developmental Studies in community college education.

Students who enroll in Developmental Studies courses are primarily those who are at risk of not completing a postsecondary degree. The data illustrate that, in addition to a lack of basic skills, there are many other reasons students fail to complete their Developmental Studies and/or postsecondary degrees. NCES defines factors related to being an "at-risk" learner:

1. Delayed enrollment between high school graduation and postsecondary entry,
2. Part-time attendance,
3. Completed high school by certificate or GED® credential,
4. Worked full time when first enrolled,
5. Child rearing,
6. Single parenting,
7. Financial independence (NCES, 2003).

These identifying factors directly parallel actual student enrollment statistics in community college Developmental Studies courses. The age range of Developmental Studies students is from age 16 to age 60, and 57 percent of all those students are Caucasian, 50 to 57 percent of whom are women, and 20 percent of whom are married (Boylan and Bonham, 1994). Eighty percent of Developmental Studies students are U.S. citizens, 10 percent are veterans, and 33 percent work 35 or more hours per week, yet 20 percent are still eligible for some form of financial aid (Knopp, 1996). Adult students (over the age of 22) comprise 40 percent of developmental education students (Oudenhoven, 2002). These at-risk learners are at risk because the demands on their lives are broad and intense. Understanding the large proportion of Developmental Studies students who are married Caucasian women over the age of 22, and who work almost full time yet are poor enough to receive some form of aid should give us pause. We need careful reflection about the kind of policy and financial support needed for Developmental Studies to work.

Immigrants to the United States are significant participants in Developmental Studies. In the year 1999–2000, public two-year colleges served more than 345,000 resident alien students, while public four-year colleges and universities served fewer than 245,000 (NCES, 2001). Approximately 60 percent of those resident aliens in community colleges took at least one remedial course (NCES, 2001).

The diversity of students requiring Developmental Studies is broad and becomes more so every year. Increasing numbers of high school graduates who need Developmental Studies support are seeking a college degree, large numbers of college dropouts return to attempt college again (Boylan, 1999), and as we have seen there is a substantial number of adults returning to college. Add to this the large immigrant population needing integration into American society, and we must ask the question, "Why are we surprised that one-third of all college students are under-prepared?" The surprise may be in the positive impact that Developmental Studies actually has on all these under-prepared learners.

LENGTH OF TIME DEVOTED TO DEVELOPMENTAL STUDIES

In the fall of 2000, 28 percent of all entering freshmen enrolled in one or more Developmental Studies course in either reading, writing, or mathematics. The time spent in developmental courses was generally limited to one year or less. There was no increase in the percentage of students enrolled in Developmental Studies courses over a five-year period between 1995 and 2000. During that same time period, however, the number of all freshmen students staying *longer* than one year in "remediation" rose from 28 percent in 1995 to 35 percent in 2000 (Hoachlander et al., 2003). Six states actually impose a time limit on completing remedial courses: Colorado, Georgia, Massachusetts, Oklahoma, South Carolina, and Texas. State time limits range from 24 credits to four semesters in any given subject area (Jenkins and Boswell, 2002). Increased enrollment of those considered to be at risk could be the reason for this 7 percent increase in time devoted to developmental work. Another consideration could be the increasing numbers of colleges that are mandating developmental work for students who do not pass assessment tests at a college-approved level.

WHO TEACHES DEVELOPMENTAL STUDIES?

In the mid-1990s, the number and variety of institutions offering Developmental Studies was large and diverse. One hundred percent of community colleges, and 78 percent of *all* higher education institutions, offered at least one developmental course in reading, writing, or mathematics (Lewis and Farris, 1996; U.S. Department of Education, 1996).

Approximately 49,500 faculty were engaged in teaching Developmental Studies in 1998 (Kozeracki, 2002). Independent colleges reported that 60 percent of faculty teaching remedial education were full time, and public community colleges reported that 33 percent of the faculty teaching Developmental Studies were full time (Shults, 2000). Whether or not this is an important issue in student success is still debated, since research comparing faculty availability, student evaluation, and student success among full- and part-time faculty finds no notable difference between the two (Roueche et al., 1995).

In 2000, 20 percent of community colleges required that full-time faculty possess training specific to remediation before teaching developmental courses, and 17 percent had such a requirement for part-time faculty (Shults, 2000). It appears preparation for the important "save" of this work is lacking among faculty in community colleges, and so are the programs that could provide formal preparation in this essential field. Four universities in the country offer graduate degrees in the field of Developmental Studies (Grubb, 1999).

THE EFFECT OF DEVELOPMENTAL STUDIES

Success is usually measured by the number of developmental students who complete their course of developmental work, move on to earn an Associate degree, and then (if that is their goal) transfer to a four-year college or university. Students who transfer to four-year institutions prior to completing a two-year degree are also included in success measurements.

A concern of Developmental Studies critics quoted in newspapers, journal articles, and potential legislation is that people don't move past developmental work into college-level study or more advanced work. It is important to remember that many of the people who enroll in the community college are the learners most at risk of failure: returning adults, high school drop-outs, immigrants, and more than 80 percent of high school graduates are not truly college ready. Of this group of students, *one-half* of those who enroll in developmental courses complete them and enroll in college-level courses (Cohen and Brawer, 1996; Illich, Hagan, and McCalllister, 2004). This is a fairly large group of people who probably would never have succeeded in college without developmental support.

Involvement in Developmental Studies also has an impact on the length of time it takes to earn an Associate degree. While state criteria tend to expect students to earn a two-year degree in four years, taking at least one or more courses in Developmental Studies further delays this achievement.

In 1976, Pat Cross estimated that only 10 percent of under-prepared students were likely to earn a degree without some kind of intervention (Boylan, 1999). A study of 2.5 million student transcripts determined that students who did not need to take remediation courses had a graduation rate of 55 percent (Adelman, 1998). Those who took one remedial course had a graduation rate of 47 percent. From one perspective this percentage can be considered a miracle of instruction and faculty support, salvaging a large group of under-prepared students who might never have succeeded in college without this extra reinforcement.

Results from a longitudinal study conducted from 1988 to 2000 found that in total, 61 percent of *all* community college students intending to earn a degree, certificate, or transfer to a four-year institution achieved their expectation within six years of their initial enrollment (Hoachlander et al., 2003). These successful students are those who enrolled in college preparatory courses in high school and were better prepared for college-level work. However, even among this group of prepared high school students, 40 percent needed math help, 20 percent needed English help, and 25 percent required reading review (Merisotis and Phipps, 2000).

THE CRITICS OF DEVELOPMENTAL STUDIES

Criticism of the impact of Developmental Studies arises from many different sources. In 1970, for example, the CUNY system in New York City adopted an open admissions policy that virtually created a space in education for every New Yorker. Twenty-five years later, high remediation rates and perceived low graduation rates led to criticism and political pressure. Eventually the CUNY board decided to phase out "remediation" at CUNY's four-year colleges. This decision raised the eyebrows of higher education leaders everywhere, and inspired several of the noteworthy studies cited in this essay: Breneman and Haarlow, 1999; Phipps, 1998; McCabe, 2000; McCabe and Day, 1998; and Roueche and Roueche, 1999.

Some critics point out that Developmental Studies detract from the education of prepared college students by "dumbing down" courses when using the mainstreaming approach, and this leads to low graduation rates (Breneman and Haarlow, 1998; Phipps, 1998; Roueche and Roueche, 1999).

Along the same line, some say the very existence of developmental courses lowers the standards and academic quality of higher education institutions by encouraging students with inadequate skills to enroll (Clowes, 1980). Others fear that participation in developmental work de-motivates college students and contributes to higher attrition rates because developmental students are stigmatized (Boylan and Bonham, 1994).

Some critics say people needing developmental skills do not really need a college education anyway. Rubenstein observed that approximately 40 percent of people with some college education and 10 percent of those with a college degree worked at jobs requiring only high school skills. In 1971, the figures were 30 percent and 6 percent, respectively. His conclusion: people with just enough education are in short supply (Rubenstein, 1998 in Merisotis and Phipps, 2000). At the same time, sustainable jobs today require some education beyond high school (Breneman and Harlow, 1998; Merisotis and Phipps, 2000). Currently 65 percent of workers need the skills of a generalist/technician, including advanced reading, writing, mathematics, critical thinking, and interpersonal group skills. Twenty years ago, it was only 15 percent (McCabe and Day, 1998). Businesses are grappling with an under-skilled workforce due to lack of education (Kozeracki , 2002).

Others have economic concerns. Some believe the existence of Developmental Studies encourages students not to put forth their best effort in high school because they can make up the work when they get to college—forcing taxpayers to pay for the same thing twice (Lazarick, 1997a) (remember, an average of 28 percent of college-prepared high school graduates need some remedial assistance in math, English, or reading). This "waste" of resources, some believe, drains from other academic priorities such as transfer, and turns colleges into overpriced high schools (Ikenberry and Stix in Davis, 1999).

Response to Criticism

Out of a $115 million national expenditure on all of higher education, approximately $2 million per year is spent on Developmental Studies (Merisotis and Phipps, 2000). This amounts to around .02 percent of the total higher education budget. From a social perspective, no matter the cost, Developmental Studies has a staggering impact on the public good. The cost of developmental education is justified if it increases the number of students who persist in college, and it does (Institute for Higher Education Policy [IHEP], 1998). This educational effort leads to multiple benefits: increased tax revenue, greater productivity, increased consumption, greater workforce flexibility, reduced crime rates, increased community service, and better quality of civic life (IHEP, 1998). Developmental education is far less costly than the alternatives, which often include unemployment, low-wage jobs, welfare participation, and incarceration (IHEP, 1998). Alexander Astin sums up the issue when he says, "Educating everyone is a whole lot less expensive, monetarily and socially and emotionally, than to carry along in society large numbers of people with minimal skills and with minimal educational development" (Astin, 2000). When we take into account the intergenerational impact of education, the effect is exponential.

Whether or not these criticisms are based in reality is still not known: data are not available around all of these issues to support or defeat the critics. However, data do support the completion and graduation of students enrolled in Developmental Studies, and do support the economic, civic, and social contributions of these college graduates who might never have completed their college education without the underpinning of Developmental Studies.

At the same time, the issues raised are certainly critical and it is fortunate they were addressed by the research cited above. However, in 1996 state legislators were surveyed and asked whether or not colleges and universities should give remedial education more attention: 34 percent believed remedial education should not receive more attention, 32 percent believed more attention should be given to remedial education, and 32 percent were neutral (Ruppert, 1996). Clearly our public educational efforts, both regarding the successes and the room for improvements, need to continue, and hopefully this chapter can be part of that education.

CHALLENGES TO THE FIELD

Although the current impact of Developmental Studies is striking and is making a crucial contribution to higher education and to society, there is room for *significant improvement*. As community colleges focus more and more on the "learning college," we need to increasingly focus on the "learning community" and the "learning world." Fifty-three percent of students enrolled in Developmental Studies still do not reach their goals. While it may be true that not all persons are able to achieve their stated goals, it is to everyone's advantage that we strive to achieve the dream of an educated community through the vehicle of community colleges. Our strategies for improvement focus on the policy level, the institutional level, and the individual classroom. These strategies grow from the multiple studies conducted during the past several years.

Policy Level Recommendations

Policy change that can integrate levels of competence is crucial in order to make Developmental Studies an increasingly effective strategy for supporting unprepared students.

- Aligning high school requirements with college content and competency expectations can assist recent high school graduates by clarifying expectations.
- Link mentoring, tutoring, and other academic advisement activities to college financial aid, with a particular emphasis on early intervention and aid programs for graduating high school seniors. Programs such as Upward Bound for every student in need could help students receive the necessary personal attention for academic success.
- High school student follow-up and high school feedback systems can link college staff with high school staff in a way that communicates expectations and develops faculty relationships for the benefit of students.
- Improved teacher preparation is crucial to increase program effectiveness. Training for 20 percent of community college faculty seems to rely too much on individual good will and not enough on factual information about the learning process.
- University involvement could expand inter-institutional work. Working on collaborative research projects, sharing best practices to develop effective and comprehensive programs at all levels of education, and cooperating to find and implement more effective programs for underprepared students are examples of potential outcomes. Cross-institutional collaboration could use technology to enhance the teaching/learning process.
- Nationally normed placement testing could occur during the junior year in high school so students identify—before they arrive in college—areas needing extra work. More developmental courses could then be done at the high school level.

Institutional Recommendations

Commitment to Developmental Studies at an institutional level is crucial. From the president, to the faculty who teach in the program, to the students, commitment and pride are important. Developmental Studies professionals operate most effectively in an environment that values their work. The value of Developmental Studies should be stated explicitly in the mission statement. Courses and services need to be highlighted in publications, and Developmental Studies needs to be seen as an integral part of the campus academic community and as part of any planning effort.

In the early years, community college leaders spoke about the right of students to attempt any level of education, often referred to as the "right to fail." Perspectives have changed since that time, with mandatory testing and placement of students in Developmental Studies programs the recommended, and common, practice. Without the intervention of Developmental Studies, too few students are retained in college, making the open door turn into a "revolving door" where students' entry is followed quickly by their exit. It is important that colleges help students understand the reality of being a college learner, including the necessity of prerequisite skills, and colleges now accept this as part of their responsibility. The National Association for Developmental Education in 1998 passed a resolution supporting institutional policies that require mandatory academic assessment of incoming students and mandatory placement of students into developmental courses, as appropriate. This resolution, discussed and passed by Developmental Studies faculty and coordinators, needs to be taken very seriously by institutions wishing to fulfill the dream of success harbored by students and faculty alike. This needs to be accomplished at the institution-wide level.

One of the facets of assessment we have not talked about extensively is that of assessing the strengths of our learners. Even though many students come to the community college with deficiencies in reading, writing, or mathematics, they also come with dazzling strengths. An important part of assessment, agreed on at the institutional level, could be assessing those strengths and using them to assist students to enroll in appropriate college-level courses where their developmental work could be a support to them. These strengths could also be used to facilitate involvement in service learning activities throughout the college and the community.

Program, Classroom, and Services Recommendations

Developmental Studies staff members need to take matters into their own hands to ensure the programs on their campuses are of the highest possible quality. Many college faculty do work hard to ensure quality, which is why we have considerable information about what works and what can improve effectiveness.

Many college faculty members ensure Developmental Studies is delivered by well-trained people. They conduct their own in-house training and make certain developmental teachers use best practice, as researched, and base their programs on student need: how students learn, knowledge of student issues, and information beyond content knowledge. In other words, the best Developmental Studies programs are student-oriented and holistic. Both cognitive and affective development occur in the classroom and through counseling, advising, and enrichment activities that draw students into the college environment.

Excellent Developmental Studies connects with the college curriculum. Exit standards for Developmental Studies are consistent with entry standards for the college and the goals and objectives are consistent with the goals of the institution. They are integrated into a seamless progression of academic standards, and they help students make the transition from one level of content to the next.

Developmental Studies needs to be well coordinated. On a regular basis, leaders can bring together the people who teach, to share problems and seek solutions. Learning Lab staff can synchronize with the teaching faculty, and advisors can communicate with developmental instructors. Everyone needs to have the same expectations of students.

Developmental Studies promotional materials need to have stated goals and objectives: what students can expect to accomplish and what the program expects from faculty, staff, and students. Critical thinking, and study skills should be found in every Developmental Studies course. Whether mainstreamed or centralized, developmental reading, writing, and math curricula should be aligned with content and skills found in college-level courses. Remedial literacy and math practices should be authentic, utilizing actual material and examples from the college curriculum, rather than drilling in skills that fragment the literacy process.

Individualized attention, supplementary tutoring, and even early-warning systems are important sources of support for academically under-prepared students.

Developmental students should be encouraged to participate in college activities, especially those related to the majors and professions to which the students aspire, to reduce their feelings of discouragement and self perceptions as academic failures.

Commonly cited elements associated with student success in developmental program lead to the following recommendations:

- Orientation, assessment, and placement are mandatory for new freshman students.
- Clearly specified goals and objectives are established for courses and programs.
- Adult learning theory is applied in the design and delivery of these courses.
- A high degree of structure is provided in these courses.
- A centralized or highly coordinated program exists.
- Counseling, tutoring, and supplemental instruction components are included.
- Attention is paid to the social and emotional development of the students.
- Regular program evaluations are conducted and findings disseminated widely.
- Graduation or certificate credit is awarded.
- Literacy activities are required across the curriculum.
- The students and the programs receive adequate financial support.
- Faculty who are eager to teach these courses are recruited and hired.
- Staff training and professional development are provided.

CONCLUSION

There are many ways to improve—nationwide—programs of Developmental Studies. Those ideas seen as best practice and outlined above could increase the success among students who require developmental support.

Developmental Studies programs provide a rich resource for community college students who are older adults, under-prepared high school graduates, recent immigrants, and workers who need advanced skills. Large numbers of would-be students are "saved" by Developmental Studies and move on to become economically and socially productive citizens, workers, and parents whose children are more likely to be college graduates.

CHAPTER 10

The Transfer Experience

OVERVIEW

Community colleges aim to fulfill the need for university preparation. Millions of students enroll in Associate degree programs to earn the freshman and sophomore years of a baccalaureate degree. We use data in this chapter to illustrate that a large number of students who begin at a disadvantaged level do transfer and succeed at four-year campuses. Who these students are, where they transfer, how their academic achievement compares with native students, and the comparative transferability of various majors are described. Faculty credentials and faculty commitment to teaching are discussed as a support to the transfer function, as are supportive statewide programs.

The reality of transfer is affected by many variables. Prior academic preparation and students' support at home, at work, and at college make a difference. Early transfer diminishes Associate degree graduation rates. Four-year schools sometimes limit transfer without academic basis. Measures of success are questioned with recommendations for appropriate and realistic standards. The challenge to the field is directed to college leaders, counselors, faculty and staff, and university colleagues.

THE DREAM

The original dream of the community college was that of transfer—the first purpose of "junior" colleges. Planners aimed to provide access to higher education for young people who might not be eligible for highly selective colleges or for those (around 75 percent of community college students) who worked full or part time and needed convenient courses close to home. The baccalaureate is an important entry point to the workforce, so seamless transfer from two-year to four-year institutions is essential.

The founding pioneers designed community colleges so people could ideally begin general education requirements and then easily transfer to the four-year college of their choice. We still dream that partnerships with universities can allow faculty to respect one another and work together for the good of students. We aspire to give greater support to caring faculty and advisors who build positive relationships with students and with colleagues in four-year universities. Some colleges aspire to process "upside down" transfer, in which students earn their professional credentials in an Associate in Science or Associate in Applied Science degree program at the community college and then earn their general education credits at the four-year university.

The ideal community college is a place where immigrants, academically disadvantaged students, and others in low socioeconomic groups can access education to move to the middle class in a way rarely possible at many four-year colleges. In this dream, transfer is central to educational access and equity. Overall, minority students comprise 31 percent of community college enrollment; 55 percent of Hispanic, Asian and Pacific Islander, and Native American students, and 46 percent of African-American students in higher education are in community colleges (Ely, 2000; Hungar and Lieberman, 2001). Our nation needs a route to middle-class status for minorities and immigrants, and transfer from an open-access community college is an important part of achieving this goal.

Since increasing the average level of schooling by even one year can increase a country's economic growth by 5 percent to 15 percent (Carnevale and Desrochers, 2003), transferring to four-year colleges can add that year or two. Consequently, the transfer role of community colleges is the one of the best business deals in higher education. It is good business for the student and family, for every business that sends their employees for upgraded skills, and taxpayers get a great return on their investment by supporting the country's economic growth.

THE UNFULFILLED DREAM

The reality of student transfer is daunting. Easy transfer can be stifled by specific and unique course requirements for each four-year degree. The biology course for a business major may be very different from the one required for a Bachelor of Arts degree, and again different for the Bachelor of Science degree. Students need strong guidance in their first semester in the community college to lead them to courses appropriate to their goal, but few faculty or staff at community colleges can pay the close attention to the future plans that students deserve because of workload and the complexity of student lives. Effective advisement is made more complex because of the multiplicity of colleges to which community college students transfer.

Many students, when they first enroll in a community college, are not sure of their goals. A student may begin by taking a biology course appropriate for an Associate in Arts degree, and then change his or her mind and decide on an accounting degree. This student will probably have to take another biology course, one that is the required science for a transfer program in accounting. There is no research suggesting one biology course is better for the accounting major and another for the literature major, yet these kinds of requirements cause four-year colleges that purport to transfer the "entire" Associate degree to place many community college courses in the "elective" category and not be counted toward the major. This results in community college graduates requiring more courses to achieve the baccalaureate than native students. Under these circumstances, helping students determine a goal early on in their education is crucial to their ability to stay in college and achieve transfer success, yet advising and counseling assistance is currently insufficient.

Advising may not happen adequately at the community college level because colleges cannot afford enough advisors to meet the need. Full-time faculty teaching loads, large class size (even though usually much smaller than university classes), and the increasing proportion of adjunct faculty make it almost impossible to undertake the personal connections students need to make good career and life decisions. In addition, students, after leaving their high schools, may decide they should be independent and self-advise. One student described this situation:

> A general idea is to not let the system give you the education—it is to seek out what's best for you and create your own education—choose the instructor that's going to suit your needs, or choose the major if that is what's important for you (Heelan, 2003).

Faculty sometimes consider student support to be a less important function than teaching and learning. Federally funded TRIO programs successfully provide essential support systems to high-risk learners, yet these programs can be marginalized by college counselors, faculty, and administrators. In addition, counseling and advising can be uneven and inaccurate.

In a study conducted by the Community College Research Center, one counselor described uneven advising:

> At the higher end, you have people who will look at as many of the variables as possible that they can cover in an hour's session to assist a student. In the middle you will see people at least doing the educational plan and exploring what that means. On the lower end, if a person wants an Associate degree it's very easy for me to get on the computer and plug in a few numbers and the computer will tell me what they need for the Associate degree. (Heelan, 2003)

Faculty in two-year and four-year colleges often do not hold one another in high regard. Four-year faculty may view community college faculty as "less than," not as well educated, or not as competent. Two-year faculty may view university faculty as not being student oriented or as more focused on research than on teaching and learning. Still other community college faculty may view the four-year school as more appropriate for the gifted learner, and they encourage these students to transfer early to the four-year school.

The "upside down" transfer is a rarity. A few specific university programs allow students with an Associate in Applied Science degree to transfer their credits and then earn their general education credits at the four-year institution. A prime example of this is the Veterinarian Program at Colorado State University, which allows all the credits for the Veterinary Technician Program at Colorado Mountain College to transfer in full.

Immigrant, ethnic minority, and low socioeconomic groups find it difficult to enroll in college. Only 36 percent of students from families in the lowest socioeconomic quartile enroll in postsecondary education, while more than 88 percent of students from the highest socioeconomic quartile do so (Boswell, 2004). This small percentage of students representing immigrant, ethnic minority, and other low socioeconomic groups who find it difficult to enroll in a community college find it equally difficult to transfer. This small percentage is further affected by the elimination of affirmative action policies at universities (Hungar and Lieberman, 2001). Affirmative action often made it possible for members of these groups to transfer to universities based on their potential for success as learners.

The complexities of applying for student aid, the shrinking financial aid pool, the increasing dependence on loans, and the ever-increasing cost of education make the financial aspects of transfer education more and more expensive and less accessible. Most four-year campuses place their emphasis on enrolling freshman, and therefore spend the bulk of their private scholarship money on new students. Few save resources for transfer students. Many campuses, especially the more selective campuses, do not even advertise the availability of transfer opportunities, and those that provide the option often acknowledge it is amorphous, with few clear guidelines for students to assess accurately their likelihood of being accepted.

Both the dream and the reality regarding transfer are documented in the rest of this chapter. There are serious challenges ahead to strengthen student transfer success.

THE REAL STORY

Definition of Transfer

Transfer can be described in many ways and definitions can be confusing. A common definition of transfer is a student who initially enrolls at a community college and subsequently enrolls at any four-year institution within a five-year period of study (Bradburn et al., 2001). This definition is clear, and has the added advantage of following some assumptions about transfer. The problem with this definition is that it leaves out almost as many students who transfer as it defines. Transfer has become a non-linear function. Where it formerly had a single beginning at a community college and a single ending at a four-year college, it now is iterative and cyclic (Adelman, 1999). The mobility of students creates a situation in which students begin and end at multiple points, sometimes even securing a degree. Some patterns include students who start at a four-year college, transfer to a community college, and transfer back to the same or a different four-year college. Students transfer among community colleges, return to community colleges intermittently throughout a four-year college degree program, or take courses simultaneously at both two-and four-year colleges. This mobility makes educational planning and advisement exponentially more difficult, and muddies the potential clarity of transfer support programs because of the many different kinds of students who are potentially eligible.

The students who are most successful in transferring from two- to four-year schools have similar attributes to those who are successful in four-year institutions: they have rigorous academic preparation in high school, they enroll full time, and they do not take time off en route to the degree (Wellman, 2002). These students are fully prepared for four-year study and succeed at a very high rate (Wellman, 2002). However, this group of students represents a very small proportion of community colleges enrollees who indicate a wish to transfer and then actually do transfer.

A "potential transfer" is more loosely defined and involves being eligible for transfer or at risk of not transferring. This definition includes *all* first-time, beginning community college students, although typically students taking solely development courses for which they receive no credit are excluded from the sample. For example, 71 percent of all beginning community college students responded that they anticipated earning a Bachelor's degree or higher when asked, "What is the highest level of education you *ever* expect to complete?"(emphasis added, Bradburn et al., 2001). However, if they did *not* enroll in an academic program, enroll continuously, or take courses toward a specific Bachelor's degree, the *actual* transfer rate and Bachelor's degree completion in five years was 36 percent (Bradburn et al., 2001).

"Swirling" through the system is a phenomenon that describes nearly 60 percent of undergraduates. Swirlers do not follow the linear pattern of attending a community college and then a four-year college. Swirlers may attend more than one community college, then more than one baccalaureate institution. As a matter of fact, recent American Association of Community College research finds 50 percent of the nation's baccalaureate recipients have taken courses at community colleges (McFee, 2007). Some swirlers attend a four-year college and then go to community college during their educational career (Adelman, 1999). Since only 40 percent of swirlers actually complete a degree, institutional-level measures of graduation or transfer rates are not very meaningful. Blaming one college for these low graduation rates is not really justified when students make choices to attend two or more institutions and do not graduate from any one of them. When determining transfer in the future, it may be more useful to follow students as they swirl rather than to follow institutions (Adelman, 1999).

Who Is a Transfer Student?

The students who actually succeed at transfer are often different from those who enroll in community college transfer programs. Students who say they want to transfer are in fact a very mixed group, including working parents, recent high school graduates, immigrants, low socioeconomic-level students, adults who have been out of college for decades, as well as bright and competent economically secure people. They all seek their first two years of general education at a community college.

Two-year students are on average 29 years old and enroll for fewer than 12 credits a semester (62 percent enroll part time) and they work full time

(AACC, 2006). Of those who are students full time, 30 percent also work full time (AACC, 2006). Four-year students, on the other hand, are on average younger, at 21 years old, and 79 percent are full-time students, with 55 percent who enroll full time working part time (AACC, 2006).

Community college students represent 55 percent of all Hispanic students enrolled in higher education (35.1 percent are at public four-year schools) and 47 percent of all black undergraduates (31.4 percent are enrolled in four-year schools) (AACC, 2006; Integrated Postsecondary Education Data System, 2006).

Thus the profile of a two-year student intending to transfer to a four-year institution describes the students who are least likely to succeed in college and to transfer: older, part-time students who work full time, come from a lower socioeconomic group, are raising a family, and who are African American or Hispanic. This is the enormous challenge of transfer from the community college: to redress potentially years of inadequate academic preparation for students confident and skilled enough to succeed in rigorous transfer-appropriate credit courses at the community college and beyond.

Predictors of Transfer Success

Twenty-six percent of students who begin their undergraduate careers in community colleges formally transfer to four-year institutions, and their Bachelor's degree completion rate is higher than 70 percent (Adelman, 1999). These percentages have been stable for 20 years, with a fluctuation rate of 1 percent or so (Hungar and Lieberman, 2001). Between 54 and 58 percent of traditional-age students who started in a four-year college earned the Bachelor's degree within six years (Adelman, 2006). Thus the difference in completion between "native" four-year college students, who it must be remembered were selected based upon grade and test score criteria, and the community college students who were given access to college based upon high school completion are actually skewed in the community college favor for those students who do transfer. The problem, of course, is the almost 75 percent of students who do not transfer.

The students most successful at transferring to the university are those who are enrolled in a rigorous academic program in high school, are enrolled in a college academic program, and are carefully advised regarding specific courses to take for a specific baccalaureate degree. Transfer rates are higher among students who are full-time students from a high socioeconomic group, and are native born Caucasians from a metropolitan area (McCormick and Carrol, 1997). At the same time, many community college transfer students do not match these characteristics, but nonetheless successfully transfer.

Using the traditional definition of transfer (beginning at a community college and transferring to a four-year college) the rate of transfer is highest among those students who were pursuing an academic major *and* taking courses applicable toward a Bachelor's degree (Bradburn et al., 2001). This is typically a very small group, hovering around 11 percent of all community college students (Bradburn et al., 2001). In other words, the actual percentage of students who say they want to transfer is quite different from the percentage of those who undertake the kind of academic program that allows for effective transfer. When students indicate an interest in a Bachelor's degree, they seldom understand the academic issues that must be factored into their enrollment strategy.

Full-time enrollment makes a big difference in student transfer success. Students who enrolled full time in their first year were about twice as likely as those who enrolled part time to transfer to a four-year institution within five years, with 50 percent of full-time students transferring, compared with 26 percent of part-timers (McCormick and Carrol, 1997). Transfer success is also associated with higher socioeconomic status—as are virtually all educational success outcome statistics (Bradburn et al., 2001). Adolescents from lower socioeconomic groups are only half as likely to even aspire to a college degree than those in the upper class, regardless of community size (Nelson, 1972).

Early transfer is prevalent, with 65 percent of students transferring without a credential (McCormick and Carrol, 1997). Seventy percent of students who transferred to a four-year college persisted to degree completion, which is higher than the average 60 percent rate among students who began at four-year institutions (McCormick and Carrol, 1997).

The classic form of transfer, in which a student earns at least a semester's worth of credits before moving to the four-year college, produces a very high likelihood of Bachelor's degree completion and is an extremely effective route to Bachelor's degree (Adelman, 1999). However, transfer works better for students who complete their Associate in Arts or Associate in Science degrees at the community college. Forty-three percent of Associate degree completers had received a Bachelor's degree in five years, compared with 17 percent of those who transferred without any credential (McCormick and Carrol, 1997).

In other words, early transfer does matter. For many students, completion of the Associate degree predicts greater success at the university. Unfortunately, at least one study found that faculty members and students at both the community college and the university influence the number of credit hours students completed before transfer (Cejda and Kaylor, 2001). Faculty (in 48 percent of the interviews) in community colleges influenced students to transfer earlier than they intended (Cejda and Kaylor, 2001). We can only presume faculty assume that students who transfer early benefit by being surrounded by people who are enrolled full time, have a rigorous academic preparation, and in general have the traditional predictors of success. It is critical that faculty understand that the data contradict these assumptions, and that there is a significant "completion effect" which is positively correlated with baccalaureate achievement.

Age is negatively associated with effective transfer. The older the age group, the lower the student transfer rate (Bradburn et al., 2001). This information must be analyzed further, however, because the older the student the more likely it is that educational goals, especially related to skill building or job change, are accomplished at the community college.

Ethnic Minority Group Transfer Success

More than 75 percent of foreign-born students who enter two-year colleges say they aspire to at least a Bachelor's degree. However, eight years after enrolling, only 20 percent have begun a Bachelor's program (Bailey and Weininger, 2002). Foreign-born students who attend high school in a foreign country are more likely to earn a Bachelor's degree (42 percent) than those who graduate from an American high school (35 percent) (Bailey and Weininger, 2002). Many variables, including socioeconomic class, rigor of high school, as well as financial aid and immigration policies, affect this statistic.

There are differences associated with the correlation of transfer rates and race/ethnicity which are important to acknowledge, understand, and monitor. Latino and African-American students who say they intend to transfer have lower transfer rates over a six-year period than other students, even when socioeconomic status and academic preparation were statistically controlled (Wassmer, Moore, and Shulock, 2004).

Some information available regarding minority enrollment in transfer programs comes from specific states. For example, 35 of every 100 Latino high school graduates enrolling in California higher education began their careers in a California community college. An average of 3 Latina/o students of this 100 transferred to California four-year colleges (Ornelas and Solorzano, 2004). In North Carolina, 30 percent of transfer students graduated from technical programs and 70 percent from college transfer programs (Fredrickson, 1998).

Although both groups were academically successful, technical program students earned slightly higher grades at the university level and students from the college transfer track had higher persistence rates (Fredrickson, 1998).

In New York City, 48 percent of the entering freshman class was born abroad, with foreign-born students enrolled in four-year colleges at about the same rate they enrolled in two-year colleges (Bailey and Weininger, 2002). In seven years, the foreign-born share of the entering cohort rose by 15 percentage points, or 45 percent (Bailey and Weininger, 2002).

Longitudinal data illustrate factors that postsecondary institutions can implement to positively affect small populations in which minority students are over-represented. Transfer success is enhanced when community college students end their first year with 20 or more credits (Adelman, 2006). Policies and advising, which drastically reduce "no-penalty" withdrawals and "no-credit" repeat of courses, are correlated with increasing transfer rates (Adelman, 2006). Helping students maintain full-time status, including summer enrollment opportunities, is connected to increasing rates of transfer, as are credit-bearing internships (Adelman, 2006).

Supporting these students as they struggle to complete their education is a Herculean task. While the transfer rate must be improved, honoring the dedicated faculty, counselors, and staff who work with students who face so many challenges is a crucial aspect of understanding community colleges.

Geographic Location and Transfer Success

Interestingly, several studies suggest there are differences between students who go to school in different geographic locations, although one study found none (Castaneda, 2002). The differences in rates of transfer among various geographical areas are made more complex by the lack of definitional agreement, with three federal government departments alone having six different definitions (Castaneda, 2002). Nevertheless, it is valuable to know that rural students are less likely than suburban or urban students to attend or even to aspire to attend college, let alone to transfer to a four-year school (Castaneda, 2002; Nelson, 1971).

Some findings about rural and metro transfer rates are in conflict with one another. One study reports students at rural community colleges are more likely to graduate (McHewitt, 1993) and another found that rural students are more likely to drop out (Castaneda, 2002). However, there seems to be agreement that non-metro African Americans lag behind both metro African Americans and metro and non-metro whites (Castaneda, 2002). Suburban African-American men and women were twice as likely to complete Bachelor's degrees as their non-metro counterparts (Castaneda, 2002). Non-metro Hispanics also lagged behind their metro counterparts, and both metro and non-metro whites, in four-year college completion (Castaneda, 2002).

BARRIERS TO THE TRANSFER PROCESS

The literature suggests that transfer problems for students really occur at the community college before they transfer to the university. Boswell, in her 2004 publication, points out that, once community college students successfully transfer to a four-year institution, they graduate at the same rate as students who begin at four-year colleges, and they obtain equal job status and earning capacity to those students who started at and graduated from four-year institutions. Problems preventing successful completion of the Bachelor's degree usually arise prior to transfer or during the transfer process (Boswell, 2004). There is strong motivation for community colleges to support the success of those students who indicate a desire to transfer, and there is strong motivation to encourage students to complete their Associate degree. What is it about community colleges that inhibits completion of the transfer degree?

The above discussion makes clear that any assessment of barriers to transfer begins with student demographics, since most community college students do not have the characteristics identified in the research as being positively associated with transfer. Thus, the fact that community college students intending to transfer, or completing transfer, are older than university students, more likely to be part time, more likely to have full-time jobs and/or be parents, is associated with lower rates of success. The speculation is that there are simply many other things in a community college student's life besides college to demand their attention. In addition, the majority of racial and ethnic minority students who go to college enroll in community colleges. Therefore the very aspects of the community college that are inviting to minority students—colleges close to home, ability to work and study, ability to attend night and weekend classes, and developmental classes that support poor skills—may attract students who will have the hardest time transferring.

Differing institutional missions between community colleges and universities are also a source of problems. Faculty attitudes, scarce advising, and fewer sources of financial support, coupled with the lack of systemic and statewide policy making, all have a negative impact on students' ability to transfer. The supportive, open-door, second-chance culture of a community college exists simultaneously with the rigor of any other academic institution, while a university culture may have fewer supportive functions and systems. Universities have increasingly limited slots for transfer students due to budget cuts and unfunded enrollment. In addition, some community college courses (not initially intended for transfer) tend to focus on applied practical learning and skill building rather than mimicking the research-oriented curricula at a traditional university. Occupational courses are especially difficult to articulate with related programs at the university. Sometimes when courses do transfer into the university, university departments do not accept the credits toward the academic major. This issue perhaps requires greater observation and analysis. Is there evidence, for example, that one science course is truly better for any given department major than another science course? Do students really perform better in their majors when their general education courses follow a particular pattern, one that is different for each major?

Parochial views of a specific institution's courses and credentials can make collaboration difficult. This can include concern about a lack of rigor, defensiveness, and turf arguments. For example, can students be taking a veterinarian course taught in the junior year at a four-year school during their sophomore year at the community college? Can community college accounting students take a second-year accounting course before taking calculus, even though the four-year sequence requires calculus first, although there is no actual calculus in the second-year accounting course? We have each seen these battles between faculty at community colleges and receiving four-year institutions waged with great heat, but almost no light. To our knowledge, there is almost never a study conducted to determine if students who take specified classes in different sequences, or slightly different general education courses, do any worse or better at a four-year college. Yet the rigidity of course requirements can be discouraging not only to potential students who wish to transfer, but also to faculty interaction. These attitudes can make it difficult for faculty from two- and four-year institutions to collaborate and come to an agreement on a core curriculum or on the transferability of courses. Fewer full-time faculty members at community colleges translate into fewer people to serve on articulation committees with university faculty, or to serve as mentors to transfer students.

Difficulties with Transfer Support Services

Since success at the community college is so crucial to transfer success, specific details about student support at the community college may be useful here. Students rarely receive information about the importance of accurate information about the process or demands of transfer, whether from a committed faculty member or a more formal transfer advisor. Too often, transfer advisement is at best a self-directed activity, and frequently occurs after several semesters in which students have been taking classes which may or may not transfer. Sometimes students know there are transfer services available only if they happen to read the printed or online catalogue. One study found that many students don't even understand the difference between the catalogue and the class schedule (Heelan, 2003). Even the nomenclature is confusing—with students aware that they want to eventually attend a four-year college, but not knowing that academics refer to this process as "transfer" or "transfer articulation." So there are students who have never obtained transfer information unless a professor tells them they need to see a counselor.

Furthermore, in a setting where establishing a goal and declaring a major are crucial, most students begin their freshman year as undeclared or liberal arts majors as a default for not really knowing what degree will take them where they want to go. In other words, they are not making an informed choice. Therefore, the often small amounts of transfer or academic advisement offered by community colleges can be inappropriate for the program in which the student is potentially, or even vaguely, interested. And, given the daunting prospect of understanding the complex requirements for multiple colleges and dozens of majors, the quality of transfer advising and information is uneven across a given college (Heelan, 2003).

Most four-year campuses do not have coherent transfer policies. While individual colleges often outline articulation agreements with certain feeder community colleges within specific programs, too many transfer agreements simply try to do a one-for-one course exchange. If a community college doesn't have the exact course (and even more flagrantly sometimes when they do), a receiving college will transfer the course as an elective credit. This means that the credit will be transferred, but generally will not move a student closer to the baccalaureate degree. Compounding the problem is that course-by-course equivalency evaluations are conducted at a departmental level by faculty or chairs who have rarely been trained in the process, and whose basis for making a decision is a single paragraph description in a course catalog. Anecdotal evidence abounds of faculty transferring a community college's two-semester, six-credit sequence in mathematics, science, or accounting as equivalent to the first three-credit course at the four-year college. The decision appears to be based upon four-year faculty assumptions about the lack of quality at community colleges. Virtually never are the decisions based upon any data that review student progress (Mellow, 1998). There are cases in which the scant personal evidence of a single student who did not perform well in one faculty member's class determined a course decision (Mellow, 1998).

Inconsistent state-level coordination of public postsecondary institutions results in inconsistent policies and practices. Lack of alignment between high school graduation standards and college entrance requirements causes new freshmen students to be unprepared for college-level work. Different placement tests at different institutions and dissimilar cut-off scores and placement standards are confusing to students and to faculty and staff as well. Inadequate data systems to track students across K-16 make it difficult to provide timely feedback, and cumbersome financial aid rules and requirements impede student transfer—especially troublesome is merit-based rather than need-based financial aid. All these barriers represent significant blocks to students attempting to transfer from two-year to four-year colleges.

ACTIVITIES TO OVERCOME TRANSFER BARRIERS

There are many activities initiated by community colleges and universities that stimulate and help ensure student success at transfer. The National Academic Advising Association has articulated a set of premises that would enhance transfer advising. They include the precepts that advisement should be focused on teaching and learning, done in a collaborative manner, be embedded in an effort to help students create an overall life plan, and be iterative, i.e., an approach that provides students with different kinds of advisement at different times in their academic careers (Gordon and Habley, 2000). These principles lead to activities that ensure transfer advisement is not a mechanical process of just securing course or program articulation, but rather an opportunity to help students further develop goals, academic standards, and life plans to expand their educational horizons.

These values are often best expressed in one-on-one and fairly extensive communication with a student within a relationship that extends over the course of a student's college career. However, since long-term, one-on-one relationships with academic advisors can be a rare occurrence at a community college, it is also important to ground all advisement in these protocols, whether the advisement is administered by peers or professionals, in person or electronically. While these values and beliefs form a thread throughout some of the literature about student support, they unfortunately do not form a consistent thread in practice and thus the support process unravels (Heelan, 2003). There are, at the same time, many examples of community college and four-year college partnerships that provide exemplary models of good practice.

Faculty Involvement

The single most important variable in the academic success of community college students is faculty expertise in teaching and learning. When this is coupled, as it so often is among community college faculty, with a sincere enthusiasm for making a difference in students' lives, the transformative capability of education is realized. This is most powerful when an institution creates a culture, reward system, and administrative infrastructure to nurture and celebrate great teaching (Heelan, 2003). It occurs at every community college where individual, committed faculty make a difference for students (Heelan, 2003).

> When I have a chance to talk to [students], I try to put the idea in their head that they better start thinking about what they're going to do, and what school they want to go to. And a lot of times, that's a revelation for them. Nobody told them that they should do some homework. They just think 'oh', maybe the second year, all of a sudden they're going to just go off to some school. I don't think they're even aware they need to apply and find out what the requirements are. From the very first moment I see them, I ask them where they're going to go and what they're going to do. (Heelan, 2003)

There are many academic practices that ensure that students focus on completing the Associate degree and transfer to the baccalaureate, including the consistent use of original documents in teaching (Reitano, 2003); the inclusion of multiple and intensive writing projects through courses in all disciplines (Gross, 2002); the inclusion of original student research in the curriculum (Wu, 2004); and a clear emphasis on critical thinking (Chaffee, 2006b).

Explicit faculty focus in class, and informally with students, is another important way to encourage degree completion and transfer. Actions as simple as bringing one's academic regalia to class and explaining the meaning of the doctoral hood, and telling students not to limit their transfer applications to local and "safe" colleges, all work to build students' knowledge of transfer (Macheski, 2002; Zaritsky, 2001). Faculty interest in transfer is also inspirational to students and helps students face the multiple hurdles that might prevent a less motivated student from completing the necessary processes to transfer successfully.

Without engaged faculty, preparing for transfer can seem like a different world. One community college student said, after coming back from an intensive summer program at an elite college, "Sometimes the community college is like the 'hood.' It's what you know, where you hang. But there is another door to another world, but students don't know how to ask about it. Faculty have to tell them" (Davis, 2005).

Faculty members influence student decision making, and some create their own private enticement for student success. "I know there are some instructors...maybe some English instructors...if the paper is not up to par they'll say, 'You have to go to tutoring; I'll give you some extra credit if you're in tutoring'" (Heelan, 2003).

The faculty and other staff members across institutions who function in this manner have a positive effect on those students who wander through their colleges with vague goals and uninformed choices.

Transfer Models

At the suggestion and provocation of LaGuardia Community College, Vassar College developed a program called Exploring Transfer. Since 1985 this Ford Foundation-supported program has been a "mini-residential college" experience, selecting community college students with no intention of Ivy League transfer to live on the Vassar campus for five weeks and attend a rigorous liberal arts or science-based academic program. Students earn Vassar credit for six credits of coursework, team-taught by a community college and a Vassar faculty member. During the first ten years of the program, 64 percent of the students went on to four-year schools, with several achieving graduate degrees (Lieberman, 1998). This model is replicated at five other elite liberal arts colleges (Lieberman, 1998). Santa Ana College and the University of California at Irvine have a similar program, achieving similar results to the Vassar model. Success is attributed to intensive faculty involvement, high academic quality and expectations, a residential experience on a prestigious four-year campus, strong academic support, and peer counseling (Lieberman and Hungar, 1998).

Santa Monica College in California focused on counseling to support its transfer effort by combining the transfer and counseling centers. The large counseling staff includes transfer experts who provide intensive orientation, sophisticated tracking efforts, and University of California application workshops (Leovy, 1999). The results are strong. black and Hispanic students made up 20 percent of the total transfers in the fall of 1997, with 517 Santa Monica students transferring to the University of California campuses, compared with 383 for the next highest transfer institution (Information Digest, 1999). Other community colleges create effective transfer paths by exchanging support staff, with the Maricopa Community College system welcoming staff from the University of Arizona on their campus to be a direct link for student transfer, and vice versa.

Another model for transfer is the creation of student cohort groups that visit highly selective colleges and honors programs that emphasize challenging coursework, independent research, and public presentation. Rockland Community College in New York, through the combination of its honors program and Beacon Program (an annual academic conference during which students from several different community colleges are competitively selected to make presentations of their scholarship), has had high rates of success in helping students transfer to selective colleges (Kahn, 2006).

Creative energy to support transfer is expressed in many ways. Technology can provide a powerful new tool for community colleges interested in transfer. Virtual interest groups that combine students, peer mentors who are almost ready to graduate, alumni who have transferred, and a faculty monitor have facilitated transfer by creating a robust and honest online dialogue among students who are interested in transferring within the same major (Arcario, 2003). The City College of San Francisco spearheaded a national transfer focus on Historically Black Colleges and Universities (HBCUs) and community colleges by creating the National Articulation and Transfer Network, and used virtual tours and related activities to link students and colleges across the country (Roach, 2001). Faculty took bus-loads of students to several HBCUs to further encourage transfer (White, 2006). The National Coalition of Cooperative Education provides scholarships to encourage transfer between co-op community colleges and co-op four-year colleges (Stonley, 2007).

Advisement Systems

Supporting academic success among students intending to transfer (or simply to graduate within a transfer-oriented program) is often keyed to individual academic tutoring and advising. Programs are typically specialized for academically under-prepared, ethnic minority students, or persons with disabilities. Programs focus on such elements as academic goal development, study skills, time management, and best strategies for learning in an academic environment. Personal counseling is also offered by many colleges as a service to all students (Cooney, 2000; Gordon, 2000; *Transfer Enhancement Plan*, 1998; Walsh, 2000*)*. Parental involvement is a particularly significant factor in the success of underrepresented groups (Gordon, 2000).

In addition to counseling centers with advising in various departments, there are, at several institutions, special forms of support for special groups. Some have federally sponsored TRIO programs that intensify advising, counseling, tutoring, and other student support services, with resulting improved retention rates. At Colorado Mountain College, high-risk students enrolled in the TRIO program had a combined transfer and graduation rate of 88 percent, compared with 37 percent retention and graduation of all other students (Bowen, 2000). These programs incorporate several key aspects: the declaration of a major at the time of enrollment, intrusive transfer advising that helps students enroll in the specific courses required for a specific major at a specific four-year institution, information about and field trips to specific transfer institutions, student support groups around individual career fields, and trips to conferences and offices related to students' chosen major (Cooney, 2000; Heelan, 2003; *Transfer Enhancement Plan*, 1998; Walsh, 2000). Other related services to support the transfer function include special centers serving ethnic minority students, women, or students who have disabilities. Services to special populations frequently use federal grants to enable them to spend, on average, an additional $1,000 per student to achieve higher graduation and transfer rates (Heelan, 2003).

Salt Lake Community College is an example of an institution that has made transfer the responsibility of everyone on campus: "All faculty are aware of the importance of student-instructor contact in student learning and development. Classroom satisfaction must start with competent, caring faculty who believe their mission is to reach individual students and have a positive impact on their lives" (Cooney, 2000). Other campuses use a similar orientation. One college created "Tutorial Tuesdays," when faculty and staff went to the college center to be present and provide whatever assistance students needed (Heelan, 2003). One student commented about "Tutorial Tuesdays":

Student: "I find it helpful. I have gone down before just like for proof-reading research papers—to give them one final look over and they're helpful."

INTERVIEWER: "Can you request a certain person?"
STUDENT: "There are a lot of people around, but if you look like you need help they just come over to you and help"(Heelan, 2003).

Here, the model, under the leadership of the president, is to make student success everyone's business. There is an early warning system for students, whereby faculty members send out an alert when a student is in trouble, which then automatically triggers a letter to that student (Heelan, 2003). Minority faculty members serve as mentors to minority students who are part of a special program, where they serve as role models and an access point for other support for students (Heelan, 2003).

In increasing numbers of institutions, mandatory advising is being explored to positively influence transfer success. When students have a problem or *are* a problem, they are directed to advising. Students with developmental needs are often directed to advising. Full-time students are required to have an advisor's signature or to attend an orientation (Heelan, 2003).

STATE AND NATIONAL TRANSFER ACTIVITIES

United States senators have begun to listen to constituent complaints about transfer problems, and some legislators now consider transfer policies more important than ever. There has been some action at the federal level to ensure college students' ability to transfer from one institution to another without unfairly losing credit for quality courses they have completed (Strout, 2006). Some senators have inserted provisions into legislation requiring colleges to publicly disclose their transfer policies, to restrict their use of accrediting agencies to determine whether to award credits, and to report on how many credits they award (Strout, 2006). While this interest is largely focused on for-profit transfer, and while many community college leaders view this kind of legislative mandate as a bureaucratic nightmare, it is significant that national leaders are concerned about some of the arbitrary standards used by institutions to accept only certain courses for transfer (Burd, 2005).

State Attempts to Ease Transfer from Two-Year to Four-Year Institutions

As discussed by Wellman in her 2002 publication, many states pay a good deal of attention to the academic policy aspects of transfer, such as core curriculum, articulation agreements, credit transfer, and statewide transfer guides which often include Web-based catalogues (Wellman, 2002). States with a statewide governance structure have higher transfer rates than other states, and they do a better job of using data as a tool to improve transfer (Wellman, 2002). For example, some states publish statewide comparison data so that students can determine which colleges provide the best transfer access (Wellman, 2002).

State-level accountability measures, however, tend to focus on two-year college transfer performance instead of also looking at the responsibilities of the four-year institutions. In several states, accountability mechanisms require five-year retention and graduation rates. Since community college students rarely complete the baccalaureate degree in five years, the measure discourages four-year institutions from serving transfer students (Wellman, 2002).

The variety of state-level initiatives to encourage community college completion and transfer are reflected in some of the following state-level examples. In Wisconsin, K-12, vocational-technical colleges, and the university system have come together to examine their different standards and identify gaps and inconsistencies that serve as barriers. The State of Minnesota charged Metropolitan State University (MSU) with supporting and assessing the formal education experience of Minnesota students, as represented in transcripts, experiential learning, etc. MSU aggregates the credits, advises students about their options for attaining a baccalaureate, develops degree plans, and offers and prescribes courses (AACC, 2004b).

Illinois identifies common curriculum requirements across associate and baccalaureate programs and across institutions in order to facilitate student transfer. All 60 public postsecondary institutions participate (AACC, 2004b). Seven states require a common course numbering system for all public institutions of higher education. All English 101 classes, for example, are the same and any college can transfer those credits (Boswell, 2004).

State Policies that Support the Transition from K-12 to Higher Education

Another important movement is the partnership growing between K-12 and the higher education community. Considering the high success rate of transfer students who have a rigorous academic high school preparation, this is a very important trend.

The Arkansas legislature created a series of directives supporting increased education attainment and alignment. Colleges and universities are directed to work with the public schools to organize information sessions about postsecondary options for seventh graders and parents. Conferences are scheduled with students and parents to define education objectives and develop a course of study for students in grades 8-12.

The Nebraska commissioner of education sends out an annual letter to all eighth graders listing requirements for college readiness. Washington State created the Running Start program, which permits high school juniors and seniors to enroll in challenging college-level courses at community college campuses at minimal cost.

Utah's New Century scholarship program pays 75 percent of a high school student's college tuition for two years of upper-division work at any public college or university in the state, if the student earns the equivalent of an Associate degree through dual or concurrent enrollment by September 1 of the year of high school graduation. Maryland passed legislation requiring improved information to local school systems concerning student performance at the college level. The Student Outcome and Achievement Report (SOAR) tracks student outcomes at the state level and helps local educators evaluate high school preparatory programs.

All of these attempts to lower the barriers for transfer students are exemplary. If broadly implemented on a national basis, they would fulfill many of our recommendations for creating a culture truly conducive to transfer education.

CHALLENGES TO THE FIELD

In addition to the excellent examples of transfer support programs already in existence, we submit these recommendations for actions that could increase the likelihood of success for community college students who say they want to transfer to four-year colleges and universities. Some recommendations are from the literature about transfer and some are our own conclusions based on our understanding of the problems community colleges face.

1. Recommendations addressing the differences in students between the community college and transfer institutions:
   - Enhance counseling, target advising services, use well-trained faculty advisors.
   - Create coordinated studies programs.
   - Increase sensitivity to older and multicultural students.

2. Recommendations addressing differences in institutional missions and capacities:
   - Provide clear and timely communication of changes in requirements.
   - Create strong and clear articulation agreements between institutions.

- Have course evaluation done by a centralized, faculty-led entity to eliminate ad hoc transfer decisions.
- Use dual admission and common course numbering to optimize the number of credits accepted in transfer.
- Encourage community college students to complete the Associate degree before transfer.
- Increase scholarships set aside for transfer students.
- Experiment with new approaches to the baccalaureate such as "upside down" transfer degrees, where students complete general education requirements at the baccalaureate institution after having completed an Associate in Applied Science degree that contains many junior-level courses.
- Provide accurate and timely information to students regarding transfer information, with emphasis on Web-based information to focus students' attention on transfer.
- Create financial incentives by guaranteeing admission at the four-year institution and by discounting tuition for community college students who complete the Associate degree before transfer.

3. Recommendations addressing faculty biases:
   - Inform both university and community college faculty of the higher transfer rate and success rate of students who complete the Associate degree.
   - Encourage ongoing relationships among university and community college faculty who support mutual exploration around their discipline areas to build respect.
   - Encourage analysis of university department curricula and student success based on their completion of particular general education courses.

4. Recommendations for addressing a lack of student support:
   - Require each student intending to transfer to declare a major.
   - Ensure that postsecondary students end their first year with 20 or more credits.
   - Create policy and advising support to drastically reduce no-penalty withdrawals and no-credit repeat of courses.
   - Increase high-demand courses in summer terms, offer credit-bearing internships in the summer, and offer other creative initiatives.
   - Create social and co-curricular activities that foster student goal clarity.

- Create clubs among students with common transfer majors and encourage visits to professionals in their field.
- Provide specific transfer advisors who work at both the community college and the transfer institution.
- Organize visits to four-year institutions selected by students.
- Provide assistance in filling out transfer institution application and financial forms.
- Model transfer activities after the federally funded TRIO programs for at-risk learners such as first-generation college students, low-income students, and students with disabilities. Attempt to replicate common TRIO program success of 62 percent participation in college after three years by reinforcing the role of support services in student retention, including tutoring, advising, and counseling.
- Continue to research the cultural and economic issues that limit African-American and Latino student transfer success to help craft effective solutions to minimize racial/ethnic disparities in transfer.

5. Recommendations for addressing state and policy issues. The Institute for Higher Education Policy and the American Association of Community Colleges and Association of American Colleges &Universities project suggest key recommendations addressing state policy:
   - Develop baseline information about statewide transfer performance.
   - Clarify state policy and plans for transfer, and set goals and measures for performance.
   - Identify and invest in core resources for transfer at the institutional level.
   - Perform statewide transfer policy audits to ensure that policies are consistent and that performance measures do not inadvertently discourage transfer.
   - Make sure articulation and credit transfer agreements are in place.
   - Focus state policy change on low-performing institutions.
   - Use financial aid as a tool to promote transfer.
   - Include private institutions in transfer planning and performance accountability.
   - Encourage joint admissions at two- and four-year colleges and dual financial aid programs to increase the number of students completing the baccalaureate.
   - Mandate student assessment and placement of students needing developmental work; establish consistent cut-off scores among institutions.

- Create structures to facilitate ongoing communication among all stakeholders regarding advising and transfer issues.
- Encourage accrediting bodies to promote transfer and access to the baccalaureate.
- Track retention, transfer, and successful completion rates and share the information among institutions.
- Allocate sufficient resources, both fiscal and human, to adequately address the growing population of transfer students. State funding for higher education must support foreseeable demands for access to an undergraduate education.

CONCLUSION

Students wishing to transfer to four-year institutions present colossal challenges to the community colleges desiring to support them in their educational careers and in the transfer process. Characteristics of most transfer students are those whose life experiences present barriers that make them the *least* likely to succeed in the transfer process. In addition to the barriers presented by students themselves, states and institutional policies as well as faculty attitudes hurl even more difficulties at potential transfer students.

These recommendations for institutional, state, and local action could increase the likelihood of success for all potential transfer students, whether they are foreign born, low income, Hispanic, African American, from low-socioeconomic groups, or attend college part time and/or have full-time jobs. If implemented, these recommendations could transform the transfer culture at community colleges and the success of the transfer dream.

Economic and Workforce Development

"Community colleges are the pivotal player in America's competitiveness. The nation's more than 1,100 community colleges and technical schools are a resource for job seekers, current employees, and business and industry leaders. Higher levels of education and training will continue to provide one of the best opportunities for the nearly 36 million Americans living in poverty to achieve economic well-being. Others will use community colleges to obtain additional skills to retain or improve their employment status. Accessing these opportunities will be key to competing for the 21 million new jobs that the Department of Labor projects will be created during the 2002-20012 period."

—DAVID D. BELLIS, Director, Education, Workforce and
Income Security Issues, U.S. General Accounting Office.

THE DREAM

Community colleges are a mainstay for American economic development, and the dream is to continue their flexible responsiveness to keep the country competitive in the coming decades. Staying connected to advances in the workplace, building bridges to business and industry, and providing training to meet workforce needs combine in a unique way at community colleges. The educational opportunities create positive changes in income for individual students/workers, for individual companies, and often for the colleges themselves.

Ideally, community colleges hire a group of faculty in occupational and paraprofessional programs who are strongly connected to their fields and maintain active links to business and industry. As members of local, regional, national, or even international economic communities, community colleges can provide excellent education for existing careers and target emerging fields to build cadres of new employees.

The dream is for community colleges' educational offerings to be capable of opening a door to every occupation, regardless of a student's starting point. The best occupational offerings create serial skills ladders—open-ended at the bottom of the scale but with a trajectory enabling students to reach the highest levels of a profession. The ideal programs start with effective assessment of incoming students so that they are accurately placed into programs. Preferably, the sequence of courses allows students to enter anywhere along a continuum that begins with very basic skills (often starting with non-credit training programs) and creates attainable steps up an educational ladder that advance students' skills, educational attainment, and eventually income. The best programs lead to well-paid work because they are tightly linked to the current practices in the field as well as to a specific local labor market. An ideal program includes internships to ensure what John Dewey would term experiential education, where "education [is] conceived as a continuing reconstruction of experience" (Dworkin, 1959, p. 27). Programs with internships also give students an entrée into specific business sectors, an especially important benefit for first-generation students.

The dream is to provide high-quality vocational programs as colleges maintain external accreditations for all employment-related programs. These up-to-date programs reflect current industry standards, and develop advisory boards of active practitioners who make sure that the programs maintain high levels of accountability and integration with the local labor market.

Since as many as one-third or more of all students come to college seeking preparation for work, the greater focus, and subsequent *esprit de corps* of tightly sequenced applied programs, can lead to higher retention rates for first-generation students. With few choices among electives, counseling and advising are easier as well.

The best occupational programs fully integrate with the liberal arts. The intellectual skills students develop through the study of the liberal arts are essential for further academic training as well as superior job performance. Great occupational programs help individuals become employees with initiative, critical problem-solving skills, and the ability to interact with a diverse set of co-workers. The best career-focused degree provides education in aesthetic, ethical, social, and international perspectives so that employees become exemplary community citizens as well as wonderful employees. Even though occupational programs at a community college focus on preparing students for immediate work, ensuring smooth transitions to occupational programs at the baccalaureate level (and higher) is also critical for continued student success. Many community colleges develop articulation with senior colleges to transfer graduates to general education degrees or other flexible structures that take all the courses in an applied degree as fully applicable toward the baccalaureate degree.

The best community college programs go beyond meeting local workforce needs to forecasting them. Colleges develop certificates and degrees that anticipate industry trends and thereby allow local economies to remain ahead of the curve in training employees for emerging businesses. When done well, community colleges' foresight attracts new businesses to a locale to take advantage of a skilled workforce. The fluid and dynamic link between local businesses and the college further cements relationships that lead to enhanced fund-raising success, expanded public awareness, and increased political good will.

The ideal community college workforce and economic development program enhances its community's ability to function effectively for all its citizens. It makes sure that all segments of a community are educated, with students distributed in various job areas among genders, races, and ethnicities. Colleges find multiple ways to link with K-12 educational systems and a range of business sectors. The community college acts as a broker between career education and entry into college and work for its community's youth.

The ideal community college leverages education in many forms and many venues to enhance the economic viability of its community, and to greatly improve individual student lives. In a very fundamental way, community colleges deliver on the American promise of economic mobility.

THE UNFULFILLED DREAM

The reality of vocational, paraprofessional, or occupational programs is much more mixed than its ideal. Problems center around currency, connectedness, and effectiveness.

Staying Current

Macro-level economic changes combine to produce rapid alterations in business and industry practices, acceleration of the globalization of markets, and local or regional changes within specific business sectors. This makes up-to-date occupational degree programs difficult to offer. When a business sector rapidly expands, as nursing has in the early 2000s or computer-related fields did in the 1990s, community colleges find good faculty hard to recruit, retain, and pay a competitive salary. Laboratories or expensive equipment can become obsolete. The ability to anticipate accurately the next wave of employment is a complex prognostication at best. Any or all of these factors can result in community colleges not being able to offer a truly state-of-the-art occupational program.

Staying Connected

The nature of the academy also can hobble the effectiveness of occupational programs. Often the degree programs' curricula are too isolated from the liberal arts; sometimes they are too narrowly focused on specific skills training, which ultimately limits students' career progression. Programs stagnate without active engagement in the field, and the heavy teaching load of community college faculty makes this a difficult hurdle to surmount. Structural issues within the academy, including full-time faculty status, tenure, and/or union rules, can make it difficult to change faculty expertise as quickly as industry requires.

Some programs are not connected with actual work in the community. Program reviews may not be consistently or rigorously conducted. Even when reviewed, programs may not be routinely updated based upon the review's recommendations. The weight of the status quo may keep a specific academic certificate or degree program longer than the industry sector warrants, resulting in the overproduction of graduates for non-existent jobs. The tension that can exist between non-credit and credit curricula and faculty make it difficult to create seamless ladders among skill sets. In addition, colleges offer degree programs that prepare students for fields such as child care, where it is difficult to secure a living wage.

Overly close ties to industry can produce other kinds of problems, where skills developed in a program are too specifically tailored for a particular company instead of broadly applicable to an industry-related career. Gender imbalances still exist in occupational programs, with nursing programs still predominantly female and automotive technology programs overwhelmingly male. Community colleges face increased competition from for-profit training institutes and colleges, where higher tuition can provide greater access to up-to-date equipment or better focus on job placement (and cynics would contend much better advertising and vigorous recruitment tactics).

Since community college students have fewer economic resources, the fact that many workforce or co-op opportunities are unpaid means that the very structure that might accelerate successful entry into the workforce is inaccessible because students need a job to pay for school. Transfer, especially of Associate in Applied Science degrees, can be very problematic and is rarely promoted actively.

Thus, the kinds of deep and ongoing relationships with many external partners that are required of an occupational program at a community college may be difficult to maintain. With national accreditation for most allied health programs, some paralegal and business programs, and many engineering programs, external mandates can help a program command the kinds of resources it needs to educate and prepare students successfully. Nevertheless, there are many vocational programs for which no external mandate exists.

Staying Effective

The final hurdle for occupational programs is the effectiveness of the occupational training itself. Great tension can exist between the amount of education students receive and the time it really takes to become proficient in the field. While beginning trial lawyers or surgeons are expected to have several years of support and ongoing development after graduating from university training, registered nurses and computer programmers often face unrealistic expectations from employers, who require them to immediately handle complex problems. On the other hand, community colleges might not be successful in requiring that graduates achieve industry standards in their applied programs. If a community college has only one faculty member in the field, the lack of standards in a specialty area may not be apparent without an external evaluation of the program. With the academy's propensity for self-evaluation, a single faculty member may have motives to not point out program deficits. Extraneous external limits to applied programs, such as state-mandated limits on the number of credit hours in an Applied Associate degree or limits on financial aid, can lead to fewer hours of training than are necessary for real competence in a field.

Overall, the reality of community college vocational programs is mixed. It ranges from community college nursing student graduates who routinely outperform baccalaureate nursing students on the national licensing exam in many states, to travel agents who are not familiar with the latest industry trends or processes. Overall, the graduates of community college occupational programs are at work every day in the United States. Dollar for dollar, the money invested in community college occupational programs produces more for the communities, its businesses, and its overall economy than any other single educational sector. This chapter highlights the many ways in which occupational programs have created and maintained active, effective, and productive employees in the United States.

THE REAL STORY

Education for a Career

College professors are often dismayed when students are narrowly focused on going to college for the sole purpose of making money. While it is universally acknowledged that college students must develop critical thinking, explore new ideas, become global citizens, and nurture a life of the mind, even students at the most prestigious colleges are relentlessly practical. People go to college mostly because it is their ticket to a lifetime of better employment. Community colleges educate most of the current and future mid-skilled workforce, accounting for 75 percent of all employees in the United States (Grubb, 1996).

Student Success: A Promise Kept

The return on investment for students and their communities from occupational programs is significant. A meta-analysis of the literature demonstrates that "completion of Associate degrees enhances wages, employment, and earnings by significant amounts, in both conventional and statistical senses. For example, men with Associate degrees earn 18% more and women 22.8% more than high school graduates, once all the differences between the two groups have been considered" (Grubb, 2002). Minority graduates of community colleges have an even greater advantage in the labor market than white students (Grubb, 1998). Over a lifetime, a student who completes an Associate degree will earn $400,000 more than a high school graduate, and these differences are exacerbating as the number of low-skilled/high-wage jobs dwindles to nearly zero in the United States (AACC, 2006). Graduates of Applied Associate degree programs earn more, on average, than graduates of the more traditional Associate in Arts degree (Elsner, 2001).

What can only be inferred, because there is currently very little data, is the generational influence of community college graduation upon family socioeconomic status. Since community college students are much more likely to be poor than are students in four-year colleges, better wages often affect generations—not only the children of the community college graduate, but other family members as well. Community colleges' power to move low-income students to the middle class is one of a diminishing set of variables that deliver on social mobility, transforming family as well as individual income. For example, at one urban community college, family (not individual) income increases 17 percent for graduates (Institutional Profile, 2005). The promises are not uniform for every graduate, and it remains true that too many community college students do not complete the credit or non-credit programs in which they are enrolled. But for the tens of thousands who do complete programs every year, their economic lives are forever changed for the better. There is also a clear wage premium for degree completers, as opposed to students who simply complete the same number or type of courses (Bailey, Kienzl, and David, 2004). Despite the bias that sometimes exists about occupational programs, students who graduate with an occupational degree do at least as well as, and often much better than, liberal arts graduates, with the magnitude of wage difference larger for women than for men (Bailey et al., 2004).

In 1996, on average the population of workers with Bachelor's degrees earned more than those with Associate degrees, but the outcomes for any one graduate vary according to the details of the career which he or she enters. Carnevale explains, in his 2005 publication, that the range of wages for graduates of two- and four-year colleges is really two overlapping bell curves. The curves differ most at the more extreme ends, with Associate degree holders more likely to be at the lower end. However, and importantly, 80 percent of Associate degree recipients earn as much as people with Bachelor's degrees. It is also the case that salaries are most alike for workers in the middle income strata between $30,000 and $50,000. It must be noted that almost one-third of Associate degree holders earn more than the median earning of Bachelor's degree holders, mostly because they are in highly paid professional or technical fields (Carnevale, 2005).

The power of a vocational program to move a poor student into the middle class is very dependent upon the career program, and sometimes on eventual placement. Veterinary technology graduates who work as assistants in veterinary offices, child development graduates who work at daycare centers, and administrative assistants who work in the public sector make on average just slightly above the minimum wage, with few benefits such as good health care or retirement programs. On the other hand, a vet tech graduate who runs an animal laboratory for a pharmaceutical company, a child development graduate who owns a chain of child care centers, or the executive assistant to the CEO of a major company can easily make more than $80,000 in 2006 dollars. Currently, graduates from programs in engineering, nursing, physical therapy, and skilled trades make a middle class salary almost upon graduation (U.S. Department of Labor, 2006). On the other hand, some data suggest that racial differences exist in the "return on investment" in occupational programs, with white students benefiting more than students of color (Bryant, 2001a).

Substantial problems limit the ability of community college applied and workforce development programs to effectively serve low-income adults. One problem is that non-credit and credit programs in basic skills are often unaligned (Prince and Jenkins, 2005). Another is the simple fact that too few students who are eligible actually move from very basic skills to workforce training and then transition into credit programs, i.e., numbers range from a low of 4 percent to a high of 30 percent in a longitudinal study in Washington State (Prince and Jenkins, 2005).

Types of Workforce and Economic Development Offerings

Community colleges take several approaches to working with business and industry for workforce and economic development. Occupationally focused Associate degrees, non-credit continuing education certificates, and programs and community leadership all play a role.

More than 90 percent of all community colleges offer academic degrees or transfer opportunities that lead to a specific career, and 96 percent offer occupational, professional, or technical training for workforce development (General Accounting Office, 2003). Seventy-nine percent of community colleges offer contract training for a specific company and 61 percent offer some form of occupational, professional, or technical training open to the general public (General Accounting Office, 2003).

Nationally, community colleges enroll significant numbers of students in applied degree programs. Percentages vary significantly by campus and region, with a national median of 33 percent in occupational workforce-related programs (General Accounting Office, 2003). Table 12.1 categorizes types of education and training typically offered in this venue.

TABLE 11.1

Basic Types of Credit and Non-Credit Vocational Programs

Type of Vocational Program	Program Description
Credit Programs	
Academic degrees	Courses leading to an Associate in Arts, Associate in Science, or other academic degree, or eligible for transfer credit to an institution that offers baccalaureate degrees in such majors as engineering, architecture, business, etc.
Occupational, professional, or technical education	Courses leading to an Associate in Applied Science or other occupationally related degree, certificate, license, or diploma (e.g., practical nurse certificate).
Non-Credit Courses or Programs	
Occupational, professional or technical education	Non-credit courses leading to a certificate, license, or diploma (e.g., non-credit certified home health aide program).
Below college-level academics (developmental)	Courses, including basic mathematics, English, English as a second language and reading that are required before students who lack college-level proficiency in those subjects can be accepted into college credit courses.
Basic Skills	Courses, including adult basic education, English as a second language, and those preparing student for the GED® high school equivalency exam.
Contract or customized training	Employee training provided under contract to businesses, government entities, or other employers.
Other	Includes personal enrichment courses and any other courses not in the above categories.

Source: Slightly amended from Table 1, p. 2 (Government Accountability Office, 2004).

The three major categories of workforce development, namely Applied Associate degree programs, continuing education, and leadership in community economic development, will be outlined in the following section.

Associate Degree and Credit-Bearing Vocational, Paraprofessional, and Technical Education

Community colleges left behind their "junior college" status when they began to provide students with vocational, paraprofessional, and technical degrees and certificates. Koos, writing in the 1920s, defined the level of vocational education at community colleges as that which prepares people for the "semiprofessions," differentiated "from trades, the training for which is concluded during the conventional secondary-school period, and...from professions, adequate preparation for which requires four or more years of training beyond the high school" (Koos, 1970; originally published in 1925, p. 20). By 1949, 70 percent of junior colleges offered "terminal" or vocational degrees, enrolling just about the same percentage of students (35 percent) as they do now (Townsend, 2001).

Nationally, community colleges offer career education in health care, business (accounting, marketing, management, or sales), a range of industries (engineering, technology, or manufacturing), social services (human services, education, or drug abuse counseling), service occupations (administrative, retail, banking, insurance, paralegal), and specialized programs that link to a region's economy, whether it is gaming in Atlantic City, silicon chip clean production in Southern California, or culinary arts in Mississippi (Government Accountability Office, 2004). Many colleges link to high schools through federally sponsored tech prep and school-to-work programs. Colleges provide certification, licensure, and Associate in Arts or Associate in Applied Arts degrees for incumbent technical workers (Bragg, 2001a). National enrollment in credit programs averages for occupational programs is concentrated as follows:

- Business and office: 27%
- Health: 26%
- Computer and data processing: 17%
- Trade and industry: 10%
- Engineering and science technology: 7%
  (National Center for Education Literacy, 1996)

Associate degrees providing education for specific career areas are developed either for transfer or for immediate employment. Associate in Arts (AA) and Associate in Science (AS) degrees are intended for transfer. Some common occupational AA degrees include media studies, human services, early childhood education, and theater design, while common AS degrees include nursing, engineering technology, hospitality management, physical therapy assistant, and Web technology. A degree intended primarily to prepare a student for immediate employment upon graduation is an Associate in Applied Science degree. There is no one national standard, but in general its narrower focus on the practices and techniques of a specific career mean the degree contains few liberal arts courses.

In general, Applied Associate degrees are intended, and often end up, containing fewer transferable credits than an Associate in Arts or an Associate in Science. Some campuses make the issue of non-transferability very explicit. The State of Washington, for example, allows community colleges to offer an Associate in Applied Science technology degree, which is deemed a workforce degree with some general education (Washington Community & Technical College System, 2003). However, the state recommends particular language in college information which says that the degree is not intended for transfer, although some colleges have bachelor-level programs that accept the degree (Seattle Community College, 2004) .

The vast scope of these vocational, paraprofessional, or technical programs can be separated into ten to sixteen categories for ease of classification. (See Table 11.2 for typology with illustrative examples.) The sixteen categories as developed by the U.S. Department of Education in 1999 (Hull, 2000) are:

- Agriculture and Natural Resources
- Arts, Audio, and Video Technology and Communication
- Business and Administrative Services
- Construction
- Education and Training Services
- Financial Services
- Health Science
- Hospitality and Tourism
- Human Services
- Information Technology Services
- Legal and Protective Services

- Manufacturing
- Public Administration and Government
- Retail and Wholesale Sales and Services
- Scientific Research, Engineering, and Technical
- Transportation, Distribution, and Logistics

Different states across the country often develop their own classifications with some variation in terminology but roughly equivalent examples of Applied Associate degree programs. Applied Associate degree programs are sometimes linked to a credit certificate or a non-credit educational experience so that working students can enroll in modules of the program, gradually working their way up to the credit program.

The variety of Applied Associate degree programs reveals the responsiveness of community college programs to the businesses and industries that surround them. Regional labor markets predominate in some occupational programs, so that one could find a plastics engineering technology program in the northeast, an oil extraction and refining degree in Mississippi, a viticulture program in California, and a nanotechnology manufacturing program in Ohio. Other Applied Associate degrees are more commonly found at community colleges across the country, including those in law enforcement, allied health, human services, and computer technology.

Applied Associate degree programs have several distinctive features. The first is how they are developed: Business or industrial practitioners are commonly partners in curriculum and course creation. The DACUM process, which is a step-by-step method of bringing practitioners together with faculty to identify necessary skills and then derive the course content, has been successfully used in the creation of many Applied Associate degree programs (Norton, 1997). A second distinctive feature is advisory boards. Other features that make occupational programs look different from liberal arts programs at community colleges are tightly sequenced series of courses, ongoing revision and updating of curriculum and equipment, oversight by external agencies, internships, and a practicum and external examination or certification process for students upon graduation.

In some ways, these programs, with their linear clarity and tight connection to an existing and specific job, have a cohesion that other programs at community colleges don't have. Programs like nursing or other highly sought after degrees may even have a series of entrance requirements—not exactly admission criteria, but a greater selectivity based on limited program slots.

TABLE 11.2
Categories of Applied Associate Degree Programs Adapted to the U.S. Department of Education Career Clusters*

1. *Agriculture and Natural Resources* – including food development, oil mining, or other natural resource extraction or management; parks, wildlife and fisheries administration; horticulture, lumber production, viticulture, enology, and wine business; wild land fire technology.

2. *Arts, Audio and Video Technology and communication* – including design, interior design, industrial design, computer-aided design, audio technology, new media, video technology, communications.

3. *Business and Administrative Services* – including marketing, real estate, management and leadership preparation, accounting, insurance, administrative assistant, entrepreneurship, aviation and airport management.

4. *Construction* – including architecture, drafting, surveying, construction and construction management, building codes and inspection, equipment operation, HVAC (heating, ventilation and air conditioning), building and industrial maintenance.

5. *Education and Training Services* - child care, pre-service education, paraprofessional education.

6. *Financial Services* – including finance, credit, customer service, consumer lending, deposit operations, securities, financial planning, mortgage lending.

7. *Health Science* – including registered and practical nursing, dental assistant, dietitian assistant, sonography, imaging systems, medical technology, occupational therapy, physical therapy, nurses assistant, health aide, health information specialist, veterinary technology, emergency medical technician, paramedic, IV therapy, optics, pharmacy technology, phlebotomy, mortuary science, electrocardiography, respiratory therapist, radiology assistant, surgical technology.

8. *Hospitality and Tourism* – including cook/chef training, culinary arts, food service, events planning, supervision and management, hospitality, tourism.

9. *Human Services* – including human services, gerontology, deaf interpreter, substance abuse counseling, disabled services, direct care attendant services, related service occupations.

10. *Information Technology Services* – including arts, media technology, communication, game design, Web site design, software application, publishing, network support and administration.

Note: *adopted in 1999
Source: Hull, 2000.

Credit-bearing certificates require students to take a limited set of courses that can often be completed in less than a year, typically with almost no liberal arts courses. Many of these occupationally related degrees lead to state or national certification and licensure, sometimes conferred only after graduates pass an external exam. In collaboration with specific labor market sectors, colleges develop credit degree and certificate programs in anticipation of a need to spur economic development. The range of credit-bearing degrees linked to employment needs in a community is broad. All regionally accredited community colleges must register their credit degree and certificate programs with appropriate federal (and usually state) agencies in order to offer them.

Community colleges try to both respond to and anticipate business and industry needs—a complex, iterative, and episodic process. Some states, such as Florida, attempt to tie program development to state-level economic forecasts through performance-based financial incentives (Florida Department of Education, 2004). Michigan's community colleges were required to align their applied credit programs to national career clusters (similar to those in Table 11.2) and to clearly specify skills and competencies to be achieved in each program, as well as the methods of assessing skills attainment (Michigan Department of Labor and Economic Growth, 2003).

When these programs make local businesses an integral part of the development and educational process, they are not only able to access the latest technological advances, but they also potentially secure a better ability to forecast new skills and industry needs (Orr, 2001). Community colleges across the country have created links to both K-12 and business and industry in a variety of ways. For example, Pima Community College in Arizona created the Summer Career Academy to improve K-12 school transitions, offering preparation for careers, specific connections to business, guest speakers, field trips, etc. (Jacobs, 2001). Some programs link national industry to several community colleges. The College of DuPage in Illinois, El Paso Community College in Texas, and the national Association of Rotational Molders created a curriculum package for incumbent worker training on industry sites, customized training, and continuing education programs for the molders (Orr, 2001). But critiques about the rigor and inclusion of liberal arts classes with technical or occupational studies maintain that some community colleges still lag behind (Dare, 2001).

Being responsive to local businesses, especially in credit programs, can have its drawbacks. If program development is too closely linked to a particular industry or local business, academic independence can be challenged.

Automotive technology programs such as the Ford Asset Program work hard to produce generic automotive technicians, yet they link their materials closely to one specific manufacturer. The benefit to students is often immediate employment in the field, but perhaps a slightly more complex transition to a different national employer in the future.

Faculty development and maintenance of labor market currency are two of the challenges for institutions that wish to hire and support vocational program faculty (Brewer and Gray, 1997). If a labor market is "hot," it is difficult to compete with industry salaries. And highly technical programs require either expensive equipment purchases or the time and connection to support faculty who can make the necessary linkages with the industry to have expensive equipment donated or made available to students. Both activities require a level of institutional support that can be difficult for community colleges to provide. The heavy teaching load of community college faculty can also limit the time faculty in vocational programs have to conduct extensive industry outreach, and it is the rare community college that provides rewards and incentives for these activities (Brewer and Gray, 1997)

Vocational, paraprofessional, and technical programs are growing at community colleges. One of the paradoxes is that students who complete Applied Associate degrees are often very interested in transfer, even though these degrees fit inelegantly into most baccalaureate degrees.

WHO ARE THE STUDENTS IN APPLIED DEGREE PROGRAMS?

Determining the exact number and demographic characteristics of community college students in degree and certificate programs aimed at developing workforce skills is challenging. Federal analysis suggests that 49 percent of credit students are enrolled in liberal arts transfer programs, and 33 percent in occupational workforce-related programs. The difficulty is to tease out the actual intention of the "transfer" student, who may be enrolled in an Associate in Science degree program that articulates with an engineering program, or an Associate in Arts program that connects with a teaching program at the baccalaureate level. Of course, many students taking liberal arts courses at community colleges are very intent upon being journalists, social workers, or forensic scientists upon their transfer, so it might be argued that almost all students are working toward a specific career goal or goals over their college careers.

One of the major federal initiatives for the development of vocational educational programs at the secondary and postsecondary levels has been the Carl Perkins Act, and the subsequent addition of the Tech Prep program. The Tech Prep program is designed to link secondary and postsecondary vocational programs to increase technical and academic rigor and currency. Since its inception in the 1980s, millions of dollars have been spent. Hershey et al. (1998) conducted the final valuation of this program. Although extremely modest, the positive results included greater dialogue between community colleges and school districts about vocational education, a slight increase in industry involvement with schools, and a slight increase in high school advisement regarding technology and technical careers. However, they did not find increases in career continuity, increases in levels of rigor, or enhanced academic course (liberal arts) integration with vocational education. There were few students taking advantage of the college credit they earned in high school, and little connection between work experience in the field and the occupation for which students were studying (Bragg, 2001b; Hershey et al., 1998).

In Ohio, when researchers documented promising practices among the best run tech prep programs, student success outcomes were still minimal (Bragg, 2001b). Over the course of the program, enrollment of tech prep high school students in community colleges increased slightly, and 65 percent were involved in some form of postsecondary education, but there were not significant differences in grade point averages or in graduation rates (Bragg, 2001b). The other troubling finding was that work still pulled these students out of school, with tech prep students more likely to be working than transfer students and thus less available to continue collegiate educational opportunities (Bragg, 2001b). Thus, despite millions of dollars, the Tech Prep program did little to make the kinds of dramatic changes in occupational programs that would have a significant impact on the U.S. workforce.

Vocational and technical education in the United States has struggled with a history of having these career programs recommended for students who were not educationally facile enough to be truly college bound. There is some evidence that this still occurs in Applied Associate degree programs, with students of lower ability sometimes tracked into vocational programs despite the increasing complexity of technical and critical thinking skills necessary (Dare, 2001). Students in career programs sometimes exhibit the double whammy of being both under-prepared academically and the least likely to think that general education courses are necessary (Perin, 2000).

Vocational programs and their students face a slightly different set of problems from transfer students. The curricula of some vocational programs, such as nursing, engineering, or technology, are intensive. The combination of the typical community college students' at-risk profile—inadequate high school preparation, the necessity of paid employment, parenthood, and inadequate study skills—combine to limit students' ability to successfully tackle some of the high-challenge, high-reward degree programs (McKlenney, 2005). Community colleges' persistent under-funding makes the lack of tutoring and other academic support services for these high-challenge degree programs problematic.

Are Vocational Students Different from Transfer Students?

Demographic Differences

While the difference between non-credit occupational and credit occupational students could be substantial, it is difficult to determine if students who major in liberal arts in community colleges with the express purpose of transferring are in fact different from students who are majoring in marketing, accounting, or nursing. More than 50 percent of all community college credit students are occupational students, and the differences between liberal arts students and students in applied programs are diminishing over time (Bailey, Kinzel, and David, 2004). While it is more likely that students in occupationally focused certificate programs are older on average, there has been a significant decrease in the socioeconomic background of vocational students over the past six years (Bailey, Kinzel, and David, 2004). Students who complete the Associate in Applied Science degree (A.A.S.) now transfer in equal or even greater numbers than students with traditional transfer degrees (Townsend, 2001). Thirty-two percent of credit students in Associate degree programs in applied fields enroll with the stated intention of transferring, and this statistic seems to be increasing by small amounts annually (Berkner, Horn, and Clune, 2000). A North Carolina study found that half of students said that they intended to transfer, despite the fact that only 20 percent were enrolled in transfer programs (Townsend, 2001). Almost one-third of all students who transferred from community colleges in the state to the University of North Carolina system were from terminal degree programs (Frederickson, 1998).

The data are complex because most studies of transfer exclude students in applied fields, and therefore underestimate the amount of transfer within occupational degree students (Townsend, 2001). Since we have already seen that the majority of students transfer before receiving an Associate degree (see chapter ten), it is not out of line to presume that many are from vocational programs (Townsend, 2001).

Four-year colleges differ in their acceptance rate of vocational degree students. In 1998, 73 percent of non-liberal arts courses from California community colleges transferred to the California State University system, but only 27 percent to the University of California system (Townsend, 2001). Some state systems have made a point of ensuring the best possible transfer opportunities for occupational degree students. Northern Arizona University and Arizona State University have developed a degree program in applied science so that A.A.S. students can transfer easily. Conversely, states such as Wisconsin have passed state-level policies that limit transferability (Townsend, 2001). Only one state, Maryland, has a state-level articulation for the Associate in Applied Science degree, and even there this is only for the Bachelor's in technology (Townsend, 2001). It is only in specific programs, such as nursing, construction, or industrial technology, with commitment from individual campuses and often a high labor market demand, that transfer agreements allowing student progress from an applied occupational Associate degree to a Bachelor's degree are found (Townsend, 2001).

Pedagogical Differences

From the time of Thomas Dewey, arguments have been made that experiential learning is effective for all kinds of learning, but this has reached its height at community colleges in vocational programs (Dworkin, 1959). Advocates of work-based learning believe that students who learn occupational skills in the workforce are exposed to a greater range of information and techniques, as well as broader job skills, co-workers, alternative applications, and the latest techniques and equipment. When work-based learning is part of a curriculum, critics say it diminishes academic rigor and academic integration because it limits the number and depth of liberal arts courses. Thus, work-based learning is considered important for vocational education because it exposes students to different pedagogies, different applications in the workplace, and the latest techniques and equipment, while critics maintain that it takes away academic rigor and academic reinforcement (Johnston, 2001).

Questions remain about the appropriate way to teach applied curricula. Much of the literature touts integration of academic and applied coursework, but little empirical research validates the efficacy of this approach (Perin, 2000). Researchers in one study of self-reported vocational-academic integration could find discernable evidence that the integration even occurred in only about 70 percent of the cases (Perin, 2000). And sadly, most community college faculty in vocational programs report rigid boundaries that separate them and their curriculum from liberal arts faculty (Brewer and Gray, 1997).

There are some disturbing trends in occupational programs for specific student populations. For example, transfer enrollments are lower for minority students in community colleges that offer the greatest number of vocational programs, but there are almost no data beyond this to help understand the effect (Bragg, 2001a).

Advocates argue that contextual learning encourages more interactive, applied, and laboratory-oriented pedagogy, while also providing students with more opportunities for cooperative learning and team building—some of the important new soft skills in the workplace (Dare, 2001). "Contextual learning provides learners with an understanding of the context for what they are learning, and builds on what they know and already understand [as a new and] valid approach to teaching and learning" (Dare, 2001, p. 86).

NON-CREDIT OR CONTINUING EDUCATION

Arguably the most flexible and most innovative aspect of community colleges' initiatives in workforce development is non-credit—sometimes called continuing education. Increasingly, community colleges are working with local, state, and national agencies to provide a range of non-credit programs that lead to specified skills or certification. An amazing variety of skills are taught in programs that prepare students to be able to work in a whole panoply of industries, organizations, and businesses.

The primary focus of most non-credit education is to help people enter into a new job or provide skills enhancement for individuals already employed (incumbent workers). The four major workforce development segments can be defined as

- Emerging workers – 22 years old or younger, seeking first full-time employment.
- Transition workers – moving from one career to another, seeking job or skill upgrades, or returning to the workforce from an absence.
- Entrepreneurial workers – self-employed and small business owners.
- Incumbent workers – currently employed and needing additional training.
  (Warford and Flynn, 2000)

Over the last fifteen years, these programs have grown so large that they are frequently the largest part of a community college's "student" population.[1] Since education is so closely tied to economic enhancement, it can be argued that nearly all of the more than 5 million non-credit students in the United States are seeking skills to enhance their job readiness, whether it is a GED® certificate or advanced micro-processing technology. Nationally, the median percentage of non-credit students in applied programs is between 1 percent and 14 percent of all students (Government Accountability Office, 2004).

Non-credit programs help individuals achieve their first job, enhance their skills, or move from public assistance into the public realm. Skill or job upgrades are the primary focus of those entering non-credit programs for the first time, and almost 50 percent of new registrants return for more training (Rivera, 2002). Colleges work closely with large employers or with sectors (banking, retail, hospitality) to customize training and education for employees who need entry-level skills. Increasingly, employers are using community colleges to move entry-level employees to the next managerial strata, or to enhance executive-level employees' ability to improve performance in a company's strategic initiatives, whether it is managing an increasingly diverse staff or supporting organizational change.

The need for new kinds of skills, and to improve skills for those already employed, have accelerated as the American workplace changes from industrial to knowledge work and ultimately enters a global economy. While all American communities need better skilled and more effective workforces, some maintain that without improved links to business, community colleges run the risk of becoming outdated (Zeiss, 2000). Additionally, for-profit organizations compete for the non-credit enrollee; since the requirements of businesses are for skills and credentials, not necessarily degrees, community colleges must become more responsive by providing non-credit certificate programs that train students for exactly the skills employers need, or industry will look elsewhere for a "consumer-driven, open learning delivery system" (Zeiss, 2000, p. 48).

---

[1] Terminology is tricky here, in that calling students in continuing education or workforce development programs "students" is not universally applied. It also is difficult to use the term broadly to apply to an incumbent worker, who receives a training session on-site at a place of work for only one hour, as opposed to applying the term to an individual who takes part in a 24-week, six-hour-a-day, five-day-a-week training session on campus, which prepares the individual to seek work.

Critics of this approach worry that linking too closely to the business community will ultimately produce narrowly skilled workers who are unable to advance in their careers. They also contend that the United States will provide public dollars to train incumbent workers for companies that should foot the bill themselves, since they will reap the corporate profit from the improved skills of their employees (Grubb, 2001).

Community colleges differ in their level of regional or state-level coordination of non-credit programs. In Michigan, for example, the state's economic development corporation, community colleges, and the Department of Labor formed a state-wide coalition to provide Web-based, open entry/open exit modules to train workers for specific job sectors, using a combination of federal and state workforce development funds to support individual student enrollment (Michigan Community Colleges and Technical Education Update, 2004).

Various Faces of Workforce Development

Non-credit courses are a principal way of helping low-income, under-educated or un-educated adults move toward middle class jobs through career ladders. "Perhaps one of the biggest benefits of non-credit programs is to provide transitional education for people who leave high school unprepared for college-level programs" (Government Accountability Office, 2004, p. 12). They are particularly useful because they are so flexible. Non-credit programs can sequence progressively educational milestones of increasing difficulty in short spurts to allow low-income adults to more easily achieve academic goals, progressive levels of employment, and incremental increases in hourly pay.

There are several examples of these career ladders (Alssid et al., 2002; Workforce Strategy Center, 2001). A retail career ladder might have a non-credit sequence that starts with very basic literacy skills linked to a job in a stock room, and next moving to basic literacy, numeracy, and interpersonal (soft) skills for an entry-level cashier job. The individual can then begin more advanced college prep skills for a shift coordinator position, culminating in a one-year college credit business certificate with a retail focus to qualify the student to enter the company's management training program. An allied health sequence might move from home health care aide to nursing assistant to certified nurse's aide to practical nurse to an Associate degree program in nursing. Since the non-credit education and training programs can be quicker, cheaper, and more flexible, they can provide quicker entry into the workforce or faster skills upgrades (Government Accountability Office, 2004).

Many individual community colleges and state-wide systems have been particularly active in providing education and training for public assistance recipients in efforts to move individuals out of poverty. For example, the State of Washington's community and technical college system created WorkFirst programs, which provide assessment and education to public assistance recipients, including pre-employment training, basic skills, parenting, and personal management and work readiness (Seattle Community College, 2004). The program combines non-credit education with work-study jobs and some credit college enrollment (Seattle Community College, 2004). The results of the program were slightly positive, with 54 percent of participants finding jobs, but only at slightly above minimum wage (Washington Community & Technical College System, 2003).

Non-credit registrations are increasing precipitously at the same time non-credit students are becoming more diverse, because they are as likely to be low-income adults as they are to be adults with some college or even a college degree (Varga, 2004). While it is a common community college practice to package a range of courses, from contract training to ESL, for individuals and companies to be delivered at their location, there are no definitive data or data set upon which to draw solid conclusions about the actual number of individuals served, no assessment of the kind or the level of training provided, and no measure of student achievement.

Measurement of non-credit students is made much more fuzzy by the lack of a clear metric that compares to the full-time equivalent (FTE) measure used in credit programs. This is discussed more extensively in chapter four, which covers measurement.

CORPORATE, CONTRACT, OR CUSTOMIZED TRAINING

Customized training is another way community colleges structure non-credit programs. In this process, a community college will work with a specific company or business sector to create an educational and training curriculum for a group of employees (often termed incumbent workers). The training is sometimes offered for credit, but usually provides a more narrowly focused non-credit experience. For example, a college might develop a series of customized workshops in physics to help a glass manufacturer's mid-level managers understand enough about fluid dynamic principles to comprehend why certain glass processes were successful or unsuccessful in fabricating a new window element. At the other end of a difficulty spectrum, a community college might create a series of contextualized English as a Second Language sessions for the Spanish-speaking janitors of a large office complex so that the janitors would be able to read and understand the warning labels on commonly used cleaning products. In every case, the college works with a company to identify to whom the training should be delivered, the content to be offered, and the educational outcomes to be achieved.

About 1 million employees were enrolled in customized training in 2003. The largest buyers of these services are private business at 53 percent, although government and non-profits account for an additional 29 percent. About one-third of the businesses served employed 100 workers or fewer, 21 percent employed 101-500, and 12 percent employed more than 500 workers (Government Accountability Office, 2004).

North Carolina stands as a leader in the provision of customized training services through coordination between state incentives and the community college system's Economic and Workforce Development Division, along with the 58 individual colleges (North Carolina Community College System, 2005). Working individually with each company, services are provided to companies that project they will create more than twelve jobs per year. Providing services for companies that range from software development to biotechnology to warehousing, a local community college will work with a company to profile needed skills, determine appropriate curricula, and then provide instructors, equipment, facilities, and educational support services to deliver the training. The system can also profile needed skills and then use community colleges to train company personnel to develop questionnaires and other assessment materials needed to interview and select new employees, and then provide pre-employment training for those selected (North Carolina Community College System, 2005). North Carolina has also established a worker training tax credit that creates additional incentives for employers to use the training, as well as job creation credits and machinery and equipment investment credits (North Carolina Community College System, 2005).

COMMUNITY LEADERSHIP FOR ECONOMIC DEVELOPMENT

The final and most complex relationship of community colleges to workforce development is in the role colleges play in economic development for municipalities, regions, and states. In this role, community colleges are thinking about ways to leverage their ability to create not only an educated workforce, but also intellectual capital that leads to new forms of economic development. This can take the form of activities that bring new companies into a region, establish business incubators, and build coalitions of businesses, colleges, and government, and a host of other unique arrangements that result in the enhancement of the overall economic viability of a community. In this role, community colleges are conveners and visionaries, as well as trainers and logisticians, who act as a lever for change and development for a community's overall economic profile.

This is a complex role to undertake. It requires a college to have a multifaceted community needs assessment that is up-to-date and ongoing, and to then wade into the political maneuvering that accompanies changes in economy delivery systems. The role may stretch a community college's ability to walk the tightrope between political, philanthropic, and corporate desires. Nonetheless, inventive programs are going on across the country, in which the colleges have been pivotal in changing the economic landscape for the better.

One of the promising practices in this arena is when community colleges help identify and grow regional business and industry clusters. Regional clusters create and support interdependence between companies based on a particular type of product or service. To be successful, the community college must undertake a careful needs assessment to identify nascent or emergent clusters and then support them by creating entities, such as a research and practice center or new curricular structures (both credit and non-credit), that will advance work skills for the cluster (Jacobs, 2001). Some community colleges have evolved "second-generation" industry centers, such as Advanced Technology Centers, whose purpose is to collaborate with software development companies or companies that build high-tech machines (Jacobs, 2001). These centers provide a place to demonstrate the use or application of advanced equipment or production systems. In addition, these second-generation centers give companies privileged access to newly trained pools of specialized labor (Jacobs, 2001). A particularly exciting development is the emergence of "third-generation" centers, where colleges have successfully gathered companies, highly trained and engaged faculty, up-to-date equipment, and curricula in order to work with industry organizations and address needs of firms collectively. "[C]olleges can build strengths and develop expertise not possible if spread over many types of business" (Jacobs, 2001, p. 6).

By nurturing regional industrial clusters, community colleges have served as catalysts for local economic development because they can integrate community and industry connections. The resulting activities have produced some exciting new models at community colleges across the country. For example, the Northeast Oklahoma Manufacturers Council developed into a state-wide strategy building organization. Other colleges have created entrepreneurial business incubators, such as NY Designs at LaGuardia Community College in New York City. Other clusters include biotechnology at Asheville-Buncombe Community College in North Carolina, and metals at Hagerstown Community College in Maryland. The most innovative community colleges also host technology and local economic development offices and train faculty from other colleges (Regional Technology Strategies, Inc., 2003).

SOURCES OF FINANCIAL SUPPORT FOR CREDIT AND NON-CREDIT OCCUPATIONAL PROGRAMS

Government Involvement

The involvement of municipal, state, regional, or national governments in workforce and economic development is both extensive and chaotic. Grants, funding from government linked through businesses to the colleges, and a host of state and local funding mechanisms can be found. Full-time equivalency (FTE) reimbursement for credit employment at state levels is variable, and sometimes is available for non-credit education. There is also variability in the extent to which community colleges receive direct access to workforce development and economic development funds at the state and federal levels.

Federal Support

The federal government's role began seriously in the 1960s with the development of "manpower" programs established to combat the unemployment spurred by the increasing technological revolution (Grubb, 2001). Manpower programs were established with the conviction that schools were not appropriate for skills training, and therefore set in motion the split between education and training that remains to this day (Grubb, 2001). The Comprehensive Employment and Training Act of 1973, evolving into the Job Training Partnership Act of 1981 and 1998, were the first federal attempts to develop a national system of workforce development (Grubb, 2001) . They were significantly overhauled in the series of welfare reform acts through the 1980s and 1990s, when the focus of the programs changed from training people for work to getting people off of public assistance (Grubb, 2001).

Over the years, these federal systems became more complex. In 1995, the General Accounting Office (GAO) counted 163 federal programs with $20.4 billion in resources devoted to workforce development, and state programs focused on using workforce training programs to spur economic development must be added to that (Grubb, 2001). The result is that there is a great deal more federal and state money connected to workforce development than ever before. In states like North Carolina, Oregon, and Oklahoma, community colleges are the linchpin of the states' workforce program (Grubb, 2001). Much remains for each system to learn about the other—colleges have a lot to teach other providers about quality instruction, and many community colleges must learn to strengthen placement, create more flexible schedules, and develop tighter curricular connections with employers (Grubb, 2001).

The federal Workforce Investment Act (WIA) is the most recent attempt to coordinate a federal-level workforce development process. Funneled through local Workforce Investment Boards (WIBs), WIA funding can support community colleges that seek to play a large role in a region's workforce development strategy. In Oregon, for example, local WIA-funded, one-stop staff collaborated with the local community college to fund a nursery consortia for skills upgrades for agricultural workers (General Accounting Office, 2003). Seventy-eight percent of local WIBs that spent funds to train incumbent workers in 2001 used community colleges to do so (General Accounting Office, 2003).

The federal Carl Perkins Vocational and Technical Education Act provides funding for promoting workforce education at the secondary and postsecondary levels and spends millions of dollars annually (although it has been slated for elimination in several recent federal budget proposals). Even this massive program has not made real headway, and there is little evidence of consistent technical or academic improvement in the curricular connection among vocational education and local industry, nor with local school districts. This is not uniformly true, and there are examples, such as those in Florida, of extensive connections among community colleges and local school districts for technical advancement. But much remains to be learned and enacted.

The Tech Prep, a national program to improve technical education by more closely linking secondary and postsecondary education, is emblematic of too many vocational programs. Spread too thin to really challenge existing systems, the dollars were politically fought over and expended without regard to the efficacy of past grants. The premise that linking students early with career focus and the attempt to accelerate students' entry into community college credit programs were untested when the federal dollars began to be distributed, and were never challenged by an examination of outcomes data. It is difficult not to conclude that the program, despite the best intentions and many individual successes, did almost nothing to advance American technological or vocational education on a national level.

State Support

State-specific programs for economic or workforce development have a wide range of funding mechanisms. Most states offer more funding for credit than non-credit programs (General Accounting Office, 2003). "On a program-by-program basis, state funding varied considerably between credit and non-credit programs. While about one-third of schools responding to our survey reported receiving about the same level of state funding for credit and non-credit occupational, professional, and technical training programs, most states fund non-credit courses to a lesser degree—and in some cases not at all" (Government Accountability Office, 2004). Nearly one-fifth of the schools are not allowed to use any public funds for training courses (Government Accountability Office, 2004).

In planning workforce-related programs, state-wide strategies are sometimes developed to address the needs of local business. Florida created a targeted list of occupations to guide program development, and the State of Washington's community colleges must show that a newly developed program's output will not exceed the need for workers in the field (Government Accountability Office, 2004).

Corporate Involvement

Applied Associate degree programs or non-credit education are worthless if they do not teach the competencies required by local employers. Thus, the close involvement of the businesses is critical if graduates are to secure jobs—preferably good jobs with appropriate wages and benefits. There are thousands of instances of such collaborations, but the following are examples of how some colleges worked with manufacturing companies to give an overall sense of how it works and what is possible.

Greenville Technical College in South Carolina uses an annual $200,000 grant from companies that benefit from the employees' education as well as state allocations to create the Upstate Training Alliance. The Alliance brings together the faculty at Greenville Tech with supervisors from the local companies, as well as the local chamber of commerce, to produce skilled workers for advanced manufacturing (Grubb, 2001). The Alliance developed the Fast Track Apprentice program for an Applied Associate in Science degree in industrial maintenance, with companies paying for all tuition and employing the students part time during the program. Graduates were eligible for full-time employment. The program not only provided trained employees, but also created a growing interest in the career field that had not existed previously (Summers, 2001).

Local manufacturers convinced Parkland Community College in East Central Illinois to develop a program in manufacturing technology, not only by providing robust workplace internships to support learning, but also by paying for almost all of the equipment the college required to teach the courses on campus (Johnston, 2001). Also in Illinois, Danville Area Community College set up apprenticeship programs in automotive, electronics, manufacturing, and computer-aided design with local companies, and enhances the career programs through articulation agreements with its local state university. In each of these examples, the strong working relationship between community college and business sector enhanced both the program and the area's companies in significant ways.

STUDENT FINANCIAL AID IN APPLIED CREDIT AND NON-CREDIT PROGRAMS

Degree Programs

Students enrolled in credit programs are eligible for the full range of financial aid. There are additional sources of support provided by companies or specialized training dollars from the state or locality that support internships or part-time employment. The informal connections students often make when some of the instruction occurs on a plant floor (often to access very expensive, specialized equipment) can also turn into summer paid employment or full-time jobs. Although no longer true, at the height of the red-hot technology boom, student interns were often lured away from education by companies offering full-time, well-paid employment and such perks as signing bonuses before graduation. Nursing students are often recruited by the hospitals where they have their clinical training, although the educational requirement that they complete their degrees makes luring them away before graduation impossible. Companies with close ties to a community college that has developed an effective degree program often offer scholarships to students, sometimes with requirements for involvement with the company during their schooling or after their graduation.

Non-Credit Programs

The greater challenge for financial support is for non-credit training. No federal student financial aid is provided for non-credit, certificate, or adult basic education. Loans, which are increasingly a part of students' overall financing package for education, are both not as available and not as recommended for non-credit students, since the actual financial return on investment for non-credit programs is not as large as that for a college degree.

The focus of the national Workforce Investment Act (WIA) is to provide skills and connections to the working poor, and to lift the poor out of poverty. Although structured in different ways across the country, WIA typically offers individual training vouchers that are used by individuals to access training, as well as some directly funded programs with colleges or companies. There are many successful examples of community colleges partnering with local Workforce Investment Boards and local companies to provide funding for training programs. The Bridge Program at the City Colleges of Chicago connected a range of partners, including community-based organizations, to recruit students and employers who provide jobs after the community colleges provide training (Jacobs, 2001).

Cabrillo Community College in rural California developed a Fast Track to Office Work program, combining education with career transition services, advisement, financial aid, and tutoring. Like many programs, Cabrillo combined both WIA funds with local employers' contributions to provide much more robust support for low-income individuals than any community-based organization, community college, or employer could do on its own (Jacobs, 2001). These programs are important because they link skill upgrades with solid academic work, providing graduates with transferable skills for upward mobility in the career for which they prepare, or for other careers (Jacobs, 2001).

WORKFORCE PROGRAM SUCCESS

The most important question is: Do these programs work? Whether tightly or loosely linked with business and industry, controlled closely by advisory boards or run entrepreneurially by faculty, are vocational programs at community colleges delivering on their promise of opening the career doors to every sector, and providing students with appropriate movement through economic strata? Some experts criticize community colleges, especially non-credit programs, asserting that most just follow grant money, be it local, state, or federal, and don't think of how to systematically create career ladders within non-credit programs.

Data Collection

The difficulty in understanding the extent and effect of community college attendance comes in part from lack of data, with the U.S. Department of Education collecting graduation and completion rates information only on full-time degree seeking students. At one school in Washington State, this was less than 20 percent of community college students (Government Accountability Office, 2004). Only about 17 percent of community colleges track outcomes from non-credit workforce development programs (Government Accountability Office, 2004). Estimates are that between one-half and two-thirds of community college students seeking a credential either get the credential or transfer. Several states have created data links between unemployment insurance earnings information and community college administrative records to collect earnings data, although each state varies in its ability to collect such data because state laws, reporting procedures, and higher education agency organizations differ by state (Government Accountability Office, 2004).

For students in remedial academic courses, about two-thirds complete those courses, and more than 60 percent complete their GED₈ credential or other adult basic education courses (Government Accountability Office, 2004). Completing these basic skills is ideally just the beginning of skills development for job attainment. (See Table 12.3.) What is needed for an effective evaluation, however, are data that examine such things as increases in business profitability, decreases in failures of local small businesses or start-ups, increases in the ability of companies to offer wages that can support a family, and increases in the number of companies in a community that offer health or retirement benefits to their workers. In short, if all workforce development activities of a community college are effective, the ultimate result should be a more prosperous community and a higher level of

TABLE 12.3
Percentage of Students Passing Below College-Level (Developmental) and Three Types of Basic Skills Courses, During Fall 2002 Term

Type of course	Median percent of students passing
Below college-level (developmental)	66%
Adult Basic Education	60%
English as a Second Language	71%
GED₈ Tests	65%

Source: Slightly amended Table 6, p. 32 (Government Accountability Office, 2004).

overall economic development. While few programs track outcomes at a level sufficient for national extrapolation, even fewer use the metric of community development as the sign of program success.

CHALLENGES TO THE FIELD

The breadth and depth of community college career and workforce development programs are noted in this chapter. There is so much activity that a challenge to the field might be simply, "Carry on!" However, in addition to the good work that is occurring, we suggest that there are additional ways to frame, fund, and evaluate vocational, technical, and paraprofessional programs. Some of these recommendations come from the research literature, and others emerge from our own understanding of how campus-based, local, and state-level workforce development programs function.

1. Recommendations addressing the development of Applied Associate degree and non-credit certificate programs:
   - Ensure that advisory boards are current and active in the field and closely supervise new program development and ongoing rigorous program review.
   - Emphasize the liberal arts in both course content and links with technical and applied courses in credit as well as non-credit education.
   - Advocate business data that are locally and regionally sensitive, and able to identify with a high degree of specificity which kinds of job opportunities exist and the kinds of qualifications needed for effective employment.
   - Advocate smooth transition from Applied Associate degrees to a range of baccalaureate degrees.
   - Link credit and non-credit educational experiences to create an educational career ladder that extends the ability of a low-income and very low-skilled adult up to the highest academic levels in a discipline.

2. Recommendations addressing the recruitment of students:
   - Create advising materials and processes that help students understand the range of occupational programs in any college, and the difference between credit and non-credit experiences.
   - Create strong and clear connections with individual businesses to help employees develop an academic career ladder that is recognized by local companies with promotions and wage increases.

- Ensure that racial and gender diversity is always a consideration in recruiting and supporting students, with specific tactics for degree programs where the balance is skewed (e.g., nursing, engineering).
- Work actively with local economic development agencies to leverage educational resources as the basis for economic development.

3. Recommendations addressing better evaluation and accounting for applied and workforce development programs:
   - Create a national full-time equivalency definition for non-credit enrollees to understand the relationship between "head count" and the actual numbers of instructional hours received.
   - Conduct studies of transfer that include all students who transfer, whether in transfer programs or not.
   - Create a measure of community college effectiveness in advancing economic development that evaluates the effect on the local community as the outcome.

CONCLUSION

Community colleges, through their range of programs, offer Associate degrees and non-credit experiences that provide excellent training to tens of thousands of individuals every year. The problems of workforce development are as important as their successes. Training may be too narrowly tied to a particular company instead of a specific industry, unrelated to jobs in a community, or not up to industry standards. It is possible that much public money is spent helping for-profit businesses and industries pay for training that they would have provided themselves, therefore wasting public resources. Job training programs designed to move individuals from poverty to self-sufficiency work well for only a small minority, and often fail at serving the "hardest to serve." And all occupationally related programs suffer from the same kinds of lack of completion rates that plague traditional liberal arts programs.

While the business pages of the *Wall Street Journal* and the *New York Times* avidly cover what is happening at elite colleges like MIT or Wharton, it is actually the success or failure of community colleges in the delivery of high-quality education to prepare individuals for high-wage jobs that will make or break America's ability to be successful in a globally competitive world.

CHAPTER 12

English as a Second Language

English as a Second Language (ESL) fulfills the community college commitment to creating the next generation of new Americans. Immigration has always existed as one of America's brightest promises, although it always was and remains a contested concept. It is no accident that the Statue of Liberty stands so tall in the New York Harbor, where it thrilled generations of individuals making the passage by ship at the turn of the twentieth century. The reality of the twenty-first century is that we should move her to the waiting room at John F. Kennedy International Airport.

Community colleges are the contemporary equivalent of the settlement houses in New York City's Lower East Side—they are the places where students learn not only language but also culture, and prepare not only for a job pushing a cart but also for a job running a company. One hundred years ago, immigrants had no equivalent to the cell phones, email, and CNN that make their native countries so close today, and the tensions between a country of origin and the new American identity are much more complex and circular. America's community colleges have slowly waded into these moving waters and are shaping the new Americans. Ten years ago, the issues of immigration were centered in a few coastal states: California, Texas, Florida, New Jersey, and New York. But it can be surprising to learn that immigrants currently make up large parts of the heartland, such as 50 percent of the population of Kansas City, Missouri. Immigrants can be found throughout the country, and rural as well as urban community colleges are providing educational services.

THE DREAM

Depending on the level of the ESL and the intentions of the students, ESL can be either primarily an academic exercise in contrastive rhetoric or a deeply personal acculturation that links lived experience with language instruction. Community colleges across the country offer programs that span the spectrum. However it is termed, whether English as a Second Language (ESL) or English for Speakers of Other Languages (ESOL), the dream of each program is to swiftly provide language instruction so that students can enter academic programs and complete degrees and certificates. Community college ESL programs hope to provide instruction to everyone from the immigrant German physician who wants to pass her board to become a practicing doctor in the United States to the agricultural worker who has completed only second grade in Guatemala—and everyone in between.

Ideally, an ESL program will have a curricular structure that provides the intensity and breadth to do many things. It simultaneously gives students the oral, written, and listening skills to manage daily life, while moving inexorably toward intensive academic English. It advances students toward academic goals while respecting the complicated lives of predominantly poor immigrants who work and care for families while going to school. And it straddles the complicated intellectual boundary of being a "basic skill" or a "prerequisite" of college-going while at the same time understanding that an equivalent level of learning French or Chinese would be considered advanced academic work for an English-speaking student at the same college.

The ideal ESL program grounds its curriculum within the principle that learning a foreign language as an adult is a lifelong process that can be hampered or accelerated by non-college issues such as language spoken at home, or level of technical or vernacular used. A highly trained nurse might understand all his coursework vocabulary and then fail in a clinical setting where he needs to understand what a patient means when she complains about feeling "woozy." The ideal ESL program allows students into academic courses when their ability to read and comprehend is adequate, but recognizes that the ability to write at an advanced level will continue to progress throughout an academic year (and many years beyond). This ESL program will also be fully integrated with all basic skills and academic courses, so that other faculty understand the difference between "ESL" mistakes (mistakes that often express different rhetorical perspectives) and "basic skills" mistakes.

Funding issues also become critical for ESL students. If students require a long series of sequenced courses to become sufficiently fluent to enter college courses, funding from state and local sources often is inadequate. The ideal ESL programs find ways to fund early learning so that students who do not start out speaking English at levels sufficient to take college classes save some of their tuition assistance for the credit courses.

THE UNFULFILLED DREAM

Immigrant students can be welcomed as the bedrock of a community's economy, or reviled as individuals who are using up the scarce resources in poor communities. Despite their explosive growth, far too many ESL programs wallow as out-stations on a community college campus. Frequently separated from all credit instruction, there may be no established pathway from basic ESL to academic English proficiency. Even if students find their way through the contortions of academic gerrymandering, the system often exhausts students' time or money.

ESL students come in too many patterns to establish clear programmatic boundaries. The varieties of students' English abilities, combined with educational, work, family, and cultural considerations, result in the group of any specific pattern being too small to cluster in an individual class. So, students who are highly educated in their home country but have virtually no English skills are in a class with students who are barely educated in their home country but have rudimentary speaking ability in English. These differences become a very thorny issue for the ESL faculty member assigned to that class.

Because ESL programs are fragmented, students can spend years working through a prescribed course sequence that exhausts all available financial aid. State assistance is possible, but federal assistance is less likely because it requires citizenship. Students often circle through non-credit sequences that are not intensive enough or sufficiently integrated within a student's lived reality to allow them to progress at a reasonable rate, and not integrated well enough with academic standards to move them into credit courses. There is ESL "recidivism" because students' home life or work life moves in and out of being monolingual in their native language, causing losses in English proficiency gained in classes.

Assessment of English language capacity is often not sensitive enough to place students in tracks that move them toward specific goals, and therefore students can spend too much time in a non-academically focused ESL program even after their goals have changed to include college. With financing of lower level courses so difficult, the range of skill levels in a single class can be far too broad for effective pedagogy. And the semester basis of most programs pushes ESL students into for-profit programs of higher cost and lower quality because they accept students on an open-access basis. These programs typically do nothing to move students toward academic programs. Students with learning disabilities are almost impossible to assess and assist.

ESL students who succeed in taking all required ESL courses often find themselves lumped with developmental students in writing and language arts courses. This delays student progress, and rarely are developmental faculty prepared to assist students with the specific linguistic problems that are linked to different linguistic rhetorical and grammatical structures.

The perception of ESL teaching as a discipline versus a developmental prerequisite can be especially problematic in overall curricular design. Often grouped with developmental departmental classes, and yet proficient in a discipline with distinct and advanced scholarship and pedagogy, ESL faculty can find themselves outside the curricular mainstream in a way that faculty of modern languages are not. If there is any academic credit provided for ESL students, it is typically institutional credit, despite the fact that the language proficiency learned by students far exceeds what would be required for native English speakers in their two semesters of college-credit bearing German or French.

Community colleges do not always reframe curriculum to respond to the specific needs of ESL students in regular curriculum. For specific groups of English language learners, especially students from Asian countries, insufficient attention is paid to oral communication, even though this can be one of the last hurdles to overcome. And even with the knowledge that learning another language as an adult is a lifelong practice, students are not provided with necessary academic support after leaving ESL or developmental classes.

Into this mix one must place the rapidly changing world of the immigrant to the United States. Students experience a tension between the traditions of their culture of origin and the evolving cultural negotiations that define their personal and academic lives in the United States, both inside and outside the classroom.

THE REAL STORY

Rising Demand for ESL in Community Colleges

A wave of new immigration swept the United States in the 1990s. Today, more than 1 million people immigrate to the United States every year (Yearbook of Immigration Statistics, 2007). The growth of a diverse, multilingual community of American residents hailing from around the globe is one of the major developments of the current era. Much of the change in who immigrates to America, and their numbers, can be traced to the impact of the 1962 Immigration Act, which changed the American preference for immigrants from specific European countries to a more balanced global eligibility. What remains difficult to measure is the power of the American dream. But the power of the dream is strong and is evidenced in the large numbers of undocumented workers who run the gamut from agricultural workers who cross a river in Texas to highly educated German professionals who do not return at the end of a tourist visa.

There are over 35 million foreign-born residents in the United States, a 65 percent increase over the past decade (U.S. Department of Commerce, 2007). Uneducated immigrants enter the United States to flee poverty and war in their homelands, and highly educated immigrants might come to capitalize on the "sky is the limit" sense of economic, social, and cultural opportunity. As immigrants and their children enter the educational system, colleges nationwide scramble to serve students with an ever-widening spectrum of cultural and educational backgrounds. In 1979, Europe accounted for 65 percent of all immigrants. Today, only 14 percent of new immigrants are European (with Eastern Europe predominating) and the majority hail from underdeveloped countries throughout the world, especially from Asia and Latin America (Alfred, 2005).

Currently, one in four students in community colleges are immigrants, and the numbers are increasing (Sheppard and Crandall, 2004). ESL programs are the largest and fastest-growing programs at many colleges. For example, ESL is now the largest academic department at Miami-Dade Community College in Florida (Sheppard and Crandall, 2004). Over the past two decades, there has been exponential growth in both credit and non-credit ESL programs at community colleges. In 1991, only 40 percent of community colleges offered ESL; now the number is closer to 90 percent (Blumenthal, 2002). While immigration used to affect primarily three key large states (California, Texas, and New York), it is now widespread. At the same time, there has been a change in the languages spoken by immigrant groups, from Spanish only (although it still predominates) to much more widely international (U.S. Census Bureau, 2005). No matter where immigrants reside, data suggest that it will be an imperative for the United States to provide educational opportunities for them. The proportion of foreign-born individuals 25 years or older with a high school education is lower (67 percent) than native born (87 percent), and the needs are as great or greater (Szelenyi and Chang, 2002).

Community colleges are now often the equivalent of the settlement houses that existed in New York City's Lower East Side a hundred years ago. Settlement houses were part of a series of programs that linked the immigrant world and its deep connection to an "old world" to the contemporary American world where new identities and modes of behavior were cultivated. No national data base produces reliable information about immigrants at community colleges (Szelenyi and Chang, 2002), and given the fluidity of immigration laws, many colleges are hesitant to provide access even to the information that they do keep. For example, in a study of more than 140 two- and four-year colleges, only eight were willing to participate in a study of immigrants in college, and only two of these routinely kept data about their students' immigration status (Szelenyi and Chang, 2002). This hesitancy becomes more pronounced with undocumented students. In urban areas with large immigrant populations, this can mean anything from students who have lived in the United States since they were infants yet are not citizens because their parents are illegal, to students who themselves have illegally gained access to the United States by crossing a desert or hiding in the belly of a container ship for a month. Counts of immigrant students at community college are also difficult because our definition of "immigrant" is fluid. In one study conducted by the American Association of Community Colleges in 1996, the data elicited were very conservative because the definition of "immigrant" consisted of undocumented aliens, legal permanent residents, and refugees (Szelenyi and Chang, 2002).

Differences in immigration status directly affect the amount of tuition students taking ESL classes are charged. One of the biggest issues is whether immigrant students should be charged the lower in-state tuition. The decision to apply the lower tuition fees has varied over the past years and continues to be in flux. For example, in-state tuition was charged to students in New York City before the terrorist attacks on the city on September 11, 2001; they were charged out-of-state tuition for the next few years, and then legislation was passed to allow the in-state tuition again in 2005. Both California and Texas charge in-state tuition for students who are able to prove residence—although the length of residence and the documentation required has been fluid (Szelenyi and Chang, 2002). No non-U.S. citizen is eligible for federal financial aid, but some states allow non-residents to apply for some types of state aid, and some community colleges use their own privately raised funds to assist students (see a fuller discussion of financial aid in chapter three) (Szelenyi and Chang, 2002). The department in which the ESL classes are housed at the college also influences the availability of aid, since only credit courses are eligible in most states (Szelenyi and Chang, 2002).

ESL Defined

English as a Second Language can be a misnomer, as increasing numbers of students at American community colleges are learning English as their third or fourth language. In most contexts, however, ESL is a process whereby students are learning English in a country where English is the native language. This distinguishes it from the learning of other modern languages, in which students' exposure to the language outside class is limited. The other key context in which community colleges teach ESL is that, for many of the classes, the presumption is that the English will be advanced to a level that will provide students with sufficient linguistic proficiency to function in classrooms where collegiate-level instruction is delivered in English.

The typical ESL program, no matter what the level, usually is directed at comprehensive learning, so that instruction is provided in listening, speaking, reading, and writing, with lessons on pronunciation as well as grammar. ESL programs want to provide students with the ability to participate in a variety of activities, including personal, civic, and work life, as well as academic study. Some ESL programs limit their aim to specific work functions (for example, enough English to be a room attendant in a hotel), but typically even contextualized vocational ESL, where the vocabulary consists of words and interactions typical to the work setting, also provide instruction in other aspects of the language.

Who Are the Students?

Diverse Immigrant Groups

While statistics will define the students in overall groups, it is also important to understand the richness and potential of this student population. For that, there's nothing like some life stories.

> *Marisol de Leon is 22 years old. She came to the United States in her teens and is a graduate of a local high school. She lives in a tightly knit Dominican-American community and says, "I've been taught that it's important to stay close to family regardless of where education and career may take you." Marisol's relationship with her family grew tense when she came out*

as a lesbian at fourteen; when her mother developed a terminal illness, however, Marisol took on a new role: "I became my mother's mother. . . I cared for her as if she were my own child." After her mother died, Marisol was determined to go to college, but had "only a minimum wage and no parents to rely on for financial assistance." She found her way to a community college where, she says, "I was in school one semester and out the next." Today, Marisol is preparing to graduate from the community college and transfer to a four-year college, and ultimately get a Master's in public health administration. And in her personal life, with her Colombian partner, Marisol says she hopes to "put a better twist" on traditional family values: "My family is going to value togetherness without everyone having to take up expected gender roles."

Mamadou Mdoup is 26 years old, from Senegal, and a liberal arts major. He works as a taxi driver to support himself, pay his tuition, and send money back to his family in Africa. A member of the college's Muslim Club, the hardest part about college for him is balancing his time. "Learning is more than books and tests," he says. "I have made sure I have time for social events, because I learn by interacting with people." When he graduates, he hopes to return to Senegal and work toward social change and a united Africa.

Sarita is 41 years old, and came to New York in the late 1980s from Peru, after a short stay in Mexico. "I decided to change my life, to look for opportunities," she explains. When she first arrived in New York, she worked as a housecleaner, working 12 hours a day. Then she found work in a travel agency serving a largely Latino community. Studying accounting at a community college, she found that the college's language and literacy tutorial programs made a big difference in helping her learn English and overcome the obstacle blocking her from improving her situation. The college was also the first place where she really got to know people from outside her own community.

Ei Sander Khine came from Myanmar with her family, refugees from the repressive Burmese government. When she was eight years old, the government squashed a wave of student demonstrations and strikes, and her memories from that time are filled with "gun shots and blood in the night." Now she lives with her extended family in a household of 18 people. Studying at home is difficult for her, due to noise and crowding, so she often stays at the college's library until it closes. Her father, who had been a teacher, now works in a restaurant, but she is studying statistics and hopes to go on to a four-year college and become a mathematics teacher herself one day.

(Mellow et al., 2004, pp. 10-13)

As these stories point out, it is difficult to identify the "average" ESL students. All of the above students share a similarity, in that they are high school graduates who are seeking ESL services at a community college. When non-credit ESL is included in the statistics, ESL programs can include teaching English to individuals whose native language skills are very limited.

International Students

There is a small minority of ESL students at community colleges who are international students, and these populations are typically of a higher socioeconomic class, well-educated in their home country, and taking ESL to pass TOEFL® tests. Their presence at the community colleges is mostly attributable to its lower cost (Blumenthal, 2002). The great majority of students at community colleges are immigrants, undocumented, refugees, and/or asylum-seekers. Their purpose in ESL classes is highly instrumental. They are seeking education for entry into basic jobs or the professional jobs available to Associate degree holders, or they are interested in transfer. As with many community college students, aspirations sometimes begin with an intention to learn enough English for a job that grows into being focused on acquiring academic English for a college degree. There are also ESL programs that community colleges deliver off-site for currently employed individuals.

There is no typical ESL student. They include nurses from the Philippines and engineers from Russia studying English to pass job-related proficiency exams; refugees from Somalia or agricultural workers from Mexico seeking basic English and literacy; Central American or Eastern European immigrants desiring access to vocational training or better employment; permanent residents from around the world seeking U.S. citizenship; U.S. citizens from Puerto Rico seeking to develop their academic English to enter a postsecondary program; and Afghan or Vietnamese women and elders wanting to help school-aged children with their homework (Sheppard and Crandall, 2004, p. 4).

Anecdotally, faculty will point out different abilities among students from various countries to respond to American classroom practices (Alfred, 2005).

Faculty with long experience teaching ESL to a wide variety of students comment that differences between Asian and Hispanic students' willingness to participate in interaction is profound, with Asian students much more reluctant to speak in class. To date, however, there does not appear to be research identifying different linguistic communities and their ability to succeed at community colleges (Gross, 2005). Additionally, faculty teach students who are transnational in personal identity, who are often as connected to their country of origin as they are anxious to be fully American (Alfred, 2005).

Generation 1.5

An emerging issue for community colleges is the students labeled Generation 1.5, which uses the nomenclature of new releases of software that indicates much of the existing structure is foundational but new programming has significantly changed the product. Generation 1.5 ESL students are adult immigrants who are enrolled in a community college (or other postsecondary education) with some amount of education in the United States, often including graduation from an American high school. Their language skills, however, are poor, particularly in academic writing and grammar. They can be highly fluent verbally, and idiomatically correct, but they make writing and grammar mistakes typical of ESL students. Students' fossilized errors often become a permanent part of their language, and it is much harder for students to "unlearn" these mistakes than it is for students who are new to learning English.

These students' profiles are also made more complex by their psychosocial orientation. Since they see themselves as American students, they are insulted by the suggestions that they need further ESL education (Sheppard and Crandall, 2004). The complexity is often played out in community colleges as placement occurs. The challenge is to determine the best initial placement—often neither developmental or ESL classes. Each program partially serves and partially under-serves this population. ESL faculty gear most of their curriculum to recent immigrants to the United States, so there is an emphasis on cultural aspects of the country as well as an assumption of greater grammatical fluency in a native language. Generation 1.5 students will be insulted by the "How to Live in America" parts of the curriculum, and at the same time unable to keep up with the content and grammar. Developmental classes, however, rarely have faculty who are trained to understand and cope with fossilized linguistic errors that emerge from a different linguistic tradition.

Generation 1.5 is increasing its presence in community colleges and is estimated to make up more than 50 percent of some ESL programs (Blumenthal, 2002). Colleges are experimenting with developing classes aimed specifically at Generation 1.5 by combining elements of developmental activities with specific focus on ESL language learning. While it is possible that some Generation 1.5 students will attend four-year colleges, their general lack of adequate high school–level literacy skills indicates that they are much more likely to be community college students (Blumenthal, 2002). Since these students are likely to be part of the growth of the workforce attributable to immigrants, finding pedagogical structures to support their learning will be particularly important (Sheppard and Crandall, 2004).

ESL CURRICULUM AND OUTCOMES

Community colleges' ESL students are so diverse that assessing the effectiveness of students progressing through curricular structures and then measuring outcomes is difficult. In part, it is hard to even ascertain which program should be evaluated, since ESL students might be literacy students, college students seeking TOEFL improvement, or Generation 1.5 (Ignash, 1995). Because of this, a comprehensive assessment outside of an individual program on an individual campus has rarely been attempted (Blumenthal, 2002). This diversity is evident in the organizational structures within which ESL programs operate on community college campuses, ranging from non-credit only to full-fledged departments with tenured faculty (Blumenthal, 2002).

The assessment conducted to place students might be as simple as determining financial need for entry into grant-sponsored programs or as involved as advanced writing, speaking, and listening assessments individually administered to each student seeking admittance (Blumenthal, 2002). The complexity of having ESL students take computerized entrance placement examinations or high-stakes "rising junior" exams is acknowledged, as are issues with learning disabilities, but there are few assessments that evaluate the effectiveness of different programs for different categories of ESL students (Rooney, 2002; Crook, 2004).

Without any national data, the localized data of student outcomes are very similar to those seen in other community college basic skills academic programs. An analysis of California's community colleges shows that retention is a significant issue, with just more than half (52 percent) of ESL students not returning for a second semester (Sengupta and Jepsen, 2006).

These data must be interpreted carefully, because even a semester of ESL could fulfill a student's desire to be employed at an entry-level job. However, it would not fulfill the goal of most community college credit ESL programs, which is to provide students with collegiate-level reading, writing, and speaking skills so they can pursue an Associate degree.

Some research has tried to determine if immigrant students are more likely to be enrolled in community colleges than in four-year colleges. Analysis of some systems, such as a study of the City University of New York, finds immigrants relatively evenly distributed throughout two- and four-year colleges, although even in this study, differences by country of origin were identified (Bailey and Weininger, 2002). Other studies find that immigrants are more likely to be enrolled in community colleges than in four-year colleges (Vernez, 1996).

Several studies have found that immigrants with high school education from their home country earn more credits and are more likely to graduate from community colleges than native-born students (Bailey and Weininger, 2002). It is hypothesized that this occurs because certain immigrants have better underlying educational skills (and perhaps educated family and family financial resources) and use community colleges primarily for their access to ESL and related support services (Bailey and Weininger, 2002).

Structure of ESL Programs

ESL programs at community colleges can be divided roughly into two types: those programs that seek to develop academic English so that students will enter credit programs, and those programs that focus on helping students enter the workforce (Vernez, 1996). ESL programs have several configurations. The curriculum ranges from free literacy ESL provided to students with little literacy in native languages and taught primarily by volunteers, to academic ESL programs taught by highly skilled faculty within a traditional credit context (although usually for institutional credit only). There are no mandated standards for the curricular structure of the ESL classes, with program reviews finding as few as four and as many as 13 different levels of ESL offered by individual community colleges (Vernez, 1996).

The departmental location of the ESL program also shows significant variability, ranging from a set of courses within a credit English department, to a stand-alone academic department, to a program within the non-credit offerings of continuing education. While most classes are open to all students who need them based upon some assessment of linguistic ability in

English, a few colleges specialize classes or ESL programs for particular ethnic immigrant groups who form large groups on a local campus. There are currently no data determining the relationship of ESL student outcomes to organizational structure, although there are calls for increased integration within the traditional academic structures (Sheppard and Crandall, 2004).

There are conceptual struggles in defining ESL as a credit course. Should ESL be defined as a "basic skills" course and placed in the curriculum as a prerequisite for all that follows? If so, the institutional-only credit allocation is logical. On the other hand, ESL experts argue that learning a language as an adult is an exalted intellectual skill, one with plateaus and iterative curves that continues throughout many years. As such, linguistic perfection is rare, and significant progress can be obtained in separate elements (such as reading and writing) but not others (such as speaking or listening). Two significant questions remain: When are second-language learners prepared to enter credit courses at a community college, and should campuses credential the learning of English differently from how they credit other college students who are learning French or Japanese?

Prerequisite Issues

Answering the first question about prerequisites asks community colleges to clarify their understanding of what a prerequisite means. For example, if students are not verbally proficient but can listen, read, and write relatively well, is it appropriate for them to enter a beginning mathematics class? Students who simultaneously take an ESL course explicitly linked to a content course do better not only in the ESL class, but also in the content class when compared to students who take the ESL course as a prerequisite and the content course subsequently (Arcario and Gantzer, 2004). These data suggest that curricular structures that require linear and sequential progress may not be as effective as connected or circular structures.

Language Credentialing

The second issue—why academic ESL classes are not evaluated in a way equivalent to other modern language classes on campus—is also fraught with challenges. Students are of course in the United States, and are typically hoping to embark on a college education that will be taught almost exclusively in English. ESL students' ability to be fluent in English is therefore fundamental to their ability to attend and succeed at the college. On the other hand, the level of academic English learning often far exceeds what the native English speaker is learning in a beginning modern language class for which they will receive college credit. One way to address this issue might be to use standardized tests to credential the native languages of foreign speakers. The problem stems from the few tests that exist; for example, the College Board offers CLEP exams in only French, German, and Spanish, and few campuses go beyond the addition of Japanese, Russian, Portuguese, Chinese, and Arabic in their attempts to credential foreign languages, although over 100 languages exist around the globe. As the countries from which students are immigrating multiply, the ability to test in Urdu or Swahili will be of increasing importance.

ESL FACULTY

The wide variety of curricular structures is reflected in the range of ways in which faculty are prepared to teach ESL (Henrichsen and Savova, 2000). There is continued conflict about the status of ESL faculty, particularly when some of the ESL programs are offered in the non-credit arena and others on the credit side (Blumenthal, 2002). Because ESL can mean everything from high-level teaching of English for professionals to basic literacy, the training of faculty is reflective of both the level and the content of the curriculum. For non-credit courses, particularly those held in conjunction with community-based organizations, volunteers are often given little training and part-time faculty predominate (Blumenthal, 2002). Even when ESL faculty are hired permanently, they might not be on a tenure track if the ESL classes on that campus receive neither institutional nor degree credit (Blumenthal, 2002; Manzo, 2005). ESL faculty complain that, because it is in a "skills" as opposed to a "content" area, the discipline is perceived by other faculty as less demanding (Blumenthal, 2002). On the other hand, calls for locating all ESL programs within community colleges are predicated in part on the belief that it is only with excellently trained faculty (minimally at the Master's degree level in linguistics or a related field) that students who need ESL will thrive (Sheppard and Crandall, 2004).

CHALLENGES TO THE FIELD

The challenges to the field in some ways can be limited to two statements: more money and more academic focus. But if we are to take seriously our commitment to creating the next generation of new Americans, ESL programs must come more fully into their own as a part of the grand scheme of community colleges. Although regional differences will affect the need differently, no part of the country can afford not to pay attention to improving ESL programs. These suggestions emerge from the research and from our own experience with running ESL programs.

1. Recommendations regarding curricular coherence:
   - Ensure seamless and intense coordination between non-credit and credit-level ESL experiences.
   - Ensure that ESL can be taught in the context of real student lives, including workplace literacy and social integration in school, health care, and community.
   - Teach college-level content courses in coordination with ESL courses whenever possible.
   - Place increased research scrutiny on the issue of modern foreign languages and ESL as a part of students' collegiate experience.
   - Develop research protocol to determine the best curricular structures for Generation 1.5 to access basic literacy skills.

2. Recommendations regarding faculty development:
   - Hold ESL faculty to the same standards as other community college faculty, with commensurate benefits and wages.
   - Provide faculty development opportunities to enhance pedagogical innovation, with particular emphasis on technology as an adjunct to learning.
   - Continue research into the best tutoring and academic services and processes to support faculty.

3. Recommendations regarding student support services:
   - Tailor academic support services for immigrant students, with specific responsiveness to different emergent issues based on students' countries of origin.
   - Expand support services to include advising on careers, job placement, immigration, health and insurance, housing, and finance management.
   - Provide practitioners who understand personal and cultural issues, such as the fear of losing one's native culture and the challenges of being connected to one's family while making one's way in an American society.

CONCLUSION

Immigrants are the foundation of our country, and America leads the world in understanding the implications of changes in technology and mobility. We can have a country with open borders, embracing the most talented and creative people from across the globe, or we can turn inward toward a past that never was by decrying that some people are "not American." Community colleges have a pivotal role in embracing the next generation of immigrants and helping the rest of the country understand that there is power not only in teaching students college-level English, but also in reciprocally using the knowledge of other cultures to enrich our own.

CHAPTER 13

Programmatic Challenges of Diverse Demographics

OVERVIEW

The greatest challenge for community colleges is embracing and supporting the most diverse classroom of learners ever to sit side by side in American higher education. With the past as a guide and demographic data as a basis, it seems possible to predict the future for community colleges. This chapter describes who is likely to attend community colleges in the twenty-first century. The data predict trends in family income, ethnicity, gender, and parental level of education, and compares student success in various geographic regions of the country. Comparisons are made between students enrolled in two-year and four-year institutions. A challenge to the field suggests changes needed to support the new traditional student.

THE DREAM

Every chapter of this book demonstrates that open admissions requires community colleges to embrace diverse skill levels, ages, genders, racial-ethnic identities, language speakers, native citizens and immigrants, and various levels of enrollment status. The dream for community colleges relative to demographics is success for anyone who can benefit from an education, where success is defined as students accomplishing their entry goals. Entry goals for diverse learners differ immensely depending on their skill level upon entry.

The enrollees at community colleges are frequently termed "nontraditional students." A common definition of nontraditional includes: adults

257

beyond traditional school age (beyond the early-twenties), ethnic minorities, women with dependent children, under-prepared students, and other groups who historically have been under-represented in higher education (Kim, 2002). What has become clear is that nontraditional students have become the tradition at community colleges. Part of the dream must be a comprehensive redefinition of the college student that encompasses the characteristics of these students, who have now become the "average" in community colleges. As we continue to dream of student success, a renewed focus on the nontraditional as traditional could have a potent influence on the way we organize and the way we funnel our resources.

The dream is then a dramatic one of believing that community colleges can solve all of the educational problems created by large numbers of students whose backgrounds would have previously excluded success in college. We dream we will be able to serve the hardest to serve learners and help them achieve their goals.

THE UNFULFILLED DREAM

Community colleges have long been open-door institutions. They make it possible for a great diversity of individuals to attempt college. In reality, these "now-traditional" students do find their way to the open door. Enrollment in higher education in general continues to grow (Phillipe and Patton, 2000). Enrollment in public four-year colleges grew by more than 13.2 percent in the late 1990s, whereas enrollment at public community colleges grew by 22 percent (Phillipe and Patton, 2000). Almost twice as many first-time freshmen are enrolling in community colleges as in other institutions, and the resulting population reflects the description of nontraditional students (Kim, 2002). These populations have attended community colleges from their inception, and their growth and their attraction to community colleges expands and intensifies.

The percentage of ethnic minorities in our nation continues to climb, but the academic progress of different races and ethnicities has not kept pace with this growth (The Education Trust, 2003). Large numbers of urban youth are not graduating from high school; there is a crisis in black and Hispanic male participation in higher education (The Education Trust, 2003). More and more people are working full or part time, the success rate of ethnic and racial groups is slim, and gender issues, skill level issues, and the different learning needs of millennials, baby boomers, Generation X and others create a need for a response from community colleges. These demographics are juxtaposed against the changing need in the twenty-first century for much higher levels of education. The challenge to community colleges is one of heroic proportions.

Many who attempt higher learning succeed and move on to better lives, and they make significant contributions to American society. At the same time, this diversity brings with it a need for diverse institutional services to respond to different requirements. We need to re-think so much of higher education—pedagogy, relationships with K-12, how we hire faculty, and the kinds of curricula we develop—because just more of the same won't help us achieve our dream. There is, to date, small evidence that community colleges are gearing up to really deal with the huge problem that demographics pose. Community colleges' ability to respond to the ever intensifying and expanding diversity is crippled by a lack of resources and sometimes by a lack of will on the part of staff. Since we have not begun to codify the different kinds of student goals in any systematic way, the assumption that racial, ethnic, age, or other categorical differences among students are associated with different individual goals is untested and currently untestable. Community colleges' ability to measure student success at meeting individual goals is seriously inadequate.

THE REAL STORY

Forms of Diversity

Nationally, ethnic and racial diversity grows annually. From 2000 to 2002, for example, Hispanic representation grew by more than 3 percent, from 35.3 percent to 38.8 percent. African-American representation in the population grew by 1 percent, from 37.1 percent to 38.3 percent (U.S. Census Bureau, 2006). This growth in diversity is projected to continue through 2050. In addition, the majority of the population in the year 2025 will be between the ages of 30 and 34, and between 60 and 74. The "traditional-aged" college students between the ages of 18 and 24 will be one of the smallest population groups nationally (U.S. Census Bureau, 2005). The student body of community colleges strongly reflects the population demographics of the nation.

In additional to age and ethnicity, there are other diverse factors to consider. Diversity in the community college comes in many forms. Learners have vastly differing skill levels, and their skill and ability to learn affects the resources required to ensure that learning occurs (The Education Trust, 2003). Ages span from 16 to 90 and each age level brings with it varied characteristics that influence the learning environment. For example, students of different ages make a mixed commitment to working full time or part time. The level of their work commitment changes the way a college can structure a learning environment, including the time of day courses are offered and their length. An individual professor's learning environment is changed with the students' varied life experiences and awareness. Diverse cultural and ethnic groups stake their requirements on the college agenda, as do men and women. Each aspect of diversity is addressed in a separate section of this chapter.

Diverse Skill Levels

The ability of students to learn at a higher level is affected by the skills with which they enter higher education. The federal government believes that learning at a higher level is predicted most clearly by entering levels of math skills (Federal Government Statistics, 2005). Higher postsecondary educational expectations among high school seniors are associated with higher levels of math performance. However, 63 percent of seniors who expected to earn a four-year college degree did not exhibit mastery of intermediate-level mathematical concepts (37 percent did exhibit intermediate-level mastery) (Federal Government Statistics, 2005).

Approximately 30 percent of all students entering both two-year and four-year American colleges and universities require developmental studies in English, reading, or mathematics. Thirteen percent of all undergraduates, about 1.6 million students, report taking one or more developmental courses in college. Another million, it is estimated, obtain remediation through tutoring programs or learning centers (Hoachlander et al., 2003). So, of the nation's more than 12 million undergraduates, about 2 million participate in developmental education during any given year (Boylan, 1999). In community colleges, an average of 28 percent of first-time freshman students are under-prepared, and they enroll in developmental courses (Hoachlander et al., 2003).

The demographics regarding diversity in college-level preparation present unique challenges for community colleges wishing to ensure student success, and these challenges are addressed extensively in chapter nine, Developmental Studies.

Diverse Age Levels

Diversity in age levels is an important factor for community college students. The average community college student, nationally, is 29, but ages range from 16 to 90-plus. This diversity brings with it immensely different expectations and needs on the part of students, as well as a richness that creates powerful learning environments. A little more than 40 percent of community college students are of "traditional" college age (21 years or younger), but an equal percentage are between the ages of 22 and 39 (AACC, 2006). This adult population sometimes is more likely to be found on campus on evenings or weekends, but the interaction between young and more mature students is a unique aspect to a community college class. Sixteen percent of students in American community colleges are 40 years of age or older (AACC, 2006). There is nothing quite like a developmental psychology class in which the mothers talk from the experience of watching their children go through Piaget's stages, the young students are close enough to adolescence to tell stories exemplifying the theoretical perspectives, and the senior citizens relate the joys and terrors of entering Erickson's generative stage. Age difference is one of the riches that community college faculty use to promote deep and meaningful learning.

Dual enrollment students are changing the age demographics of community colleges. In 1997, 4 percent of students were younger than 18. This percentage grew dramatically over the next several years due to the increased popularity of dual enrollment programs within states and among high school juniors and seniors. Dual enrollment increased nationally from 96,913 students in 1993 to 123,039 in 1995 (Bryant, 2001b). In 2001, there were 48 states involved in dual enrollment programs. This is a 406 percent increase between 1996 and 2001 (Andrews, 2005). This increase, projected to continue over the next five to 10 years, poses special concerns to community college leaders: integrating the young into classes with older students, developing their social skills, and simply accommodating their numbers without increased financial support from the state. This is a challenge because as these young students increase each year, so does the percentage of their course load that is college level.

Thirty-five percent of community college students in 1997 were aged 18 to 22. This is the largest of any group of students. Enrollment in community colleges of this age group has remained basically constant (Bryant, 2001a).

Recent high school graduates are projected to increase in the future. A little more than 47 percent of those who enter college for the first time begin their postsecondary studies at a public two-year institution (AACC, 2006). Of the students who enroll for the first time in a public institution within one year of high school graduation, 54 percent enroll at a community college (Kojaku and Nunez, 1999). Community colleges are currently a destination for graduating high school seniors, and demographic projections into the future suggest the number of young, recently graduated high school students entering community colleges will only continue to increase (Kojaku and Nunez, 1999).

While the number of high school graduates will increase in most states, there is considerable variation in high school graduation rates from region to region. Eight states will experience declines from 1996 through 2009 and increases in most states will range from 1 percent to 103 percent (Gerald and Jussar, 1999). The U.S. Department of Education estimates that because of the growing number of 18 year olds in the population, the number of high school graduates in 2009 will be 23 percent higher than in 1997 (Gerald and Jussar, 1999). This 23 percent increase of high school graduates will make itself keenly felt in community colleges around the country.

The millennial generation was born between 1982 and 2002, and this group of young students appears to possess characteristics presenting unique challenges to higher education. The millennial generation is characterized as special, sheltered, confident, team-oriented, achieving, pressured, and conventional (Howe and Strauss, 2000). These students are sheltered from learning from mistakes, since their parents are going to unprecedented lengths to protect their children from harm (Howe and Strauss, 2000). The millennial generation respects their elders, follows the rules, and seeks to create positive changes in their local communities (Howe and Strauss, 2000). They've done service-learning since elementary school, and most say they identify with their parents' values and that they trust and feel close to their parents (Howe and Strauss, 2000). These newer community college students have baby-boomer parents who tend to see their college-aged students as children rather than adults (Conneely, Good, and Perryman, 2001; Donovan, 2003). Baby-boomer parents of the millennial generation see college less as a place for their learners to discover and grow and more as an investment in both of their futures. This has implications for college graduates taking their place as adults in society. They are tending now to be seen as emerging adults from ages 18 to 25

(Donovan, 2003). It predicts that there will be increased parental involvement in their children's college educations and support for the role of *in loco parentis* on the part of college staff. This shift will be difficult to make since colleges have moved dramatically away from *in loco parentis* during the 1960s (Donovan, 2003).

Several other age groups (all considered nontraditional) attend community colleges and include: 22 to 24 year olds (13 percent); 25 to 29 year olds (14 percent); and 30 to 39 (17 percent). Generation X is a moniker used to describe students born between 1961 and 1981. They are viewed as castaways, at risk, neglected, aggressive, slackers, and alienated (Howe and Strauss, 2000), and they bring an exceptional set of needs to their community college education. They were raised in daycare, and were set aside to make room for their parents' fulfillment. They are underachievers and grew up amidst major political, social, economic, and cultural turmoil. They have an edgy skepticism about them. They are characterized as selfish, apathetic, complaining, and alienated. These students have been in higher education for a few years, and have already presented their behavioral, often addictive, personalities in community college classrooms. They have a need to learn how to live in a community, how to respect themselves, and how to love and be loved as well as how to learn.

Students aged 47 and older represent 16 percent of the community college population. This age distribution has increased slightly since 1993, and given the aging baby-boomer population, it is projected to expand much more over the next ten years (Phillipe and Patton, 2000). The percentage of those aged 66 to 74 doubled from 8.4 percent in 1991 to 19.9 percent in 1999 (Manheimer, 2005). The biggest growth in student population is projected to be in community-based, non-credit educational programs.

Baby boomers are usually described as those born between 1945 and 1960. Manheimer, in his 2005 publication, explains that they are older parents who delayed childbirth until they had achieved some of their personal goals. Baby boomers are caught between their children (often returning home to the nest, creating the cluttered nest) and their aging parents. Between 2005 and 2020, this large cohort of post-World War II-born individuals will face decisions about work, retirement, use and availability of discretionary time and money, and continued learning. About 22 percent of the population will be over the age of 65. Never before in history will there have been such a demographic shift toward later life (Manheimer, 2005). Based on the increase in older learner programs from 1950 to 2005, this age group will continue to be a growing and significant demographic for community colleges, and programmatic changes are necessary in order to meet the evolving and genuine needs of this age group.

Prior to the mid-1980s, continuing education focused on a failure model of aging, with a concentration on ameliorating the problems of the elderly. This educational model is changing to a successful or productive outlook on aging, and a new image of the robust, engaged, thriving senior adult eclipses the earlier stereotype of the despondent, dependent, disengaged older person (Manheimer, 2005). Educational programs that hold on to programs for "elders, retirees, or seniors" either will dwindle or be unable to attract the "neo elder" (Manheimer, 2005). Due to decreases in financial support, lifelong learning programs to support older learners will have to remain market driven, and increasingly will require full fees or some form of co-payment for enrollment. Without dramatic change, programs will attract a frailer, older population. The new elder plus the old elder group present a special set of needs for continuing education.

This vast diversity in age levels is important for community colleges because different ages of students bring various needs to their college experience. Among the factors driven by age is the number of students who work. Working, in turn, affects enrollment status.

Diverse Enrollment Status

Reverse transfer students are one group of older students who work. They are baccalaureate degree "non-completers" who return to community colleges to finish coursework. Degree completers of one or more baccalaureate degrees return to the community college to develop skills for employment (Andrews, 2005). It is imperative that community colleges continue to develop new career-oriented programs offered in specialized time frames that can provide the skills needed for this group of working learners.

Job retraining students paid $63 billion to be educated in a variety of venues (Drury, 2001). These older students, affected by changes in their work environments, seek new skills to achieve new jobs, and they can afford to attend school only part time. These students affect enrollment status in community colleges. These students helped push the part-time enrollment to a high of approximately 65 percent of the total community college enrollment (Phillipe and Patton, 2000). By comparison, in four-year colleges, only 22 percent of students attend part time (Phillipe and Patton,

2000). This percentage has stayed constant since 1991, and is projected to remain unchanged through 2010 (Phillipe and Patton, 2000).

Part-time enrollment among this group of learners is attributed to both family and job constraints. The largest percentage of part-time students are aged 35 and older. It is interesting to note that full- and part-time students who are more likely to work part time are younger than 19 through age 22, comprising 35 percent of students (Bryant, 2001b). Students aged 23 to over 40 (59 percent of students) are more likely to work full time. The 59 percent of students working full time will only continue to grow and expand during the next ten years. Working students need courses offered at different times of day and often seek courses offered for longer periods of time, one day or night a week, rather than for the traditional one hour every day. Working students bring very special concerns as well as gifts to community colleges, especially the 58 percent of them who are women (Bryant, 2001b). Yet it is important to remember that time is not expandable, and maintaining academic intensity is increasingly difficult for individuals who work full time, may have families, and seek to study.

Women and Men in Community College

Gender differences among the number of students attending two- and four-year institutions are slim. The percentage of women in two-year institutions in 1991 was 57.8 percent (54.5 percent in four-year), compared with 58 percent (54.5 percent in four-year) in 1997 (Phillipe and Patton, 2000).

Women make up 58 percent of community college students, and they bring with them special concerns. Adult women in community colleges report high levels of stress resulting from parenting, financial constraints, and health concerns for themselves and for their children. In addition, persisting women differ from non-persisters in that non-persisters integrate themselves even less into college life than other community college students do (Goldsmith and Achambault, 1997 in Bryant, 2001b; Johnson et al., 2000). Concerns exhibited by the majority of community college students necessitate specialized orientation, academic and financial advising, peer support, and specialized co-curricular activities to ensure greater engagement in the college. While it is unlikely that adult women students will be attracted to a Friday night dance, an early warning system for adult female students might help students anticipate and better manage problems that arise.

Racial and Ethnic Diversity

Nearly three in 10 Americans are members of an ethnic or racial group that is categorized as "non-white" (U.S. Census Bureau, 2000). Although increasingly a misnomer in many localized areas, "minority" students or "students of color" are common nomenclature to refer to students of African-American, Asian and Pacific Island, Hispanic, and Native American descent. The level of minority students' enrollment has grown at both two-year and four-year institutions. However, community colleges are the primary providers of higher education for minority students. In community colleges, minority students comprised 25 percent of the student body in 1992, and 34 percent of students in 2006 (AACC, 2006). This increase in minority student enrollment is projected to continue (Donovan, 2003).

Nationally, the Hispanic population is the fastest growing minority population, and is estimated to increase to 15.4 percent by 2015 (Donovan, 2003). Asian and Pacific Islanders are estimated to grow from 5.4 percent to 8.4 percent, and African-American students will increase nationally by 400,000 by 2015 (Donovan, 2003). Community colleges are ideal starting places for minority students if and only if the colleges are able to provide the rigorous academic preparation necessary for continued educational advancement. As discussed in chapter nine, Developmental Studies, and chapter ten, The Transfer Experience, programs which provide a specialized focus on minority students are often required to ensure progress.

Students representing racial-ethnic groups often come to higher learning with several barriers to learning. For example, research has demonstrated that black students transfer at a higher rate from larger community colleges where daycare facilities are provided, and when schools are located in affluent communities with a high percentage of black residents (Blau, 1999). The transfer rate is lower when black students are concentrated in particular programs (e.g., vocational) in predominately white schools (Blau, 1999). Latino students' attitudes toward themselves and their community college experiences are strongly related to interactions with the faculty and self-image (Vasquez and Garcia-Vasquez, 1998). These issues require community colleges to ensure that adequate role models and faculty and staff representatives of each group, as well as sufficient structural support systems like daycare and tutoring facilities, are present.

Recent immigrants are a significant proportion of students attending community colleges. Immigrants are 10 percent more likely to attend a community college than a four-year school (Szelenyi and Chang, 2002). The educational needs and experiences of international and immigrant students frequently differ from one another, especially regarding English-language acquisition and vocational training (see chapter twelve). Immigrant students face cultural adjustment, discrimination, and citizenship and language difficulties and consequently these students often require counseling and advising beyond the services normally provided (Szelenyi and Chang, 2002). Nineteen percent of students report being bilingual or cite English as their second language, a steady increase compared with ten years ago (Donovan, 2003). Increasing numbers of immigrants are undocumented and even though they graduate from high school, in some areas they are not eligible to attend college. After years of lawmaker and activist effort, in 2001, only Texas and California passed legislation allowing in-state tuition for undocumented students (Szelenyi and Chang, 2002).

Other Demographic Information

First-generation learners attending postsecondary education are less likely to succeed in attaining a degree than their counterparts whose parents attended postsecondary education. This success differential is noticeable in both the number of credits earned during the first year and the persistence shown in pursuing a degree over time (Federal Government Statistics, 2005). As increasing percentages of Americans seek higher education, it seems likely that increasing numbers will be children of parents who did not attend college. This group of learners requires unique support systems. They need to learn the language and culture of higher education before they can successfully navigate the system. For example, they need to understand financial aid and they need to learn the amount of time it takes to study for each credit enrolled; additionally, developmental student will need math, science, and reading skills.

POVERTY AMONG COLLEGE STUDENTS

Today's college students are likely to be raised in a single parent household (32 percent), to live below poverty level (23.1 percent), or to have a mother who works outside the home (89.4 percent) (Donovan, 2003). These factors are relevant to all the students attending community colleges, and many of those students *are* the parent who works outside the home.

The average American is getting poorer. While household income rose by 30 percent between 1967 and 2005, it did not increase at all between 2002 and 2005 (Donovan, 2003). Thus, the actual average purchasing power of American households has declined over those three years from $44,482 to $44,389 (Donovan, 2003). The ability of the community college learner to pay tuition is decreasing while, due to declining state funding support, actual tuition is increasing. For the fourth consecutive year, the poverty rate rose in the United States (Donovan, 2003), and it now stands above 13 percent. Since community colleges traditionally offer an education for less money per credit than do other institutions of higher learning, a greater portion of learners with low incomes come to the community college. Increasingly, these learners find it difficult to secure financial aid, and are taking out loans to support their education. Low-income learners are already leaving the community college deeply in debt, and this trend is doomed to continue (Federal Government Statistics, 2005).

CHALLENGES TO THE FIELD

While we in community colleges currently work diligently to serve the diverse demographic attending our institutions, we have mixed results in ensuring student success among diverse learners. The chapters on transfer and Developmental Studies provide ample data to support this concern. To move persistently toward achieving the community college dream, we must make changes to our approach to supporting diversity, and we need specific programs designed for specific groups.

- We need to redefine the concept of the nontraditional learner in the community college. The new has become the old, and vice versa. We could perhaps refer to them as our "now traditional" learner. Our programmatic responses need to reflect that redefinition.
- Monitoring and facilitating high school flow from school districts to community colleges remains an important role for community colleges' collaboration with schools. Activities can include curriculum articulation and assistance in promoting student advancement from one grade to the next through programs like Upward Bound and Talent Search.
- Community college and political leaders must work together to provide in-state tuition for immigrants, including those who are undocumented.

This has been achieved in two politically conservative states, Texas and California, and their success can serve as a model for others. Visibility and persistence among community college leaders is an important priority during the national immigration debate.

- We need to develop academic, personal, and career counseling that are directed toward the various groups needing special support. Some programs can be used for several groups; for example, women and African-American students demonstrate a higher need for daycare. The desire for English proficiency and citizenship support is unique to immigrant students; however; their need for help dealing with discrimination and cultural adjustment is shared by other students representing racial-ethnic groups. These programs need to include specialized orientation, academic and financial advising, peer support, and role models. An early warning system is necessary to anticipate and better manage problems that arise.
- As the community colleges attract younger learners in dual enrollment programs and recent high school graduates who have been protected by their parents, we may need to adopt an increased *in loco parentis* philosophy. We may need to expand opportunities for these plugged in and protected learners to develop social skills.
- There is a continued need to teach Generation X students how to learn and how to respect themselves and others, including their teachers and one another.
- As colleges continue to provide for the growing population of the "new elder," they need to work directly with this group to design relevant learning programs for lively and robust individuals.

Conclusion

Based on demographic data, community colleges will continue to serve populations that are diverse, challenging, and complicated. Each age group, each racial-ethnic group, women, immigrants, and students with varying skill levels have grown in population during the past 15 years, and they are projected to continue to grow—many in large numbers. In the past, community colleges have referred to most of these groups as "nontraditional." It is time for us to change the way we think about community college students, and to no longer refer to the student population as nontraditional. This student group *is* now our traditional population.

Community colleges have been challenged in the past to meet the needs of these many and diverse groups, and too often practitioners consider it someone else's job to reach out to them. We attempt, here, to identify a few potent means of addressing some of the challenges facing community college learners and their educators. If we can learn from the best practices of our colleagues how to support diverse learners, we can then truly be the pace-setters for a democratic society.

~ Summary
Minding the Dream

~ OVERVIEW

Minding the dream of America's community colleges requires us to enact the highest purpose of our intentions to make a high-quality education available for all. It demands that we refine and use our best process and our best practices. This chapter assembles in one place recommendations that, if implemented in their entirety, could truly realize the dream for community colleges. As practitioners with almost 60 combined years of service who are passionate about the students who enroll in the community college, we write this book as an expression of the values and beliefs we have tried to implement in the colleges where we have worked. We have made many mistakes and at the same time we have implemented many of the practices and recommendations from whatever seat we held: adjunct or full-time faculty member, dean, vice president, and president. Where these practices have been tested, we have seen positive student success outcomes. If every community college could implement all the recommendations described here, no one could deny the powerful impact we would have on the 48 percent of undergraduates enrolled in higher education in this country.

Most of the recommendations result from research done by our colleagues in the community college field. The citations giving them credit for their work are contained in the chapter involving the relevant issue. We thank these colleagues, many of them scholar-practitioners, for their ground-breaking work. We challenge our readers to implement these recommendations to the fullest extent possible.

FINANCING THE DREAM

Every vision and challenge described in this book has financial implications. Every added response to our learners' needs costs money. We cannot pass this expense on to our students because our financial dream is affordability. The existing low levels of public funding for community colleges compared to other forms of higher education results in a difference in the number of full-time faculty, more students attending part time, and low levels of intensive academic support for at-risk students. Funding for these needs attenuates the real affordability of community colleges.

The quality of an education balances on the fulcrum of money, and community colleges run on a shoestring, so that budget constraints hobble our ability to offer the services needed. This shows up in many ways described in chapter three. What needs to be done includes both data collection to prove our success and our need, followed up with funding support.

We need to *work with governments to create national benchmarks* or indices, similar to a Standard & Poor's rating scale, that evaluate the relative contribution of local, state, and federal dollars. These national benchmarks or indices that create a "value" standard can relate tuition to educational value. This standard can be used by students and elected officials to determine the best use of tax dollars in higher education.

We need to establish a definition of non-credit and collect national data on non-credit courses and workforce development activities; we need to use this information to fund non-credit courses that could move low-income adults to college and ultimately to greater employment and productivity.

The national benchmarks scale described above needs to be used to structure state and local statutes that *regularize the funding for community colleges* and create greater consistency in funding programs. Funding benchmarks must take into account local cost-of-living indices, and could be used as the basis for creating a pool of equity dollars that could be distributed using equalizing factors.

This approach to benchmarking and funding would increase availability of state and federal tuition assistance for community college students' living expenses, indexing the entire need as not simply based upon individual campus tuition. Benchmarking should ultimately create mechanisms to provide tuition assistance for non-credit courses. It would also ensure that states provide funding, at a minimum, which creates equity on a full-time equivalency (FTE) basis between high schools and community colleges.

Community colleges need to use the leverage we have gained as a result of the extent of our influence and our proven success using national benchmark data to convince federal and state governments to *re-evaluate and re-calibrate federal and state tuition assistance programs* so that a greater amount of tax dollars do not automatically flow to the most expensive programs.

Using our national data, community colleges will be able to prove that we have indeed been able to accomplish amazing outcomes on very little funding. An exciting calculation is what might happen to higher education in America if we were provided equitable and consistent funding.

Exposing the ways in which state and federal policies affect community colleges, and creating mechanisms to benchmark best state and local funding practices, are beginning steps to regularize and rationalize the crazy quilt of funding structures at use across the country. Finding ways to fund the need for expanded services is crucial if community colleges are to continue in their efforts to serve almost half of all the undergraduates in the country.

MEASURING SUCCESS WITH A MORE EXACT GAUGE

Increasing numbers of government leaders, as well as many of our own colleagues, are demanding to know just how effective is our work. We are challenged as a nation of community colleges to prove that what we do for learners works. Many standard yardsticks for four-year colleges (time to graduation, acceptance rates, IPEDS standards of "first-time, full-time") do not provide a complete measure of community college effectiveness, yet comprehensive measures that might provide some insight into community college success (percentage of developmental students who graduate, percentage of students who pass national certifying examinations) have not been used nationally. We are confronted with a need to address this dilemma.

We can *create coordinated strategies* across states and regions and establish national indices and benchmarks as a beginning accountability measure. We can collect and focus on improving teaching and learning, and ensure that information is then presented to the public in clear language that everyone can understand. We can articulate the community college's distinct mission, and then link all accountability metrics to those roles.

We need to work with the federal government and the states to distinguish between *institutional-level and state-level accountability.* We need to pay special attention to how students flow across institutions, including from high school to college and between colleges, as well as patterns of returning adult student enrollment and graduation between public, private, and for-profit colleges. We need to establish campus-level standards for learning, especially for general education, and decide how these learning outcomes can be measured. Then we can consistently report on these outcomes to the general public.

We need to work with the federal government to *revamp IPEDS data* to include measures that respond to community colleges. While the federal government maintains focus on educational equity, federal data collection can improve its ability to track students across institutions and across the country. Also, the federal government must improve national research, the actual equivalent of clinical trials research, on student learning.

There are *few true outcome measures* universally used by community colleges across the country. Graduation rates and professional licensure examination scores are among these few. Others include: transfers from community colleges, faculty teaching loads, credits at graduation or time-to-degree, faculty/staff diversity, job placement rates, non-instructional costs as a percentage of overall costs, program duplication, satisfaction surveys (alumni or employers), sponsored research dollars obtained, student test scores, and workforce training indicators.

We have the capacity to *influence federal and state and accreditation* agencies to incorporate many more of the sporadically used measures that truly demonstrate our effectiveness. We need the will to implement them in a universal manner, and then we need to use our national data to demonstrate success and to leverage respect for our unique measures.

GOVERNANCE THAT HOLDS THE
COMMUNITY COLLEGE DREAM IN TRUST

Governance, at its highest level, is about holding an organization in trust so it can reach its greatest potential or, as we propose in this book, to achieve the dream of the community college mission. Governance occurs at several levels in a community college: The community, represented by a board of trustees; the president, hired by a board of trustees to represent them; an administration; and the faculty and staff. Tom Peters' philosophy of involving everybody in everything could be a theme for governance that can transform a community college. The president, administration, faculty, and staff have been explored in other parts of the governance chapter. Boards of trustees are also an important area of concern. Trustees and presidents need to work together nationally to clarify and strengthen trustee activity in areas that support and enhance the needs of community colleges.

We need to ask governing boards to help institutions *gain perspective on the major issues of the day*, do good environmental scanning, understand and articulate the inherent risks in future endeavors and directions, and use board meetings to discuss strategic issues for the future.

Trustee education can guide new trustees to understand that they do not lead in the traditional manner, as the president leads. Their mandate does not give them the authority to do so. Effective colleges help trustees understand that shared governance limits everyone in the institution's role to a certain extent. In addition, in the few days a year trustees are able to devote to their college, it is impossible to understand the complexities of the organization they hold in trust.

Trustees function as advocates, overseers, guardians of public interest, and as social conscience is highly prized and needed in governing community colleges. In these roles, they are able to help define reality in the community, point presidents in the right direction, and urge them to get going. They can do effective external environmental scanning to identify looming problems and issues, and they can also engage in national dialogue about challenges like those described in this book.

For example, trustees can engage in regular board dialogue about such difficult issues as changes in local economies and regional economic structures; how to respond to the changing demographic realities; how the campus should respond to the need for advances in science and technology; how effective standards of quality can be set (for faculty and for teaching); how global perspectives and issues can be addressed; and how students can be helped with values, ethics, and related issues.

In the words of John Carver, effective boards act on behalf of the owners, who are the community at large, but not simply the "customers"—the students). Boards lead rather than monitor, are future-oriented, focus outward not inward, are proactive not reactive, are actively linked with their ownership, are actively linked with other governing boards, and ensure executive performance. With powerful people holding the community college in trust and holding their collective finger to the wind, and interacting with leaders in the local, state, and national community, we can make great strides in realizing our community college dream.

PEDAGOGY AND STRUCTURE FOR LEARNING

We in community colleges have always prided ourselves that our students succeed because of our great teaching. The paradox, which we invite our readers to consider, is that not enough of our students are succeeding. We believe potential barriers to our students' success are the practices we employ for teaching them. We continue to teach the way we were taught, usually by lecture in a classroom. Learners who we have always considered not traditional are now our traditional student. We need to adapt our pedagogy to learners who are not "college material" because of their prior academic preparation, their significant language barriers, and their past failures in traditional school settings using traditional pedagogy, and their considerable life experience if they are older learners. We need to become colleges deeply focused on student learning (not the teacher) and create policies that motivate and support new pedagogies.

An important new college policy is *requiring innovative, inquiry-based liberal education*. Through multiple experiences across courses and semesters, students can move toward achieving general learning goals. While completing courses in required areas of knowledge, students can simultaneously develop designated competencies (like writing), use modes of inquiry (like deductive reasoning), and engage with selected themes (like science and society). Creative combinations may occur, such as applying quantitative skills in a humanities course. We need to know exactly what, and to what extent, we want our graduates to know and be able to do when they graduate with an Associate degree, and we need to actually assess the knowledge and skills demonstrated. When graduates are not able to demonstrate knowledge and skill at the level we deem appropriate, we need to change what we do until a greater percentage of learners succeed.

Another college policy is our *class size policy*. Aware of the difficulty of large class sizes while implementing creative new options, colleges need to re-consider their class size policies. Course cancellation policies, related to class size, often force innovative projects to be scuttled before they have a chance to become known by learners and to build a strong registration. These policies, too, may need to be adapted in order to sustain pedagogical innovation.

Innovative approaches to *integrating technology* can be invented to engage the new learner and to take maximum advantage of their immersion in multiple technologies. This could involve outsourcing or co-sourcing technology efforts.

Faculty development experts need to be guides at community colleges to support new faculty roles and to help them learn the skills to assess student learning.

Leaders of community colleges need to *create an environment* in which faculty and staff come together and speak from their hearts about issues of substance: student learning, new roles, and new learning strategies. These conversations of consequence can be part of a general culture of inquiry and quality engendered by the leader.

Funding sources must become aware of the factors that can increase our effectiveness and our "output": A learning emphasis, the resources required to keep small class sizes, low-enrollment courses, technology innovations, and large-scale organization changes to support a new pedagogy.

Higher learning, the transformation of individuals in their learning, knowing, and doing, continues to be a challenge for community colleges as we attempt to make our dream a reality. Sixteen years after our first exploration of the role of learning as opposed to that of teaching, we continue to focus more on the needs of our teachers (hours taught, courses taught, and time spent directly with students) than on the direct needs and outcomes of learners. We have learned much in 16 years about ways to increase student progress along the road of transformation: new pedagogies exist that are truly democratic in their diversity, multiple entry points, and interactivity; new technologies enhance the learning process; faculty roles have evolved; leadership roles continue to be important; and organizational changes that support technology are needed. Our knowledge exists, and our practice and the funding for implementation lag far behind. To accomplish our community college dream, we have many challenges and much hard work ahead.

LEADERSHIP THAT TARGETS THE DREAM

Leading a community college is very different from leading a four-year school because community colleges are not just another form of higher education. Community colleges are a movement for greater social justice and for a real implementation of democracy. In other words, our work must truly be oriented toward what is diverse and inclusive, have multiple entry points, and be interactive. We want *all* the learners who come to us to succeed, and we need leaders at every level (presidents, vice presidents, deans, and faculty and support staff) to believe this and to take the risks and make the investments that can bring to fulfillment what we imagine.

New leaders must be prepared for the mission, the dream of community colleges. Leaders need to understand our reason for existence so they can lead the many people who work in the colleges who neither understand the mission nor have the will to implement it. Distributed education or distance learning doctoral programs for mid-career professionals are essential for preparing persons already employed in community colleges. These doctoral students and current leaders can support the field by helping explore which are the best leader behaviors to implement the crucial competencies and activities needed for community colleges in this new century. Successful leaders can share their stories with their colleagues.

Colleges need to find ways to *persuade faculty members to consider leadership* positions by appealing to their sense of the greater good as well as to their enlightened self-interest. To this end, colleges need to formalize a leadership development policy and program to prepare future leaders among faculty, support staff ,and administrators who represent every ethnic group. The program needs to be assigned to a responsible individual, perhaps the staff development officer.

Elements of *institutional policy* that would be worthy of attention include: sabbaticals, extended leave for administrators, and financial support for persons pursuing longer-term leadership programs, including advanced degrees. It would be valuable for the common good if colleges would consider these programs a service to the entire field as well as to individual institutions. In addition, new leaders need trained mentors and coaches as guides as they face the challenges presented by our colleges' need for diversity, inclusivity, interactivity and multiple entry and exit points.

There are many *barriers for leaders* confronting these challenges: Faculty members who choose to teach only the people who are like themselves, long-term administrators who believe things should be the way they have always been and who believe the only really important activity occurs in the college-level classroom, community leaders who want services not available to them, students with powerful needs not being met, and state and federal governments demanding accountability. Leaders who can both engage their college personnel and achieve results that make the dream a reality are in great demand.

THE INTERNATIONAL CONNECTION

China is the country with the largest number of English speakers in the world, and India is close behind. These two examples demonstrate a need for global awareness and connection. Fortunately, community colleges are perfectly positioned and, in many ways, are already responsive to that need. There is much for us to learn from other countries, and there is much for us to share with others; those learning opportunities need both institutional, governmental, and media support.

Dialogue between students, faculty, and staff of community colleges with colleagues around the globe deepens understanding and awareness for all participants. Some colleges promote internationalization in their curriculum and exchange programs in non-credit services. Some community colleges are discussing ways to expand educational opportunities for the poor, women, and those in minority status around the globe. Activities described in chapter eight are those that create linkages among faculty and campuses and create networks of trust and knowledge that can ground America's future in global collaboration, connection, and mutual gain. We encourage readers to rise to the global challenge in each community college in the country.

COMMITTING TO DEVELOPMENTAL STUDIES

Developmental Studies Programs can be the centerpiece for the democratic college if they meet all the major hallmarks of democracy: working with diverse learners, providing a special entry point for learning, and being interactive. Developmental Studies Programs are the centerpiece for keeping real opportunity open to all learners, and they are the centerpiece for access to the American Dream. It is crucial that we meet the challenge of student success in the developmental curriculum. Forty-nine percent is a good success rate, and we need to be better. We need to annually set goals for increasing our success among these diverse learners. Our challenges lie at the policy level, at the institutional level, and at the classroom level. Community college leaders at all levels need to rise to the challenge and to implement the activities that realize the vision.

Policy changes integrate competence among all levels of education, both secondary and higher education. Agreeing on appropriate competence levels from kindergarten though the senior year in college is crucial in order to make Developmental Studies an effective strategy for supporting unprepared students.

Policy agreements can align high school requirements with college content and competency expectations. Early intervention and financial aid programs targeted at students at the K-12 level can link mentoring, tutoring, and academic guidance with a guarantee of college financial aid. Programs like the TRIO Program's Upward Bound for every student, for example, can help ensure that all high school students receive the personal attention they need in this area. High school student follow-up and high school feedback systems can link college staff with high school staff in a way that communicates expectations and develops faculty relationships for the benefit of students. Policy regarding teacher preparation is crucial to increase program effectiveness. Collaborative research among secondary schools, community colleges, and universities can ensure best practices are developed that support effective and comprehensive programs for under-prepared learners at all levels of education. Placement testing can take place during the junior year in high school so students know before they arrive in college those areas in which they need extra work, and more developmental work can then be done at the high school level.

Institutional commitment to face the challenges of Developmental Studies is crucial. From the president, to the faculty who teach in the program, to the students, commitment and pride are important. Developmental Studies professionals operate most effectively in an environment that values their work. In fact, the value of Developmental Studies should be stated explicitly in the mission statement. Courses and services need to be highlighted in publications, and Developmental Studies needs to be seen as an integral part of the campus academic community and as part of any planning effort.

Mandatory testing and placement of students in Developmental Studies programs needs to occur. For many years, in community colleges we talked about the learner's right to fail. This, as we know, resulted in more than the open door; it resulted in the revolving door. Facing reality and helping students face their reality as college learners is our responsibility. In 1998, the National Association for Developmental Education (NADE) passed a resolution supporting institutional policies that require mandatory academic assessment of incoming students and mandatory placement of students into developmental courses, as appropriate. This resolution, discussed and passed by Developmental Studies faculty and coordinators, needs to be taken seriously by community college presidents and everyone in the institution wishing to fulfill the dream of success harbored by students and faculty alike.

Assessing the strengths of our learners is also important. Even though many students come to community college with deficiencies in reading, writing, or mathematics, they also come with dazzling strengths. An important part of assessment, agreed on at the institutional level, could be assessing those strengths and using them to help students enroll in appropriate college-level courses where their developmental work could be a support to them. These strengths could also be used to facilitate involvement in service learning activities throughout the college and the community.

Developmental Studies program and classroom staff members need to take matters into their hands to ensure the programs on their campuses are of the highest possible quality. Many college Developmental Studies faculty members work hard to ensure quality, which is why we have considerable information about what works and what can improve effectiveness.

Many college faculty members ensure Developmental Studies programs are delivered by well-trained people. They conduct their own in-house training and make certain that developmental teachers use best practice as researched and base their programs on student need. A need exists to focus on how students learn, knowledge of student issues, and far more than content knowledge. In other words, the best Developmental Studies programs are student-oriented and holistic.

Excellent Developmental Studies programs connect with the college curriculum. Exit standards for Developmental Studies are consistent with entry standards for the college, and the goals and objectives are consistent with the goals of the institution. They are integrated into a seamless progression of academic standards, and they help students make the transition from one level of content to the next. Critical skills, critical thinking, and study skills are found in successful Developmental Studies courses. Whether mainstreamed or centralized, effective developmental reading, writing, and math curricula are aligned with content and skills found in college-level courses. Remedial literacy and math practices utilize actual material and examples from the college curriculum rather than drilling in skills that fragment the literacy process.

Individualized attention and supplementary tutoring are important sources of support for academically under-prepared students. This can include early-warning systems.

Both cognitive and affective development occur in the classroom and in the counseling department, where there are advising and enrichment activities that engage learners in the college environment. Students enrolled in Developmental Studies programs who participate in college activities, especially those related to the majors and professions to which they aspire, increase their feelings of self-confidence and their self-perceptions as an academic success.

Many Developmental Studies programs are well coordinated. On a regular basis, leaders bring together the people who teach to share problems and seek solutions. Learning lab staff synchronize with the teaching faculty, and advisors communicate with developmental instructors. Everyone has the same expectations of students.

Effective promotional materials for Developmental Studies programs have stated goals and objectives and identify what students can expect to accomplish and what the program demands from faculty, staff, and students.

It is the implementation of these activities by the Developmental Studies programs that brings our community college success rate for students in Development Studies to 49 percent. If *all* community colleges implemented *all* these activities, why couldn't our success rate could be 99.5 percent!

ALL-ENCOMPASSING TRANSFER SUCCESS

Community college pioneers aspired to provide access to all of higher education for an extraordinarily diverse group of young people who might not be eligible for college right out of high school and for the 75 percent of community college students who work full time and need convenient courses close to home. Community college planners dreamed that people could earn their general education requirements and then easily transfer to the four-year college of their choice. The baccalaureate continues to be an important entry point to the workforce, and it is essential for students to be able to transfer from two-year to four-year institutions.

We still dream that *partnerships with universities* can allow faculty to respect one another and work together for the good of students and for a particular field. We dream we have caring and supportive faculty and counselors who build positive relationships with students and with colleagues in four-year universities. We dream of "upside down" transfer, where students earn their professional credentials and work while at the community college and then earn their general education credits at the four-year university. We dream that people can work, raise their families, and earn their degrees close to home. To fulfill this dream, we have many challenges to confront. Again, programs and examples currently exist to guide us as we strengthen our transfer function in community colleges.

The *students most successful at transferring* to the university are those who are enrolled in a rigorous academic program in high school, are enrolled in a college academic program, and are carefully advised regarding specific courses to take for a specific baccalaureate degree (14 percent of all high school graduates). Successful transfer students are more likely to be those who *complete* the Associate degree rather than transfer early. Transfer rates are higher among students who are full-time, from a high socioeconomic group, and are native born Caucasians from a metropolitan area. This highly successful population is a very small group of people, and this statistic most certainly does not fully reflect who we are as community colleges. Many of our students (now traditional) are part-time, working students (33 percent) from middle to lower socioeconomic groups (20 percent). Many of our students are not native born (20 percent), and a very high percentage of our learners represent diverse racial and ethnic groups (43 percent). Approaches to achieving success with these diverse learners is well documented, and we invite leaders at all levels to respond to these challenges.

We need to *enhance counseling and advising* services and invite only well-trained faculty to act as advisors. This includes an increased sensitivity to older and multi-cultural students, learners who work, and parents who are students.

Differing missions between community colleges and universities are addressed by providing clear and timely communication of requirement changes, clear articulation agreements between institutions, dual admission agreements, common course numbering systems, and a milieu that optimizes the amount of credits accepted in transfer. We can, at both the community college and the university, encourage community college students to complete the Associate degree. Increased scholarships set aside for transfer students who have completed the Associate degree can support this end. Another financial incentive can guarantee admission at the four-year institution by discounting tuition for community college students who complete the Associate degree before transfer. It could be worthwhile for the university. Those universities who keep track of GPAs for native juniors and for transfer students are well aware that transfer students are their very best juniors.

Some colleges use *new approaches to the baccalaureate degree*. One possibility is the use of the upside down transfer degree that allows students to complete general education requirements for the baccalaureate after having completed an Associate of applied science degree that contains many junior level courses.

Faculty bias is a challenge we can handle by informing both university and community college faculty of the higher transfer and success rate of students who complete the Associate degree. We can encourage ongoing relationships among university and community college faculty that support mutual exploration around their discipline areas. These relationships can build the mutual respect that will in the end benefit students. In addition, we can encourage analysis of university department curricula and student success based on their completion of particular general education courses.

Lack of student support is a major challenge for community colleges. Some colleges are finding ways to make resources available through federal grants to TRIO programs at a cost less than $1,000 per student. TRIO programs follow all the best knowledge from research and best practice, and they ensure that each student intending to transfer declares a major. TRIO support staff form social committees that foster student goal clarity, create clubs among students with common transfer majors, encourage visits with people from their field, provide specific transfer advisors who work at both the community college and the transfer institution, make sure students visit four-year institutions selected by students, and provide assistance in filling out transfer institution application and financial forms. These services focus on at-risk learners. Among TRIO participants, 62 percent were still in college after three years. Imagine our transfer success rate if all community college students received such robust support. There are particular groups of students for whom we need further research into relevant cultural and economic issues. This research can help us to craft effective solutions to minimize racial/ethnic disparities in transfer.

Policy level challenges exist and so do clear methods of addressing them. The Institute for Higher Education Policy and the American Association of Community Colleges (AACC) and the Association of American Colleges and Universities (AAC&U) project suggests the following key approaches to policy-level issues.

Effective colleges develop baseline information about statewide transfer performance, clarify state policies and plans for transfer, and set goals and measures for performance. We can perform statewide transfer policy audits, to ensure that policies are consistent and that performance measures do not inadvertently discourage transfer. We can ensure articulation and credit transfer agreements are in place and encourage joint admissions. College-mandated student assessment and placement of students needing developmental work can occur and successful colleges can establish consistent cut-off scores among institutions. We can create structures to facilitate ongoing communication among all stakeholders regarding advising and transfer issues. Such structures include encouraging accrediting bodies to promote transfer and access to the baccalaureate. We can track retention, transfer, and successful completion rates, share the information among institutions, and allocate sufficient resources to adequately address the growing population of transfer students. State funding for higher education must support foreseeable demands for access to an undergraduate education.

Most students who actually transfer from the community college are those persons identified in the literature as *least* likely to succeed in the transfer process. In addition to the barriers presented by students themselves, states and institutional policies, as well as faculty attitudes, hurl barriers at potential transfer students. These recommendations for institutional, state, and local action could increase the likelihood of success for all potential transfer students. If implemented, these recommendations could transform the transfer culture at community colleges and the success of the transfer dream.

A GLOBALLY AGGRESSIVE WORKFORCE

America is relying on community colleges for continued success in generating a workforce prepared for an information-based economy. Community colleges are responding to that challenge in an admirable and exciting manner. There are many things we can learn from our successful colleagues and their best practices that will sustain our efforts and enable community colleges to continue to enhance service to business and industry.

Associate of Applied Arts degrees are a significant part of employee training. Emphasizing the liberal arts as well as technical skills ensures that we will continue to have workers who can think. Both programs and noncredit courses based on local and regional data provide a high degree of effective employment, and local advisory board members who are current and active in their field provide effective and rigorous oversight.

Inclusion of liberal arts courses in these degrees allows for a smooth transition to a range of baccalaureate degrees in several forward-thinking partnerships between community college and university programs. Replication of those efforts can ensure an educational career ladder that supports low-level skilled workers to the highest level in any field or discipline, and assures business and industry the needed skilled workers. Many students who eventually transfer to a baccalaureate degree are not enrolled in transfer programs; they are enrolled in applied programs not originally intended to transfer. A study of the vast numbers of these learners could encourage reverse transfer programs that allow students to take liberal arts courses at the junior and senior level at the university, and take their applied courses at the freshman and sophomore level at the community college.

Identifying the right people in workforce training, both in industry and among potential learners, is an important factor. Identification needs include creating effective connections with businesses and economic development agencies, advising learners, and helping business and industry leaders, as well as learners, understand the range of career programs and non-credit training opportunities. Community colleges can assist integration in career fields by ensuring racial and gender diversity in career programs.

Nationally, there are opportunities for strengthening the impact of workforce training and development. Creating a national standard for non-credit offerings that defines a full-time enrolled and a part-time enrolled learner will enable colleges and the government to better assess productivity definitions for workforce training. A national measure for assessing community college effectiveness in supporting economic development could help the public understand the impact we have on local communities.

While community colleges are extraordinarily effective at preparing America's workforce, the work goes largely unnoticed and unsupported financially. Implementing more of the strategies described above, and in greater detail in chapter five, could strengthen workforce training effectiveness and enhance national visibility and support for community college efforts.

ENGLISH AS A SECOND LANGUAGE: AN EDUCATIONAL FAULT LINE

As immigration levels rise and language challenges grow in our country, the community college becomes increasingly important in preparing new citizens to speak clearly and to participate fully in American society.

ESL content, in the most creative programs, is linked to college-level content with a seamless and intense coordination between non-credit and credit-level courses. Effective ESL courses use the context of learners' lives as course content, including the workplace, social structures, educational interactions, healthcare issues, and community involvement. Place increased research scrutiny on the issue of modern foreign languages and include ESL as a part of a students' collegiate experience.

Develop research protocol to determine the best curricular structures for Generation 1.5 to access basic literacy skills.

Faculty standards and faculty development opportunities are the same for ESL faculty as for other faculty members in colleges who are serious about preparing the next generation of the United States' immigrant citizens. In addition, there is more to learn regarding the best approach to tutoring and support for ESL learners and for ESL faculty members.

DEMOGRAPHICS

The challenges presented to community colleges by the national demographic and by the demographic of the student population are of heroic proportions. There are many ethnic minorities in our nation due to birth rates and to unprecedented levels of immigration. Community colleges need to respond to a range of concerns: more and more learners work full- or part-time; the documented success rates of ethnic and racial groups need improvement; and there are gender issues, skill level issues, and different learning needs between millennials, baby boomers, the X generation, the "new elder," and others. These demographics are then juxtaposed against the changing need in the twenty-first century for much higher levels of education.

While we in community colleges currently work diligently to serve the diverse demographic attending our institutions, we have mixed results in ensuring student success among diverse learners. The chapters on transfer and on Developmental Studies provide ample data to support this concern. To move persistently toward achieving the community college dream, changes need to be made to our approach to supporting diversity and *we need specific programs designed for specific groups*.

We need to re-define the concept of *nontraditional learners* in the community college. The new has become the old, and vice-versa. Our programmatic responses can reflect a re-definition of the traditional community college learner.

Monitoring and facilitating high school flow from school districts to community colleges remains an important role for collaboration between community colleges and schools.

Creative leaders in community colleges in some settings have *worked with political leaders* to provide in-state tuition for immigrants, including those who are undocumented. This has been achieved in several fairly conservative states, and their success can serve as a model for others.

Responsive colleges can develop *academic, personal, and career counseling* that is directed toward the various groups needing special support. Some programs can be used for several groups; for example women and African-American students demonstrated a higher need for daycare. English proficiency and citizenship support is unique to immigrant students, however their need for dealing with discrimination and cultural adjustment is shared by other students representing racial/ethnic groups. These programs include specialized orientation, academic and financial advising, and peer support. An early warning system and intrusive advising are used to anticipate and better manage problems that arise.

As the community colleges attract younger learners in dual enrollment programs and recent high school graduates who have been protected by their parents, we may need to adopt an *increase in loco parentis* philosophy.

For those learners representing Generation X there is a continued need to *teach learners how to learn,* how to respect themselves and others, including their teachers and their fellow students.

As colleges continue to provide for the growing population of *the "new elder,"* they need to work directly with these students to design relevant learning programs for lively and robust individuals.

Based on demographic data, community colleges will continue to serve populations that are diverse, challenging, and complicated. Each age group, each racial/ethnic group, women, immigrants, and those with varying skill levels have grown in population during the past 15 years, and they are projected to continue to grow—many in large numbers. It is time for community colleges to find these learners to be our traditional learners and to pour our resources into their success.

Conclusion

We believe this work demonstrates the promise of community colleges, while not ignoring the unfulfilled portion of the dream. We celebrate seeing the best of that promise realized in hundreds of colleges across the country and the scholar practitioners who have carefully gathered and shared their data about the promise. We believe the American community college is the single most democratic form of higher education; we believe the future of America, especially her ability to keep and educate a middle class, requires great community colleges to survive.

We believe this book on the process and the practice of community colleges is necessary reading for individuals who are a part of the higher learning community, especially the community college sphere—board members, faculty members, administrators, advocates, students of higher education, policy makers, and state officials. We intend to help a general audience understand community colleges, and provide a thoughtful call-to-arms for educational policy makers interested in the future of American higher education.

We're still dreaming. We are minding the dream—we still care about it, fret about it, and believe in it. We trust that our readers who have reached this concluding portion of the book also will Mind the Dream. Minding the dream means we dedicate ourselves to a public good so good it transforms individual lives while it strengthens a potent middle class.

This book is a tribute to the people who dreamed the dream, those who enact the dream, the scholar-practitioners who continuously seek perfection in the dream, who are committed to the least among us and celebrate each step into democracy's light. We rest this book on their bones and sinew, on their breath and heartbeat. They are the living embodiment of hope for an educated America.

༂ Bibliography

Accuplacer. (2006). Accuplacer Tests. Retrieved January 8, 2006, from www.college-board.com/highered/apr/accu/accu.html.

ACT. (2006). Facts about the ACT. Retrieved January 8, 2006, from www.act.org/.

Adelman, C. (1996, October 4). The truth about remedial work. *The Chronicle of Higher Education*, p. A56.

Adelman, C. (1998). The kiss of death: An alternative view of college remediation. *National Crosstalk: A Publication of the National Center for Public Policy and Higher Education, 6*(3), 11.

Adelman, C. (1999). *Answers in the tool box: Academic intensity, attendance patterns, and bachelor's degree attainment.* Washington, DC: U.S. Department of Education.

Adelman, C. (2000). *A parallel postsecondary universe: The certification system in information technology.* Washington, DC: U.S. Department of Education.

Adelman, C. (2003). *The empirical curriculum: Changes in postsecondary course-taking, 1972–2000.* Washington, DC: U.S. Department of Education.

Adelman, C. (2005). *Moving into town—and moving on: The community college in the lives of traditional-aged students.* Washington, DC: U.S. Department of Education.

Adelman, C. (2006). *The toolbox revisited: Paths to degree completion from high school through college.* Washington, DC: U.S. Department of Education.

Adelman, C., Daniel, B., & Berkovits, I. (2003). Postsecondary attainment, attendance, curriculum, and performance: Selected results from the NELS:88/2000 Postsecondary Education Transcript Study (PETS), 2000. *Education Statistics Quarterly, 5*(3). Retrieved January 15, 2004, from http://nces.ed.gov/programs/quarterly/Vol_5/5_3/4_2.asp.

Alexander, B. (2004, September/October). Going nomadic: Mobile learning in higher education. *Educause Review, 39*(5), 28–35. Retrieved January 16, 2006, from www.educause.edu/pub/er/erm04/erm0451.asp?bhcp=1

Alfred, M. V. (2005). Overlooked in academe: What do we know about immigrant students in adult and higher education? *New Horizons in Adult Education, 19*(1).

Alfred, R. (1998). *Shared governance in community colleges.* Denver, CO: Education Commission of the States.

Alfred, R., Ewell, P., Hadgins, J., & McClenney, K. (1999). *Core indicators of effectiveness for community colleges.* Washington, DC: American Association of Community Colleges.

Alssid, J. L., Gruber, D., Jenkins, D., Mazzeo, C., Roberts, B., & Stanback-Stroud, R. (2002). *Building a career pathways system: Promising practices in community college-centered workforce development.* Brooklyn, NY: Workforce Strategy Center.

Al-Tal, A. Y., & Ashour, M. (1993). Community colleges in Jordan: Issues and challenges. *Community College Review, 21*(2), 51–65.

Amaury, N. (2005) *Reexamining the community college mission.* Unpublished manuscript.

American Association of Community Colleges. (1996). *Employment status of community college students.* Washington, DC: Author.

American Association of Community Colleges. (2004). *Competencies for community college leaders.* Washington, DC: Author.

American Association of Community Colleges. (2006). *Fast facts about community college.* Retrieved May 11, 2006, from www.aacc.nche.edu.

American Council on Education. (2004). *Shifting ground: Autonomy, accountability and privatization in public higher education.* Washington, DC: Author.

Andres, L. (1999). *Investigating transfer: The student's perspective.* Vancouver: British Columbia Council on Admissions and Transfer.

Andrews, H. A. (2005). *Enrollment trends in community colleges.* ERIC Clearinghouse for Community Colleges. (ERIC Document Reproduction Service No. ED477914)

Annual Almanac of Higher Education. (2005). *The Chronicle of Higher Education.* Retrieved December 12, 2005, from http://chronicle.com/free/almanac/2005/.

Arcario, P. (2003). *Year end report-title v.* Long Island City, NY: LaGuardia Community College, CUNY.

Arcario, P., Eynon, B., & Clark, E. J. (2005). Making connections: Integrated learning, integrated lives. *Peer Review, 7*(4), 15–18.

Arcario, P., & Gantzer, J. (2004). *Analysis of linked ESL and content courses.* Unpublished manuscript, Long Island City, NY: LaGuardia Community College, CUNY.

Arenson, K. W. (1999, November 24). Opponents of a change in CUNY admissions policy helped pass a compromise plan. *The New York Times,* p. B3.

Arenson, K. W. (2006, February 9). Panel explores standard test for colleges. *The New York Times,* p. A1.

Argyris, C. (1999). *On organizational learning.* Malden, MA: Blackwell Publishing Inc.

Arnett, J. J. (2000). Emerging adulthood: A theory of development from the late teens through the twenties. *American Psychologist, 55,* 469–80.

Ashburn, E. (2006, June 2). No-confidence vote taken at Clark. *The Chronicle of Higher Education, 52*(39), pp. A23–A24.

Asonevich, W. J. (2005, August 29). Building college governance - a case study. *Community College Week,* pp. 4–5.

Association of American Colleges and Universities. (2004). *Our students' best work: A framework for accountability worthy of our mission.* Washington, DC: Author.

Association of Community College Trustees. (2005). *An overview of exemplary community college governance.* Retrieved February 26, 2006, from www.acct.org/ Acct/files/ccLibraryFiles/FILENAME/000000000336/An%20Overview%20to% 20Exemplary%20Governance.pdf.

Association of Community College Trustees. (2006). *About the ACCT.* Retrieved February 26, 2006, from www.acct.org/Template1.asp?sid=1.

Association of Community College Trustees. (2006). Standards of good practice for trustee boards. Retrieved July 9, 2007, from www.acct.org/CenterEffective Governance.asp?bid=89.

Association of Governing Boards of Universities and Colleges. (1992). *Trustees & troubled times in higher education.* Washington, DC: Author.

Astin, A. (1998). Remedial education and civic responsibility. *National Crosstalk, 6*(3), 12–13.

Astin, A. (2000). An interview: Alexander W. Astin, *National Crosstalk, 1,* 2–3.

Astone, B. (2005). *LaGuardia community college institutional profile.* Long Island City, NY: LaGuardia Community College, CUNY.

Bachelet, M. (2006, January 16). A leader making peace with Chile's past. *The New York Times,* pp. A1, A8.

Bailey, T., Alfonso, M., Scott, M., & Leinback, T. (2002). *The education outcomes of occupational postsecondary students: Evidence from 1990s.* New York: Community College Research Center, Teachers College at Columbia University.

Bailey, T., Calcagno, J. C., Jenkins, D., Kienzl, G., & Leinbach, T. (2005). *The effects of institutional factors on the success of community college students* (No. 24). New York: Community College Research Center, Teachers College at Columbia University.

Bailey, T., Kienzl, G., & David, M. (2004). *Who benefits from postsecondary occupational education? Findings from the 1980s and 1990s.* New York: Community College Research Center, Teachers College at Columbia University.

Bailey, T., Leinback, T. D., Scott, M., Alfonso, M., Kienzl, G., & David, M. (2003). *The characteristics of occupational sub-baccalaureate students entering the new millennium.* New York: Community College Research Center, Teachers College at Columbia University.

Bailey, T., Leinbach, T., Scott, M., Alfonso, M., Kienzl, G., & Kennedy, B. (2004). *The characteristics of occupational students in postsecondary education.* New York: Community College Research Center, Teachers College at Columbia University.

Bailey, T., & Weininger, E. (2002). *Performance, graduation and transfer of immigrants and natives in City University of New York community colleges.* Unpublished manuscript, New York: Community College Research Center, Teachers College at Columbia University.

Baker, M., Hansen, T., Joiner, R., & Traum, D. (1999). The role of grounding in collaborative learning tasks. In P. Dillenbourg (Ed.), Collaborative learning: Cognitive and computational approaches. Oxford: Elsevier Science.

Barr, R. B., & Tagg, J. (1995, November/December). From teaching to learning: A new paradigm for undergraduate education. *Change Magazine*, pp. 13–25.

Barrett, H. C. (2005). *Researching electronic portfolios and learner engagement.* The Reflect Initiative. Retrieved October 5, 2007, from http://electronicportfolios .com/reflect/whitepaper.pdf.

Baum, S., & Payea, K. (2004). *Education pays: The benefits of higher education for individuals and society.* New York: The College Board.

Begin, S. (2005, June 20). High-tech magnets: schools use economic partnerships to attract other funding. *Crain's Detroit Business, 21*(25), 33.

Bellis, D. (2004). *Public community colleges and technical schools:Most schools use both credit and noncredit programs for workforce development.* Washington, DC: Government Accountability Office.

Bensimon, E. M., & Soto, M. (1997). Can we rebuild civic life without a multicultural university? *Change Magazine, 29,* 42–44.

Berkner, L., Horn, L., & Clune, M. (2000). *Descriptive summary of the 1995–96 beginning postsecondary students: Three years later, with an essay on students who started at less-than-4-year institutions.* Washington, DC: National Center for Education Statistics.

Bers, T. H. (2004). Assessment at the program level. *New Directions for Community Colleges, 126,* 43–52.

Bierman, S., Ciner, E., Lauer-Glebov, J., Rutz, C., & Savina, M. (2005). Integrative learning: Coherence out of chaos. *Peer Review, 7*(4), 18–20.

Birnbaum, R. (1991a). The latent organizational functions of the academic senate: Why senates do not work but will not go away. In R. Birnbaum (Ed.), *Faculty in governance: The role of senates and joint committees in academic decision making* (Vol. 75, pp. 7–25). San Francisco: Jossey-Bass.

Birnbaum, R. (Ed.). (1991b). *Faculty in governance: The role of senates and joint committees in academic decision making* (Vol. 75, p. 75). San Francisco: Jossey-Bass.

Birnbaum, R. (2004). The end of shared governance: Looking ahead or looking back. In W. G. Tierney & V. M. Lechuga (Eds.), *Restructuring shared governance in higher education* (Vol. 127, pp. 5–22). San Francisco: Jossey-Bass.

Blau, J. R. (1999). Two-year college transfer rates of black American students. *Community College Journal of Research and Practice, 23*(5), 525–31.

Bloom, B. S. (1956). *Taxonomy of educational objectives, handbook: The cognitive domain.* New York: David McKay Company, Inc.

Bloom, D., & Sommo, C. (2005). *Building learning communities—early results from the opening doors demonstration at Kingsborough Community College.* New York: MDRC.

Blumenstyk, G. (2005, January 7). Watch the wind in for-profit colleges' sails. *The Chronicle of Higher Education, 51*(45), A19.

Blumenthal, A. J. (2002). English as a second language at the community college: An exploration of context and concerns. *New Directions for Community Colleges, 117,* 45–53.

Boggs, G. R. (2003). Leadership context for the twenty-first century. In W. E. Piland & D. B. Wolf (Eds.), *New Directions for Community Colleges: Questioning the community college role.* San Francisco: Jossey-Bass.

Bolman, L., & Deal, T. (1997). *Reframing organizations: Artistry, choice and leadership* (2nd ed.) San Francisco: Jossey-Bass.

Boston, C. (2003). *Cognitive science and assessment.* ERIC Clearinghouse on Assessment and Evaluation (ERIC Document Reproduction Service No. ED481716).

Boswell, K. (2002). *An overview of the current economic climate in the states.* Paper presented at Doing more with less: Community colleges and the new economy, Annual Policy Forum, Washington, DC.

Boswell, K. (2004). Bridges or barriers. *Change, 36*(6), 8.

Boswell, K., & Wilson, C. D. (2004). *Keeping America's promise.* Denver, CO: Education Commission of the States.

Boylan, H. R. (1999). Demographics, outcomes, and activities. *Journal of Developmental Education, 23*(2), 5.

Boylan, H. R., & Bonham, B. S. (1994). Seven myths about remedial education. *Research and Teaching in Developmental Education, 10*(2), 5–12.

Boylan, J. I., Bliss, L., & Bonham, B. (1997). Program components and their relationship to performance. *Journal of Developmental Education, 20*(3), 2–9.

Bradburn, E. M., Hurst, D. G., & Peng, S. (2001). *Community college transfer rates to 4-year institutions using alternative definitions of transfer.* Research and Development Report. Washington, DC: National Center for Education Statistics.

Bragg, D. D. (2001a). Opportunities and challenges for the new vocationalism in American community colleges. *New Directions for Community Colleges, 115,* 5–Bragg, D. D. (2001b). *Promising outcomes for tech prep participants in eight local consortia: A summary of initial results.* Columbus, OH: National Dissemination Center for Career and Technical Education.

Bragg, D. D., & Hamm, R. E. (1966). *Linking college and work: Exemplary policies and practices of two-year college work-based learning programs.* Berkeley, CA: National Center for Research in Vocational Education.

Braham, B. (1992). *Self-esteem and getting ahead.* Belmont, CA: Southwestern Publishing, Thomson Higher Education.

Braunstein, A., McGrath, M., & Pescatrice, D. (2000–2001). Measuring the impact of financial factors on college persistence. *Journal of College Student Retention: Research, Theory and Practice, 2*(3), 191–203.

Brawer, F. B. (1996). *Community colleges international,* Los Angeles, CA: ERIC Digest (ERIC Document Reproduction Service No. ED393504).

Brender, A. (2003, November 14). Japan's junior colleges face a grim future. *The Chronicle of Higher Education,* p. A39.

Breneman, D. (2006, October). *Post-secondary research centers.* Paper presented at the Kick-off Meeting of the National Post-Secondary Research Center, Teachers College, New York City, NY.

Breneman, D. W., & Haarlow, W. N. (1998). *Remedial education: Costs and consequences.* Remediation in higher education. Washington, DC: Thomas D. Fordham Foundation.

Breneman, D. W. & Haarlow, W. N. (1999, April 9). Establishing the real value of remedial education. *The Chronicle of Higher Education,* pp. B6–B7.

Brevard Community College. (2007). *Center for service learning mission and purpose.* Retrieved July 6, 2007, from www.brevard.cc.fl.us/index.php?subnavframe=/csl/content/sub_nav.html&mainframe=/csl/content/mission_purpose.html

Brewer, D., & Gray, M. (1997). *Connecting college and community in the new economy: An analysis of community college faculty-labor market linkages.* Berkeley, CA: RAND Corporation.

Brickman, B. N., & Nuzzo, R. (1999). Curricula and programs for international and immigrant students. *Journal of Intensive English Studies, 13,* 53–62.

Bringle, R. G., & Hatcher, J. A. (1997). Reflection: Bridging the gap between service and learning. *College Teaching, 45*(4),153–58.

Brookfield, S. D. (2005). Overcoming impostorship, cultural suicide and lost innocence: Implications for teaching critical thinking in the community college. *New Directions for Community Colleges, 1*(130), 49–57.

Brown, C. H. (2001). Two-year colleges and tech prep partnerships: A Texas perspective. *New Directions for Community Colleges, 115*(Fall), 51–62.

Bryant, A. N. (2001). *The economic outcomes of community college attendance.* Los Angeles, CA: ERIC Clearinghouse for Community Colleges. (ERIC Document Reproduction Service No. ED467981).

Bryk, A. S., & Schneider, B. (2002). *Trust in schools* (1st ed.). New York: Russell Sage Foundation.

Bundy, C. (2005). Global patterns, local options? Some implications for South Africa of international changes in higher education. *Perspectives in Education, 23*(2), 85–98.

Burcham, J. (2004, November 23). Dominican Republic to open four community colleges. *Community College Times,* p. 2.

Burd, S. (2004, October 29). A house divided over tuition-control bill. *The Chronicle of Higher Education,* p. A27.

Burd, S. (2005, February 25). Republican bill to renew higher education act mirrors last year's legislation. *The Chronicle of Higher Education,* p. A28.

Burke, J. (1997). *Performance-funding indicators: Concerns, values, and models for two- and four-year colleges and universities.* Albany, NY: State University of New York, Rockefeller Institute of Government.

Burke, J. C. (2005a). The many faces of accountability. In J. C. Burke (Ed.), *Achieving accountability in higher education—balancing public, academic and market demands* (pp. 1–54). San Francisco: Jossey-Bass.

Burke, J. C. (2005b). *Achieving accountability in higher education—balancing public, academic and market demands.* San Francisco: Jossey-Bass.

Callan, P., & Finney, J. E. (2005). State-by-state report cards. In E. D. Heller (Ed.), *The states and public higher education policy—affordability, access and accountability* (pp. 198–215). Baltimore: The Johns Hopkins University Press.

Campus Compact. (2007). *About Campus Compact.* Retrieved July 14, 2007, from www.compact.org/about/.

Carey, K. (2004). *The funding gap.* Washington, DC: The Education Trust.

Carnevale, A. P. (2005). Community colleges and career qualifications. *American Association of Community Colleges Issue Papers.* Retrieved May 24, 2005, from www.aacc.nche.edu/Content/NavigationMenu/ResourceCenter/Projects_Partnerships/Current/NewExpeditions/IssuePapers/Community_Colleges_and_Career_Qualifications.htm.

Carnevale, A. P., & Desrochers, D. M. (2001). *Help wanted, credentials required—community colleges in the knowledge economy.* Princeton, NJ: Educational Testing Service, Inc.

Carnevale, A. P., & Desrochers, D. M. (2003). *Why learning? The value of higher education to society and the individual—keeping America's promise.* Denver, CO: Education Commission of the States.

Carver, J. (1990). *Boards that make a difference: A new design for leadership in nonprofit and public organizations.* San Francisco: Jossey-Bass.

Carver, J.C., & Mayhew, M. (1997). *Reinventing your boards.* San Francisco: Jossey-Bass.

Casazza, M. E. (1999). Who are we, and where did we come from? *Journal of Developmental Education, 23*(1), 2–7.

Casazza, M., & Silverman, S. (Eds.). (1996). *Learning assistance and developmental education.* San Francisco: Jossey-Bass.

Cashman, K. (1998). *Leadership from the inside out.* Provo, UT: Executive Excellence Publishing.

Castaneda, C. (2002). Transfer rates among students from rural, suburban and urban community colleges: What we know, don't know, and need to know. *Community College Journal of Research and Practice, 26,* 439–49.

Cejda, B. D., & Kaylor, A. J. (2001). Early transfer: A case study of traditional-aged community college students. *Community College Journal of Research and Practice, 25,* 621–38.

Center for Community College Policy. (2000). *State funding for community colleges: A 50 state survey.* Denver, CO: Education Commission of the States.

Center on Juvenile and Criminal Justice. (2002). *Is Maryland's higher education system suffering because of prison expenditures?* Retrieved January 17, 2006, from www.cjcj.org/pubs/mary/maryreport.html.

Central Piedmont Community College. (1995). *Meeting the needs of the workforce.* Unpublished manuscript.

Chaffee, J. (2006a). *Critical thinking across the curriculum—a year in review.* Unpublished manuscript, Long Island City, NY: LaGuardia Community College, CUNY.

Chaffee, J. (2006b). *Thinking critically.* Boston: Houghton Mifflin Company.

Chaker, A. M. (2005, July 19). Tuition increases start to slow. *The Wall Street Journal.* Retrieved July 19, 2005, from http://online.wsj.com.

Chaney, B., Muraskin, L., Calahan, M.,& Rak, R. (1997). *Third-year longitudinal study results and implementation study update: National study of student support services.* Washington, DC: U.S. Department of Education.

Cheslock, J. J., & Hilmer, M. J. (2001). *How college enrollment strategies affect student labor market success.* Unpublished manuscript.

Christopherson, K. A., &.Robison, M. H. (2001). *The socio-economic benefits generated by Colorado Mountain College.* Community College Benefits Inc. Retrieved August 8, 2001, from www.coloradomtn.edu/info/public/economicexecutivesummary.pdf.

Citron, R., Dillon, C., & Boyd, T. (2001). Teaching and learning in the new information age: State-system policies for technology. In B. K. Townsend & S. B. Twombly (Eds.), *Community colleges—policy in the future context* (Vol. 2, pp. 223–39). Westport, CT: Ablex Publishing.

Clem, B. (2005). Pedagogy of a radical multiculturalism. *MELUS, 30*(2), 123–37.

Cleveland, H. (2002). *Nobody in charge: essays on the future of leadership.* San Francisco: Jossey-Bass.

Clowes, D. A. (1980). More than a definitional problem: Remedial, compensatory, and developmental education. *Journal of Developmental & Remedial Education, 4*(1), 8–10.

Coastline Community College. (2007). *Distance learning.* Retrieved July 7, 2007, from www.coastline.edu.

Cohen, A., & Brawer, F. (1996). *The American community college.* San Francisco: Jossey-Bass.

Cohen, A. M. (2001). Governmental policies affecting community colleges. In B. K. Townsend & S. B. Twombly (Eds.), *Community colleges—policy in the future context* (Vol. 2, pp. 3–22). Westport, CT: Ablex Publishing.

Cohen, C. (2004). *Revenues and expenditures for public elementary and secondary education: School year 2001–02 (NCES 2004–31).* Washington, DC: U.S. Department of Education, National Center for Education Statistics.

College Board. (2004). *Pricing and financial aid.* Retrieved August 8, 2005, from www.collegeboard.com/press/article/0,38993,00.html

College Board. (2005). *2004–2005 college costs: Keep rising prices in perspective.* Retrieved August 8, 2005, from www.collegeboard.com/article/0,3868,6-29-0-4494,00.html

Colorado Mountain College. (1998). *Student access and success task force report.* Carbondale, CO: Author.

Commission on the Future of Community College. (1988). *Building communities: A vision for a new century.* Washington, DC: American Association of Community Colleges.

Conneely, J. E., Good, C., & Perryman, K. (Eds.). (2001, Summer). *Balancing the role of parents in the residential community* (Vol. 94). San Francisco: Jossey-Bass.

Cooney, F. (2000). *General studies majors at Salt Lake community college: A secondary analysis of the Fall 1999 new student survey.* Salt Lake Community College.

Cooper, J. E., & Pagotto, L. (2003). Developing community college faculty as leaders. *New Directions for Community Colleges, 123,* 27–37.

Cooperrider, D. L., Whitney, D. L, & Starvos, J. M. (2004). *Appreciative inquiry handbook: The first in a series of AI workbooks for leaders of change.* San Francisco: Berrett-Koehler Publishers.

Coughlin, E. (1999). Professional competencies for the digital age classroom. *Learning and Leading with Technology, 27*(3), 22–27.

Council for Aid to Education *(2000). Voluntary support of education 1999.* New York: Author.

Cronholm. L. (1994). Why one college jettisoned all its remedial courses. *The Chronicle of Higher Education.* Retrieved September 24, 1999, from http://chronicle.com/weekly/v46/i05b00601.htm.

Crook, D. (2004). *City University of New York data indices for strategic planning.* New York: City University of New York.

Dannemiller, K., James, S. L., & Tolchinsky, P. D. (2000). *Collaborating for change: Whole-scale change.* San Francisco: Berrett-Koehler Publishers.

Dare, D. E. (2001). Learner-centered instructional practices supporting the new vocationalism. *New Directions for Community Colleges, 2001*(115), 81–91.

Davis, F. (2000). *Issues in community college governance.* [Issues Paper No. 7]. Washington, DC: W. K. Kellogg Foundation.

Davis, J. H. (Writer/Director). (2005). Exploring transfer: Twentieth anniversary video [Video]. Long Island City, NY: LaGuardia Community College and Vassar College.

Davis,. J. L. (1999). *Developmental course taking in community colleges.* Unpublished manuscript.

Day, J. C., & Newburger, E. C. (2002). The big payoff: Educational attainment and synthetic estimates of work-life earnings. *Current population reports.* Washington, DC: U.S. Census Bureau. Retrieved October 5, 2007, from www.census.gov/prod/2002pubs/p23–210.pdf.

Day, P. (2004). Personal communication.

Day, P. (2006). Personal communication.

DesignShare. (2007). Home page. Retrieved July 9, 2007, from www.designshare .com/index.php/home.

Diaz, D. M.., Justica, N. T., & Levine, L. (2002). *Making content accessible to promote second language acquisition: The ESL intensive program at Hostos Community College*. CUNY. (ERIC Document Reproduction Service No. ED477556).

Dictators of the world. (2006). Retrieved May 17, 2006, from www.strategy-planet.com/tropico/dictators.shtml

Dillenbourg, P. (Ed.). (1999). *Collaborative learning: Cognitive and computational approaches*. Oxford: Elsevier Science.

Dirks, T. (2005). Personal communication.

Donovan, J. (2003). Changing demographics and generational shifts: Understanding and working with the families of today's college students. *Journal of Student Affairs, 12*. Retrieved October 5, 2007, from www.colostate.edu/Depts/SAHE/JOURNAL2/2003/Donovan.htm.

Dougherty, K. J. (2001). State policies and the community college's role in workforce preparation. In K. B. Townsend & S. B. Twombly (Eds.), *Community colleges—policy in the future context* (Vol. 2, pp. 129–47). Westport, CT: Ablex Publishing.

Dougherty, K. J., & Bakia, M. (2000). Community colleges and contract training: Content, origins and impact. *Teachers College Record, 102*(1), 197–243.

Douglas, B., & Harmening, T. (1999). *Comparative financial statistics for public two-year institutions fiscal year1998*. Washington, DC: National Association of College and University Business Officers.

Dowd, A. C. (2004). Community college revenue disparities: What accounts for an urban college deficit. *The Urban Review, 36*(4), 251–70.

Dowd, A. D. (2005). *Data don't drive: Building a practitioner culture of inquiry to assess community college performance*. Boston: Lumina Foundation for Education. Retrieved January 21, 2006, from www.luminafoundation.org/publications/datadontdrive2005.pdf.

Dowdy, H. B. (1996). *A manual for trustees: Role, responsibilities, relationship*. North Carolina Community College System (ERIC Document Reproduction Service No. ED388374).

Draut, T. (2007). *Strapped: Why America's 20- and 30-somethings can't get ahead*. New York: Doubleday.

Drury, R. L. (2001). The entrepreneurial community college: Bringing workforce, economics and community development to Virginia community colleges. *Inquiry, 6*(1), 26–33.

Dworkin, M. S. (1959). *Dewey on education - selections*. New York: Teachers College Press.

Easley, J. I. (2005). The political tension of education as a public good: The voice of a Martin Luther King scholar. *Education and Urban Society, 37*(4), 490–505.

Education Commission of the States. (1997). *State postsecondary structures sourcebook: State coordinating and governing boards.* Denver, CO: Author.

Education Trust, The. (2003). A new core curriculum for all. *Thinking K-16, 7*(1), 1–32. Washington, DC: Author.

Ehrenberg, R. G. (2004a). Conclusion: Looking to the future of shared governance. In R. G. Ehrenberg (Ed.), *Governing academia* (pp. 276–80). Ithaca, NY: Cornell University Press.

Ehrenberg, R. G. (Ed.). (2004b). *Governing academia.* Ithaca, NY: Cornell University Press.

Ehrenberg, R. G., Klaff, D. B., Kezsbom, A. T., & Nagowski, M. P. (2004). Collective bargaining in American higher education. In R. G. Ehrenberg (Ed.), *Governing academia* (pp. 209–32). Ithaca, NY: Cornell University Press.

Elsner, P. A. (2001, June/July). Connecting our partners. *Community College Journal, 71*(6), 18–23.

Ely, D. P. (2000). *The field of educational technology: Update 2000. A dozen frequently asked questions.* Retrieved July 10, 2007, from http://library.educationworld.net/a5/a5-69.html.

Ennis-Cole, D., & Lowhon, T. (2004). Teaching, technology, and support in the new millennium: A guide for new community college teachers. *Community College Journal of Research and Practice, 28,* 583–92.

Ewell, P. T. (1994). A matter of integrity: Accountability and the future of self regulation. *Change Magazine, 26*(6), 24–29.

Ewell, P. T. (2005). Can assessment serve accountability. In D. E. Heller (Ed.), *The states and public higher education policy—affordability, access and accountability* (pp. 104–124). Baltimore: The Johns Hopkins University Press.

Eynon, B. (2005). *ePortfolio's impact on student retention, satisfaction and pass rates.* Unpublished manuscript, Long Island City, NY: LaGuardia Community College, CUNY.

Eynon, B. (2006a). E-portfolio. Long Island City, NY: LaGuardia Community College, CUNY. Retrieved July 19, 2006, from www.lagcc.cuny.edu\eportfolio.

Eynon, B. (2006b). Why do digital stories. Long Island City, NY: LaGuardia Community College. Retrieved April 19, 2007, from www.lagcc.cuny.edu/ctl/dfl/dfl2_0304/nov5seminar/.

Fain, P. (2006, June 23). Crisis of confidence: Three current and former college presidents discuss the recent spate of failures at the top. *The Chronicle of Higher Education, 52*(42), pp. A28–A30.

Farren praises cross border scheme. Wider Horizons, Department for Learning and Employment, Northern Ireland. Retrieved September 15, 2000, from http://archive.nics.gov.uk/el/000616b-el.htm.

Federal Government Statistics. (2005a). The white house demography. Retrieved January 23, 2006, from www.whitehouse.gov/fsbr/demography.html.

Federal Government Statistics. (2005b). The white house, social statistics briefing room. Retrieved July 9, 2006, from www.whitehouse.gov/fsbr/demography.html

Finkelstein, J. (2002). *Maximizing retention for at-risk freshmen: The Bronx Community College model.* (ERIC Document Reproduction Service No. ED469657).

Fischer, K. (2005, May 27). States increase spending on student aid by smallest amount in 6 years, survey finds. *The Chronicle of Higher Education,* pp. 1–7.

Fitzgerald, J. (2000). *Community colleges as labor market intermediaries: Building career ladders for low wage workers.* Boston: The Center for Urban and Regional Policy, Northeastern University.

Florida Department of Education. (2004). *Enrollment by program (2002–2003).* Retrieved May 22, 2005, from www.fldoe.org/CC/facts_glance.asp.

Frederickson, J. (1998). Today's transfer students: Who are they? *Community College Review, 26,* 43–54.

Freedman, J. O. (2004). Presidents and trustees. In R. G. Ehrenberg (Ed.), *Governing academia* (pp. 9–27). Ithaca, NY: Cornell University Press.

Friedman, T. L. (2006, July). *The world is flat: a brief history of the 21st century.* Plenary session. Paper presented at the Campus of the Future, Annual Meeting of the National Association of College Business Officers, Honolulu, HI.

Furhman, S. (2006, October 11). Welcome speech on the celebration of the opening of the postsecondary research center at Teachers College, New York, New York.

Gardner, H., & Laskin, E. (1995). *Leading minds: An anatomy of leadership.* New York: Basic Books.

General Accounting Office. (2003). *Workforce training - employed worker programs focus on business needs, but revised performance measures could improve access for some workers.* Washington, DC: Author.

George, B. (2003). *Authentic Leadership: Rediscovering the Secrets to Creating Lasting Value.* San Francisco: Jossey-Bass.

Gerald, D. E., & Jussar, W. J. (1999). *Projections of education statistics to 2009.* Washington, DC: National Center for Education Statistics.

Gershwin, M. C. (2005). What economic developers must know about community colleges: Economic development America. Retrieved August 2, 2006, from www.iedconline.org/EDAmerica/Fall2005/myths_2html.

Gill, A. M., & Leigh, D. E. (2000). Community college enrollment, college major and the gender wage gap. *Industrial and Labor Relations Review, 54*(1), 163–81.

Gilmour, J. (1991). Participative governance bodies in higher education: Report of a national study. In R. Birnbaum (Ed.), *Faculty in governance: The role of senates and joint committees in academic decision making. New directions for higher education report* (Vol. 75, pp. 27–40). San Francisco: Jossey-Bass.

Girardi, A. G., & Stein R. B. (2001). State dual credit policy and its implications for community colleges: Lessons from Missouri for the 21st century. In B. K. Townsend & S. B. Twombly (Eds.), *Community colleges - policy in the future context* (Vol. 2, pp. 149–72). Westport, CT: Ablex Publishing.

Goff, D. G. (2003). *What do we know about good community college leaders: A study in leadership trait theory and behavioral leadership theory.* (ERIC Document Reproduction Service No. ED476456).

Goldsmth, D. J., & Archambault, F. X. (1997). Persistence of adult women in community college re-entry program. *Community College Review, 29*(3), 77–93.

Gordon, V. N., Habley, W. R., & Associates. (2000). *Academic advising: A comprehensive handbook.* San Francisco: Jossey-Bass.

Government Accountability Office. (2004). *Public community colleges and technical schools.* Washington, DC: Author.

Graves, E. (2004). Performance funding in community based organizations. In D. C. Smith, & W. J. Grinker (Eds.), *The promise and pitfalls of performance-based contracting.* New York: Structured Employment Economic Development Corporation.

Green-Anderson, G. (2007). Personal communication.

Greenleaf, R. (1982). *The servant leader: Robert Greenleaf Center for Servant Leadership.* New York: Paulist Press.

Gross, N. (2002). *Final report: Writing in the disciplines.* Unpublished manuscript, Long Island City, NY: LaGuardia Community College, CUNY.

Gross, N. (2005). Personal communication.

Grubb, N. W. (1991). The decline of community college transfer rates: Evidence from national longitudinal surveys. *Journal of Higher Education, 62*(2), 194–222.

Grubb, N. W. (1996). *Working in the middle: Strengthening education and training for the mid-skilled labor force.* San Francisco: Jossey-Bass.

Grubb, N. W. (1997). Not there yet: Prospects and problems for "education through occupations." *Journal of Vocational Education Research, 22*(2), 133–39.

Grubb, N. W. (1998). *Learning and earning in the middle: The economic benefits of sub-baccalaureate education.* New York: Community College Research Center, Teachers College at Columbia University.

Grubb, N. W. (1999). *Honored but invisible.* New York: Routledge.

Grubb, N. W. (2001). From isolation to integration: Post-secondary vocational education and emerging systems of workforce development. *New Directions for Community Colleges, 115,* 27–37.

Grubb, N. W. (2002). Learning and earning in the middle, part 1: National studies of pre-baccalaureate education. *Economics of Education Review, 21,* 299–321.

Grubb, N. W., Badway, N., Bell, D., Bragg, D., & Russman, M. (1997). *Workforce, economic and community development: The changing landscape of the entrepreneurial community college.* (A Joint Publication of the League for Innovation in the Community College, National Center for Research in Vocational Education, National Council on Occupational Education). Mission Viejo, CA: League for Innovation in the Community College (ERIC Document Reproduction Service No. ED413033).

Grubb, N. W., & Lazerson., M. (2004, October 29). Community colleges need to build on their strengths. *The Chronicle of Higher Education,* B16.

Grubb, N. W. & Worthen, H. (1999). Remedial/developmental education: The best and the worst. In N. W. Grubb (Ed.), *Honored but invisible.* New York: Routledge.

Hadedorn, K. S. (2004, Fall). The role of urban community colleges in educating diverse populations. *New Directions for Community Colleges, 127,* 21–34.

Hamel, G., & Valikangas, L. (2003). The quest for resilience. *Harvard Business Review, 81*(9), 52–63.

Hammond, M. S. (2001). Career center and needs assessment: Getting the information you need to increase your success. *Journal of Career Development, 23*(3), 187–97.

Hammond, T. H. (2004). Herding cats in university hierarchies: Formal structure and policy choice in American research universities. In R. G. Ehrenberg (Ed.), *Governing academia* (pp. 91–138). Ithaca, NY: Cornell University Press.

Harbour, C. P. (2002). The legislative evolution of performance funding in the North Carolina community college system. *Community College Review, 29*(4), 28–50.

Harbour, C. P. (2003). An institutional accountability model for community colleges. *Community College Journal of Research and Practice, 27,* 299–316.

Harbour, C. P. (2005). Assessing a state-mandated institutional accountability program: The perceptions of selected community college leaders. *Community College Journal of Research and Practice, 29*(6), 445–62.

Haring. E. (2005). personal communication.

Harmening, T., & Douglas, B. (1999). *Comparative financial statistics for public two-year colleges: Fiscal year 1998, September.* Washington, DC: National Association of College and University Business Officers.

Harrigan, A. (2004). *Cope program outcomes.* Long Island City, NY: LaGuardia Community College, CUNY.

Harris, B. W. (1998). Looking inward: Building a culture for student success. *Community College Journal of Research and Practice, 22*(4), 401–19.

Hebel, S. (2002). Who shall be educated? The case of restricting remediation at the City University of New York. *Education and Urban Society, 37*(2), 174–92.

Heelan, C. (2001). *Leadership 2020: Task force report.* Unpublished manuscript, Washington, DC: American Association of Community Colleges.

Heelan, C. (2003). Advising for student success. Unpublished manuscript, New York: Community College Research Center at Teachers College, Columbia University.

Heller, D. E. (Ed.). (2001). *The states and public higher education policy: Affordability, access and accountability.* Baltimore: The Johns Hopkins University Press.

Heller, D. E. (Ed.). (2004). *State oversight of academia.* Ithaca, NY: Cornell University Press.

Heller, D. E. (2001). The three corners of the accountability triangle. In D. E. Heller (Ed.), *The states and public higher education policy—affordability, access and accountability* (pp. 296–324). Baltimore: The Johns Hopkins University Press.

Henrichsen, L. E., & Savova, L. P. (2000). International and historical perspectives on the preparation of ESOL teachers. *TESOL Journal, 9*(3), 3–4.

Hermalin, B. E. (2004). Higher education boards of trustees. In R. G. Ehrenberg (Ed.), *Governing academia* (pp. 28–48). Ithaca, NY: Cornell University Press.

Hershey, A. M., Silverberg, M. K., Ownes, T., & Hulsey, L. K. (1998). *Focus for the future: The final report of the national tech prep evaluation.* Washington, DC: Department of Education, Planning and Evaluation Service.

Higginbottom, G. H., & Romano, R. M. (2001). SUNY general education reform and the community colleges: A case study of cross purposes. In B. K. Townsend and S. B. Twombly (Eds.), *Community colleges - policy in the future context* (Vol. 2, pp. 243–60). Westport, CT: Ablex Publishing.

Higher education services corporation annual report 2003–2004. (2005). Albany, NY: Higher Education Services Corporation.

Hilmer, M. J. (1997). Does community college attendance provide a strategic path to a higher quality education? *Economics of Education Review, 16*(1), 59–68.

Hilmer, M. J. (1998). Post-secondary fees and the decision to attend a university or a community college. *Journal of Public Economics, 67,* 329–48.

Hoachlander, G., Sikora, A., Horn, L., & Carroll, C. D. (2003*). Community college students: Goals, academic preparation, and outcomes. NCES 2003-164.* Washington, DC: National Center for Education Statistics, U.S. Department of Education

Hood, L. (2003). *Immigrant students, urban high schools: The challenge continues.* New York: Carnegie Corporation of New York.

Hopkins, D. (Ed.). (2003). *Understanding networks for innovation in policy and practice.* Paris: OECD Publications Services.

Howe, N., & Strauss, W. (2000). *Millennials rising: The next great generation.* New York: Vintage Books.

Huber, M. T., Hutchings, P., & Richard, G. (2005). Integrative learning for liberal education. *Peer Review, 7*(4), 4–8.

Hughes, K. (2007, January-February). Plenary session. Paper presented at the Workforce Development Institute, San Diego, CA.

Hull, D. M. (2000). *Education and career preparation for the new millennium.* Waco, TX: CORD.

Hungar, J. Y., & Lieberman, J. (2001). *The road to equality: Report on transfer.* New York: Ford Foundation.

Hurley, R. G. (2002). Identification and assessment of community college peer institution selection systems. *Community College Review, 29*(4), 1–27.

Ignash, J. M. (1995). Encourage ESL student persistence: The influence of policy on curricular design. *Community College Review, 23*(3), 17–24.

Ignash, J. M. (1997). Who should provide postsecondary remedial/developmental education? *New Directions for Community Colleges, 25*(4), 5–20.

Ignash, J. M., & Towsend, B. K. (2001). Statewide transfer and articulation policies: Current practices and emerging issues. In B. K. Townsend & S. B. Twombly (Eds.), *Community colleges - policy in the future context* (Vol. 2, pp. 173–92). Westport, CT: Ablex Publishing.

Illich, P. A., Hagan, C., & McCallister, L. (2004). Performance in college-level courses among students concurrently enrolled in remedial courses: Policy implications. *Community College Journal of Research and Practice, 28,* 435–53.

Information digest 1999. (1999). Oakland: University of California.

Institute for Higher Education Policy (1995). *Opportunity endangered.* Washington, DC: Association of Community College Trustees.

Institute for Higher Education Policy. (2005). *The investment payoff: States gain major payoffs from investment in higher education: A 50 state analysis of the public and private benefits of higher education.* Washington, DC: Author.

Introduction to career clusters. (2003). Retrieved May 22, 2005, from www.michigan .gov/documents/Career_Cluster_Intro_105340_7.pdf.

Jackson, K. L., & Glass, J. C. (1998). A new role for community college presidents: Private fund raiser and development team leader. *Community College Journal of Research and Practice, 22*(6), 575–90.

Jacobs, J. (2001). Community colleges and the workforce investment act: Promises and problems of the new vocationalism. *New Directions for Community Colleges, 115,* 93–99.

Jacobs, J., & Pope, N. (2007, January/February). *The new inter-relationships between credit and non-credit workforce development programs.* Paper presented at the Workforce Development Institute, San Diego, CA.

Jacobs, J., & Teahen, R. C. (1997). The shadow college and NCA accreditation: A conceptual framework: Shadow colleges invisible students, high -profile systems. *NCA Quarterly, 71*(4), 472–78.

Jenkins, D., & Boswell, K. (2002). *State policies on community college remedial education: Findings from a national survey.* New York: Ford Foundation.

Jenkins, M., Brown, T., & Walker, R. (2005). *VLE surveys: A longitudinal perspective between March 2001, March 2003 and March 2005 for higher education in the United Kingdom.* London: University Colleges and Information Systems Association.

Johnson, L. G., Schwartz., R. A., & Bower, B. L. (2000). Managing stress among adult women students in community colleges. *Community College Journal of Research and Practice, 24,* 289–300.

Johnston, G. H. (2001). Work-based learning: Finding a new niche. *New Directions for Community Colleges, 115,* 73–80.

Jurgens, J. C. (2000). The undecided student: Effects of combining levels of treatment parameters on career uncertainty, career indecision and client satisfaction. *The Career Development Quarterly, 48*(3), 237–51.

Kahn, R. (2006). Personal communication.

Kane, T. J., & Rouse, C. E. (1999). The community college: Educating students at the margin between college and work. *Journal of Economic Perspectives, 13*(1), 63–84.

Kaplan, G. E. (2004a). Do governance structures matter? In G. T. William & V. M. Lechuga (Eds.), *Restructuring shared governance in higher education* (Vol. 127, pp. 23–34). San Francisco: Jossey-Bass.

Kaplan, G. E. (2004b). How academic ships actually navigate. In R. G. Ehrenberg (Ed.), *Governing academia* (pp. 165–208). Ithaca, NY: Cornell University Press.

Katopes, P. (2007). Personal communication.

Kearns, K. P. (1998). Institutional accountability in higher education. *Public Productivity & Management Review, 22*(2), 140–56.

Keener, B. (2002). Resource development in community colleges: A national review. *Community College Journal of Research and Practice, 26*, 7–23.

Keimig, R. T. (1983). *Raising academic standards: A guide to learning improvement* (ASHE-ERIC Higher Education Report # 4). Washington, DC: Association for the Study of Higher Education (ERIC Document Reproduction Service No. ED233669).

Kemper, K. M. (2003). The search for cultural leaders. *Review of Higher Education, 26*(3), 23.

Key terms and concepts related to critical pedagogy and educational theory and practice. Critical Pedagogy on the Web. Retrieved November 12, 2005, from http://mingo.info-science.uiowa.edu/~stevens/critped/terms.htm.

Kezar, A. (2004). What is more important to effective governance: Relationships, trust and leadership, or structures and formal processes. In W. G. Tierney & V. M. Lechuga (Eds.), *Restructuring shared governance in higher education, 127*, 35–46. San Francisco: Jossey-Bass.

Kim, K. A. (2002). Exploring the meaning of nontraditional at the community college. *Community College Review, 30*(1), 74–89.

King, J. (2007a). *The American college president.* Washington, DC: American Council on Education.

King, J. (2007b). *Report to the commissioners of the ACE center for policy analysis on the American college president study.* Washington, DC: American Council on Education.

King-Simms, S. (2006, April). *Career pathways to economic success.* Paper presented at the American Association of Community Colleges National Conference, Long Beach, CA.

Kirp, D. L. (2003). *Shakespeare, Einstein and the bottom line.* Cambridge, MA: Harvard University Press.

Kisker, C. B., & Carducci, R. (2003). Community college partnerships with the private sector - organizational contexts and models for successful collaboration. *Community College Review, 31*(3), 55–74.

Klein, J. T. (2005). Integrative learning and interdisciplinary studies. *Peer Review, 7*(4), 8–11.

Knopp, L. (1996). Remedial education: An undergraduate student profile. *American Council on Education Research Briefs, 6*(8), 1–11.

Knowles, M. S., Holton, E., & Swanson, R. (2005). *The adult learner: The definitive classic in adult education and human resource development* (6th ed.). London: Elsevier, Inc.

Kojaku, L. K., & Nunez, A. M. (1999). *Descriptive summary of 1995–96 beginning postsecondary students with profiles of students entering 1- and 4-year institutions.* Washington, DC: Office of Educational Research and Improvement.

Kolomechuk, D. (2006). Personal communication.

Koos, L. V. (1970; originally published 1925). *The junior-college movement.* Westport, CT: Greenwood Press.

Kozeracki, C. A. (2002). Issues in Developmental Education. *Community College Review, 29*(4), 83–100.

Lanaan, F. S. (2001a). Accountability in community colleges: Looking toward the 21st century. In B.K. Townsend & S.B. Twombly (Eds.), *Community colleges— policy in the future context* (Vol. 2, pp. 57–76). Westport, CT: Ablex Publishing.

Lanaan, F. S. (Ed.). (2001b). *Transfer student adjustment* (Vol.114). San Francisco: John Wiley and Sons, Inc.

Lance, L., & Moretti, E. (2002). *The effects of education on crime: Evidence from prison inmates, arrests, and self-reports.* Unpublished manuscript, Joint Center for Poverty Research.

Lange, A. (1918). The junior college—what manner of child shall this be? School and Society, as cited in D. Bragg, The New Vocationalism in American Community Colleges, *New Directions for Community Colleges, 7,* 211–16.

Lazarick, L. (1997a). Back to the Basics: Remedial Education. *Community College Journal, 68*(2), 10–15.

Lazarick, L. (1997b). *Remedial education at higher education institutions in fall 1995. Washington,* DC: National Center for Educational Statistics.

League for innovation executive leadership institute. (2007). Retrieved April 27, 2007, from www.league.org/2/conferences/eli/2007/about.cfm.

Lee, B. A. (1991, Fall). Campus leaders and campus senates. *New Directions for Higher Education, 19*(3), 41–61.

Lee, E. W. C., & Young, E. C. (2003). Pioneering the community college movement in Hong Kong. *International Journal of Lifelong Education, 22*(2), 147–58.

Leovy, J. (1999, August 7). Black, Latino students lag in transfers to UC campuses. *Los Angeles Times,* p. A1.

Levine, J. S. (2001). The buffered and the buffeted institution: Globalization and the community college. In B. K. Townsend & S. B. Twombly (Eds.), *Community colleges—policy in the future context,* (Vol. 2, pp. 77–97). Westport, CT: Ablex Publishing.

Levine, J. S. (2002). The revised institution: The community college mission at the end of the twentieth century. *Community College Review, 28*(2), 25.

Lewin, K. (1951). *Field theory in social science.* New York: Harper.

Lewin, T. (2006, September 7). Report finds U.S. students lagging in finishing college. *The New York Times,* p. A23.

Lewis, L., & Farris, E (1996). *Remedial education at higher education institutions in fall 1995.* Washington, DC: National Center for Education Statistics.

Lieberman, A. (2000). Networks as learning communities: Shaping the future of teacher development. *Journal of Teacher Education, 51*(3), 221–27.

Lieberman, D. A., & Guskin, A. E. (2003). The essential role of faculty development in new higher education models. In C. M. Wehlburg & S. Chadwick-Blossey (Eds.), *To improve the academy* (Vol. 21, pp.257–72). Boston: Anker Publishing Company, Inc.

Lieberman, J., & Hungar, J. (1998). *Transforming students' lives: How exploring transfer works and why.* Washington, DC: American Association of Higher Education.

Liebowitz, M., Haynes, L., & Milley, J. (2001). *Driving change in community colleges, volume 1: Building systems for advancement to self-sufficiency.* Boston: Jobs for the Future.

Liebowitz, M., Haynes, L., & Milley, J. (2001). *Driving change in community colleges, volume 2: An analysis of change in two community colleges.* Boston: Jobs for the Future.

Lindsay, J. M., & Daalder, I. H. (2005). *America's role in the world: Challenges to American business and higher education.* Washington, DC: Business-Higher Education Forum.

Lingenfelter, P. E. (2004). The state and higher education: An essential partnership. In W. G. Tierney & V. M. Lechuga (Eds.), *Restructuring shared governance in higher education* (Vol. 127, pp. 47–59). San Francisco: Jossey-Bass.

Lochner, L., & Morreti, E. (2004). The effect of education on crime: Evidence from prison inmates, arrests, and self-reports. *American Economic Review, 94*(1), 155–89.

Lohmann, S. (2004). State oversight of academia. In R. G. Ehrenberg (Ed.), *Governing academia* (pp. 71–90). Ithaca, NY: Cornell University Press.

Long, B. T. (2005). *State financial aid: Policies to enhance articulation and transfer* (No. 8A25). Boulder, CO: Western Interstate Commission for Higher Education.

Lovell, C. D. (2001). Federal policies and community colleges: A mix of federal and local influences. In B. K. Townsend & S. B. Twombly (Eds.), *Community colleges—policy in the future context,* (Vol. 2, pp. 23–37). Westport, CT: Ablex Publishing.

Lovell, C. D., & Trouth, C. (2002). State governance patterns for community colleges. *New Directions for Community Colleges, 117,* 91–100.

Ludema, J. D., Diana, W., Mohr, B., & Griffin, T. (2003). *The appreciative inquiry summit: The practitioner's guide for leading large-group change.* San Francisco: Berrett-Koehler Publishers.

Macheski, C. (2002). Personal communication.

Magnesson, K. (1995). *Five processes of career planning.* Washington, DC: U.S. Office of Education: Office of Educational Research and Improvement (ERIC Document Reproduction Service No. ED404581).

Manheimer, R. J. (2005). The older learner's journey to an ageless society: Lifelong learning on the brink of a crisis. *Journal of Transformative Education, 3*(3), 198–220.

Manzo, K. K. (2005, January 3). Report calls for beefed-up ESL programs. *Community College Week*, p. 11.

Marable, M. (2006, September). *Dealing with difficult dialogue by opening the classroom.* Paper presented at the LaGuardia Community College Opening Sessions, Long Island City, NY.

Marlow-Ferguson, R. (Ed.). (2002a). *Denmark* (Vol. 1). New York: Gale Group.

Marlow-Ferguson, R. (Ed.). (2002b). *Germany* (Vol. 1). New York: Gale Group.

Matus-Gorssman, L., Goodman, S., Melissa, D., & Seupersad, R.(2002). *Students' perspectives on juggling work, family, and college.* New York: MDRC.

Maxwell, M. (1997). *What are the functions of a college learning assistance center?* (ERIC Document Reproduction Service No. ED413031).

McCabe, R. H. (2000). *No one to waste: A report to public decision-makers and community college leaders.* Washington, DC: Community College Press.

McCabe, R. H., & Day, P. R., Jr. (Eds.). (1998). *Developmental education: A 21st century social and economic imperative.* Mission Viejo, CA: League for Innovation in the Community College and the College Board.

McCants, J. (2004). *Pathways to improving practice: Fact sheet 6.* National TRIO clearinghouse and pathways to college network. Retrieved July 10, 2007, from www.pathwaystocollege.net/pdf/PIP6.pdf.

McCormick, A. C., & Dennis, C. (1997). *Transfer behavior among beginning postsecondary students: 1989–1994.* Washington, DC: National Center for Educational Statistics, U.S. Department of Education.

McKlenney, K. (2006). *Community college survey.* Retrieved April 14, 2006, from www.ccsse.org/aboutccsse/aboutccsse.cfm.

McKlenney, K. (2005). Personal communication.

McKlenney, K. (2006). Personal communication.

McPhee, S. (2006). En Route to the Baccalaureate: Community College Outcomes. AACC-RB-06-1, Washington, D.C.: American Association of Community Colleges.

Mellander, G. A., & Mellander, N. (1994). *Towards an Hungarian community college system.* Fairfax, VA: George Mason University.

Mellow, G. (1998, September 7). Overcoming the stigma. *Community College Week*, pp. 4–5.

Mellow, G. (2005). *China's national imperative as a learning country and its implications for the development of a community college system.* Unpublished manuscript. Long Island City, NY: LaGuardia Community College.

Mellow, G., Eynon, B., & Van Slyck, P. (2004). The face of the future: Engaging in diversity at LaGuardia Community College. *Change, 35*(2), 10.

Mellow, G.,& Talmadge, R. (2005). Creating the resilient community college. *Change, 37*(3), 59–66.

Melvine, J. (1997, March). *Meta-analysis of transfer success: Community college vs. native students' academic performance.* Paper presented at Learning, Technology and the Way We Work: National Conference on Higher Education, American Association for Higher Education. Washington, DC.

Merisotis, J. P., & Phipps, R. A. (2000). Remedial education in colleges and universities: What's really going on? *The Review of Higher Education, 24*(1), 67–85.

Michigan community colleges and technical education update. (2004). Retrieved May 22, 2005, from www.mccte.msu.edu/updates/mist/index.asp.

Miller, M. T., Vacik, S. M., & Benton, C. (1998). Community college faculty involvement in institutional governance. *Community College Journal of Research and Practice, 22*(7), 645–54.

Milliron, M. D. (2003). *On the road to dotcalm in education.* League for innovation in the Community College. (White Papers) Retrieved December 14, 2006, from www.league.org/publication/whitepapers/0305.htm.

Milliron, M. D., & De Los Santos, G. (2004). Making the most of community colleges on the road ahead. *Community College Journal of Research and Practice, 28*, 105–122.

Mills, C. W. (1957). *The power elite.* New York: Harper.

Mitchell, O. S., & Lung Hsin, P.(1994). *Public sector governance and performance.* National Bureau of Economic Research, Inc. Retrieved from http://edirc.repec.org/data/nberrus.html.

Murray, W. H. (1951). Goethe couplet: The Scottish Himalaya expedition: Daily Celebrations website. Retrieved June 18, 2006, from www.dailycelebrations.com /082899.html.

Napoli, A. R., & Wortman, P. W. (1998). Psychosocial factors related to retention and early departure of two-year community college students. *Research in Higher Education, 39*(4), 419–55.

National Association of State Student Grant and Aid Programs. (2004). *34th annual survey report on state sponsored student financial aid: 2002-2003 academic year.* [Electronic version]. Retrieved February 18, 2005, from www.nassgap.org/researchsurveys/34th%20NASSGAP%20Survey%20Report.pdf.

National Center for Developmental Education. (1998). Facts about developmental education, *Journal of Developmental Education, 21*(3), 40.

National Center for Education and the Economy. (2007). *Tough choices or tough times: Executive summary.* Washington, DC: Author.

National Center for Education Literacy. (1996). *National postsecondary student aid study.* Washington, DC: National Center for Education Statistics.

National Center for Education Statistics. (1996). *Remedial Education at Higher Education Institutions.* Washington, DC: Office of Educational Research and Improvement, U.S. Department of Education.

National Center for Education Statistics. (2001). *National Postsecondary Aid Survey: 1999–2000.* Washington, DC: U.S. Department of Education.

National Center for Education Statistics. (2003). *Trends in nontraditional under-graduates.* Retrieved July 10, 2007, from http://nces.ed.gov/pubs/web/9757c.asp.

National Center for Education Statistics. (2006a). *Integrated postsecondary education data system.* Washington, DC: Author.

National Center for Education Statistics. (2006b). *Table 345. Current-fund expenditures per full-time equivalent student in degree-granting institutions by type and control of institutions: Selected years, 1970–71 to 2000–01.* Retrieved December 14, 2006, from www.nces.ed.gov/fastfacts/display.asp?id=75.

National Council for Research on Women. (2006). *Gains and gaps: A look at the world's women.* New York: Author.

National Institute for Literacy. (2001). *Correctional education facts.* Retrieved October 5, 2007, from www.nifl.gov/nifl/facts/correctional.html.

National Panel Report. (2000). *Greater expectations: A new vision for learning as a nation goes to college.* Washington, DC: Association of American Colleges and Universities. Retrieved January 16, 2006, from www.greaterexpectations.org/.

National Student Clearinghouse. (2006). *Educational verification and more.* Retrieved January 8, 2006, from www.studentclearinghouse.org/colleges/Tracker/pdfs/Schoolsbrochure.pdf.

Nelson, J. (1972). High school context and college plans: The impact of social structure on aspirations. *American Sociological Review, 37,* 143–48.

Nettles, M., Cole, J. (2001). A study in tension: State assessment and public colleges and universities. In D. E. Heller (Ed.), *The states and public higher education policy — affordability, access and accountability* (pp. 198–218). Baltimore: The Johns Hopkins University Press.

New Jersey virtual community college consortium. (2006). Retrieved December 14, 2006, from www.njvccc.cc.nj.us/.

No child left behind act of 2001. (2001). pp. 1425–2094. Washington, DC: United States Congress.

Noel-Levtiz Inc. (2005). *Making sense of the retention puzzle.* Retrieved January 7, 2006, from www.noellevitz.com/NR/rdonlyres/A922CEFE-4ABF-4217-BD9D-1F951DC14FFB/0/RETENTIONPUZZLE_0405.pdf.

North Carolina community college system business and industry services. (2005). Retrieved May 22, 2005, from www.ncccs.cc.nc.us/Business_and_Industry/.

Northern Virginia Community College. (2000). *Evaluation of NVCC counseling and career center services: Research report.* (2000). Annandale: Author (ERIC Document Reproduction Service No. ED453877).

Norton, R. E. (1997). *DACUM Handbook* (2nd ed.). Leadership training series, No. 67. Columbus, Ohio: Center on Education and Employment, Ohio State University.

O'Banion, T. (1997). *A learning college for the 21st century.* Phoenix, AZ: Oryx Press.

O'Banion, T. (2002). Leadership that lasts. *Community College Journal, 73*(1), 34–37.

Ohmann, R. (2000). Historical reflections on accountability. *Academe, 81*, 24–29.

Okundade, A. A. (2004). What factors influence state appropriations for public higher education in the United States. *Journal of Education Finance, 30*(2), 123–38.

Oleks, T. (2005). *Increasing student learning and student satisfaction during electronic coursework.* Boston: Council for the Study of Community Colleges.

Olson, L. (2005, January 6). Financial evolution. *Education Week, 24*(17), p. 8.

Organisation for Economic Co-Operation and Development. (2003). *Networks of innovation - towards new models for managing schools and systems.* Paris: Author.

Ornelas, A., & Solorzano, D. G. (2004). Transfer conditions of Latina/o community college students: A single institution case study. *Community College Journal of Research and Practice, 28*, 233–48.

Orr, M. T. (2001). Community colleges and their communities: Collaboration for workforce development. *New Directions for Community Colleges, 115*, 39–49.

Orr, M. T., & Brag, D. (2001). Policy directions for k-14 education—looking to the future. In B. K. Townsend & S. B. Twombly (Eds.), *Community colleges—policy in the future context* (Vol. 2, pp. 101–127). Westport, CT: Ablex Publishing.

Oudenhoven, B. (2002). Remediation at the community college: Pressing issues, uncertain solutions. *New Directions for Community Colleges, 117*, 35–44.

Owen, H. (1997). *Open space technology.* San Francisco: Berrett-Koehler Publishers.

Park, J. (2005, January 6).Finance snapshots. *Education Week*, p. 60.

Parker, A. (1999). A study of variables that predict dropout from distance education. *International Journal of Educational Technology.* Retrieved July 3, 2007, from http://smi.curtin.edu.au/ijet/v1n2/parker/.

Parsad, B., Lewis, L., & Greene, B. (2003). *Remedial education at degree-granting post-secondary institutions in fall 2000.* Jessup, MD: U.S. Department of Education.

Pascarella, E. T. (1999). New studies track community college effects on students. *Community College Journal, 69*(6), 8–14.

Pascarella, E. T., & Terrenzini, P. (1991). *How college affects students.* San Francisco: Jossey-Bass.

Pascarella, E. T., Edison, M., Nora, A., Hegedorn, L. S., & Terenzini, P. T. (1998). Does community college versus four-year college attendance influence students' educational plans. *Journal of College Student Development, 39*(2), 179–93.

Payne, E. M., & Lyman, B. G. (1996). Issues affecting the definition of developmental education. In J. L. Higbee and P. L. Dwinell (Eds.) *Defining developmental education: Theory, research & pedagogy.* Annual Monograph of the National Association for Developmental Education. Carol Stream, IL: National Association for Developmental Education.

Perin, D. (2000). *Curriculum and pedagogy to integrate occupational and academic instruction in the community college: Implications for faculty development.* New York: Community College Research Center, Institute on Education and the Economy/Teachers College at Columbia University.

Perin, D. (2002). The location of developmental education in community colleges: A discussion of the merits of mainstreaming vs. centralization. *Community College Review, 30*(1), 27–44.

Peterman, D. (1999). *Measuring the economic benefits of community college attendance using community college, unemployment insurance, and state agency data.* ERIC Document Reproduction Service No. ED433076.

Petrides, L. A., McClelland, S. I., & Nodine, T. R. (2004). Using external accountability mandates to create internal change. *Planning for Higher Education, 33*(10), 44–50.

Phillipe, K. A., & Patton, M. (2000). *National profile of community colleges: Trends and statistics.* (3rd ed., pp 1–75). Washington, DC: Community College Press.

Phipps, R. A. (1998). *College remediation: What it Is, what it costs, what's at stake.* Washington, DC: Institute for Higher Education Policy.

Phipps, R., & Merisotis, J. (2000). *Quality on the line: Benchmarks for success in internet-based distance education.* Washington, DC: Institute for Higher Education Policy.

Piland, W. E., & Wolf, D. B. (2003, September). In-house leadership development: Placing the colleges squarely in the middle. *New Directions for Community Colleges, 123,* 93–99.

Polgreen, L. (2006, January 17). Liberia's Harvard-trained 'queen' is sworn in as leader. *The New York Times,* p. A3.

Polonio, N. A. (2005, October 28). Best practices for community college boards. *The Chronicle of Higher Education,* pp. B18–B19.

Pope, M. L. (2004). A conceptual framework of faculty trust and participation in governance. In W. G. Tierney and V. M. Lechuga (Eds.), *Restructuring shared governance in higher education* (Vol. 127, pp. 75–84). San Francisco: Jossey-Bass.

Pope, M. L., & Miller, M. T. (2000). Community college faculty governance leaders: Results of a national survey. *Community College Journal of Research and Practice, 24*(8), 627–38.

Preskill, H., & Tzavaras, C. T. (2006). *Reframing evaluation through appreciative inquiry.* Thousand Oaks, CA: SAGE Publications.

Prince, D., & Jenkins, D. (2005). *Building pathways to success for low-skill adult students: Lessons for community college policy and practice from a longitudinal tracking study.* New York: Community College Research Center of Teachers College at Columbia University.

Pulley, J. L. (2001, May 4). College fund raising reached record $23.5 billion in 1999–2000. *The Chronicle of Higher Education,* p. 28.

Pusser, B., & Turner, S. E. (2004). Non-profit and for-profit governance in higher education. In R. G. Ehrenberg (Ed.), *Governing academia* (pp. 235–57). Ithaca, NY: Cornell University Press.

Quigley, M. S., & Bailey, T. W. (2003). *Community college movement in perspective - Teachers College responds to the Truman commission.* Lanham, MD: The Scarecrow Press, Inc.

Raftery, S. (2005). Developmental learning communities at Metropolitan Community College. *New Directions for Community Colleges, 129*, 63–72.

Reitano, J. (2004, September). *Creating general knowledge through the use of original documents.* Paper presented at the Opening Sessions, LaGuardia Community College, Long Island City, NY.

Richardson, R. C., Baracco, K. R., Callan, P. M., & Finney, J.E. (1998). *Designing state higher education systems for a new century.* Westport, CT: Oryx Press.

Richardson, R., Jr., & de los Santos, G. E. (2001). Statewide governance structures and two-year colleges. In B. K. Townsend and S. B. Twombly (Eds.), *Community colleges - policy in the future context* (Vol. 2, pp. 39–55). Westport, CT: Ablex Publishing.

Richardson, R., Jr., & Smalling, T. R. (2005). Accountability and governance. In J. C. Burke (Ed.), *Achieving accountability in higher education - balancing public, academic and market demands.* San Francisco: Jossey-Bass.

Rifkin, T. (2000). *Improving articulation policy to increase transfer.* Unpublished manuscript.

Rivera, L. A. (2002). *Comparative analysis of noncredit workforce development education progress at public community colleges in Texas.* Unpublished doctoral dissertation. University of Texas, Austin, TX.

Rizzo, M. (2004). *A (less than) zero sum game? State funding for public higher education: How public higher education institutions have lost.* Ithaca, NY: Cornell University Press.

Roach, R. (2001, April 4). Community colleges, historically black colleges forge new bonds. *Community College Week*, p.2.

Roblyer, M. D. (1999). Is choice important in distance learning? A study of student motives for taking internet-based courses at the high school and community college levels. *Journal of Research on Computing in Education, 32*(1), 157–71.

Rocconi de Quintanilla, I. (2005, June 10). Peruvians visit U.S. community colleges virtually. *Community College Times*, Retrieved May 11, 2006, from www .aacc.nche.edu/Template.cfm?Section=GlobalAwareness&template=/Content Management/ContentDisplay.cfm&ContentID=14891&InterestCategoryID =310&Name=International%20News&ComingFrom=InterestDisplay.

Rodgers, C. (2002). Defining reflection: Another look at John Dewey and reflective thinking. *Teachers College Record, 104*(4), 842–66.

Romero, M. (2004, November/December). Who will lead our community colleges? *Change Magazine, 26*, p. 30.

Romero, M., & Purdy, L. (2004). The community college leadership. *Community College Journal, 36*(6), 30.

Rooney, G. (2002). *Providing support services for college students with learning disabilities who are not native English speakers: The challenge of the LD/ESOL student.* ERIC Digest (ERIC Document Reproduction Service No. ED469337).

Rossiter, M. (2002). *Narrative and stories in adult teaching and learning.* (ERIC Document Reproduction Service No. ED473147).

Roueche, J. E., & Roueche, S. (1999). *High stakes, high performance: Making remedial education work.* Washington, DC: Community College Press.

Roueche, J. E., Roueche, S., & Milliron, D. (1995). *Strangers in their own land: part-time faculty in American community colleges.* Washington, DC: Community College Press.

Ruffel, C. (2000). *The governance game: In search of effective pension board planning: Plan sponsor.* Retrieved November 11, 2006, from www.cortex-consulting.com/articles/TheGovernanceGame.pdf.

Ruppert, S. (1996). *The politics of remedy: State legislative views on higher education.* Washington, DC: National Education Association.

Rust, E. B., Jr., & Reed, C. B. (2004). *Public accountability for student learning in higher education: Issues and options.* Washington, DC: American Council on Education.

Sanchez, J. R., & Lanaan, F. S. (1997). The economic returns of a community college education. *Community College Review, 25*(3), 73–87.

Sanchez, J. R., & Lanaan, F. S. (1998). Economic benefits of a community college education: Issues of accountability and performance measures. *New Directions for Community Colleges, 104*, 5–15.

Sanchez, J. R., Lanaan, F. S., & Wiseley, C. W. (1999). Post-college earnings of former students of California community colleges: Methods, analysis and implications. *Research in Higher Education, 40*(1), 87–113.

Sanford, K. (1999). The needs of beginning teachers: preparing for the journey. *Teaching and Learning: The Journal of Natural Inquiry, 13*(2), 15–23.

Santa Rita, E., & Scranton, B. (2001). *Counseling faculty handbook.* New York: Bronx Community College of the City University of New York.

Schaffer, F. (2005). *The Perez case - interpretations.* Unpublished memorandum. New York: City University of New York

Schwan, H. (2005). Security and international students. *Community College Journal, 75*(4), 28–31.

Scott, V. (2005). Personal communication.

Seattle Community College. (2004). *The college transfer advantage.* Retrieved May 22, 2005, from www.sbctc.ctc.edu/data/data.asp#RS.

Sehoole, C. T. (2004). Trade in educational services: Reflections on the African and South African higher education system. *Journal of Studies in International Education, 8*(3), 297–316.

Sengupta, R, & Jepsen, C. (2006). *California's community college students.* San Francisco: Public Policy Institute of California.

Serban, A. M. (2004). Assessment of student learning outcomes at the institutional level. *New Directions for Community Colleges, 126*, 17–27.

Shaw, K. M., & Rab, S. (Eds.). (2003). *Market rhetoric versus reality in policy and practice: The workforce investment act and access to community college education and training* (Vol. 586). Thousand Oaks, CA: SAGE Publications.

Sheppard, K., & Crandall, J. (2004). *Adult ESL and the community college.* New York: Council for the Advancement of Adult Literacy.

Shulman, J. (2005). Personal communication.

Shults, C. (2000). Remedial education: Practices and policies in community colleges. *Research Briefs, No. 11.*.Washington, DC: Community College Press.

Shults, C. (2001). *The critical impact of impending retirements on community college leadership.* Washington, DC: American Association of Community Colleges.

Smart, J. C. (2003). Organizational effectiveness of 2-year colleges: The centrality of cultural and leadership complexity. *Research in Higher Education, 44*(6), 673–703.

Smith, B.L., McGregor, J., Matthews, R., & Gabelnick, F. (2004). *Learning communities: Reforming undergraduate education.* San Francisco: Jossey-Bass.

Smith, C. J. (2000). *Trusteeship in community colleges: A guide for effective governance.* Washington, DC: Association of Community College Trustees.

Smith, J. (2005). Final report of the New York State tuition assistance corporation: Annual report. Albany, NY: New York State Higher Education Corporation.

Sosin, J. (2002). *National leadership dialogue series: Higher education's role in serving the public good.* Report from Kellogg Forum on Higher Education for the Public Good, Ann Arbor, MI.

Spence, R., & Kiel, B. (2003). *Skilling the American workforce "on the cheap."* Washington, DC: The Workforce Alliance.

Sperling, C. B. (2003). How community colleges understand the scholarship of teaching. *Community College Journal of Research and Practice 27,* 593–601.

Starks, G. (Ed.). (1994). *Retention and developmental education: What the research has to say.* Clearwater, FL: H.H. Publishing.

Starobin, S. S. (2002). Community colleges in Japan and the social status of Japanese women. *Community College Journal of Research and Practice, 26*(6), 493–503.

Stonley, P. (2007, June). *Cooperative education scholarship opportunities.* Paper presented at the 9th Annual Corporate Symposium of the National Commission for Corporate Education, Boston, MA.

Strout, E. (2006, February 10).Community colleges struggle when it comes to soliciting private donations. *The Chronicle of Higher Education,* p. A25.

Sullivan, L. G. (2001). Four generations of community college leadership. *Community College Journal of Research and Practice, 25*(8), 559.

Sum, A. (2007, June). *The literacy challenge facing the nation's schools and employers.* Paper presented at the 9th Annual Corporate Symposium of the National Commission for Corporate Education, Boston, MA.

Summers, J. J., Beretvas, S. N., Svinicki, M. D., & Gorin, J. S. (2005). Evaluating collaborative learning and community. *The Journal of Experimental Education, 73*(3), 165–88.

Summers, M. D. (2001). The role of leadership in successful vocational initiatives. *New Directions for Community Colleges, 115,* 17–25.

Swan, K. S., Fredericksen, E. E., Pickett, A. M., & Pelz, W. E. (2000, October/November). *Course design factors influencing the success of online learning.* Paper presented at the WebNet 2000 World Conference on the WWW and Internet Proceedings, San Antonio, TX.

Swigart, T. E., & Ethington, C. D. (1998). Ethnic differences in estimates of gains made by community college students. *Community College Journal of Research and Practice, 24*(4), 703–713.

Szelenyi, K., & Chang, J. C. (2002). Educating immigrants: The community college role. *Community College Review, 30*(2), 19.

Talmadge, R. A, & Glick, M. (2006, Summer). Appreciative inquiry and strategic planning: An appreciative approach to strategic planning at LaGuardia Community College. *Leadership: Journal for Post-Secondary Leaders, 13.1,* 3–9.

Tierney, W. G., & Lechuga, V. (Eds.). (2004). *Restructuring shared governance in higher education.* 127. San Francisco: Jossey-Bass.

Tierney, W. G., & Minor, J. (2004). A cultural perspective on communication and governance. In W. G. Tierney and V. M. Lechuga (Eds.), *Restructuring shared governance in higher education,* 27, 85–94. San Francisco: Jossey-Bass.

Tollefson, T. A. (1996). *Emerging patterns in state level community college governance: A status report.* U.S. Department of Education Educational Resources Information Center (ERIC Document Reproduction Service No. ED437076).

Tollefson, T. A. (2000). Martorana's Legacy: Research on State Systems of Community Colleges. Annual Meeting of the Council for the Study of Community Colleges (ERIC Document Reproduction Service No. ED443461).

Townsend, B. K. (2001). Blurring the lines: Transforming terminal education to transfer education. *New Directions for Community Colleges, 115,* 63–71.

Townsend, B. K., & Twombley, S. B. (Eds.). (2001). *Community colleges—policy in the future context.* Westport, CT: Ablex Publishing.

Transfer enhancement plan: A report prepared by the transfer task force. (1998). San Francisco: City College of San Francisco.

Trombley, W. (2000). *California's improved financial aid program.* San Jose, CA: National Center for Public Policy and Higher Education.

U.S. Census Bureau. (2000). *Population estimates.* Washington, DC: Author.

U.S. Census Bureau. (2001). *Profile of the foreign-born population in the United States.* Retrieved September 23, 2004, from www.census.gov/prod/2002ubs/p.23–206.

U.S. Census Bureau. (2003). *Population estimates.* Washington, DC: U.S. Census Bureau Population Division.

U.S. Census Bureau. (2005). *International data base.* Retrieved April 14, 2006, from http://geography.about.com/gi/dynamic/offsite.htm?zi=1/XJ&sdn=geography &zu=http%3A%2F%2Fwww.census.gov%2Fipc%2Fwww%2Fidbsum.html.

U.S. Census Bureau. (2006). *Population estimates.* Washington, DC: U S Census Bureau Population Division.

U.S. Department of Education. (2003). *Beginning postsecondary students longitudinal study, second follow up.* Washington, DC: National Center for Educational Statistics.

U.S. Department of Education. (2006a). *Enrollment in postsecondary institutions, fall 2004, graduation rates, 1998 & 2001 cohorts; and financial statistics, fiscal year 2004.* Washington, DC: Author.

U.S. Department of Education. (2006b). *A test of leadership: charting the future of U.S. higher education; a report of the commission appointed by secretary of education Margaret Spellings.* Washington, DC: Author.

U.S. Department of Labor. (1998). College enrollment and work activity of 1997 graduates. Washington, DC: U.S. Bureau of Labor Statistics.

U.S. Department of Labor. (2006). *National compensation survey: occupational wages in the United States, June 2006.* Washington, DC: U.S. Bureau of Labor Statistics.

Varga, P. (2004). *Faces of the future.* Washington, DC: American Association of Community Colleges.

Vasquez, L. A., & Garcia-Vasquez, E. (1998). The impact of a differential social power system on Latinos' attitudes toward the high school and the community college experience. *Community College Journal of Research and Practice, 22*(5), 531–40.

Vaughan, G. B. (2004, October 29). Diversify the presidency. *The Chronicle of Higher Education,* p. B3.

Vaughan, G. B. (2005, October 28). Selling the community college: What price access? *The Chronicle of Higher Education,* p. B12.

Vaughan, G. B., & Weissman, I. M. (1998). *The community college presidency at the millennium.* Washington, DC: Community College Press.

Vernez, G. (1996). *How immigrants fare in U.S. education.* Santa Monica, CA: RAND Corporation (ERIC Document Reproduction Service No. ED399320).

Viniar, B. (2001). Personal communication.

Virginia State Council for Higher Education. (1997). *Transfer in Virginia: An update.* Richmond, VA: Virginia State Department of Education.

Walsh, J. (2000). *Unique and effective practices for TRIO student support service programs.* Unpublished report, Kankakee, IL: Kankakee Community College.

Warford, L. J., & Flynn, W. J. (2000). New game, new rules: The workforce development challenge. *Leadership Abstracts, 13*(2), 1–4.

Warren, D. (2007). Personal communication.

Washington Community & Technical College System. (2003). *Washington Community Colleges Correctional Education Annual Report.* Retrieved May 22, 2005, from www.sbctc.edu/data/data.asp#CorrectionsEd.

Wassmer, R., Moore, C., & Shulock, N. (2004). Effect of racial/ethnic composition on transfer rates in community colleges: Implications for policy and practice. *Research in Higher Education, 43*(6), 651–71.

Watkins, T. G. (1998, July/August). *Community College Journal of Research and Practice, 22*(5), 479–90.

Watson, S. (2007). Personal communication.

Weiger, P. (1999, September 20). Inputs and outputs: New equation for measuring accountability and success. *Community College Week, 12*(3) p. 6.

Weisbord, M., & Janoff, S. (1995). *Future search: Action guide for finding common ground in organizations and communities.* New York: Berrett-Koehler Publishers.

Weissman, J., Bulakowski, C., & Jumisko, M. K. (1998). Using research to evaluate developmental education programs and policies. In J. M. Ignash *Implementing effective policies for remedial and developmental education: New directions for community college (100)*, 73–80.

Wellman, J. (2002). *State policy and community college-baccalaureate transfer.* San Jose, CA: National Center for Public Policy and Higher Education.

Wheatley, M. J. (2004). *Finding our way: Leadership for an uncertain time* (1st ed.) San Francisco: Berrett-Koehler Publishers.

White, F. (2006). Personal communication.

Wikipedia. (2005). Wikipedia: http://en.wikipedia.org/wiki/Answers.com.

Williams, C. (2005). Personal communication.

Williams, D., Gore, W., Broches, C., & Lostoski, C. (1987). One faculty's perception of its governance role. *Journal of Higher Education, 58*(6), 629–57.

Wilson, J. D. (2004). Tiebout competition versus political competition on a university campus. In R. G. Ehrenberg (Ed.), *Governing academia* (pp. 139–61). Ithaca, NY: Cornell University Press.

Wolff, R. A. (2005). Accountability and accreditation - can reforms match increasing demands? In J. C. Burke (Ed.), *Achieving accountability in higher education - balancing public, academic and market demands.* San Francisco: Jossey-Bass.

Woolis, D. (2006). *The algorithms of social innovation: Online communities, new analytics, and napsterization.* Retrieved June 9, 2007, from http://blog.kpublic.com/archives/2006/03/the_algorithms_of_social_innov_1.html.

Workforce Strategy Center. (2001). *Workforce development: Issues and opportunities.* Brooklyn, NY, and San Francisco: Author.

Wu, C. (2004). *Final report: National Institute of Health bridges to the future grant.* Long Island City, NY: LaGuardia Community College.

Wyoming Community College Commission. (1999). *Community college governance.* Cheyenne, WY: Wyoming Community College System.

Yin, R. K. (1994). *Case study research: Design and methods.* Beverly Hills, CA: SAGE Publications.

Yoo, J. (2001). Sources and information: Post secondary vocational education. *New Directions for Community Colleges, 115,* 101–108.

Zang, Y., & Chang, T. (2007). *An interim report on the student support services program: 2002–03 and 2003–04, with select data from 1998–2002.* Prepared for the U.S. Department of Education. Washington, DC: American Institute for Research.

Zaritsky, J. (2001). Personal communication.

Zeiss, T. (2000). Community/workforce development: A mandate for relevancy. *Community College Journal, 70,* 47–49.

Zemsky, R. M. (2005). The dog that doesn't bark - why markets neither limit prices nor promote educational quality. In D. E. Heller (Ed.), *The states and public higher education policy — affordability, access and accountability* (pp. 275–95). Baltimore: The Johns Hopkins University Press.

Zook, G. F. (1947). *Higher education for American democracy: A report* (No. C2:5 UNI). Washington, DC: President's Commission on Higher Education.

Zumeta, W. (2001). Public policy and accountability in higher education: Lessons from the past and present for the new millennium. In D. E. Heller (Ed.) *The states and public higher education—affordability, access, and accountability* (pp. 155–97). Baltimore: The Johns Hopkins University Press.

Zwerling, L. S. (1976). *Second best: The crisis of the community college.* New York: McGraw-Hill.

Zwerling, L. S. (Ed.). (1986). The community college and its critics. *New Directions for Community Colleges, 54,* 53–60. San Francisco: Jossey-Bass.

ᕉ Index

U.S. Department of Education, 71; categories in, 219–20
Utah: New Century scholarship program in, 205

Vassar College: Exploring Transfer program at, 200
Venter, J. Craig, 17
Vermont, 33; college tuition in, 37
Vietnam, 4, 6, 12
Vietnam War, 6
vocational programs: in community colleges, 73–74, 210, 213, 215, 218, 224, 226; as credit, 217; as experiential learning, 226; as non-credit, 217; transfer students, 224; workforce, education of at, 214
Voluntary Support of Education Report, 43

Walden University, 144
Washington State, 65, 219, 235; Running Start program, 205; WorkFirst programs, 230
Weisbord, Marvin, 97
welfare reform acts, 233
Wells, H. G., 149

White, M'Shell, 28
Whitman, Christine Todd, 72
Whitman, Walt, 13
Wisconsin, 204, 226
women: education of, 151
women's movement, 6
work-based learning, 226
workforce: baccalaureate, as entry point to, 282; education of at, 214; workforce development, 49, 64, 66, 216, 237–40, 285; workforce development, and financial support, 234, 235; workforce development, and manpower programs, 233; workforce development, and state support programs, 235; workforce training, 286; as underskilled, 179
Workforce Investment Act (WIA), 66, 234, 237
Workforce Investment Boards (WIBs), 234, 237
World Bank, 152
WorldCom, 54
Wyoming, 33

Zook, George F., 6

❧ About the Authors

Dr. Gail O. Mellow became president of LaGuardia Community College in Queens, New York City, in 2000. LaGuardia Community College, part of the City University of New York (CUNY), is one of the most ethnically diverse campuses in the United States, serving more than 50,000 full- and part-time students from over 160 countries who speak 110 native languages. She has served on several national higher education boards and their commissions, including the American Association for Higher Education, the American Council on Education, The National Commission on Adult Literacy, The Community College Research Center at Teachers College (Columbia University), The Center for an Urban Future, and the American Association of Community Colleges. Dr. Mellow is a coauthor of three books.

Dr. Cynthia Heelan is the retired president of Colorado Mountain College, president of Cynthia Heelan & Associates, and an adjunct faculty member at the Fielding Graduate University. She consults with educational organizations to lead and plan in ways that engage the entire institution's heart and voice. Dr. Heelan has served community colleges for thirty-two years. She is a past chair for the American Association of Community Colleges Board of Directors; past board member of the Higher Learning Commission of the North Central Accrediting Association, the Colorado Rural Workforce Consortium Board, and the Community College Research Center at Teachers College (Columbia University); past chair of the Colorado Literacy Commission and the Minnesota Association of Continuing Adult Education; and member of numerous state, regional, and local boards and advisory groups.